Contents

KU-677-225

3 Data Compilation and Editing 151

4 Mapping and Visualization 263

5 Geographic Analysis 339

Introduction

1

ArcGIS® Desktop lets you perform the full range of GIS tasks—from geodatabase design and management to data editing, from map query to cartographic production and sophisticated geographic visualization and analysis. It is where the core work of GIS occurs. This book gives you an overview of the ArcGIS Desktop system and shows you how to access the basic functions of the software.

This chapter introduces ArcMap™, ArcCatalog™, and ArcToolbox™—the basic framework of ArcGIS Desktop—including the structure of each, the functions each performs, and how they're used together. It also provides insight into the underlying design concepts of ArcGIS, and describes where to get help.

Chapters 2 through 5 get you started with the specific tasks you'll perform as you use ArcGIS. They're organized around the major functional areas of the software. Each chapter contains an overview and then describes common tasks.

The book covers the functions most people will use, plus a number of specialized tasks that you may need for specific applications. It illustrates the various tasks you can perform, shows where to access them in the user interface, and shows how to get started with a particular task using basic or default settings.

The tasks presented here, plus many additional tasks and functions, are described in detail in the Desktop Help system (discussed at the end of this chapter).

In addition to providing an overview of ArcGIS Desktop, this book can be used as a quick reference to the interface and to common tasks. The book includes functions available in ArcInfo®—the full-function ArcGIS Desktop product—as well as in the ArcView® and ArcEditor™ products (these products are described later in this chapter, as well as in the book *What is ArcGIS 9.2?*).

ArcGIS Desktop quick tour

Most of your GIS work will revolve around maps, so exploring a map is a good way to start getting familiar with the software. The following brief tour introduces the two main integrated ArcGIS Desktop applications—ArcMap and ArcCatalog—along with ArcToolbox. You'll see what they look like and get a sense of what they do.

ArcMap is the application you'll use to make maps, edit data, and display the results of your analysis. ArcCatalog is the application you'll use to search for, preview, and manage your geographic data. It's also used to build GIS databases. You'll use the tools in ArcToolbox for processing geographic data—both to create databases and to perform geographic analysis. (The next section, 'The ArcGIS Desktop framework', describes ArcMap, ArcCatalog, and ArcToolbox in more detail, and introduces the ArcGIS Desktop extension products.)

ArcGIS uses a standard Windows® interface, for the most part—many buttons will be familiar, and many menu options are found where you'd expect them to be (Open, Save, and Print are found on the File menu, Copy and Paste are on the Edit menu).

To begin the tour, select the ArcGIS program group from the Start menu, and select ArcMap. When prompted, click the option to open An existing map, select Browse for maps from the list, and click OK. Browse to the Using_ArcGIS_Desktop folder under the tutorial data distributed with ArcGIS Desktop (the default location is C:\ArcGIS\ArcTutor). Select MexicoPopulationDensity.mxd and click Open.

What you're looking at is a map layout view of the population density of Mexico (in 1990). Each state is color-coded based on the number of people per square mile. The rulers along the top and side of the view show you the size of the map were you to print it—in this case 8.5 x 11 inches. The map displayed on the screen is not a static image of a map (as a printed map would be), but rather is interactive—you can change the data that is displayed, change its appearance, change the scale of the map by zooming in or out, and more.

Before continuing, if others in your organization will be running through this tour, make a copy of the map. Click the File menu and click Save As. Give the copy a different name— this is the map you'll be working with.

The table of contents on the left side of the ArcMap window controls which map themes, or layers, are displayed on the map (right now the boxes all have check marks in them indicating all the layers are displayed). Layers higher in the table of contents are displayed on top of lower ones. Click the check box for Rivers to turn it off so it's easier to see population density.

Uncheck this box to turn off the layer

The display window (the right-hand panel) is currently showing a layout view. Layout view is where you can see what a map will look like when it's printed. It's also where you add map elements, such as legends, scalebars, titles, and text, and create the map layout.

The map is missing a north arrow. Click North Arrow on the Insert menu, select a north arrow from the panel that appears, and click OK.

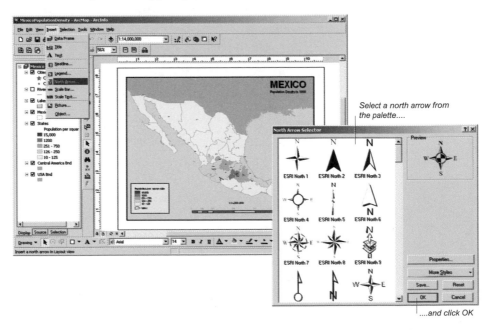

Select a north arrow from the palette....

....and click OK

The north arrow appears on the map, surrounded by a box—drag it above the legend at the left side of the map.

Drag the north arrow here

To print the map, click Print on the File menu. To make sure the whole map fits on the page click Scale Map to fit Printer Paper. You may also need to click Setup to change the printer paper orientation to landscape.

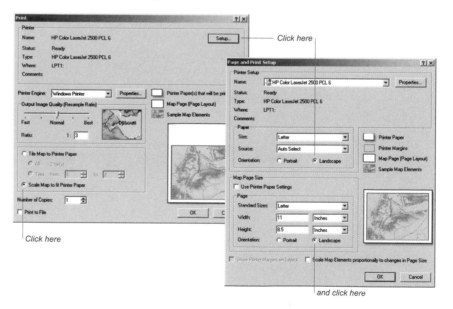

Click here

Click here

and click here

While layout view lets you add and arrange map elements in preparation for printing, much of the initial work with a map—such as which layers you display, and which color schemes and symbols you choose—is done more efficiently in data view. Data view lets you focus exclusively on the map body—the geographic data.

To switch to data view, click Data View on the View menu.

Switch to Data View

Now the geographic features fill the screen and the map elements no longer appear. However, you can see that the data content from the layout view is all here. If you go back to layout view, all the map elements will still be present.

Suppose you want to emphasize the country boundary. In the table of contents, right-click Mexico Bnd to display the context menu for that layer (this menu gives you options for working with the layer) and click Properties. The Layer Properties dialog box gives you options for how the layer is displayed.

Right-click....

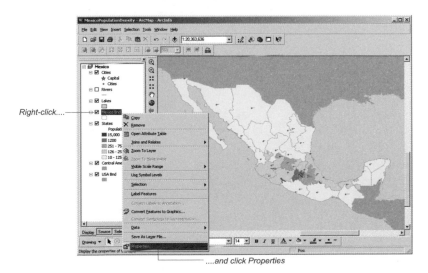

....and click Properties

Click the Symbology tab, and click the button showing the current symbol. The Symbol Selector dialog box appears—this is where you set and modify the symbols you use to draw features, such as line colors and widths, area fills, and so on. Set the outline width to 2, then click Outline Color and pick a color that is easier to see, such as a dark red or brown.

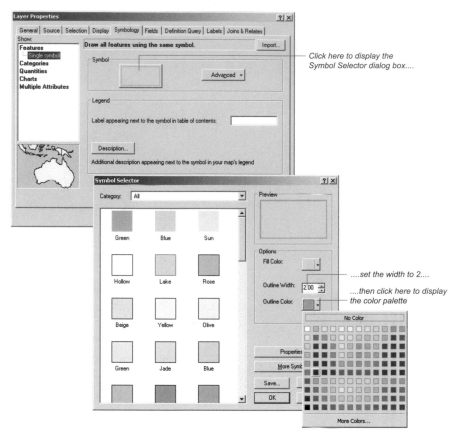

Click here to display the Symbol Selector dialog box....

....set the width to 2....

....then click here to display the color palette

It would be helpful to show major roads on the map, but they're not in the table of contents—you have to find the roads dataset and add it to the map. If you knew exactly what the dataset is called and where it is located on disk, you could use the Add button and browse to the file. If you need to search, though, use ArcCatalog.

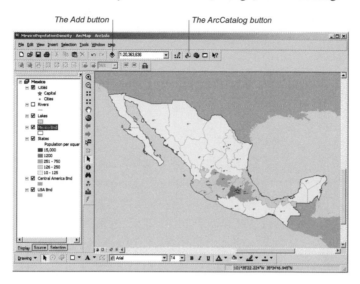

The Add button

The ArcCatalog button

Click the ArcCatalog button (or open ArcCatalog from the ArcGIS program group on the Start menu). The ArcCatalog window opens.

In the Catalog tree view (the left-hand pane) navigate to Mexico_data under the Using_ ArcGIS_Desktop folder. There are two possibilities listed: click mex_roads and click the Preview tab. This looks like too many roads to display for a map of the entire country.

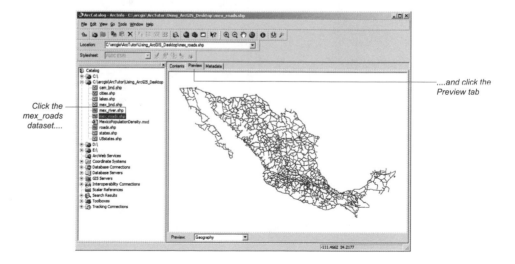

Click the mex_roads dataset....

....and click the Preview tab

Now preview the other dataset: roads. By clicking the Metadata tab you can view a description of the dataset. The metadata confirms that this is major roads.

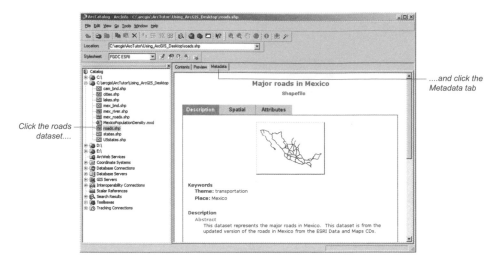

Click the roads dataset....

....and click the Metadata tab

To add roads to the map, drag the dataset name from the tree view in ArcCatalog and drop it anywhere on the map display in ArcMap.

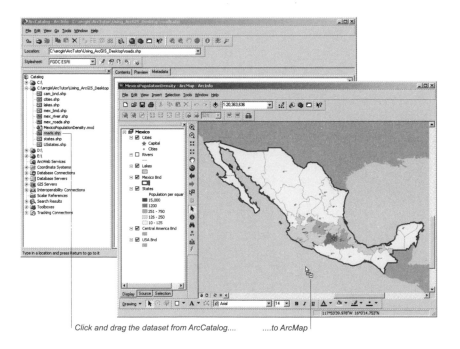

Click and drag the dataset from ArcCatalog....   ....to ArcMap

When you drag the roads onto the map they're drawn automatically, using a default symbol. Click the roads symbol in the ArcMap table of contents—this is a shortcut to the Symbol Selector dialog box. Set the line width to 0.1 and pick a color for the line from the color palette. (The default symbol color is different each time you add a dataset to a map—so if you added roads again they would draw in a different color. Once you save the map, the symbol specifications are also saved.)

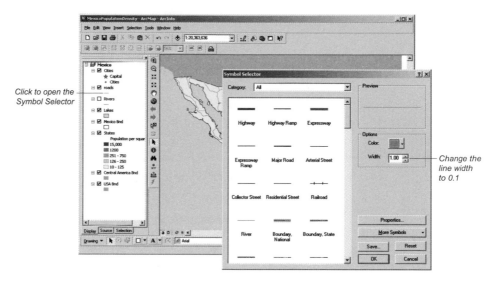

Click to open the Symbol Selector

Change the line width to 0.1

Each layer has an attribute table that contains the descriptive information associated with each feature. Open the attribute table for the states by right-clicking States in the table of contents (to open the context menu) and clicking Open Attribute Table.

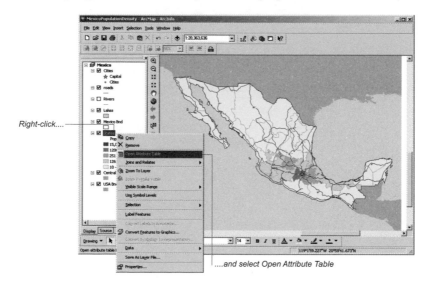

Right-click....

....and select Open Attribute Table

The information in the table can be used to symbolize features (the states are color-coded on the map based on the values in the population density field). You can also explore and query the information in the attribute table as you would in a spreadsheet. You could, for example, get the mean population density for the states, and then find the states having a density greater than the mean. Scroll the table to the right, if necessary, right-click the column heading POP90_SQMI (1990 population per square mile), and select Statistics.

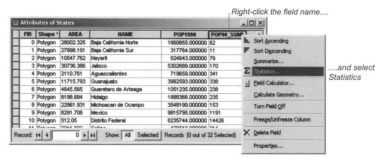

Right-click the field name....

....and select Statistics

The mean density for the states is about 633 people per square mile. Close the statistics box before going on.

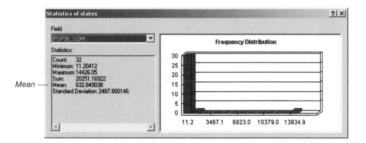

Mean

Use ArcToolbox to find the most densely populated states. Open ArcToolbox by clicking the "Show/Hide ArcToolbox Window" button.

The ArcToolbox button

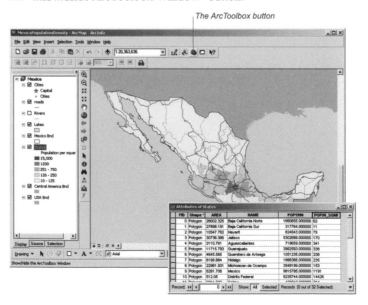

ArcToolbox includes a wide variety of data management and analysis tools. Expand the Data Management Tools toolbox (by clicking the plus sign next to the toolbox), then expand the Layers and Table Views toolset. Open the Select Layer By Attribute tool by double-clicking it.

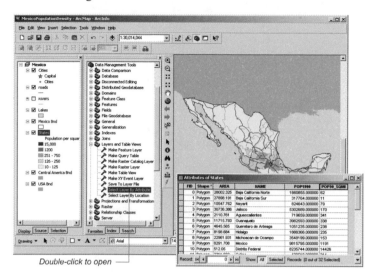

Double-click to open

Use the drop-down arrow to select States as the Layer Name.

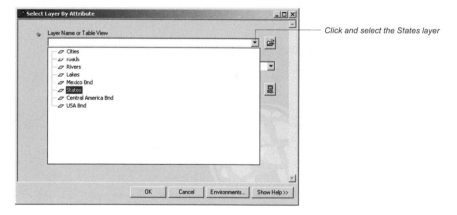

Click and select the States layer

Click the SQL button to open the Query Builder. Create a query to find states having a density greater than the mean by double-clicking "POP90_SQMI" in the Fields box, clicking the "greater than" (>) button, and typing 633.

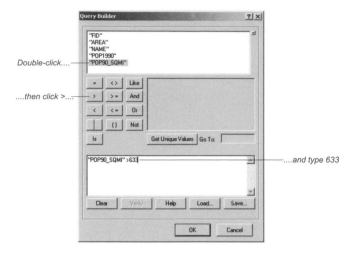

Click OK to close the Query Builder—your expression appears in the box on the Select Layer By Attribute dialog box. When you click OK on the dialog box, a status box appears telling you the command has been completed (you can close this box) and the states having a population density greater than the mean of 633 people per square mile are highlighted in the attribute table.

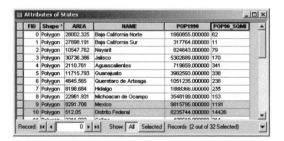

Many of the tools in ArcToolbox are also available through other parts of the interface. (In ArcMap, if you click Select by Attributes on the Selection menu or click Options on the attribute table window and click Select By Attributes, you get a similar query builder dialog box.) ArcToolbox collects all the tools in one place, and gives you a direct, common interface for using them.

If necessary, click the refresh button on the ArcMap window to see the selected states highlighted on the map. At this point, you can close the ArcToolbox window and the attribute table window.

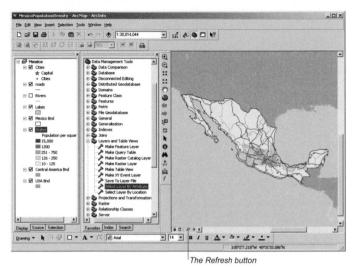

The Refresh button

To get a closer look, zoom to the selected states by right-clicking States in the table of contents, pointing to Selection, and clicking Zoom To Selected Features.

Right-click....

....click Selection....

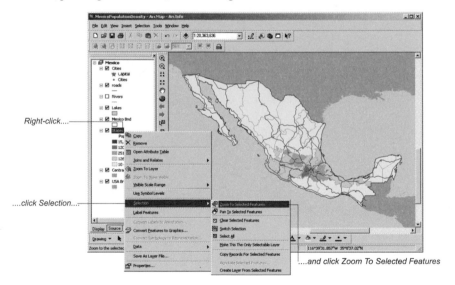

....and click Zoom To Selected Features

The map zooms in to the selected states—those with a population density greater than the mean.

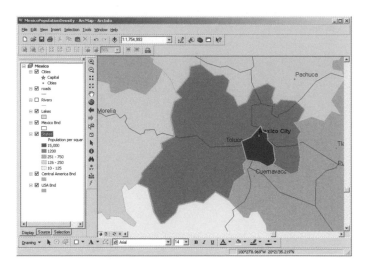

When you're done exploring the map, click File and click Exit. When prompted whether to save changes to this map, click No (unless you made a copy of the map as suggested earlier and want to save your changes).

The goal of this overview tour was to introduce the core components of ArcGIS Desktop— ArcMap, ArcCatalog, and ArcToolbox—and show how they work together. You'll learn more about each of these in the next sections and in Chapters 2 through 5.

Step-by-step tutorials for learning specific parts of the software are found in the Help system (in the 'Getting more help' topic under 'Getting Started'). See also 'Additional Resources for Learning and Using ArcGIS Desktop' at the end of this book.

The ArcGIS Desktop framework

ArcGIS Desktop is structured around ArcMap, ArcCatalog, and ArcToolbox. This section describes each in more detail, and presents the ArcGIS Desktop extension products. Using these together, you can perform the full range of GIS tasks including geographic data management, data compilation and editing, mapping and visualization, and geographic analysis.

ArcMap ArcMap is the central application in ArcGIS Desktop for display and manipulation of geographic data, including mapping, query and selection, and editing.

ArcMap lets you create and work with map documents. A map document is composed of data frames, layers, symbols, labels, and graphic objects. ArcMap has two main windows you use to work with map documents: the table of contents window, and the display window. The table of contents lets you specify the geographic data that will be drawn in the display window, and how the data will be drawn. The display window can show either a data view (just the geographic data) or a layout view (a page showing how the data and any map elements—such as legends—are arranged). You'll read more about these windows later in this section.

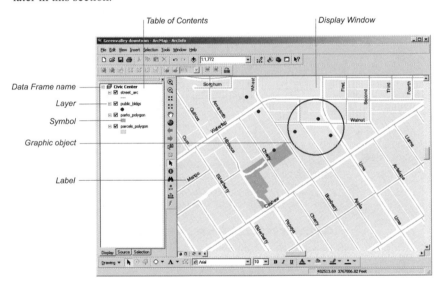

Map documents

A map document is a file stored on disk. When you start ArcMap you either create a new map document or open an existing one. You add data, change the way the data is displayed, and create new data while working in the map document. When you save a new map document, a filename extension of .mxd is appended to the file name. When you reopen the map document, it looks as it did when you last saved and closed it.

Data frames

The container in a map document that holds data is called a data frame. You can think of a data frame as a "window" onto a patch of the earth's surface, scaled down to fit in the ArcMap display. You display and work with the data in a data frame in ground units, such as feet, meters, or kilometers.

When you open a new map document, there is one data frame, named Layers. In many cases, your map will only need a single data frame. Complex maps may require several data frames. Data frames are both a way of grouping data in a map document and a way of showing multiple maps on a single layout page. One common use of this is to show different views of the same area. Another common use is to use one data frame to show a map of the area of interest and use another data frame to show a reference map of the wider area. You add data frames to a map document from the Insert menu.

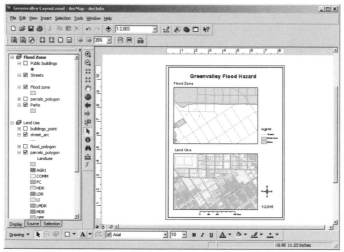

A layout with two data frames showing two different views of the same area. Both data frames have the same map extent.

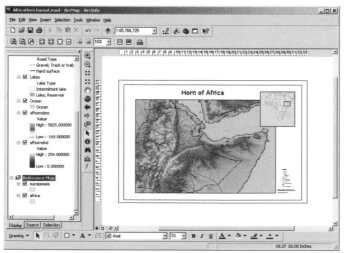

A layout with two data frames showing the area of interest and an inset area reference map. The data frames have different map extents.

Layers

Each data frame contains one or more layers that you create by adding datasets to a map document (a dataset being a file, or set of files, stored on disk containing GIS data—the basics of GIS data are discussed in Chapter 2, 'Geographic Data Management'). Each dataset, and hence each layer, contains geographic features of the same type—roads in one layer, rivers in another, county boundaries in a third, and so on. Layers you've created in a map document are stored with the document when you save it, and appear when you reopen the document.

A layer contains information about how to display the dataset, but not the data itself. Rather, a layer references the underlying dataset wherever it is stored on disk, so ArcMap doesn't have to store a copy of the data in each map document the dataset is added to. Any changes to the underlying dataset automatically appear in any of the layers created from the dataset.

You can create as many layers from the same dataset as you want in a single map document, in the same or in different data frames. For example, from a dataset of counties you could create one layer that shows the county boundaries with a thick red line and no fill color, and another layer showing the counties color-coded by population. You could add the same counties dataset to another map document to create a layer showing the counties in a solid green color.

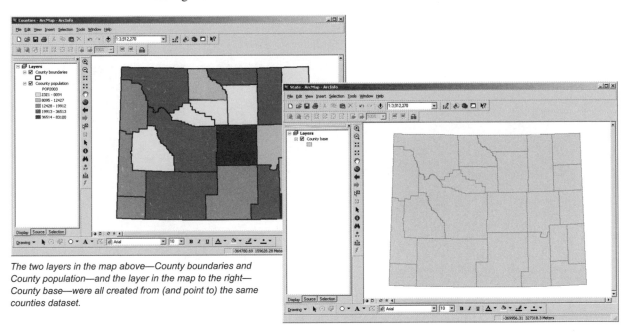

The two layers in the map above—County boundaries and County population—and the layer in the map to the right—County base—were all created from (and point to) the same counties dataset.

You can also create layers that contain a subset of geographic features from the dataset (this is known as a selected set). For example, from a layer of roads, you could select just the major highways and create a layer showing these. Creating a selected set does not create a new dataset—it only marks the particular features in the underlying dataset as "selected." The layer created from the selected set contains the selection definition, so appears when you reopen the document.

A layer in a map document can be saved as a "layer file" (it's named with an extension of .lyr) that can be added to other map documents. A layer file is essentially a map document layer that has been saved to disk. As with a layer on a map, a layer file stores the name and location of the underlying dataset along with the symbol settings for drawing the layer and the definitions of any selected sets (it doesn't store the GIS data). Unlike adding a dataset to a map, when you add a layer file to another map document it appears the same as on the original map document from which it was created—the features are drawn using the same symbols, and any selected sets are implemented. (You can, of course, modify the layer once it's added to the new map document.)

You can also export any layer in a map document to create a new dataset. You'd most likely do this if you've created a selected set of features and want to save only those features to a new dataset—perhaps to send to another ArcGIS user, or to use in analysis. Unlike a layer file, the new dataset contains the GIS data, but no symbol settings or selected set definitions.

Layers have an associated attribute table that contains descriptive information (obtained from the underlying dataset) about the features in the layer—for example, the name of each park, its size, and which agency maintains it.

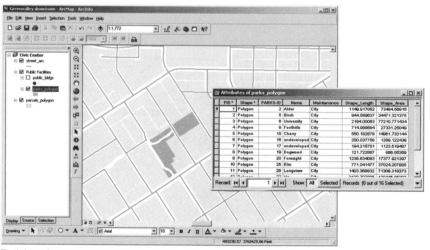

Each layer has an associated attribute table that displays descriptive information about each feature in the layer.

Symbols

To display geographic data and to better communicate the information on the map, graphic symbols are used—lines, colors, patterns, and so on. Symbols are a set of properties that get applied to a particular feature or geographic object.

You render the features in a layer by assigning symbols, such as blue lines for rivers and a green color fill for parks. You can also symbolize features based on descriptive information in the layer attribute table. For example, you could symbolize parcels by assigning a color to each landuse code: all residential parcels yellow, all commercial parcels red, all vacant parcels gray.

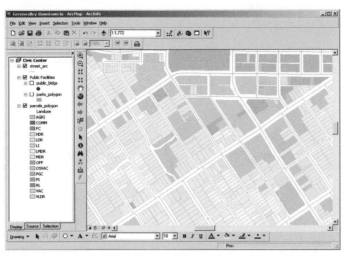

Landuse can be mapped by assigning a different color symbol to each landuse category—parcels are drawn using the color for their assigned landuse value.

When you add data to create a layer, or when you draw a graphic object, a default symbol is used. You can modify the properties of the default symbol or apply another predefined symbol from a palette (and then modify it if necessary).

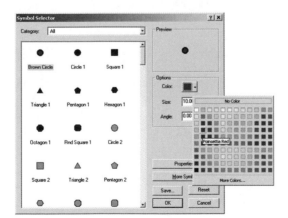

You choose symbols from the Symbol Selector dialog box. You can use a symbol as is, or modify it. You can add symbols to the palette by opening additional styles.

ArcMap includes a number of styles. You can access these—and the symbols they contain—when you're making a map or when you're creating your own symbols.

Predefined symbols are stored in styles. A style is a folder that contains other folders, one for each symbol type—all the line symbols in one folder, all the color symbols in another, all the marker symbols in a third. Many industries, such as forestry or real estate, use standard symbols on their maps, so styles are often specific to a particular industry. ArcMap provides a number of styles for various industries. You can save any symbols you modify in an existing or new style. You can also create new symbols entirely from scratch and store them in a style.

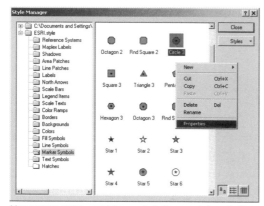

You access styles—and the symbols they contain—via the Style Manager.

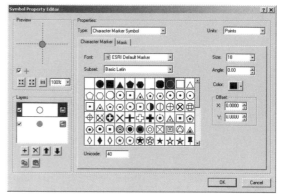

You can modify any of the existing symbols, or create your own, using the Symbol Property Editor.

Labels

Labels are used to identify geographic features on your map, such as labeling streets with their name. There are several ways to create labels in ArcMap:

- You can label features with their name or other information from the layer attribute table by specifying a field in the table. Text labels are placed automatically and can't be moved or edited individually.

- You can create annotation features. Annotation features are usually associated with individual geographic features and can be placed and edited individually. When you move a feature, the annotation automatically moves with it. Annotation can also be stored as a separate dataset and added to different maps.

- You can label features using graphic text. Graphic text is placed and edited individually, but is not linked to features. It is often used to label one feature, or a few. Graphic text is stored only with the map document in which it was created.

Feature labels (street names in this map) are created for each feature. They're placed automatically and can't be edited individually.

Graphic text is used to quickly label individual features. It can also be used to create labels for general locations not represented by specific features, such as the civic center area shown on this map.

Graphic objects

Graphic objects, such as circles or boxes, are used to highlight the data that's displayed in the map document. Graphic objects, along with graphic text, are also used to create map elements, such as titles, neatlines, legends, scalebars, and north arrows, that describe the information on your map.

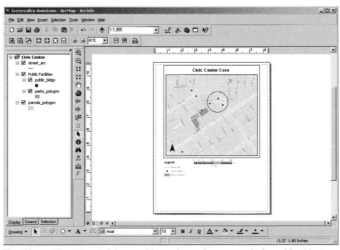

The title, north arrow, scalebar, and legend are all composed of graphic objects, as is the blue circle on the map.

The ArcMap interface

The ArcMap interface consists of the two main windows—the table of contents and display windows—along with a number of standard and specialized toolbars and menus.

The table of contents

The table of contents lists the data frames and layers in the map document, and shows you the current symbols for each layer. Use the check boxes to turn layers on and off. Drag layers up or down in the table of contents to change the drawing order (layers higher in the list draw on top).

Click and drag a layer to change the order.

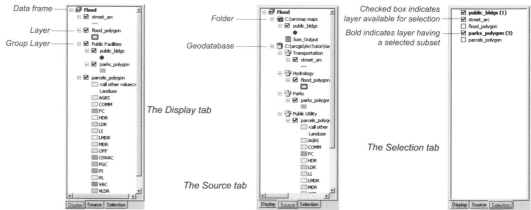

The table of contents is also where you control how layers are drawn, via context menus (right-click a layer name to display the menu). You can change the colors and patterns used to draw features, label features, and more.

The tabs at the bottom of the table of contents window present different views of the layer list. The Display tab is the default, and is the one you'll use when displaying and querying data—it shows a simple list of all the layers, organized by data frame (group layers are used to manage several layers as a unit). The Source tab is useful when you're editing data—it shows the layers organized by where their underlying dataset is stored (either in a folder or a geodatabase). It also lets you see other nonlayer data stored with your map, such as tables not associated with a geographic dataset. The Selection tab gives you an overview of selected subsets of data that are currently active, and lets you set selectable layers.

Data frame

Layer

Group Layer

The Display tab

Folder

Geodatabase

The Source tab

Checked box indicates layer available for selection

Bold indicates layer having a selected subset

The Selection tab

The display window

The display window displays the layers and graphic objects in the map document. It has two views that you switch between: data view and layout view.

Data view shows you one data frame at a time, including the currently displayed layers in that frame, along with any labels or graphic objects drawn inside the data frame. In data view, the display window is the data frame—the layers in the active data frame appear in the window.

Layout view shows you all the data frames in the map document and their contents on a layout page along with map elements you've created, such as titles, legends, and scalebars. In layout view, the data frame is embedded on the page—the frame itself is treated as a graphic element, as reflected by the context menu for the data frame on the layout page. It can be moved, resized, and so on.

Data View

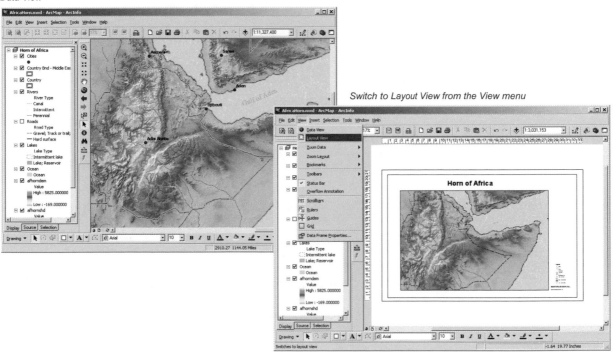

Switch to Layout View from the View menu

Data view is mainly where you do map display, query, and editing. You set the scale and map extent to control the geographic area that's displayed. You can interactively zoom in and out and pan the data (you can also set the map scale explicitly, in the scale window). You work with the contents of the data frame in ground units, such as feet or meters.

Layout view is where you compose page layouts for printing and publishing. You work with the layout in page units—usually inches or centimeters. Layout view activates tools for navigating around the page, for adding standard map elements, such as legends and scale bars, and for arranging the map data and map elements on the page. Simple map elements, such as titles and neatlines, are associated with the map page. Other map elements, such as legends and scalebars, are associated with a data frame and are dynamic—they change to reflect the layers and the map scale displayed in the data frame.

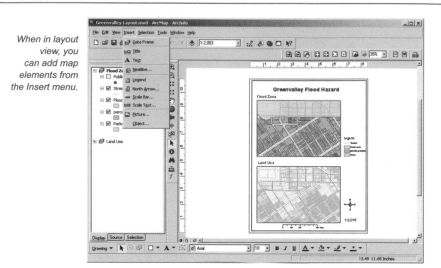

When in layout view, you can add map elements from the Insert menu.

While in layout view you can still work with the data that's displayed in a data frame just as you do in data view—zoom in and out, pan, turn layers on and off, change symbols, and even edit the data.

Only one data frame is active at a time. The active data frame appears in bold in the table of contents. When you add layers to the map they're added to the active data frame. In layout view, the active data frame is outlined with a dashed box—you need to make a data frame active before you can work with the data in the frame. To make a data frame active, click it in layout view or right-click the data frame name in the table of contents and select Activate from the context menu.

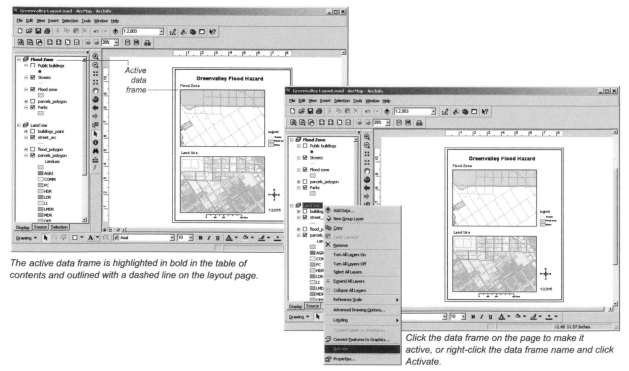

The active data frame is highlighted in bold in the table of contents and outlined with a dashed line on the layout page.

Click the data frame on the page to make it active, or right-click the data frame name and click Activate.

Toolbars and menus

ArcMap has several standard toolbars you use to manage the map document and navigate the map display. These are displayed when you first open ArcMap. The Tools toolbar contains tools that let you zoom and pan the geographic data (the data contained in the data frame). It's active in both data view and layout view. The Layout toolbar contains tools for navigating the layout page—it's active only in layout view.

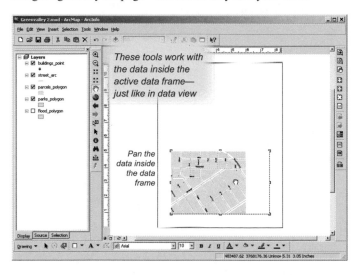

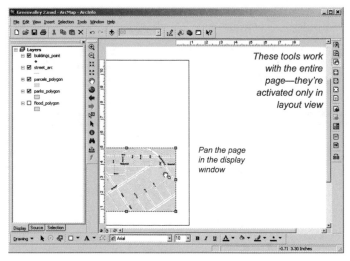

A number of specialized toolbars are used for specific tasks. These are accessed from the View menu (point to Toolbars).

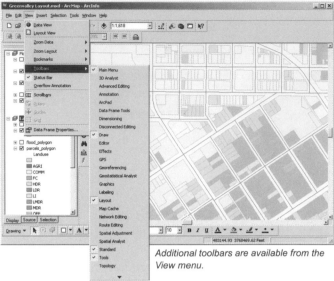

Additional toolbars are available from the View menu.

You use context menus in ArcMap to access the setting, properties, and other options for data frames, layers, and graphic objects (for example, you open a layer's attribute table from the context menu). Right-click a data frame name or layer name in the table of contents to display the context menu. Right-click a graphic object in the display window to display its context menu.

Right-click a component to display the context menu. Click Properties to display the properties dialog box.

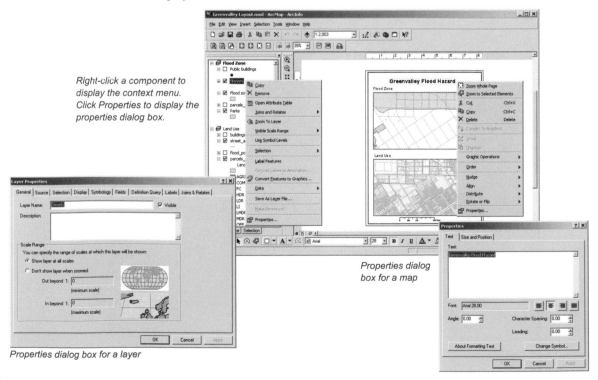

Properties dialog box for a map

Properties dialog box for a layer

Each context menu includes a Properties option, displayed at the bottom of the menu. By clicking it you'll open a Properties dialog box. Symbols and labels are properties of a layer. Layers have other properties you can access and modify, using the various tabs on the properties dialog box (as do data frames and graphic objects). For example, transparency (on the Display tab) can be used to let layers drawn underneath show through.

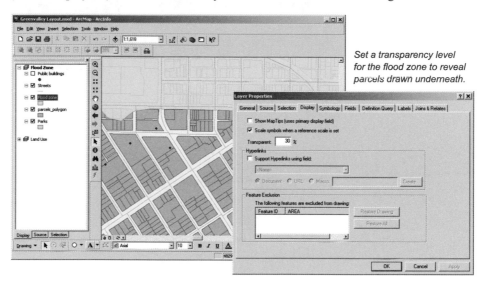

Set a transparency level for the flood zone to reveal parcels drawn underneath.

ArcMap tasks

ArcMap is used to display geographic data and create maps, interactively query and explore data, and edit geographic data.

Display data and create maps

To display geographic datasets, you'll add layers to and remove layers from the map document, change symbology and labels, zoom and pan on the map extent, and so on. This work will be done in data view. When you want to make a map for printing or publication, you'll switch to layout view, add map elements, such as titles and legends, arrange the data frames and map elements on the page, and then print the map or export it to a standard graphic format. Displaying data and making maps are discussed in Chapter 4, 'Mapping and Visualization'.

Query and explore geographic data

A map document can be thought of as an interactive map that lets you not only display geographic data, but also get information about the features in the document. The Tools toolbar includes the Identify tool that lets you point to one or more features in the display window and list the descriptive information (contained in the layer attribute table) for those features. It also includes the Find tool that lets you find and zoom to specific features or locations. ArcMap includes several ways to select a subset of features—you can point to one or more features on a map or draw a box around them, you can select features based on their spatial relationship to other features, such as parcels within 100 feet of a park, or you can select features using their attributes—for example, you can select all the vacant parcels in a parcel layer. Query and selection is discussed in Chapter 4, 'Mapping and Visualization', and Chapter 5, 'Geographic Analysis'.

The parcels within 100 feet of a park have been selected and are highlighted in blue on the map.

Once selected, you can create a layer from the features or you can export the selected features to a new dataset. ArcMap also includes tools to summarize or get statistics on attribute values, such as the minimum and maximum parcel sizes. These tools are available on the layer's attribute table.

Edit geographic data

ArcMap is where you create new features in a dataset, or modify the shape or location of existing features. You also add and edit attributes in tables, and can create editable map text (annotation). Most of the time the data in the map document is essentially locked—you can change its appearance (via layers on a map) but not its shape or position. To delete features or move a feature's coordinates, you start an edit session. You open the edit session, specify the layer to edit, create or modify features, save them, and close the edit session when you're done. Even though you specify a layer on the map to edit, the edits are made to the underlying data source. Editing is discussed in Chapter 3, 'Data Compilation and Editing'.

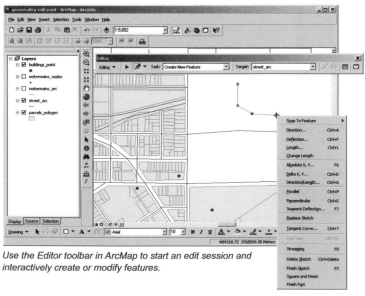

Use the Editor toolbar in ArcMap to start an edit session and interactively create or modify features.

ArcCatalog   The ArcCatalog application helps you manage your GIS information—GIS datasets, map
documents, layer files, and much more. GIS data comes in a variety of data formats and file
types. There is also associated descriptive information about the geographic features (stored
in tables) and information about the datasets, such as when the data was collected, when
it was updated, and how accurate it is. Much of this data and information you'll compile
from various sources. ArcCatalog was designed to help you organize and manage your
geographic data in all its various forms.

ArcCatalog has two main windows in which you work: the catalog tree view, and the
display window.

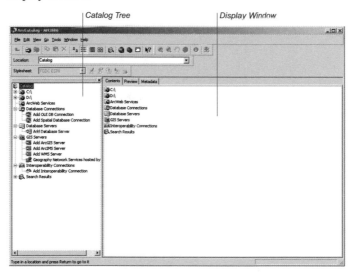

Viewing data in ArcCatalog

ArcCatalog displays folders, databases, and other items for which connections are currently
established. When you open ArcCatalog, connections are automatically established to
folders on your local disk drives. You can add connections to subfolders to make them
easier to access. You can also add connections to databases on shared database servers or
on the internet.

Once a connection to a folder, GIS database, or GIS server is established, you can browse
through its contents with ArcCatalog. You can look for the map you want to print, draw a
dataset, examine the values in a table, and find out which coordinate system a raster uses or
read its metadata document to learn about how it was created.

When you close ArcCatalog, all the current connections are retained and are available the
next time you open ArcCatalog. The connections are also available when browsing for
data in ArcMap and ArcToolbox—even if ArcCatalog isn't currently open. (You can also
establish new connections when browsing for data in ArcMap and ArcToolbox.)

The ArcCatalog interface

The Catalog tree view shows the current connections in ArcCatalog. Add and remove
connections using the Connect and Disconnect buttons. The tree view shows you how
your data is organized in folders and subfolders, and lets you reorganize it. Right-click a
top-layer folder, point to New, and click Folder to create a subfolder. The tree view is also
where you perform basic data management tasks, such as moving, copying, deleting, or
renaming datasets and files.

Right-click an entry in the tree to copy, delete, or rename it. Drag a tree entry to move the data to another folder.

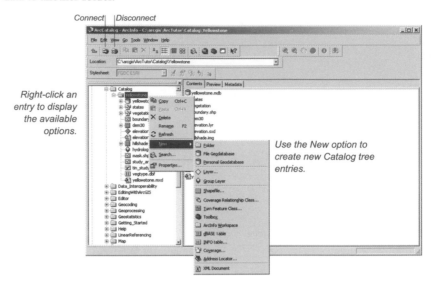

Connect | *Disconnect*

Right-click an entry to display the available options.

Use the New option to create new Catalog tree entries.

The display window shows information about the currently selected entry in the catalog tree view. The information that appears is controlled by the three tabs at the top of the display window.

The Contents tab displays the contents of a folder or geodatabase as a list, icons, or thumbnails of the datasets. In this mode, ArcCatalog lets you quickly browse and find particular datasets.

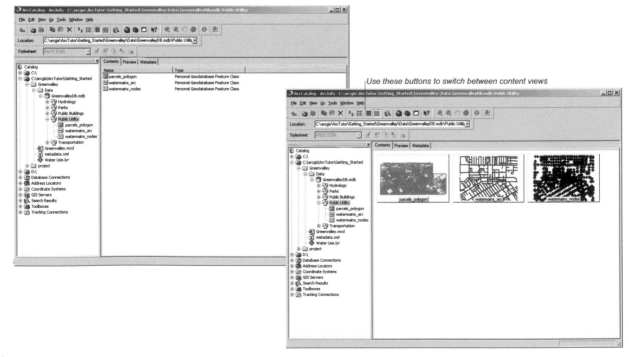

Use these buttons to switch between content views

The Preview tab displays the geographic features or the table for the selected dataset. Use the drop-down menu at the bottom of the window to select which to display. Preview mode is useful for perusing datasets before adding them to a map in ArcMap or processing them using the tools in ArcToolbox. It's also a quick way to view the resulting processed dataset. (Open ArcMap or ArcToolbox directly from ArcCatalog using the buttons on the toolbar).

The Preview tab

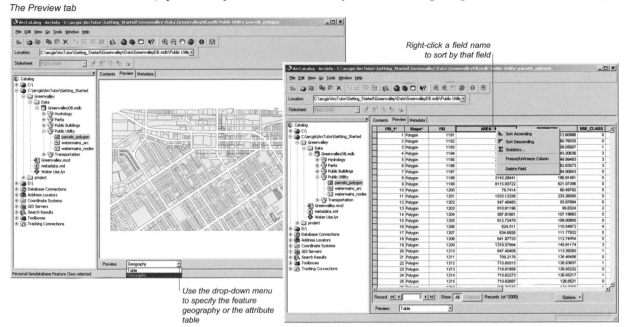

Right-click a field name
to sort by that field

*Use the drop-down menu
to specify the feature
geography or the attribute
table*

The Metadata tab displays the documentation for the currently selected dataset, including the geographic parameters, the source information and permissions for use, processing history, attribute value definitions, and so on. You can display the information using one of several standard metadata formats, or create a custom format. A set of buttons on the toolbar allows you to create and edit the metadata text.

Select the metadata style   *Use these buttons to create and modify metadata text*

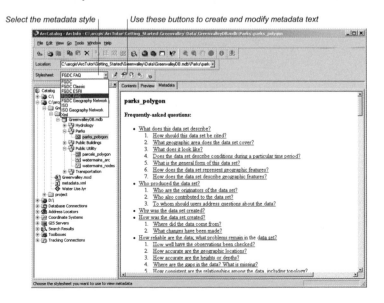

Why use ArcCatalog to manage ArcGIS data, and not Windows Explorer?

Unlike other data (a photo or a Word document), geographic datasets often consist of a set of files, rather than a single file. When listed in Windows Explorer, the datasets appear as a list of system folders and files. ArcCatalog displays and manages the datasets as single entities. Accessing them directly in Explorer—for example to delete or copy them—or in another program can corrupt the datasets; use ArcCatalog to delete, copy, rename and otherwise work with the datasets.

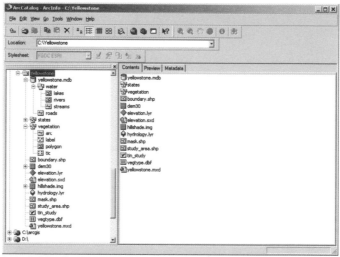

In ArcCatalog the datasets appear as single entities with identifying icons.

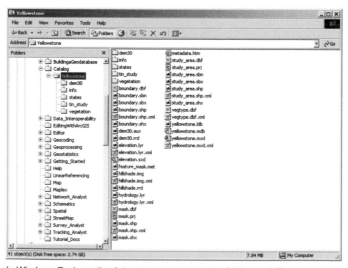

In Windows Explorer, the datasets appear as system folders and files.

The icons in ArcCatalog show you at a glance what kind of dataset it is—for example, shapefile, coverage, or layer file. ArcCatalog also lets you preview the data, using thumbnails. Right-clicking a dataset in the Catalog tree provides additional operations not available in Windows Explorer, such as Export, and lets you access the dataset's properties.

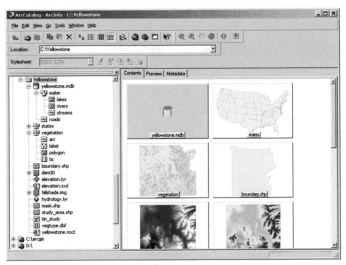

ArcCatalog lets you preview datasets as thumbnails. The Catalog tree shows the workspace structure and contents.

Using ArcCatalog to compile data

In addition to using ArcCatalog to organize, preview, and document data, you use ArcCatalog to implement database designs and compile GIS data.

ArcCatalog is where you'll import datasets from other GIS formats.

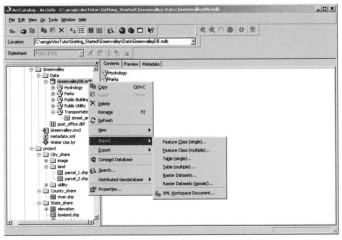

Use ArcCatalog to import datasets.

ArcCatalog also lets you prepare datasets for editing and updating—you can set up rules so that edits to one feature class are reflected in another or that moving one feature moves associated or connected features; you can also define additional fields before adding attribute values when editing in ArcMap. You may also use ArcCatalog to assign the spatial reference for a dataset, so its coordinate system is defined.

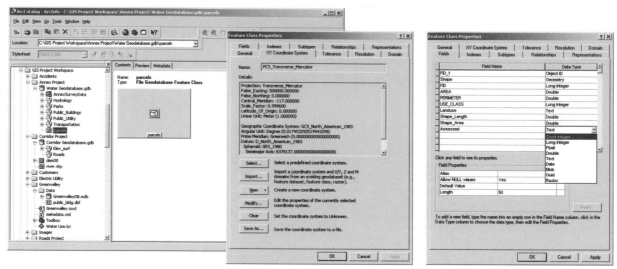

Use the Properties dialog box in ArcCatalog (right-click a dataset and click Properties) to specify the spatial reference for a dataset or add fields to the dataset.

You also use ArcCatalog to create new (empty) datasets before creating the geographic features themselves in the datasets (by importing or by editing in ArcMap). ArcCatalog lets you define parameters and rules to ensure data integrity for your database. Right-clicking an entry in the tree and clicking New displays the appropriate options for creating new databases or datasets, or for creating rules for the database.

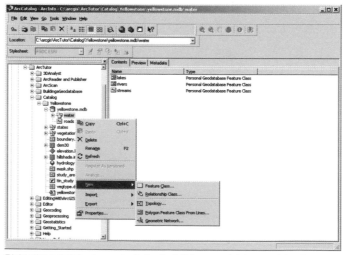

Right-click a Catalog tree entry to begin defining new databases, datasets, or rules for ensuring data integrity.

Using ArcCatalog to build databases and compile GIS data is discussed in Chapter 2, 'Geographic Data Management', and Chapter 3, 'Data Compilation and Editing'.

ArcToolbox   Much of your GIS work will involve using ArcMap and ArcCatalog to manage, display, and query geographic data. A good deal of your work will also involve processing geographic data to create new datasets, known as geoprocessing. Geoprocessing is used in virtually all phases of GIS—for data automation, compilation, and data management; analysis and modeling; and for advanced cartography.

A typical geoprocessing operation takes one or more input datasets, performs an operation, and returns the result of the operation as an output dataset. The Union tool, for example, combines features from separate datasets into a single dataset.

Inputs to Union   *Output from Union*

Land parcels   *Soil types*   *Land parcels and soil types*

There are geoprocessing functions for spatial analysis operations, for converting data from one format to another, for simple data management operations such as copying datasets, for data integration operations such as appending map sheets, and many other operations. These geoprocessing functions are collected as tools in ArcToolbox, grouped by category in toolboxes and toolsets. Some of these same functions can also be accessed through toolbars, menus, and dialog boxes in ArcMap and ArcCatalog.

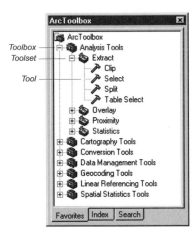

Additional geoprocessing toolsets come with many of the ArcGIS extensions (described later in this chapter), such as ArcGIS Spatial Analyst, which includes raster modeling tools, and ArcGIS 3D Analyst™, which includes terrain analysis tools. ArcGIS Geostatistical Analyst adds kriging and surface interpolation tools. When the extensions are installed, the tools appear as new toolsets in ArcToolbox. Some may also appear in menus or toolbars in ArcMap or ArcCatalog.

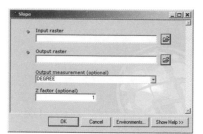

Opening the Slope tool from the Surface Toolbox opens a dialog box that prompts you for the tool parameters.

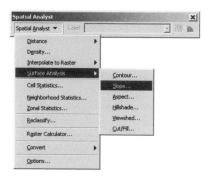

The Slope tool can also be run from a similar dialog box opened from the Spatial Analyst toolbar.

Not all ArcToolbox tools create new datasets (and thereby perform geoprocessing, strictly speaking), but all allow you to at least manage or manipulate your data in some manner.

Using ArcToolbox

To open ArcToolbox, click the Show/Hide ArcToolbox Window button on the ArcMap or ArcCatalog toolbar, or click ArcToolbox in the Window menu. The ArcToolbox window is initially docked in the ArcMap or ArcCatalog window. You can drag it to dock it along any edge or have it float as a separate window.

The ArcToolbox button

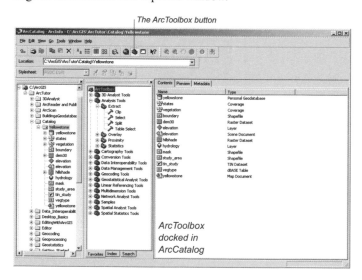

ArcToolbox docked in ArcCatalog

When you open ArcToolbox click the plus sign next to a toolbox to see the available toolsets, and open a toolset to see the individual tools.

You can also browse an alphabetical list or search for a tool by name (click the tabs at the bottom of the ArcToolbox window). Once you find the tool you want, use Locate to display the tool in the toolset—this is useful since you can see related tools in the toolset.

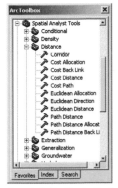  

Search for tool in ArcToolbox using the functional list, an alphabetical index, or by searching for a keyword.

You run a tool from any of the tabs by double-clicking it (or right-clicking and clicking Open) to display a tool dialog box. The dialog box prompts you for the input data and output dataset, as well as any required or optional parameters. The required parameters are indicated by a green dot. Once you enter a valid parameter, the dot disappears. If the input you enter isn't valid—for example, if a dataset you enter doesn't exist—the dot turns red. If you've opened ArcToolbox from ArcMap, you can select the input data from the layers that are currently displayed on your map, using the drop-down menu on the dialog box. For optional parameters, ArcGIS often supplies default values, which you can use or change. Click OK to run the tool—a Status window shows you the progress of the tool and tells you whether the process completed successfully.

Running a function from ArcToolbox opens a dialog box.

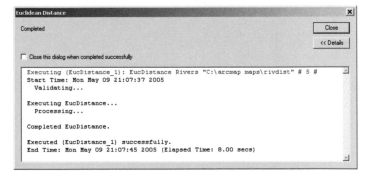

When you run the tool, a status window appears—it tells you the progress of the operation and notifies you when it completes.

You can run any of the functions that appear as tools in ArcToolbox from a command line. This is an efficient way to run a function if you're already familiar with it—you type the function name, the input and output, and the parameters on a single line.

To open the Command Line window, click the button on the ArcMap or ArcCatalog toolbar, or click Command Line on the Window menu. As with ArcToolbox, the Command Line window can float or be docked inside the ArcMap or ArcCatalog window.

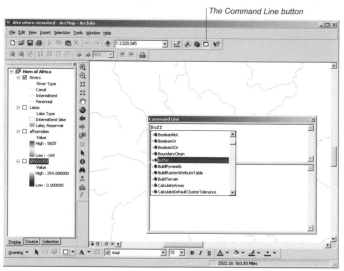

Click the Show/Hide Command Line Window button on the ArcMap toolbar; when you start typing in the window, an alphabetical list of functions is displayed.

You type the command in the upper half of the window. As you type, the command usage is displayed. Press Enter to run the command—the status appears in the lower half of the window.

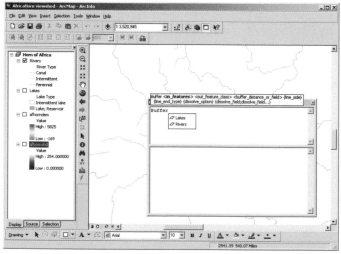

The command usage and other prompts are displayed as you type.

If you're working in ArcMap, results produced from running tools via the dialog box or command line will be added to your display by default (you can turn this off). In some cases, the result of a function is simply a chart that appears in its own window or a statistical value that appears in the status/results window.

Customizing the toolbox

You can create your own toolbox and add tools from other toolboxes—for example, you might collect tools you use often into one toolbox for easy access. To create a new toolbox, right-click anywhere in the ArcToolbox window and click New Toolbox. You can create toolsets inside a toolbox to further organize your tools (right-click the toolbox name, click New, and click Toolset).

To add a tool, right-click the toolbox or toolset name, click Add, and click Tool. In the dialog box that appears use the check boxes to specify which existing tools to add.

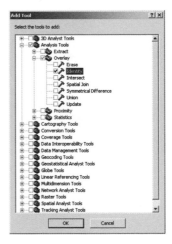

In addition to adding existing tools to a toolset, you can add your own custom tools from type libraries, executable programs, and ActiveX controls. Use Add From File on the Add Tool dialog box.

Setting the geoprocessing environments

Every tool dialog box has an Environments button. When geoprocessing tools are run, default environment settings set for the application are applied to all applicable tools. Examples of environment settings include the current workspace from which to take input data and place resulting datasets, or the geographic extent to apply to results. These settings can be changed in the Environment Settings dialog box.

Automating multistep processes

In many instances, the geoprocessing work that must be done is repetitive, involving a large number of datasets or large datasets with numerous records. In addition, many geoprocessing tasks involve a multistep process—you use the result of one function as input to the next. Complex tasks may involve many such operations.

ArcGIS Desktop provides two ways to automate repetitive or multistep geoprocessing: scripts and models. Scripts are useful for batch processing multiple inputs, such as when converting multiple datasets to a different format. Models provide a graphic way of creating and expressing a multistep process or method, such as when performing spatial analysis.

The scripts and models you create become tools in a toolbox (often a custom toolbox you create) and are run just like other tools—either through a dialog box or command line, or embedded in yet other scripts or models.

Creating a script

Scripts can be written in any Component Object Model (COM)-compliant scripting language, such as Python®, JScript®, or VBScript™, or they can be ARC Macro Language (AML™) scripts or executable files. Any of the functions in ArcToolbox can be included in a script. In fact, to include a function in a script you type it the same way you would if you were running it interactively in the Command Line window—the usage is the same. Functions can be embedded in other script statements including branching and iterative statements.

Scripts can be run from within their scripting application, or they can be added to a toolbox and run like any other tool from a dialog box, the command line, a model, or another script. To add a script, right-click a toolbox or toolset, click Add, and click Script. This opens the Add Script dialog box, which prompts you for a name for the script and other descriptive information, as well as the name of the file containing the script. You also specify any required or optional input parameters.

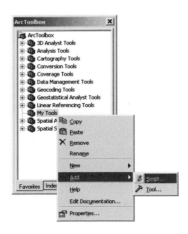

When you run the script in ArcToolbox—the same way as with any other tool—a dialog box opens that prompts the user for the input and output datasets and any parameters.

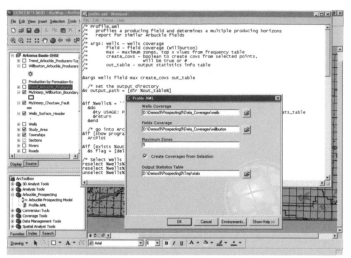

Add scripts to toolboxes and run them by supplying values for parameters.

Creating a model

Models are created within a toolbox or toolset in ArcToolbox—click the toolbox or toolset, click New, and click Model to open the ModelBuilder™ window.

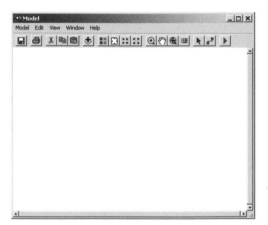

Many GIS tasks—especially analysis tasks—are not individual operations but sequences where the result of one operation becomes input to the next. While you could run the individual operations (tools) one at a time, ModelBuilder gives you a way to connect the operations using a flow diagram and then run all the operations in sequence, at one time.

The basic structure of a model is an input dataset connected to a function producing an output dataset.

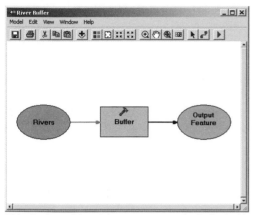

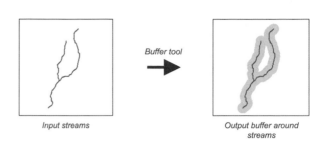

Input streams

Output buffer around streams

This simple model contains one process—the Buffer tool is used to create an output of buffer zones that are a certain distance around the input streams.

You can drag tools from ArcToolbox, and datasets from ArcMap or ArcCatalog, onto a model and connect these to create an ordered sequence of steps to perform GIS tasks. Use the buttons to connect datasets to tools, and to automatically align the model elements. Double-click a tool to open its dialog box and define the parameters (or right-click the tool and click Open).

To build the model, drag and drop tools from ArcToolbox and datasets from ArcCatalog onto the ModelBuilder window. Then connect them in sequence.

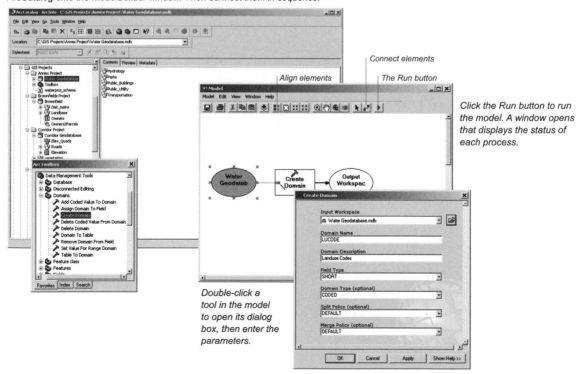

Click the Run button to run the model. A window opens that displays the status of each process.

Double-click a tool in the model to open its dialog box, then enter the parameters.

The parameters you define—including the domain codes, in this example—are stored with the model, so if you want to change them and re-create the domain, you just edit the model and rerun it. Or, you can copy the model and modify it. Once the model is constructed, you run it in the ModelBuilder window, or from within ArcToolbox as with any other tool.

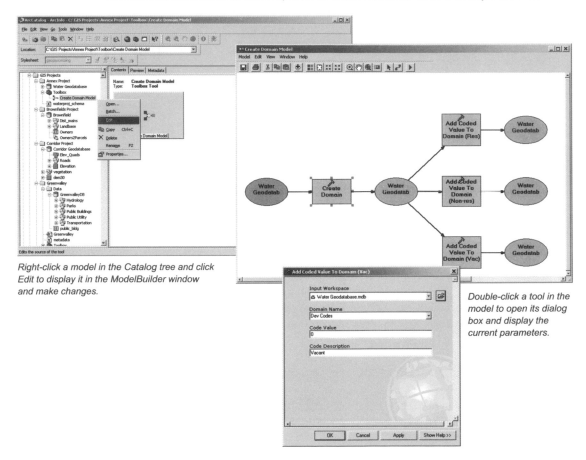

Right-click a model in the Catalog tree and click Edit to display it in the ModelBuilder window and make changes.

Double-click a tool in the model to open its dialog box and display the current parameters.

You can connect multiple inputs, functions, and outputs to create quite complex models. Models can include scripts, and even other models.

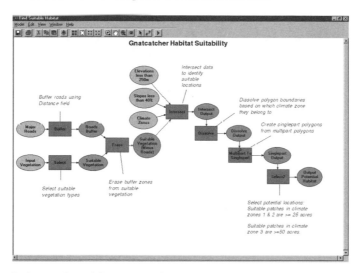

Scripts and models are a good way to save your methods and procedures. A model can be exported as a graphic file or to a script for additional editing or for sharing with other GIS users.

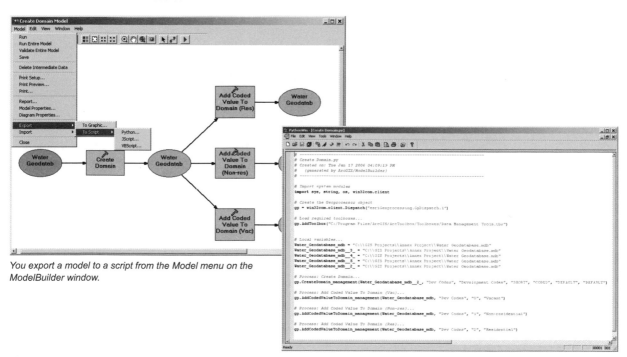

You export a model to a script from the Model menu on the ModelBuilder window.

ArcGIS Desktop Extensions

ArcGIS Desktop extensions add specialized functionality for data compilation, cartographic production, and advanced geographic analysis. Any of the extension products can be started from either ArcCatalog or ArcMap—you first need to enable the extension from the Tools menu, and then open the extension's toolbar from the View menu (click View and point to Toolbars).

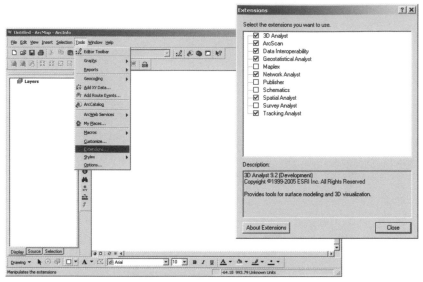

To enable an extension, click Extensions on the Tools menu and check the extension you want to enable.

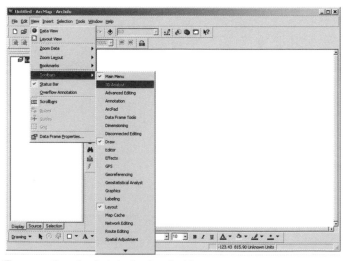

Then open the extension's toolbar from the View menu.

Some extensions add tools to ArcToolbox; some add a toolbar to ArcMap or ArcCatalog; and some do both.

Here is a brief description of each extension product. The licenses for the products are sold separately, except as noted below.

Data Compilation Extensions

- *ArcScan for ArcGIS* is used to generate data from scanned maps and manuscripts. It vectorizes features from raster data and includes integrated raster-vector editing tools. A complimentary ArcScan™ license is included with ArcEditor and ArcInfo.

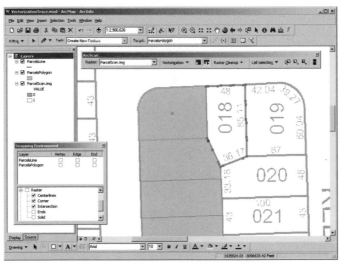

Creating parcel features from a scanned map

- *ArcGIS Data Interoperability* adds the ability to directly read, transform, and export more than sixty common GIS data formats. It also includes tools to build converters for complex or specialized data formats.

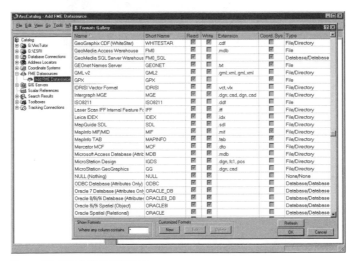

Converting data between formats

- *ArcGIS Schematics* generates database-driven schematic diagrams of GIS networks, such as electrical, water, or telecommunications networks. It lets you create multiple schematic representations of a network and place schematic views on maps and in documents.

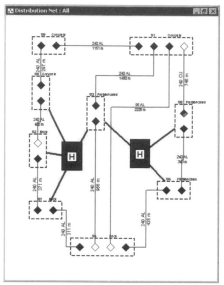

Creating a schematic diagram for a physical network

Cartographic Production Extensions

- *Maplex for ArcGIS* adds advanced label placement for cartographic production and simplifies the labor-intensive process of placing map text. It detects labels that overlap and automatically moves them, and includes tools for custom label placement. A complimentary Maplex™ license is included with ArcInfo.

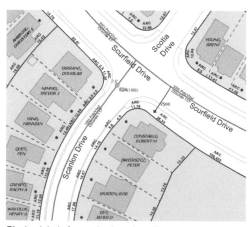

Placing labels for production of a utility network map

- *ArcGIS Publisher* is used to publish data and maps for use with ArcReader™. It enables the creation of a published map file (PMF) format for any ArcMap document. PMFs are used in ArcReader, and allow you to freely share your ArcMap documents with any number of users.

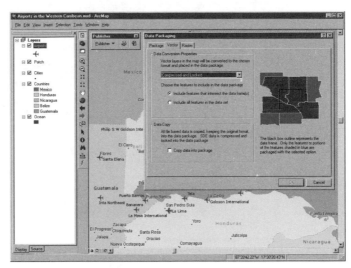

Publishing a map as a PMF file for display in ArcReader

Geographic Analysis Extensions

- *ArcGIS Spatial Analyst* provides advanced modeling and analysis for raster datasets, including terrain analysis (creating shaded relief, slope, and aspect from a Digital Elevation Model), creation of distance and cost surfaces, and raster overlay.

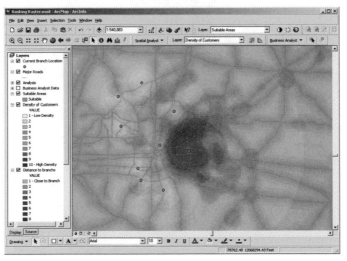

Selecting the best location for a business

• *ArcGIS 3D Analyst* enables visualization and analysis of surface data, including creation of perspective views. It provides advanced tools for three-dimensional modeling, such as cut–fill, line of sight, and terrain modeling.

Creating a perspective view

• *ArcGIS Geostatistical Analyst* provides statistical tools for predicting values across a surface from a set of sample points. It includes exploratory spatial data analysis tools for identifying outliers, trends, and spatial autocorrelation.

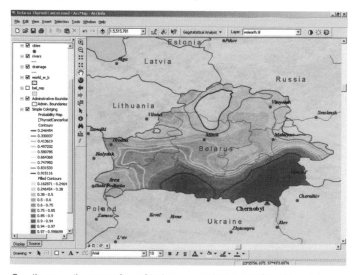

Creating a continuous surface of toxic exposure from a set of sample points

- *ArcGIS Network Analyst* is used for transportation network analysis. It allows you to find the shortest path between two points, allocate resources to a center, or find the most efficient route between several stops.

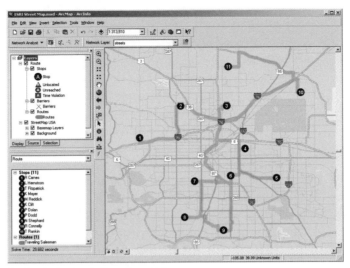

Finding the best route through a set of stops

- *ArcGIS Tracking Analyst* allows you to view and analyze temporal data—you can track feature movement through time (such as the location of a hurricane over the course of a week) and track attribute values for features over time (such as population for a county over several decades). It also lets you create time-based animations.

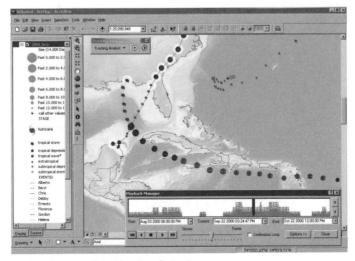

Tracking the strength and location of a hurricane

ArcGIS Cornerstones

There is a set of cornerstones underlying the design of ArcGIS. Understanding these cornerstones will help you understand how ArcGIS is built and, in turn, how to use the software effectively.

A tiered product structure

ArcGIS Desktop is sold as three software products, each providing a higher level of functionality.

- The first level of functionality, called ArcView, provides mapping, data use, and analysis tools along with simple editing and geoprocessing.

- The second level, called ArcEditor, includes all the functionality of ArcView and adds advanced geographic data editing capabilities.

- The highest level of functionality is ArcInfo, the full-function, flagship GIS Desktop product. It includes the functionality of both ArcView and ArcEditor, and extends it with tools for advanced data management and analysis. It also includes the legacy applications for ArcInfo Workstation (including ArcPlot™, ArcEdit™, and AML).

The reason for the three products is that not everybody needs the full functionality of ArcInfo—at least initially. Your organization may have purchased one of the products, or some combination—for example, one ArcInfo license for advanced processing, and three ArcView licenses for people who mainly need to display and query geographic data.

All three products include ArcMap, ArcCatalog, and ArcToolbox. The available functionality of each depends on the product you're using. For example, if you buy ArcView you get about 80 tools within ArcToolbox; ArcEdit provides over 90 tools; and if you buy ArcInfo you get about 250 tools within ArcToolbox.

An extendable product

ArcGIS Desktop is designed around core functionality that can be extended for specialized applications. The core functionality included in ArcMap, ArcCatalog, and ArcToolbox covers the tasks that the vast majority of users will need at some point in their GIS work. Because of the range of GIS applications and tasks, though, some users may never need the advanced functionality available in ArcGIS Desktop for particular tasks. For example, a water utility that uses GIS to build and maintain a database of its pipes and pumps, and perhaps its customers, will likely never need to use advanced raster analysis capabilities. Conversely, a forest research lab will likely never need to include schematic drawings of a utility network in its GIS. To allow for flexibility in building your GIS, ArcGIS Desktop includes extension products (described earlier) that provide advanced capability for data compilation, cartographic production, and advanced geographic analysis. That allows you to buy and install only the advanced functionality you'll use.

A flexible user interface

ArcGIS Desktop provides a flexible user interface that allows you to perform many of the same tasks in different ways, depending on the type of work you're doing and the framework you're using. For example, you can add a field to a table in either ArcCatalog, ArcMap, or ArcToolbox. That allows you to perform this common task whether you're using ArcCatalog to add a field while building a new dataset, you're using ArcMap to add a new field and calculate attribute values while doing analysis, or you need to add a field to a dataset while using ArcToolbox to build a model.

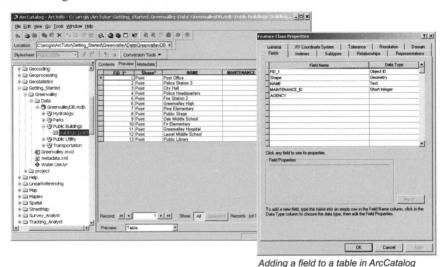

Adding a field to a table in ArcCatalog using the Properties dialog box.

Adding a field from an attribute table in ArcMap.

Adding a field using an ArcToolbox dialog box.

Similarly, the interface often provides defaults you can use for particular functions. You can accept the defaults, or modify them. For example, when specifying what symbols to use to draw features, such as the color and size you want points representing buildings to appear on your map, you can:

- Use the default symbol assigned when the data is added to the map
- Change some basic properties of the symbol, such as color and size
- Access and modify any of the properties that make up the current symbol
- Create your own symbol from scratch by defining the various properties

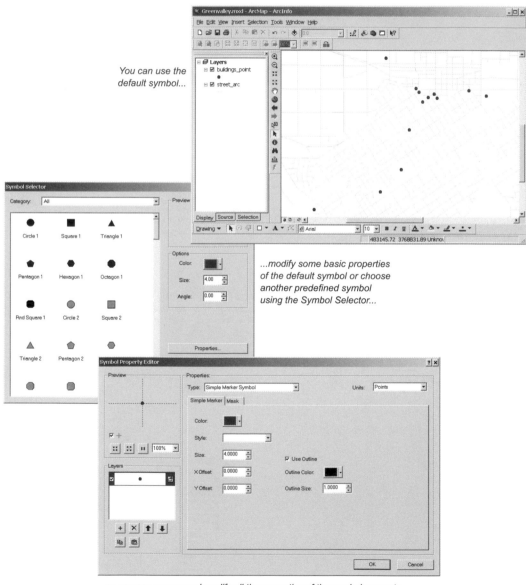

You can use the default symbol...

...modify some basic properties of the default symbol or choose another predefined symbol using the Symbol Selector...

...or, you can access and modify all the properties of the symbol or create symbols from scratch using the Symbol Property Editor.

ArcGIS Desktop provides a range of interface options that allow users at different skill levels to work efficiently—from wizards and dialog boxes to a command line interface. For example, tools in ArcToolbox can be run using a dialog box that prompts for inputs—helpful for less experienced users—or can be entered on a command line, a more direct way for advanced users to run the tools.

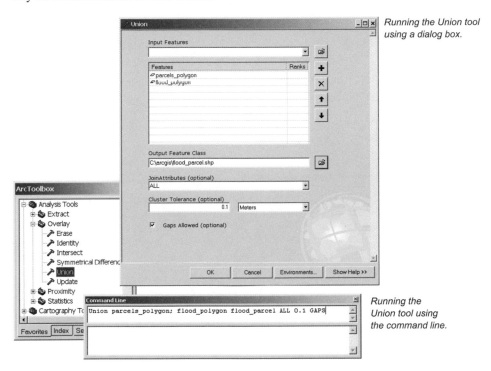

Running the Union tool using a dialog box.

Running the Union tool using the command line.

You can customize the interface, specifying which menus to display and which buttons to include, for example.

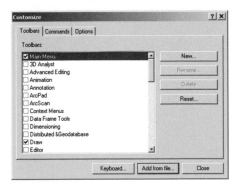
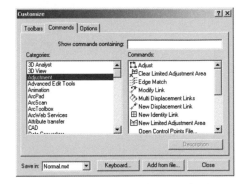

The ArcGIS Desktop interface is customizable (click Customize from the Tools menu in ArcMap or ArcCatalog). Use the Toolbars tab to specify which toolbars to display, by default. Use the Commands tab to add buttons (commands) to the various toolbars.

Flexible data support

Another cornerstone of ArcGIS Desktop is its ability to access GIS data in any format and to support a range of database configurations.

ArcGIS is designed to work with just about every type of geographic data, from a broad array of sources. Some data formats ArcGIS can read directly, such as geodatabase datasets, shapefiles, coverages, and many raster formats. Data in other GIS formats must be converted to an ArcGIS format before you can display and work with the data—ArcGIS Desktop includes converters for many standard GIS formats. Some data, such as CAD data, can be read and displayed by ArcGIS Desktop, but must be converted to an ArcGIS format to take advantage of the full functionality of the software.

ArcGIS Desktop also lets you set up databases that will meet the needs of one person, a small department or workgroup, or an enterprise that requires that many people to be able to access and edit the database concurrently. If you already use a commercial DBMS—or need your GIS to work with such a system—you can take advantage of this by creating ArcSDE® geodatabases.

Types of geographic data and how to manage data are discussed in Chapter 2, 'Geographic Data Management'.

A generic application approach

ArcGIS Desktop was designed to be used across a range of disciplines for a huge variety of tasks. It is not industry or application specific. The software provides a comprehensive set of tools and functions that users combine in the way that best addresses the task at hand. Many users customize the application toolbars and menus to reflect the tasks and workflows they perform most frequently.

ArcGIS Desktop can also be used with other ArcGIS applications in a way that allows GIS to be available on different hardware platforms and for a range of GIS users—from the general public to casual GIS users to GIS specialists. For example, maps created in ArcMap can be published using the ArcGIS Publisher extension. The maps can be distributed on CD/DVD or over the Internet and read by non-GIS users using ArcReader™, a simple, standalone map display software application.

The book *What is ArcGIS?* describes the complete ArcGIS system and how ArcGIS Desktop can be used with other ArcGIS applications to publish data and maps on the Internet, used by people throughout an organization to access a centralized GIS database, or used in conjunction with handheld devices to collect and update data in the field.

Getting help

Chapters 2 through 5 describe the basics of a number of common tasks performed in ArcGIS Desktop. More information on these and other tasks is available in the ArcGIS Desktop Help system. The Help system contains both task-based (step-by-step) and conceptual information, and includes a GIS dictionary. There are also several online sources of help available.

Desktop Help

Help can be accessed from an ArcGIS application (ArcMap or ArcCatalog) via the Help menu on the Main menu, from the Start Programs menu, or by pressing the F1 key on the keyboard. The Help viewer contains a navigation pane—with Contents, Index, Favorites, and Search tabs—and a topic pane for viewing Help topics.

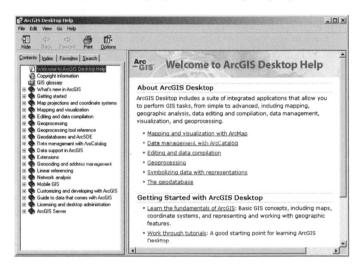

Use the Contents to look up general topics. Conceptual topics in the contents list are indicated by a page icon. Task-based topics include step-by-step instructions and tips for performing specific tasks. They're indicated by an icon showing a page with a numbered list. Some of these topics also have short, animated tutorials available.

You can scroll through the Index or search by entering keywords that identify your task.

The Favorites tab lets you keep a list of often-visited topics.

Use the Search tab to enter keywords, phrases, or complete sentences. Once you've entered your search, click the Ask button. The results are ranked and provide links to the topic.

The Help system also lets you get information about the buttons and menu commands you see on the interface. When you position the mouse pointer over a button for a second or two, the button's name pops up (this can be turned on or off on the Options tab of the Customize dialog box).

After clicking the What's This? button on the standard toolbar, you can click any button or menu option to display a description of it.

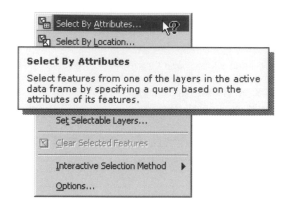

When you click the Help button in the upper-right corner of a dialog box, then click an item, a description is displayed. Some dialog boxes also have a Help button on the bottom; clicking it opens a Help topic with detailed information about the particular task.

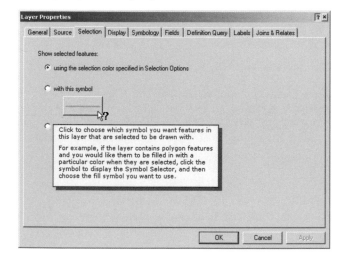

All ArcToolbox tools have associated help. The Show/Hide Help button on the tool dialog box displays (or hides) a Help panel with a description of the tool and information about the tool parameters. Clicking the Help button at the top of the panel takes you to the topic in the Desktop Help system where you'll find complete information about the tool.

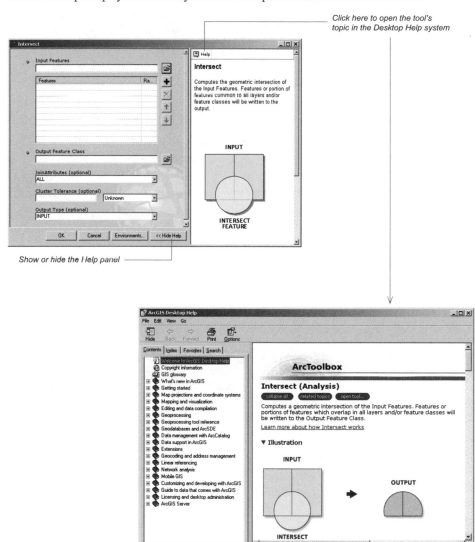

Click here to open the tool's topic in the Desktop Help system

Show or hide the Help panel

Online Help In addition to the Desktop Help System, there are several online resources for getting help with the software. These can also be accessed from the Help menu.

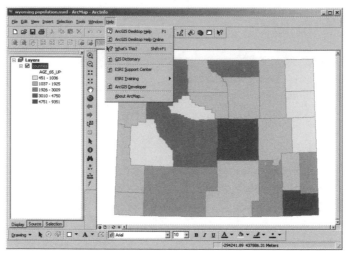

Online resources, including Desktop Help Online, a GIS Dictionary, the ESRI Support Center, training resources, and developer support are available from the Help menu.

Desktop Help online

The entire Desktop Help system is also available online. The online version features links to common tasks and to specific applications.

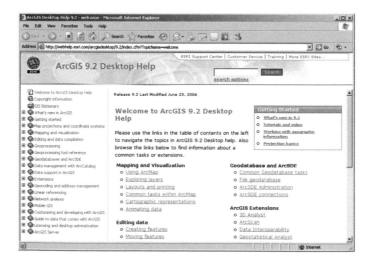

ESRI Support Center

This online site provides users with information and help for all of ESRI's software products. You can access it directly from *http://support.esri.com*, or you can launch it from the Help menu in ArcGIS.

The site includes:

- The Knowledge Base, which lets you search ESRI's database of technical articles, white papers, system requirements, and product documentation.

- Downloads of the latest software updates, service packs, samples, user-contributed ArcScripts℠, data models, geoprocessing models and scripts, and evaluation software.

- User forums for ESRI's community of GIS professionals to browse and post focused questions, or actively help others.

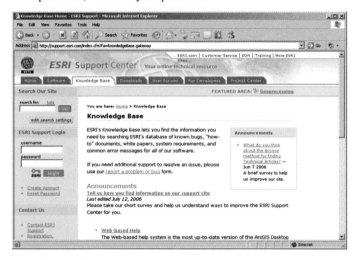

Developer Help

The ESRI® Developer Network (EDN℠) at *edn.esri.com* provides information about creating your own user interfaces, tools, and special applications. This site contains sample code, technical documents, downloads of developer tools and add-ins, and discussion forums for ESRI's developer community.

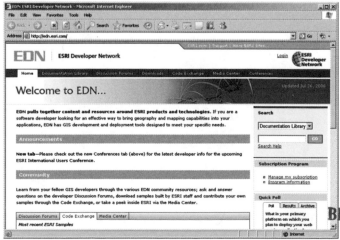

Geographic Data Management

GIS data concepts

Underpinning all your GIS work, no matter what it is, are geographic datasets that contain the data you need to build databases, make maps, and perform analyses. One of the main roles of ArcGIS Desktop is to help you organize and manage this geographic data efficiently. First, though, it's useful to review some of the basics of GIS data. While similar in some respects to data created and stored in a database program or graphics software, GIS data has some unique characteristics.

What is GIS data?

GIS data is a digital representation—or model—of features or phenomena that occur on or near the earth's surface. Many types of geographic features and phenomena can be modeled in ArcGIS and stored as GIS data, including:

- A physical object—either natural or man-made—such as a stream, or a light pole. Some objects are stationary while others are mobile, such as a delivery truck or an animal with a radio transmitter.

- A defined object that isn't necessarily visible on the ground, but that can be displayed on a map. Areas defined by boundaries, such as a county boundary, are a prime example. Many boundaries are legally defined, such as parcel or congressional district boundaries, while some are formed by physical features, such as the boundary of a watershed.

- An event that occurs for some relatively short period of time, such as a burglary, or an earthquake. While the event itself is ephemeral, the location—and date and time—of the occurrence can be captured and stored.

- A locator, such as a street address, or a milepost on a highway. The locator doesn't represent a physical object—simply a location that is important or useful to identify. Locators are often used to fix the location of events or mobile objects—for example, a street address is often used to identify the location of a burglary or to identify the location of customers or students (people move around, but in GIS their location is usually fixed to their home address).

- A spatial network representing linkages between objects or events. Often the network is defined on top of other geographic objects, such as a bus route which is a geographic feature defined from a set of streets and stops, themselves geographic features.

- A phenomenon that can be measured at any given location, such as elevation above sea level, soil moisture in the ground, or the concentration of ozone in the air.

What these geographic entities all have in common—from a GIS standpoint—is that they have a location that can be captured and stored, and they have properties, termed attributes in ArcGIS. The attributes might be descriptions—such as the zoning code of a parcel or the name of a stream, or they might be measurements—such as the population of a county or the magnitude of an earthquake. Linking the location of the object or event with its attributes makes it possible to create highly customized maps, to perform spatial queries, and to perform analyses that take into account the spatial relationships between objects.

How do you represent feature geography in a GIS?

There are a number of models for representing this variety of geographic entities, however two in particular are the most common. One represents geographic entities as geometric shapes (feature classes); the other represents them as cell values (rasters). Typical representations of feature classes are points (such as wells), lines (such as roads), and polygons (such as census tracts). Feature classes are stored as coordinate pairs that reference locations on the earth's surface. A well, for example, might be represented as a point in a features class, with coordinates as 119 degrees west longitude and 34 degrees north latitude. A line or polygon can be represented as a series of coordinate pairs that can be connected to draw the feature. This approach views features as discrete objects on the earth's surface, and the representation is referred to as vector data.

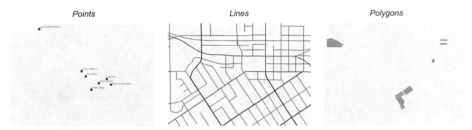

Building location points, street centerlines, and park boundary polygons are examples of feature classes.

In contrast, rasters represent geographic features by dividing the world into discrete square or rectangular cells laid out in a grid. Each cell describes the phenomenon being observed. For example, the cell values in a vegetation raster represent the dominant vegetation type in each particular cell.

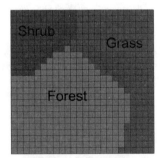

A raster of vegetation types.

Cell values can also be any measured or calculated value, such as elevation, slope, rainfall, vegetation type, or temperature.

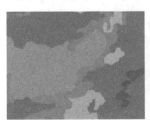

The raster data structure is commonly used for continuous categorical data (such as land cover), digital elevation models, and photo and satellite images.

While most geographic features can be represented using either of these approaches, using one or the other is often more appropriate. For example, linear features, such as roads, are often represented using feature classes. Phenomena that occur everywhere and are measured on a continuous numeric scale—such as elevation or air quality—are usually represented as rasters. Quite often you'll work with both types of data simultaneously when creating a map or when performing analysis. ArcGIS includes tools that allow you to convert data between features classes and raster data, if necessary.

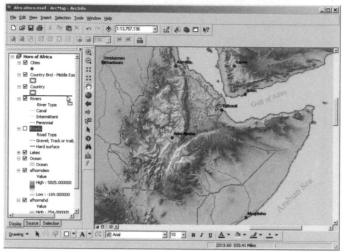

This map display was created by drawing feature classes of cities, country boundaries, rivers, and waterbodies on top of a raster dataset of shaded relief.

Features of a similar type within a designated area are stored in a single dataset. Datasets are homogeneous collections of geographic elements. Roads in a town would be stored in one dataset, landuse zones in another, census tract boundaries in a third, buildings in a fourth, and so on. The various datasets are often thought of—and portrayed—as layers of information for that place.

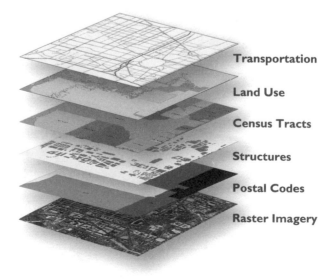

Each dataset represents a type of information for a place.

During mapping and 3D visualization, datasets are symbolized, labeled, and displayed as map layers.

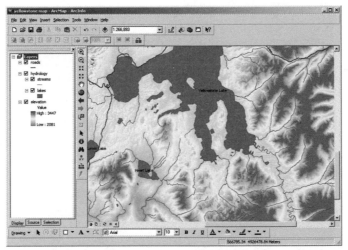

This map display includes four datasets: a polygon dataset of lakes, line datasets of roads and streams, and a raster dataset of elevation.

In geoprocessing, operators are applied to datasets to create new datasets—for example, to create a dataset of 30 meter buffer polygons around road centerlines.

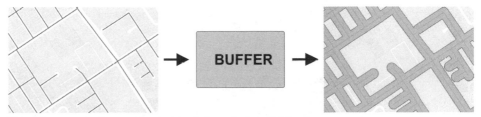

You apply geoprocessing operators to datasets to create derived datasets.

Datasets are also the most common way of sharing data among GIS users.

Cities	Feature Class	Thu 9/23/2004 3:54 PM
CitiesAnno	Feature Class	Thu 9/23/2004 11:06 AM
Roads	Feature Class	Mon 10/4/2004 10:55 AM
RoadsAnno	Feature Class	Thu 9/30/2004 8:58 AM
ParkBoundaries	Feature Class	Tue 9/28/2004 8:56 AM
States	Feature Class	Thu 9/23/2004 3:54 PM
Streams	Feature Class	Thu 9/23/2004 11:06 AM
UtahRelief	Raster Dataset	Mon 10/4/2004 10:55 AM
150mNaturalColor	Raster Dataset	Thu 9/30/2004 8:58 AM

Datasets can be listed in ArcCatalog, and can be copied and distributed to other GIS users.

You also work with the individual data elements contained in each dataset—the individual parcels, wells, or buildings—and their associated attributes. For example, you can list the descriptive attributes and properties of an individual building by pointing at it on a map. Text labels can be used to annotate selected buildings.

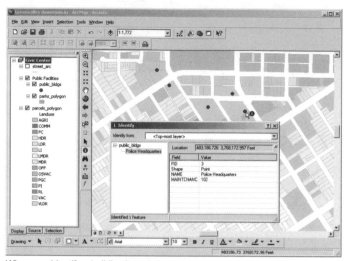

When you identify a building by pointing at it, you're working with the individual data elements in a dataset.

During editing, you edit the geometric shapes of individual parcels—for example, dragging a corner to expand the boundary of a park. Spatial selection allows you to graphically select a group of features on the map— for example, the parcels that are within a quarter mile of a freeway.

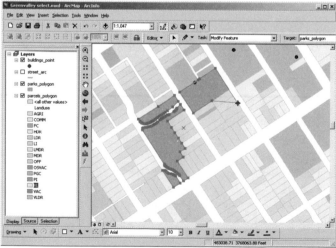

You work with individual data elements when you edit features, in this case, a park boundary.

How do you reference the location of a dataset on the Earth's surface?

A key concept of GIS data is that geographic datasets represent a location on or near the Earth's surface. This sets GIS data apart from graphics software where objects are simply stored in page units. Because the data is tied to an actual location on the surface of the earth, you can't just create it from scratch, as you would when creating a drawing on a blank page in a graphics program. (While you could draw a map on a blank page, the length or shape of features, and the distances between them, would likely not be accurate.)

Datasets are stored using coordinates that correspond to positions on the Earth's surface. The coordinates should accurately represent these positions to ensure that the feature shapes and their relationships to other features reflect actual conditions on the ground. Describing the correct location of features requires a framework for defining real-world locations. This process is called georeferencing. Georeferencing is accomplished by specifying a coordinate system for the dataset.

Georeferencing allows you to display on a single map various datasets—from different sources—and have them register correctly, or to combine datasets representing information about the same location to derive new data and information. If datasets were only in page units, two datasets representing the same location likely wouldn't register, depending on where they happened to appear on the page. Once georeferenced, the datasets refer to the same location on the ground, and register correctly.

Each GIS dataset has a set of properties that define the specific details about its coordinate system. Once specified, the coordinate system definition is maintained with the dataset.

One coordinate system for describing the position of geographic locations on the Earth's surface uses spherical measures of latitude and longitude. Latitude and longitude are measures of the angles (in degrees) from the center of the Earth to a point on the Earth's surface. This reference system is often referred to as a geographic coordinate system.

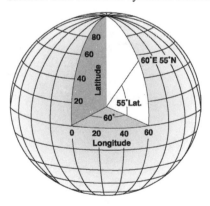

Although longitude and latitude can locate exact positions on the surface of the globe, this coordinate system doesn't allow you to measure distances or areas accurately or display the data easily on a flat computer screen or map.

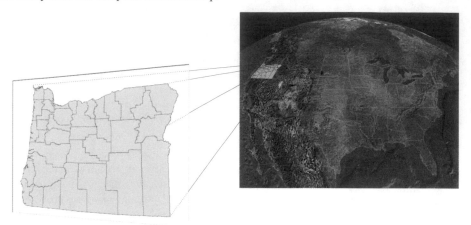

The GIS displays—on a flat computer screen or map—geographic features that occur on the surface of the spherical Earth.

To appear correctly on a screen or map page, the features have to be transformed to a flat plane. Projected coordinate systems include this transformation and specify the origin and units of the coordinates (feet or meters, usually).

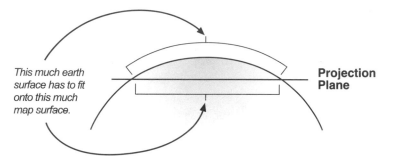

Projected coordinate systems use two axes: one horizontal (x), representing east–west, and one vertical (y), representing north–south (Cartesian coordinates). The point at which the axes intersect is called the origin. Locations of geographic objects are defined relative to the origin, using the notation (x,y), where x refers to the distance along the horizontal axis, and y refers to the distance along the vertical axis. The origin is defined as (0,0).

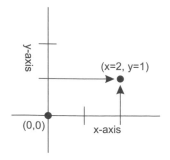

Typical units of measure in projected coordinate systems are feet or meters. So, in fact, the coordinate values are often six or seven digits—especially since the origin of the coordinate system may be far from your study area.

Each feature's coordinates are stored in these geographic units: points as x,y pairs; lines as a series of x,y pairs that define the shape of the line; the same for polygons. For raster datasets, the coordinates of the origin of the grid (usually the upper left or lower left corner) are stored, along with the cell size. Thus the extent of the raster and the geographic location of each value for individual cells can be calculated.

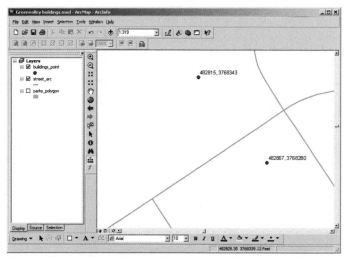

These buildings (represented as points) are labeled with their x,y coordinate values. The distance between them (about 82 feet) can be calculated in the GIS by storing the geographic coordinate values instead of the page units.

Projected coordinates can be defined for both 2D (x,y) and 3D (x,y,z) datasets, where x,y measurements represent the location on the Earth's surface and z would represent height above or below a point of reference such as mean sea level.

Unlike a geographic coordinate system (latitude–longitude), a projected coordinate system has constant lengths, angles, and areas across the two dimensions. However, all map projections representing the Earth's surface as a flat map, create distortions in some aspect of distance, area, shape, or direction. Many map projections are designed for specific purposes. One map projection might be used for preserving shape while another might be used for preserving the area (conformal versus equal area). In any case, the distortions are primarily an issue if your study area covers a large part of the globe (a country or continent), or the entire globe itself. If your study area is a county or city, these effects are small.

Many standard coordinate systems are established for the globe or for various regions—the UTM (Universal Transverse Mercator) system, for example, has a defined coordinate system for each 6-degree swath of longitude around the globe. UTM is used worldwide; in the United States, the State Plane system is another commonly used coordinate system. Other countries and regions often have their own local systems that use a local set of geographic controls.

A coordinate system specifies a datum, in addition to a map projection. A datum is a mathematical representation of the shape of the Earth's surface. A datum is defined by a spheroid, which approximates the shape of the Earth and the spheroid's position relative to the center of the Earth. A local datum aligns its spheroid to closely fit the Earth's surface in a particular area; its origin point is located on the surface of the Earth. The coordinates of the origin point are fixed, and all other points are calculated from this control point.

More than one coordinate system can become a standard for data from a specific region, and other coordinate systems may also be used. So, you may face the prospect of dealing with various datasets for the same location but that are in different coordinate systems.

By recording and storing the coordinate system properties for each dataset (the map projection, datum, spheroid, and geographic units), ArcGIS can automatically transform the locations of GIS datasets on the fly into any appropriate coordinate system (the coordinate system of the dataset stored on disk is not changed). It's then possible to map and combine information from multiple datasets regardless of their coordinate system. Alternatively, you can transform a dataset to create a new dataset in the specified coordinate system, using tools in ArcToolbox.

You can see a dataset's coordinate system by viewing its metadata in ArcCatalog or ArcMap, or by viewing its properties in ArcCatalog. See 'Defining coordiniate systems and projecting datasets' in Chapter 3 for more on assigning coordinate systems.

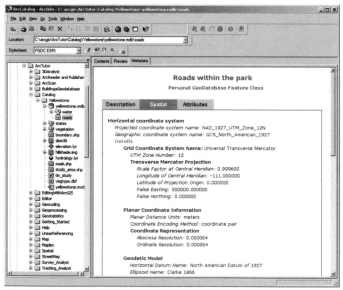

Metadata for a dataset includes a description of the dataset's coordinate system.

How do you represent feature attributes in a GIS?

In ArcGIS, attributes for feature classes are stored and managed in tables, which are based on a series of relational data concepts. These include:

- Tables contain rows.

- All rows in a table have the same columns.

- Each column has a type, such as integer, decimal number, character, date, and so on.

- Relationships are used to associate rows from one table with rows in another table. This is based on a common column in each table.

- A series of relational functions and operators, SQL (structured query language), is available to operate on the tables and their data elements.

Tables and relationships play a key role in ArcGIS, just as they do in traditional database applications. In ArcGIS, tables have an added dimension: each row in a table represents—and is linked to—a geographic element in the dataset. Additional tables can be linked to the geographic elements by a common field. For example, information on parcel owners might be stored in a separate table—the parcel identification number (PIN) serves as a link between this table and the parcels attribute table. This would allow you to associate multiple owners with a single parcel or a single owner with multiple parcels.

Feature class table

Shape	ID	PIN	Area	Addr	Code
	1	334-1626-001	7,342	341 Cherry Ct.	SFR
	2	334-1626-002	8,020	343 Cherry Ct.	UND
	3	334-1626-003	10,031	345 Cherry Ct.	SFR
	4	334-1626-004	9,254	347 Cherry Ct.	SFR
	5	334-1626-005	8,856	348 Cherry Ct.	UND
	6	334-1626-006	9,975	346 Cherry Ct.	SFR
	7	334-1626-007	8,230	344 Cherry Ct.	SFR
	8	334-1626-008	8,645	342 Cherry Ct.	SFR

Tables can be linked through a common field—in this case, the Parcel Identification Number.

Related ownership table

PIN	Owner	Acq.Date	Assessed	TaxStat
334-1626-001	G. Hall	1995/10/20	$115,500.00	02
334-1626-002	H. L Holmes	1993/10/06	$24,375.00	01
334-1626-003	W. Rodgers	1980/09/24	$175,500.00	02
334-1626-004	J. Williamson	1974/09/20	$135,750.00	02
334-1626-005	P. Goodman	1966/06/06	$30,350.00	02
334-1626-006	K. Staley	1942/10/24	$120,750.00	02
334-1626-007	J. Dormandy	1996/01/27	$110,650.00	01
334-1626-008	S. Gooley	2000/05/31	$145,750.00	02

This combination of geography and descriptive information provides the foundation for the ArcGIS information model, which is often referred to as the geo-relational model.

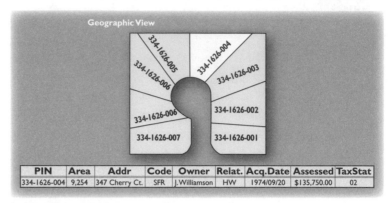

The GIS information model includes both geographic and tabular data, and is often referred to as the geo-relational model.

The geo-relational model enables key GIS tasks, such as using attribute values to label and symbolize features. Because the tabular information is linked to the geographic objects (which in turn have a geographic location), it also allows you to perform spatial queries and analyses. You can, for example:

- Point at a feature on the map and display its attributes.

- Select a feature in a table and see it highlighted on the map.

- Select a subset of features that have certain attribute values—that is, that meet some criteria you specify.

- Use statistics to find geographic clusters of features having similar values.

In the raster data model, tables function in a different way. If the raster dataset represents categorical information, such as the soil type in each cell, each row in the table represents a category rather than an individual cell. The table stores the number of cells in each category. You can also store additional attributes for each category—a soil name, crop classification, and so on. If the raster dataset represents continuous measurements, such as elevation or soil moisture, each cell potentially has a unique value, so only that value is stored with the raster, and a table is unnecessary.

An overview of geographic data management

ArcGIS provides a great deal of flexibility in the types of data you can view and analyze—data stored using different data models (vector, raster, TINs, and so on), data in different file formats (feature classes, shapefiles, or coverages), datasets covering different geographic areas, datasets from various sources and in different coordinate systems, and so on. ArcGIS Desktop also lets you work with or import a wide variety of other data types, including images (.bmp, .jpg, and so on), CAD files, other geographic data formats (such as DLG or TIGER®) and tables (in text format or spreadsheet formats such as Excel). To be able to efficiently find and use all this data, you'll need to organize it.

The main mechanism for organizing your geographic data in ArcGIS is to define a workspace. A workspace—by definition—is any folder containing your GIS data. Workspaces also contain other files and documents you collect and create in the course of your work.

Workspaces are viewed and managed in ArcCatalog. Here is a workspace named Yellowstone, containing several datasets and associated files. These are the most common types of datasets and files you'll work with.

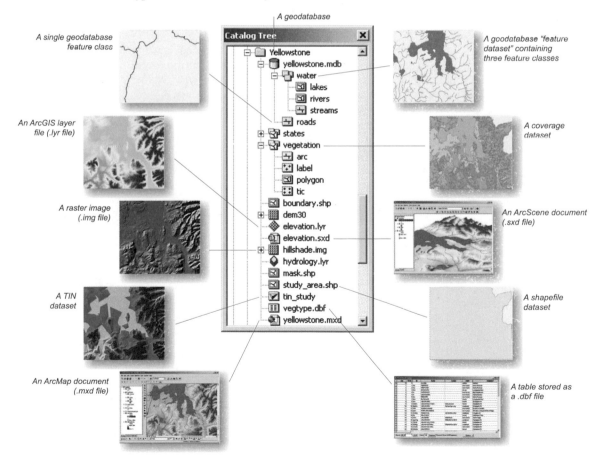

A geodatabase

A single geodatabase feature class

A geodatabase "feature dataset" containing three feature classes

An ArcGIS layer file (.lyr file)

A coverage dataset

A raster image (.img file)

An ArcScene document (.sxd file)

A TIN dataset

A shapefile dataset

An ArcMap document (.mxd file)

A table stored as a .dbf file

A geodatabase is both a format for storing datasets and a way of organizing related datasets. Geodatabases are the primary way geographic data is stored in ArcGIS—they are discussed in more detail later in this section.

ESRI shapefiles and coverages were used in earlier versions of ESRI software (ArcView GIS 3 and ArcInfo Workstation, respectively). Much geographic data is still available in these formats, and the datasets are still widely used in ArcGIS Desktop.

ArcMap documents, ArcScene™ documents, and layer files are created as you build maps and 3D views. You'll read more about them in Chapter 4, 'Mapping and Visualization', and Chapter 5, 'Geographic Analysis'.

Organizing and managing workspaces in ArcCatalog

ArcCatalog is the primary application for organizing and managing workspaces and datasets.

If you're collecting existing data, you set up a structure and copy the datasets into it (or import them). If you're creating new data (by digitizing, for example), you first create the individual datasets, and then create the features within them (see Chapter 3, 'Data Compilation and Editing', for more on creating features by editing).

Setting up a workspace structure

When possible, you'll want to define the structure for your data organization before starting a map or a GIS project. In the case of building a large, multiuser database this is essential.

Your workspaces may consist of a single file folder containing many datasets and other related documents that are organized around themes or projects. For example, if you have a statewide GIS, you might have your data organized by county. Many users organize their projects by theme, such as workspaces for roads, water, parcels, administrative boundaries, and so forth. In other situations, you may want to organize workspaces around a project such as a road development project or new power plant project. You can also organize workspaces within workspaces. For example, you may have a project workspace "New power plant", and within that workspace you may have subfolders organized for each dataset or for each project task, such as "New dam," "New road," or "New transmission lines".

This statewide workspace contains a folder for each county. The content of the county workspaces is consistent.

This simple project workspace organizes datasets in folders, by the type of data.

This workspace for a major project contains subworkspaces for each element of the project. The workspaces contain the components specific to that element.

Quite often you'll set up a geodatabase (or several geodatabases) within a workspace—the geodatabase contains the geographic datasets and related tables while other files and documents (maps documents, layer files, and so on) are stored in folders within the workspace.

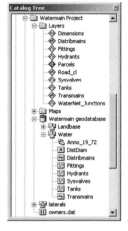

This typical workspace contains folders to contain layer files and maps as well as a geodatabase to contain geographic datasets and relationships.

Using ArcGIS geodatabases

A geodatabase is a collection of geographic datasets of various types used for representing features, images and tabular and other data types. While you can set up workspaces without geodatabases—containing only shapefiles, coverages, rasters, and so on—creating a geodatabase to store and organize your GIS data has several advantages:

• You can specify rules and create specialized datasets that more closely mimic the behavior of geographic entities, such as creating a geometric network to model the flow of water through a system of pipes and valves.

• A geodatabase lets you set up a structure that ensures relationships between datasets are made explicit and are maintained. You can make sure that datasets referencing the same location on the Earth's surface spatially register with each other correctly. In addition, you can specify that when you edit features in a geodatabase, all related features are also edited (so if you move a junction box, the connected electrical lines also move).

• You can also set up rules to ensure data integrity (for example, a rule might state that parcel boundaries cannot cross—any that do are flagged as errors).

• Storing data in a geodatabase is an efficient way to manage related datasets as a single unit.

The three most common dataset types are feature classes, raster datasets, and attribute tables. You'll typically start by building a number of these fundamental dataset types. You'll have a set of feature classes (roads, streams, boundaries, and so on). Most of the time, you'll also have a set of imagery and raster datasets to work with (an elevation surface, orthophotos, or satellite images). And you'll have a number of tables, such as dBASE™ files, Microsoft® Access™ tables, Excel® spreadsheets, and so forth.

Fundamentally, all geodatabases will contain this same kind of content. This collection of datasets can be thought of as the starting point for your geodatabase.

Then, as necessary, you'll extend your geodatabase with specialized capabilities to model how geographic features "behave" in the real world, to maintain data integrity, and to work with spatial relationships. These extended datasets are built from existing datasets plus rules and properties that define behavior or relationships.

The three primary datasets in the geodatabase (feature classes, raster datasets, and attribute tables) as well as other geodatabase datasets are stored using tables. Vector and raster geometries are stored and managed in attribute columns along with traditional attribute fields. (This is unlike shapefiles and coverages, where the geometry is stored in a set of files and the attributes are stored in a related table.) The extended functions that define feature behavior, data integrity, and spatial relationships are also stored in the database.

Basic geodatabase datasets

Feature classes are homogeneous collections of common features, each having the same spatial representation, such as points, lines, or polygons, and a common set of attribute columns—for example, a line feature class for representing road centerlines. Feature classes are similar to shapefiles or coverages in that they represent geographic features as points, lines, and polygons.

Raster datasets are commonly used for representing and managing imagery, digital elevation models, and other spatially continuous phenomena.

Tables are used to store all the properties of geographic objects (these are referred to as feature attribute tables). This includes holding and managing feature geometry in a "Shape" column. Tables also store attributes in related tables that can be linked to the feature class or raster (these are referred to as standalone tables).

Extending your geodatabase

On top of building the basic datasets in your geodatabase, you can add datasets to ensure data integrity, manage the relationships between geographic features and between tables, and allow for specialized data types.

Ensuring spatial data integrity with feature datasets and topologies

A "feature dataset" is a specific element in a geodatabase (not to be confused with the generic term "dataset") that holds one or more feature classes (sort of like a folder holds files). When you define a feature dataset, you specify the coordinate system. Any feature classes must have this same coordinate system, so you ensure that they register correctly (if they're not in the right coordinate system, you'll have to transform them first—see 'Defining coordinate systems and projecting datasets' in Chapter 3).

A topology is a set of rules you specify that defines spatial relationships between adjacent or connected features in a feature class, or between feature classes (for example, you'd specify that census tracts share common boundaries and that they nest within counties—that ensures that boundaries don't overlap). Topologies define explicitly in the GIS relationships you can see by looking at a map. By defining a topology, you ensure these spatial relationships are maintained. Topologies are created within feature datasets.

Ensuring attribute data integrity with domains and subtypes

Attribute domains are used to specify a list of values, or a range of numeric values, for attributes. This ensures that only valid attribute values are assigned to features and avoids misspellings and other data entry errors. Subtypes are used to specify default attribute values for categories within a feature class. For example, for a roads feature class you could use a Road Type attribute to assign default speed limit values (25 mph for residential streets, 45 mph for major roads, and so on). When you assign the Road Type value for a feature, the Speed Limit value is automatically assigned. This ensures that the different classes of road are assigned the correct speed limit. Subtypes can also be used to define behavior for categories of features.

Building relationships between features and tables

Relationship classes are used to build tabular relationships between feature classes and other tables using a common key. For example, you could build a relationship class between a feature class of parcels and a table of parcel owners. The parcel owner information is stored and maintained in a separate table, for efficiency (some owners may own more than one parcel—if you need to update the information, you only need to edit one record). When necessary, you can retrieve the owner information by selecting a parcel, or find all the parcels owned by someone by selecting the owner in the related table. You can build relationship classes between any two tables. The owner table could in turn be related to a table of property tax information.

Adding specialized datasets to your geodatabase

You can add a number of specialized datasets to your geodatabase to use in specific applications, such as surface modeling or network analysis:

Terrains—used for modeling triangulated irregular networks (TINs) and for managing large LiDAR and sonar point collections.

Network Dataset—used for modeling connectivity and flow for a transportation network, such as roads or rail.

Geometric Network—used for modeling outage and flows for a utilities network, such as electrical, water, or telecommunications.

Address Locator—used for assigning locations to a set of street addresses.

Linear Referencing—used for locating events along linear features with measurements, such as a highway with mile markers.

All of these datasets are discussed later in this chapter.

Types of geodatabases

ArcGIS provides three types of geodatabases, designed for different work environments—from people using GIS by themselves, to small workgroups where several people need to access GIS data for various tasks, to large corporations or agencies (known as enterprises) that have many people accessing and editing GIS data, and where the GIS is integrated into other applications and databases.

File and personal geodatabases are designed for use by one or a few people. They support the full information model of the geodatabase, including topologies, raster catalogs, network datasets, terrain datasets, address locators, and so on. File and personal geodatabases can be edited by one person at a time—they do not support having multiple versions of a geodatabase that can be worked on by different people simultaneously. The file geodatabase is a new geodatabase type released in ArcGIS 9.2. Personal geodatabases, which were introduced in ArcGIS 8, use the Microsoft Access data file structure (the .mdb file).

ArcSDE geodatabases are designed to be accessed and edited simultaneously by many users. In addition to the capabilities of file and personal geodatabases, ArcSDE geodatabases can handle transactions that occur over a long period (such as continuous updating), can manage simultaneous editing and updating by many users, and can track the changes in the database over time, through versioning. ArcSDE geodatabases are primarily used in workgroup, department, and enterprise settings. The Personal and Workgroup editions of ArcSDE use SqlExpress. The Enterprise edition of ArcSDE allows you to create geodatabases that work with a variety of DBMS storage models (IBM® DB2®, Informix®, Oracle®, and Microsoft SQL Server).

Comparison of geodatabase types

	Storage	Notes
File geodatabase	A file system folder containing a system file for each dataset	Single-user editing, multiple readers Each dataset can be up to 1 TB in size No versioning support
Personal geodatabase	All contents held in a single Microsoft Access database file (.mdb)	Single-user editing, multiple readers 2 GB size limit for each Access database (effective size for performance is 250MB to 500MB) No versioning support
ArcSDE geodatabase	Any of a number of relational databases: • Oracle • Microsoft SQL Server • IBM DB2 • IBM Informix	Requires ArcSDE Multiuser editing, scales to many users Supports versioning and long transactions Size and number of users up to DBMS limits

ArcGIS provides for flexibility in storing datasets. You can load datasets stored in a file system geodatabase into a multiuser or personal DBMS geodatabase, and can export from a DBMS geodatabase. You can also work with datasets stored in both file system and DBMS geodatabases simultaneously.

The process for designing and building a geodatabase

One way to build a geodatabase is to create datasets and load data into the geodatabase as needed during your GIS projects. It's often more efficient, though, to spend some time and thought designing your geodatabase ahead of time and collecting as much of the required data as possible before beginning your project. This will save time and effort later when you're doing analysis and making maps.

If you have experience designing large relational databases, you already have the background you need to set up a workgroup or enterprise geodatabase. The specific tasks for building a geodatabase are described later in this chapter. If you're new to database design and you're designing a single-user or small workgroup geodatabase, a process you can follow is outlined below, to get you started. There are also a couple books on geodatabase design published by ESRI Press, as well as additional resources in the Help system and at ESRI's Web site. These are listed in the appendix.

Designing a geodatabase consists of identifying the types of information products you'll create with the GIS, listing the data themes required to create these products, and defining the specifications for each data theme. These specifications are implemented as datasets in the geodatabase (feature classes, rasters, topologies, relationship classes, and so on). You will probably want to prototype the design before fully implementing it, and regardless, you'll definitely want to document your design.

Here, in brief, are the major steps in the process.

Identify the products you'll create and manage using the GIS

Your geodatabase design should reflect the work of your organization. When designing a geodatabase, you'll have a set of applications in mind—the maps, analytical models, web mapping applications, data flows, database reports, 3D views, and other products you'll create with ArcGIS Desktop. Defining what these products are helps determine the data themes you'll need in the database, and how they're represented. For example, there are numerous alternatives for representing surface elevation   as contour lines and spot height locations (hilltops, peaks, and so on), as a continuous terrain surface (a TIN), or as shaded relief. Contour lines as height locations would be appropriate for a topographic map, while a continuous terrain surface would be appropriate for an engineering or hydrology application.

Identify the data themes needed to create the products

Next, list the themes you'll need for your applications. For each product, list all of the input data themes that are required. These are the geographic features and phenomena that will comprise the geodatabase, and allow you to create your products. If your application is to create a topographic map, you'll need elevation, hydrology (streams, rivers, lakes, wetlands), transportation (roads, trails, rail lines, ferry routes), transmission lines, and so forth. A good place to start is by listing all the data themes you currently use in your applications, and their sources. It might also help to organize the themes by broader categories—transportation, hydrology, land surface, and so on.

ESRI and its user community have developed a series of geodatabase data model templates that provide a jump start on your geodatabase designs. These designs are described and documented at *http://support.esri.com/datamodels*. At this stage of the design process you can use them as a checklist to make sure you're including all the data themes you'll need. They also include the detailed specifications for each data theme (see the next step), so you can use them as examples of how to define the various themes. When it's time to build your geodatabase, you can download the applicable templates, modify them per your own geodatabase design, and then populate the geodatabase with your data, saving you the effort of creating the geodatabase structure from scratch.

Here is an example description of a data theme for ownership parcels in a cadastral application.

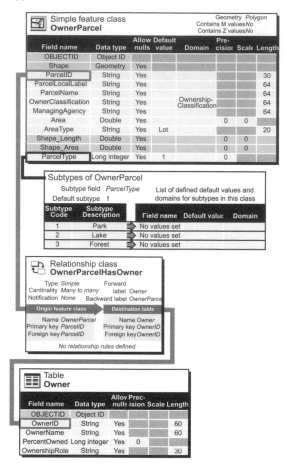

Create the specifications for individual data themes

Once you have identified and described the thematic layers in your design, the next step is to develop specifications, or schema, for representing the contents of each thematic layer in the physical database. The description of each thematic layer will result in a specification of geodatabase datasets, such as feature classes, tables, relationship classes, raster datasets, subtypes, topologies, domains, and so on.

These then become the individual geodatabase datasets you create in ArcCatalog (or that you copy from a data model and modify). Then you import the actual data into each feature class, or create new data by digitizing or scanning features in the feature class.

Here are the characteristics of each data theme that you'll want to define:

- The coordinate system—this may be predetermined by local or regional standards, or by data that you're already using. You may use different coordinate systems for different applications (and geodatabases).

- How the data themes will be represented geographically—some may be simple feature classes (wells represented as point features); some may require special datasets (an elevation surface represented as a terrain, or utilities as a geometric network). The map scale is also an issue for the geographic representation of features. You might want to represent buildings as point features when zoomed out, and as polygons (the building footprint) when zoomed in. In this case you'll need to create two feature classes for the data theme.

- The attributes of each data theme—the fields (column names), the data type for each (whether numeric or character, the field length, and so on), and the valid values or value ranges. You'll also want to define the table structure for each data theme— whether all the attributes are held in the theme's attribute table, or whether there are related tables and, if so, which fields will be used as the common keys for building relationships.

- The relationships with other features. Consider how each map layer will be displayed in an integrated fashion with other layers. For modeling and analysis, consider how information will be used with other datasets (that is, how they are combined and integrated). This will help you to identify key spatial relationships and data integrity rules, to be implemented as feature datasets and topologies.

Here's a simple example for a parcels geodatabase.

Feature Class	Representation	Notes
Street centerlines	Line	Street segments split at each intersection. Usually contain address ranges and network properties.
Soil types	Polygon	Usually have many descriptive attributes in related tables.
Parcels	Polygon	Topologically integrated with parcel boundaries and corners.
Parcel boundaries	Line	Has coordinate geometry and dimension attributes. Participates in a topology with parcels and corners.
Parcel corners	Point	Surveyed corners of parcels. Participates in a topology with parcel polygons and boundaries.
Parcel annotation	Annotation	Provides text labels for lot dimensions, taxation, and legal description information.
Building footprints	Polygon	Contains outlines of building and structures.

Specify editing workflows and map display properties

If your GIS work will involve data editing or updating data on an ongoing basis, it's useful to define up front the editing procedures and integrity rules—for example, you'd specify that all streets are split where they intersect other streets, street segments connect at endpoints, and so on. You can ensure that these rules are implemented in the geodatabase. It's also useful to define display properties for maps and 3D views, such as symbology, standard map scales, and text fonts. These will be used to define map layers.

Build and test a prototype design

If you're building a large, multiuser database, you'll want to test your prototype design. Build a sample geodatabase copy of your proposed design using a file geodatabase or a personal geodatabase. Load a subset of data and build maps, run key applications, and perform editing operations to test the design's utility. You can then make changes to the design before loading all the data.

The process of implementing your geodatabase design involves building the geodatabase structure, and then populating it with your data. There are two ways to build the geodatabase structure.

- Use ArcCatalog tools to create the various geodatabase datasets. There are a number of tools in ArcCatalog that let you create new feature datasets, feature classes, tables, relationship classes, topologies and other geodatabase datasets. These tools are discussed as separate topics later in this chapter.

- Use an existing geodatabase data model template. This can be one (or more) of the data models available at the ESRI Web site (*http://support.esri.com/datamodels*), or a template that someone else provides to you. That saves you the step of defining the geodatabase structure using the ArcCatalog tools. You'll likely use the tools, though, to modify the templates to match your design. The process for importing and modifying a geodatabase data model template is discussed as a separate topic later in this chapter.

Importing data to a geodatabase and editing are discussed in Chapter 3, 'Data Compilation and Editing'.

Document your geodatabase design

Once you've solidified your geodatabase design, you'll want to document it for reference. Various methods can be used to describe your database design and decisions: drawings, map layer examples, schema diagrams, reports, and metadata documents. The data models section at *http://support.esri.com/datamodels* has sample geodatabase documentation from a variety of industries.

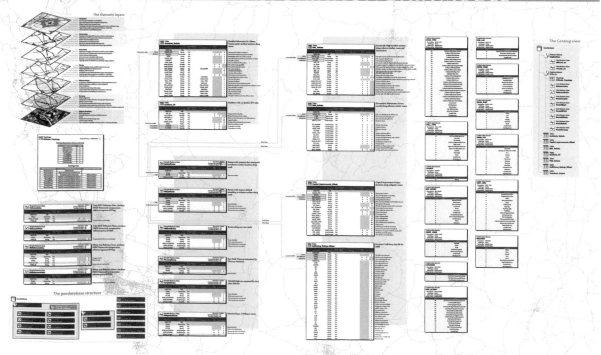

A sample geodatabase data model document showing the various datasets and associated attributes, as well as the links between tables.

Finding and connecting to data

ArcCatalog lets you find and connect to data stored on your computer or another computer on your network, on a CD or DVD, in a database management system, or on a GIS server on your local network or the Internet. Once connected, you can browse or search for data across the connections.

Establishing a data connection

While you can add data directly to a map from your local disk drive without setting up a connection, establishing the connection allows you to preview the data, review the metadata, and more easily manage your data sources.

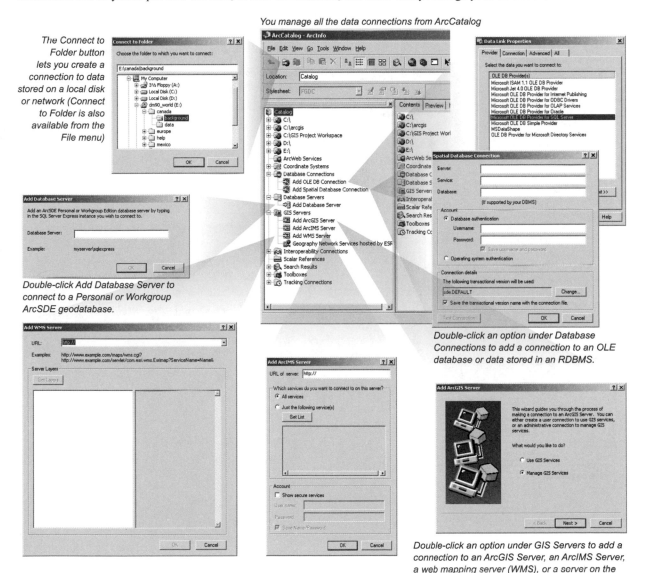

The Connect to Folder button lets you create a connection to data stored on a local disk or network (Connect to Folder is also available from the File menu)

You manage all the data connections from ArcCatalog

Double-click Add Database Server to connect to a Personal or Workgroup ArcSDE geodatabase.

Double-click an option under Database Connections to add a connection to an OLE database or data stored in an RDBMS.

Double-click an option under GIS Servers to add a connection to an ArcGIS Server, an ArcIMS Server, a web mapping server (WMS), or a server on the Geography Network.

Some connections may be established once, for databases you access on an ongoing basis; others may be connections you set up on an as-needed basis to access data for a particular map. If the connection is not currently valid (the data has moved or the server is unavailable), a small red x will appear next to the connection's name.

You can have more than one connection to the same data source—for example, a connection to a CD at the highest level and additional connections to folders and subfolders on the CD.

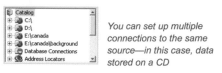

You can set up multiple connections to the same source—in this case, data stored on a CD

Once you're done accessing the data or no longer need the connection, you can disconnect by right-clicking the connection and selecting Disconnect Folder.

The established connections appear in the Catalog tree

Right-click the connection and select Disconnect Folder

Database and server connections

Storing geographic data in a relational database management system lets many people within an organization access the same set of data. Storing data on an ArcGIS or ArcIMS® server lets people both inside and outside an organization access the data. These connections are often established by a GIS or database system administrator. One special server connection is to the Geography Network℠, a clearinghouse for GIS data supplied by users worldwide. When you connect to the Geography Network you get a list of currently available images and feature data you can preview, and add to your map.

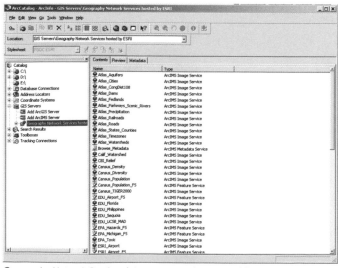

Geography Network Services lets you access images and features and services

Previewing data and maps

Using ArcCatalog, you can preview data from any source you've connected to.

Previewing what's in a folder or geodatabase

Use the Contents tab to see what's in a folder or geodatabase containing geographic datasets. You can view the contents as a list or as thumbnails, among other options.

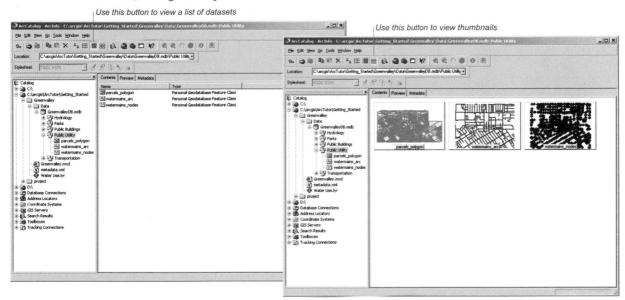

Use this button to view a list of datasets

Use this button to view thumbnails

Previewing a feature's geography or attributes

Select a feature class in the tree view and select the Preview tab. Then specify whether you want to preview the feature's geography or attribute table.

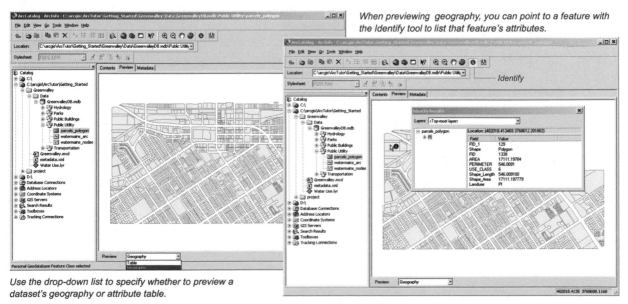

When previewing geography, you can point to a feature with the Identify tool to list that feature's attributes.

Use the drop-down list to specify whether to preview a dataset's geography or attribute table.

You can preview an attribute table associated with a feature class or another data table in a compatible format—for example, .dbf. You can explore the table to make sure, for example, that it's the most current version.

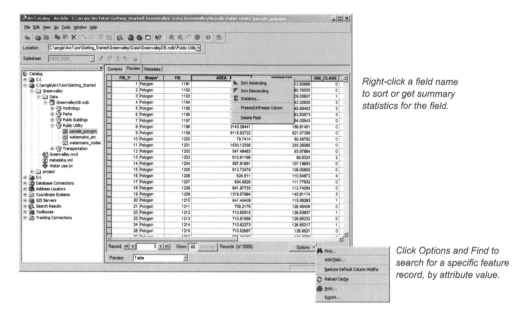

Right-click a field name to sort or get summary statistics for the field.

Click Options and Find to search for a specific feature record, by attribute value.

Reviewing a dataset's characteristics

Metadata is useful for confirming the version of the data, its source and processing history, and the spatial reference system it's in. (Your metadata may not look like this—there are many different standard and custom formats. See 'Documenting your database with metadata' in this chapter for more information.)

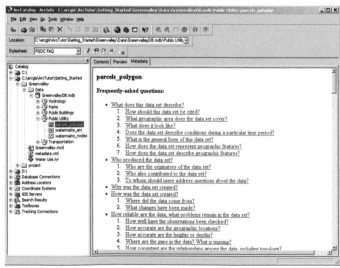

The Metadata tab displays myriad information about a dataset.

Creating a thumbnail

Before you can display a dataset as a thumbnail when previewing a folder or geodatabase, you need to create a thumbnail for the dataset. With the Preview tab selected, click the Create Thumbnail button.

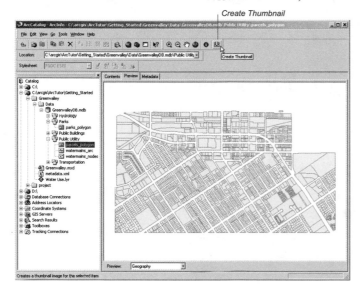

Create Thumbnail

Searching for data and maps

The ArcCatalog Search tool will look on disks, in databases, and on GIS servers for data that matches criteria you specify. Your search is saved in ArcCatalog. As data is found that satisfies your criteria, shortcuts to those data sources are added to the search's list of results. You can modify the search's criteria and run the search again. The Search tool uses metadata to evaluate whether a data source satisfies your criteria. Having good metadata documentation is essential for finding useful data.

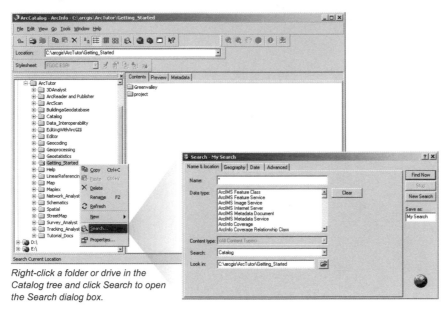

Right-click a folder or drive in the Catalog tree and click Search to open the Search dialog box.

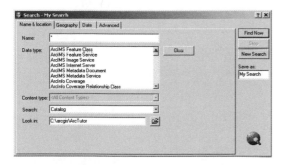

Use the Name & location tab to specify the name of a dataset (wildcards can be used); the specific data type, or types, you're searching for, such as shapefiles or rasters; and the location to search.

Remove the current box

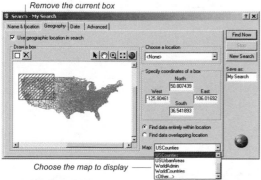

Choose the map to display

Use the Geography tab to define the geographic area in which to search. Draw a box on the map (by clicking and dragging the cursor). Use the buttons to zoom and pan the display. Alternatively, enter the coordinates of the bounding box. Refine your search by choosing a location from within the box, using the drop-down arrow.

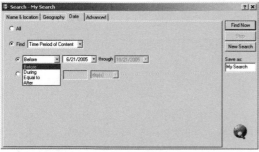

Use the Date tab to search for data created or published before or after a given date or within a date range.

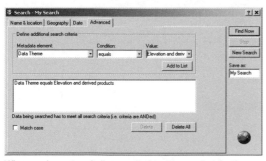

Use the Advanced tab to search other entries in the metadata, such as keywords, the data theme type, or the source. Use the dropdown arrows to create a query; then add it to the list.

When you've entered all your criteria, enter a name for the search (the default is My Search). Then click Find Now (available from any of the tabs) to begin the search.

When you click Find Now in the Search dialog box, your search is saved in the Search Results folder and automatically selected in the Catalog tree. When an item is found that matches your search criteria, a shortcut to that item is added to the Search Results list. Once you've found the item that you want to use, you can work with the shortcut as if you were working with the item itself. You can preview the item's data and metadata in the appropriate tabs. You can drag and drop a shortcut onto a map or an ArcToolbox tool. When you delete a shortcut you delete the shortcut itself, not the actual item.

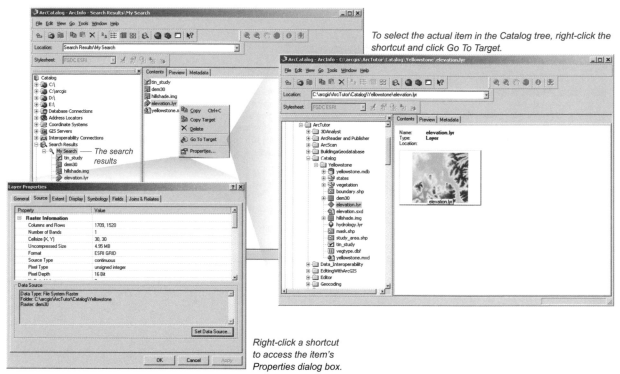

To select the actual item in the Catalog tree, right-click the shortcut and click Go To Target.

Right-click a shortcut to access the item's Properties dialog box.

You can delete or rename searches the same way you would delete or rename any other item in ArcCatalog. To see the criteria for a search, select it and select the metadata tab. To rerun a search, or to modify the criteria and then rerun it, right-click the search and click Properties—that opens the Search dialog box.

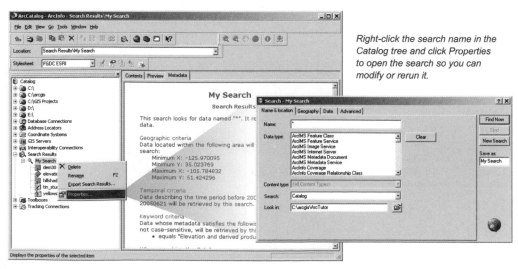

Right-click the search name in the Catalog tree and click Properties to open the search so you can modify or rerun it.

Organizing your data with ArcCatalog

ArcCatalog lets you organize your datasets in workspaces, manage datasets and workspaces, and manage how the data is displayed in the Catalog tree.

Creating a new workspace

Right-click any existing folder in the Catalog tree to add a new folder. You can then create new datasets in the workspace, or copy them in from other locations. You can also add subfolders to further organize your data.

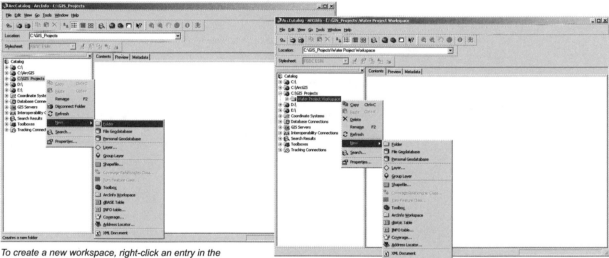

To create a new workspace, right-click an entry in the Catalog tree, select New, and click Folder. A folder is added under the entry, with the default name New Folder—type over the name to rename it.

Right-click the new workspace to add subfolders or to create new GIS datasets in the workspace.

Managing workspaces and datasets

Right-click a workspace or dataset to copy, delete, or rename it (when you delete a workspace, all its contents are also deleted). To move a workspace, simply drag it to a new location.

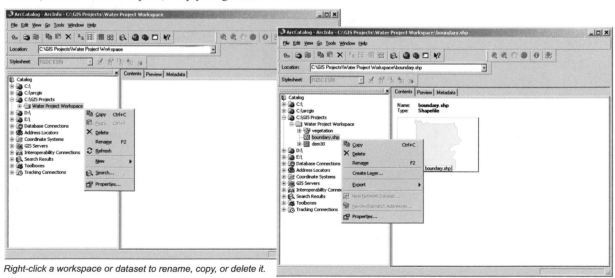

Right-click a workspace or dataset to rename, copy, or delete it.

To copy a dataset into your workspace, navigate to the folder containing the dataset. Right-click the dataset name and click Copy. Then right-click your workspace name in the Catalog tree and click Paste. You can also copy a dataset by holding down the Ctrl key while dragging and dropping. (Without the Ctrl key, dragging and dropping moves the dataset.)

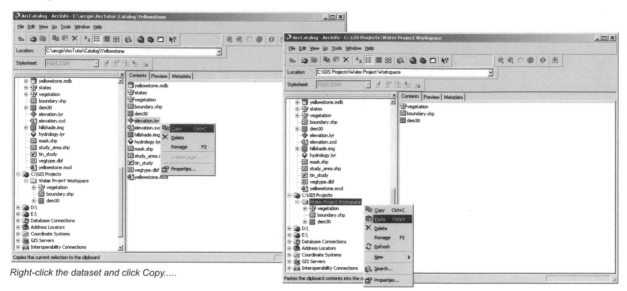

Right-click the dataset and click Copy.....

....then right-click the workspace name and click Paste.

Exploring an item's properties

To learn more about a dataset or other item, right-click it to open its Properties dialog box. You can, for example, display the source information for the dataset, view its coordinate system parameters, and display a list of its attributed fields. Different data formats have different properties dialog boxes.

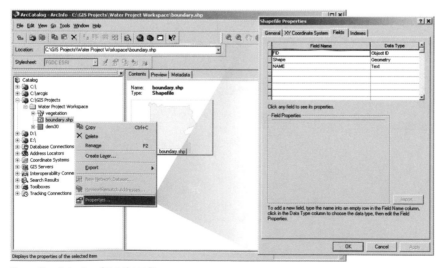

Properties dialog box for a shapefile.

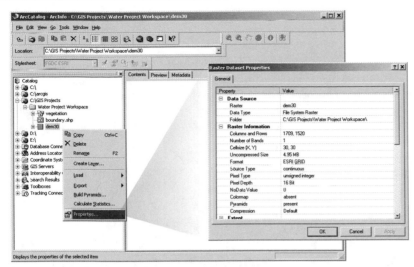

Properties dialog box for a raster.

Managing the ArcCatalog display

You can customize ArcCatalog to show only the folders and items with which you want to work. When you first start ArcCatalog, the Database Connections, Database Servers, GIS Servers, Address Locators, Search Results, and Toolboxes folders are visible. If you don't use data that is stored in a remote database or provided by a GIS server, you can hide those folders, for example. Similarly, you might only want to see the shapefiles in a folder, not the coverages and CAD drawings.

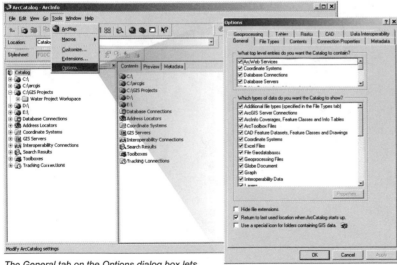

The General tab on the Options dialog box lets you specify which top-level folders to display in the Catalog tree, and which types of data will be visible.

Many files that you would see in a folder in Windows Explorer aren't initially visible in the Catalog tree. Some of these files may contain information that you need when working with geographic data. To see these files, you must add their types to the Catalog tree's file types list. You can also remove file types that you no longer need.

Some of the file types you want to use may already be registered with the operating system, such as Microsoft Word documents. You can add file type information for these files to the Catalog tree. When you double-click a file whose type is registered with the operating system, the Catalog tree will open it in the appropriate application. You can also add your own file type by defining the file extension, description, and icon you want to use to represent those files. For example, to see ArcView GIS 3 project files in the Catalog tree, you would add apr to the file types list, since project files have a .apr extension.

To specify file types to display in ArcCatalog, select Options on the Tools menu.

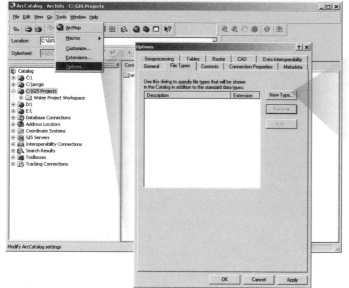

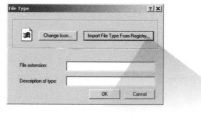

On the File Types tab, click New, then type a file extension, or select a file type from the Registry list.

Documenting your database with metadata

Documentation of each item in your database is critical for sharing tools, data, and maps; for searching to see if the resources you need already exist; and for maintaining records of your data and projects. Dataset documentation includes a description of the dataset, its spatial reference and accuracy, its source and processing history, descriptions of its attributes and definitions of categories and codes, and information on how the data may be used and shared. In ArcGIS, documentation is stored in metadata and is accessed via the Metadata tab in ArcCatalog. Once created, metadata is copied, moved, and deleted along with the dataset when you use ArcCatalog for these tasks. Any item in ArcCatalog—including datasets, tables, folders, and geodatabases—can have metadata.

Selecting the metadata stylesheet

Every time you start ArcCatalog, metadata is initially presented with the default metadata stylesheet. Each stylesheet in ArcCatalog presents the same body of metadata, but using a different format. To change the metadata's appearance, choose a different stylesheet from the drop-down list on the toolbar.

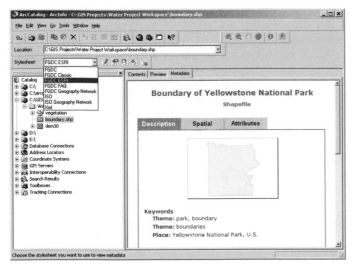

Use the Stylesheet drop-down arrow to select the metadata stylesheet to use. The information in the metadata remains the same—only the way it is displayed changes. The Stylesheet drop-down arrow is active when you select the Metadata tab.

To change the default stylesheet, use the Options dialog box on the Tools menu. You won't see the change until the next time you start ArcCatalog.

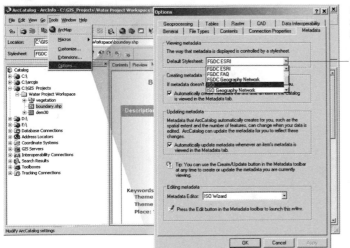

Use Options on the Tools menu to set the default stylesheet (on the Metadata tab). Your selection will be the default the next time you open ArcCatalog.

Select the default stylesheet

Stylesheets with filenames that begin with "FGDC" present metadata stored in the XML elements defined by the Federal Geographic Data Committee (FGDC) Content Standard for Digital Geospatial Metadata.

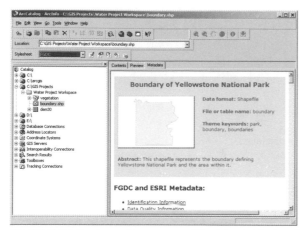

The FGDC stylesheet presents a summary of the dataset at the top of the metadata.

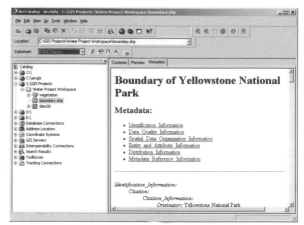

The FGDC Classic stylesheet provides a set of links to quickly jump to the pertinent section of the metadata.

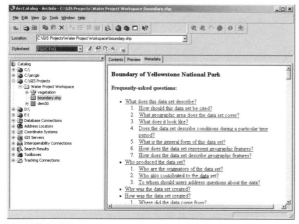

The FGDC FAQ stylesheet presents a set of frequently asked questions so you can jump right to the information you need. It's useful for datasets accessed by many users.

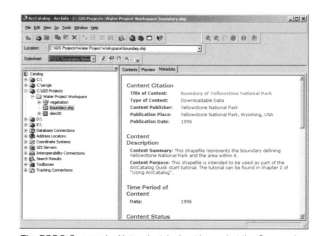

The FGDC Geography Network stylesheet is used at the Geography Network data clearinghouse. It uses a citation format so users can quickly see if the dataset will be useful for their purposes.

Stylesheets beginning with ISO present metadata stored in the XML elements defined by the ISO standard 19115, Geographic Information–Metadata. In addition to the existing stylesheets, you can customize the metadata stylesheets provided by ESRI and add your own XSLT stylesheets to ArcCatalog.

Printing metadata

When you print a copy of a dataset's metadata in ArcCatalog, the metadata will print exactly as you see it in the Metadata tab. If you're using the FGDC ESRI stylesheet, click the appropriate tab on the metadata page and expand the appropriate headings so that you can see the information you want to print.

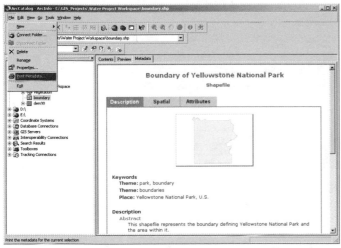

With the Metadata tab selected, choose Print Metadata from the File menu.

Editing metadata documentation

Metadata consists of properties and documentation. Properties, such as the extent of a shapefile's features, are derived by ArcCatalog and added to the metadata. Documentation is descriptive information you enter using a metadata editor—for example, legal information about using the resource.

Two metadata editors are provided with ArcCatalog. One lets you create complete documentation following the FGDC's Content Standard for Digital Geospatial Metadata. The other editor lets you document your data following the ISO standard 19115, Geographic Information—Metadata; it supports only the core metadata elements as defined by that standard. Use the Metadata tab on the Options dialog box to select the editor you want to use.

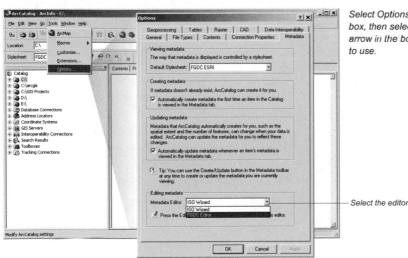

Select Options on the Tools menu to open the dialog box, then select the Metadata tab. Use the drop-down arrow in the bottom box to select the metadata editor to use.

The editor selected in the Options dialog box will appear when you click the Edit Metadata button on the Metadata toolbar.

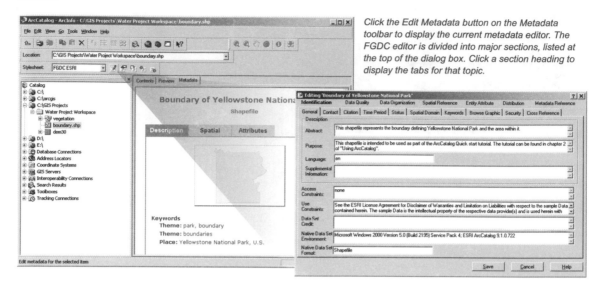

Click the Edit Metadata button on the Metadata toolbar to display the current metadata editor. The FGDC editor is divided into major sections, listed at the top of the dialog box. Click a section heading to display the tabs for that topic.

The ISO editor is presented as a wizard. You can step through the panels using the Next button, or click a topic on the list to jump to that panel.

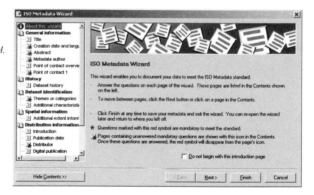

Before you start writing documentation, you need to decide which metadata standard you're going to follow. If you don't have any metadata yet and don't need to create metadata according to a specific standard, the ISO editor might be right for you. If you have a requirement to create FGDC metadata, if you already have FGDC metadata, or if you want to create detailed metadata, the FGDC editor would be a good choice. Once you've decided which metadata standard you're going to follow, use the editor that corresponds to that standard. Whichever editor you use, the information you enter will still appear in any of the style sheets.

A metadata document in ArcCatalog can contain both FGDC and ISO content. These two standards can exist in parallel in the same metadata document because they each use a completely different set of XML tags to store their information. Therefore, if you provide a title using the FGDC editor and you later switch to the ISO editor, the information you previously added won't appear in the editor.

Importing and exporting metadata

If you have metadata that was created outside of ArcCatalog, you can import it if it's stored in one of the input formats supported by the FGDC's metadata parser utility.

You might export metadata to publish it on a data clearinghouse website. Exporting to HTML format creates a file that represents the selected item's metadata exactly as you see it in the Metadata tab. Exporting to XML format creates an exact copy of the item's metadata in a new XML file; this lets you work with metadata for geodatabase items outside ArcCatalog.

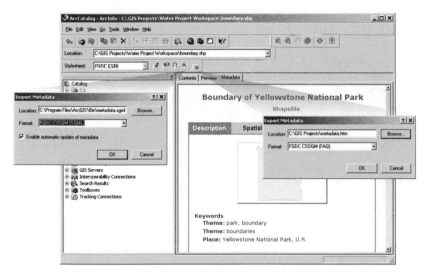

Use the buttons on the Metadata toolbar to import a dataset's metadata from (or export it to) one of several standard formats.

Creating a geodatabase

The process for building a geodatabase is to create the design for the geodatabase, build the structure for the geodatabase (the schema) in ArcGIS, and then import existing data into the geodatabase, or create new datasets within it. There are two ways to turn a geodatabase design into a geodatabase structure: create an empty geodatabase and then use ArcCatalog tools to create the various components (as defined in the design); or copy an existing schema or geodatabase template and modify it, if necessary.

After the geodatabase is constructed, you can import data (see 'Collecting, importing, and converting GIS data' in Chapter 3). You may want to start by importing a subset of data to test the design. You can then make changes to the geodatabase design before loading all your data.

Creating a geodatabase using ArcCatalog tools

To build a geodatabase using tools in ArcCatalog, you first create the geodatabase, which is initially empty. You then use the tools provided in ArcCatalog to create or import the feature datasets, feature classes, tables, geometric networks, topologies, and other items in the geodatabase. These tools are described in separate sections in this chapter. Use these same tools to modify a geodatabase you've imported from a template.

There are three kinds of geodatabases: file geodatabases, personal geodatabases, and ArcSDE geodatabases. A file geodatabase stores datasets as a folder of files on your computer. A personal geodatabase stores datasets in a Microsoft Access file on disk. They both look the same in ArcCatalog (except for the extension—.gdb and .mdb, respectively), although they vary in functionality and performance. A file geodatabase can be up to 1TB in size (versus up to 2GB for a personal geodatabase) and will perform searches and queries faster than will a personal geodatabase. A personal geodatabase, however, provides the advanced table operations found in Microsoft Access (some GIS applications may require these).

You create a file or personal geodatabase within a folder (usually for a workspace you've set up) by right-clicking the folder.

Right-click a folder, click New, and click either File Geodatabase or Personal Geodatabase.

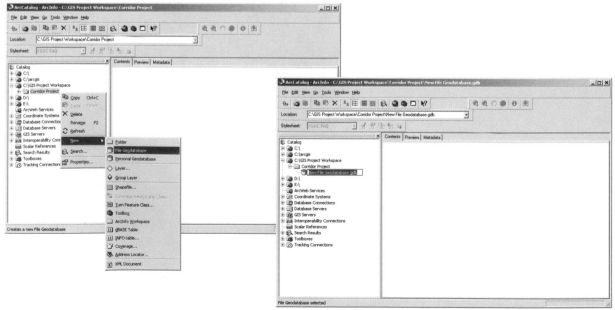

A new, empty geodatabase is created in the folder—type over the name to rename the geodatabase.

An ArcSDE geodatabase stores datasets in a DBMS. To create an ArcSDE geodatabase you first add a Database Server connection (for Personal and Workgroup ArcSDE) or a Spatial Database connection (for Enterprise ArcSDE). See 'Finding and connecting to data' earlier in this chapter. You can then create the geodatabase from this connection.

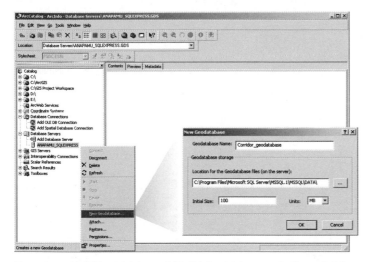

To create an ArcSDE geodatabase, right-click the database connection and click New Geodatabase. You'll be prompted to name the geodatabase, for a location to store it (it will still appear under the server connection in the Catalog tree), and for a maximum storage size.

Creating a geodatabase by copying a template

A quick way to build a geodatabase is to use the design of an existing geodatabase that meets the needs of your application. Other ArcGIS users in your region or your industry may have already built a geodatabase structure you can use or modify. Ask them to export their schema to a file and send it to you. ESRI also provides a number of data model templates at *http://support.esri.com/datamodels*. You create an empty geodatabase, then import the schema file.

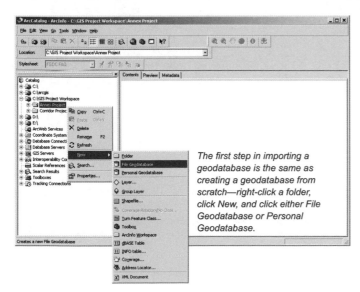

The first step in importing a geodatabase is the same as creating a geodatabase from scratch—right-click a folder, click New, and click either File Geodatabase or Personal Geodatabase.

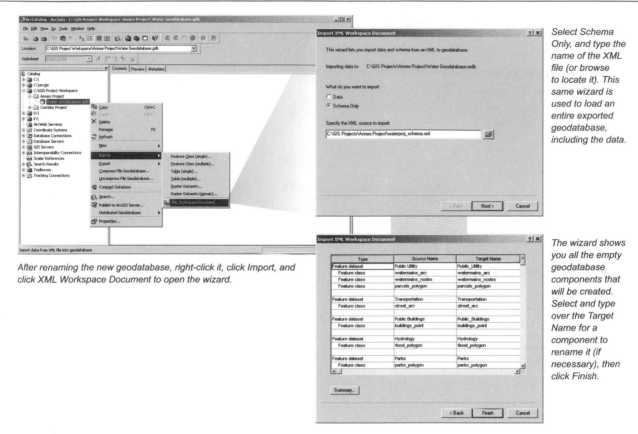

Select Schema Only, and type the name of the XML file (or browse to locate it). This same wizard is used to load an entire exported geodatabase, including the data.

After renaming the new geodatabase, right-click it, click Import, and click XML Workspace Document to open the wizard.

The wizard shows you all the empty geodatabase components that will be created. Select and type over the Target Name for a component to rename it (if necessary), then click Finish.

The result is a new schema with no data but with all the feature datasets, feature classes, tables, topologies, relationships, geometric networks, domains, subtypes, and field properties from the source geodatabase. You can then review the schema and modify it to suit your needs, deleting some items and adding or changing others.

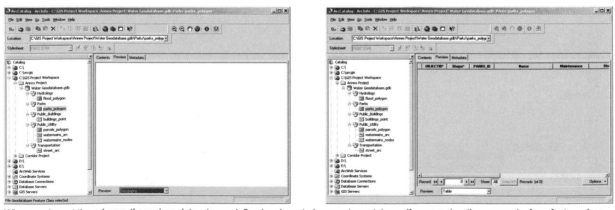

When you import the schema, the various datasets are defined and created as empty containers. If you preview the geography for a feature class, for example, you'll see that the preview panel is blank—there are no features to preview. If you preview the attribute table for the feature class, you'll see that the columns have been created but there are no records in the table.

Once your schema is ready, import the existing data into the defined geodatabase datasets.

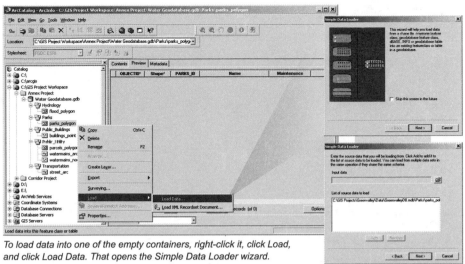

To load data into one of the empty containers, right-click it, click Load, and click Load Data. That opens the Simple Data Loader wizard.

The first panel of the Simple Data Loader wizard explains what it does.

Browse to the dataset containing the data to load, then Add it to the list (you can load multiple datasets of the same type at one time).

This panel shows the geodatabase and feature class the data will be loaded into.

Here's where you specify which attributes correspond to which fields in the table (if the field names aren't the same).

The default is to load all the features, but you can load a subset of features—select Load only the features that satisfy a query, then use the Query Builder button to specify the selection criteria.

The final panel shows you a summary of the data that will be loaded. Click Back to make changes, or click Finish to load the data.

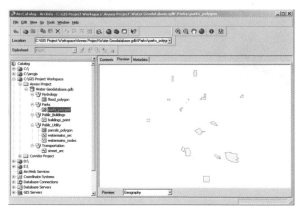 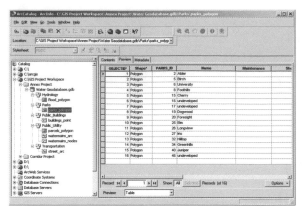

Once the data is loaded, the feature class now contains features. The feature geography can be previewed in ArcCatalog, and the features can be added to a map in ArcMap. The feature attribute table contains the attribute values for each feature.

Another way to copy the schema of a geodatabase is to use the Extract Data wizard in ArcMap. It allows you to modify the spatial reference of the new schema you create and to set a map extent for the data you want to copy into your geodatabase. This is useful because the spatial reference requirements of your new geodatabase will probably be different from those of the source geodatabase.

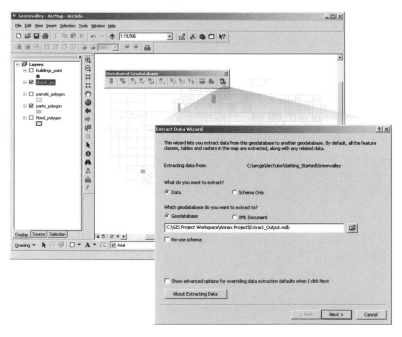

The Extract Data Wizard is available from the Distributed Geodatabase toolbar in ArcMap. To open the toolbar, click the View menu and point to toolbars.

Creating feature classes and tables

Feature classes and tables are two of the basic datasets in a geodatabase. Feature classes store geographic features of the same type and their associated attributes—for example, you'd create one feature class for roads, another for streams, and a third for parcels. Standalone tables store additional descriptive information that can be related to the geographic features. When building a geodatabase structure (or schema) from a design, after creating the geodatabase you'll create and define the empty feature classes and tables. You first create the empty feature class or table. You then define any additional fields containing descriptive data. Later you'll add data to the datasets by importing or editing.

Creating a feature class

Feature classes contain both the geometric shapes of each feature as well as their descriptive attributes.

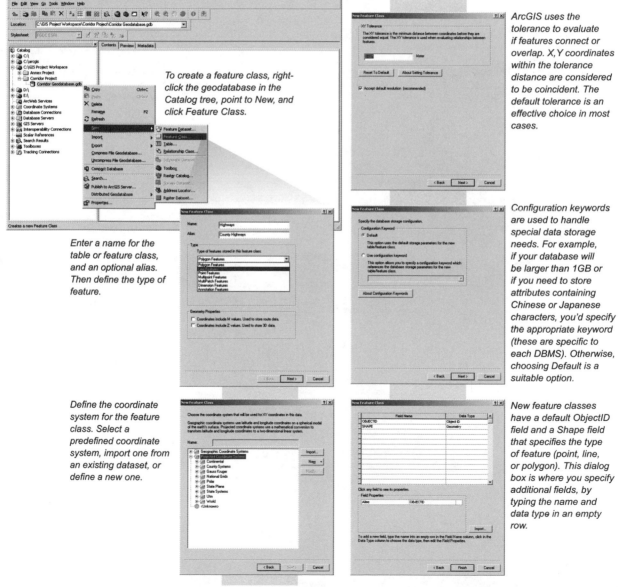

To create a feature class, right-click the geodatabase in the Catalog tree, point to New, and click Feature Class.

ArcGIS uses the tolerance to evaluate if features connect or overlap. X,Y coordinates within the tolerance distance are considered to be coincident. The default tolerance is an effective choice in most cases.

Enter a name for the table or feature class, and an optional alias. Then define the type of feature.

Configuration keywords are used to handle special data storage needs. For example, if your database will be larger than 1GB or if you need to store attributes containing Chinese or Japanese characters, you'd specify the appropriate keyword (these are specific to each DBMS). Otherwise, choosing Default is a suitable option.

Define the coordinate system for the feature class. Select a predefined coordinate system, import one from an existing dataset, or define a new one.

New feature classes have a default ObjectID field and a Shape field that specifies the type of feature (point, line, or polygon). This dialog box is where you specify additional fields, by typing the name and data type in an empty row.

Feature classes store features in vector format. Vector data is often used to represent features that have a discrete location in space—such as wells, streets, rivers, states borders, and parcel boundaries—as opposed to being continuous across space, such as elevation or rainfall, often represented using rasters (see 'Managing raster datasets in a geodatabase' in this chapter). The most common vector types are points, lines, polygons. Annotation, which is used to label features, is also stored as feature classes (see 'Creating and editing annotation' in Chapter 3). Multipoints are often used to manage arrays of very large point collections, such as LiDAR data. Multipatches are a 3D geometry used to represent the outer surface of buildings or other objects having volume.

You can also specify whether the feature class includes Z or M values. Z values are most commonly used to represent elevations, but they can represent other surface measures. M values are used to interpolate distances along linear features, such as along roads, streams, or pipelines. A common example is a highway milepost measurement system.

The coordinate system for each dataset is for georeferencing. It can be imported from an existing dataset, or you can create a custom coordinate system by defining its properties (you'll likely either import a coordinate system or select a predefined one). Most organizations use one coordinate system—appropriate for their geographic location—for all their data. Feature classes can also be created within a feature dataset in the geodatabase (see the next section, 'Ensuring spatial data integrity'). In this case, the spatial reference will be defined for the feature dataset, so you don't need to specify it.

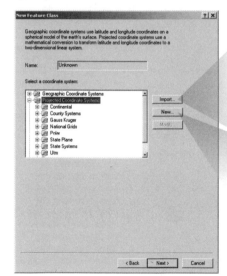

Use the Import option to assign the feature class the coordinate system of an existing dataset.

Use the New option to define the parameters of a geographic or projected coordinate system.

Creating a standalone table

The process for creating a standalone table containing only tabular data is similar to the process for creating a feature class containing geographic features. The main difference is that you don't specify a coordinate system, tolerance, or feature type.

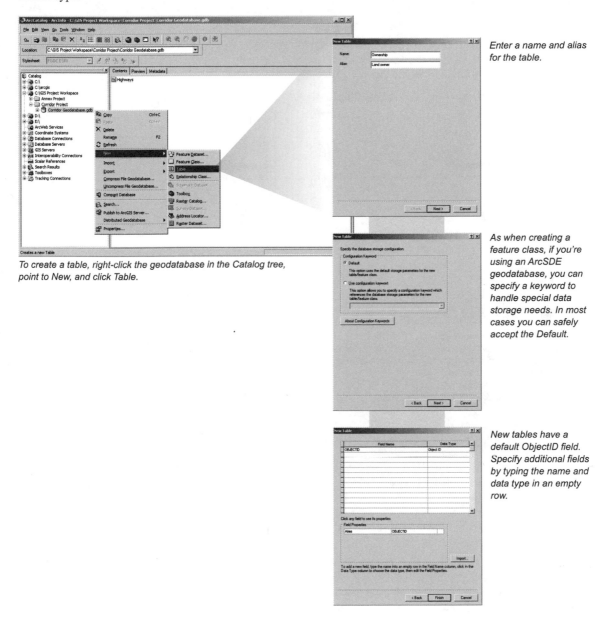

Enter a name and alias for the table.

To create a table, right-click the geodatabase in the Catalog tree, point to New, and click Table.

As when creating a feature class, if you're using an ArcSDE geodatabase, you can specify a keyword to handle special data storage needs. In most cases you can safely accept the Default.

New tables have a default ObjectID field. Specify additional fields by typing the name and data type in an empty row.

Specifying additional fields

All tables and feature classes have required fields that are automatically created. Tables have an ObjectID field, and a simple feature class has an ObjectID field and a Shape field. The ObjectID uniquely identifies each object, or feature, while the Shape field stores each feature's geometry (the coordinates). These fields have properties you can modify, such as their aliases and geometry type, but the fields cannot be deleted. Beyond these required fields, you can add any number of fields to a table or feature class to store descriptive information.

To add a field, type the field name in an empty row, select a data type for the field, and then specify the field properties that appear in the box below (or accept the defaults). At this point you're only defining the fields in the table—you add data to the table later by importing it or by editing the table and entering the data.

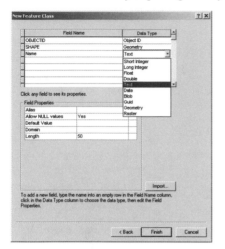

To add a field, type the field name in an empty row, and click the Data Type box in that row to select the field type. Then modify the field properties, as necessary, by clicking the box to the right of the property name and typing a value or selecting from the drop-down list.

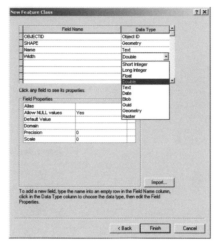

The field properties vary somewhat, depending on the data type. Numeric types include Precision and Scale.

Data types include numbers, text, dates, and binary large objects ("BLOBs"—used to store and manage binary information such as symbols and CAD geometries). Numbers can be short integers, long integers, single-precision floating point numbers (often referred to as "floats"), and double-precision floating point numbers (commonly called "doubles"). If you just need to store whole numbers, such as 12 or 12345678, specify a short or long integer. If you need to store fractional numbers that have decimal places, such as 0.23 or 1234.5678, specify a float or a double. When choosing between a short or long integer, or between a float or double, choose the data type that takes up the least storage space required. The short integer type stores integers between -32,768 and 32767; use long integer for numbers outside this range (either smaller or larger). The float type stores fractional numbers between -3.4E-38 and 1.2E38; use the double type for numbers outside this range.

If you're specifying numeric fields for a table in a file or personal geodatabase, you need only specify the data type. If you're specifying numeric fields for an ArcSDE geodatabase, you additionally specify the precision, which is the maximum length of the field, and scale, which is the maximum number of decimal places. For example, if you specify a float with a precision of 4 and a scale of 2, the field will accept 12.34—there are four digits (defined by the precision) and two of them are to the right of the decimal point (the scale).

Another way to add fields to a table or feature class is to import them from an existing dataset. When you do this, any fields you may have just defined are automatically deleted, so import before defining any additional fields you may need. You can modify the properties of the imported fields, just as with fields you define.

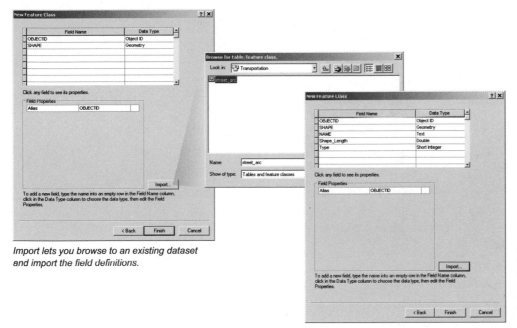

Import lets you browse to an existing dataset and import the field definitions.

After selecting the dataset to import from and clicking Add on the browser window, the field definitions are added to your new feature class or table.

When defining a table's fields in an ArcSDE geodatabase, be aware that each DBMS has its own rules to define which names and characters are permitted. The table designer checks the names you type using a set of common rules, but each database is slightly different. If you want more control over a field's data types or structure, create the table directly in the DBMS.

Modifying a feature class or table definition

You can change any of the field properties—including the geometry—anytime before pressing the Finish button. To delete a field you've added, select it by clicking the box at the left side of the row, then press the Delete key on your keyboard.

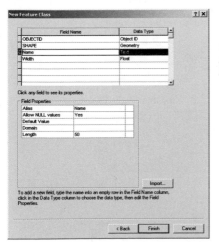

To delete a field, select the row, then press the Delete key on your keyboard.

Once you press Finish, the fields and their properties are saved. You can modify some of the properties by opening the feature class or table properties dialog box (right-click the feature class or table in the Catalog tree and click Properties). On the General tab, you can change the alias. On the Fields tab you can delete a field you've added (as described above) or change the alias or default value for a field by typing in the appropriate box. You cannot modify the feature class geometry, or field types or lengths. You can add new fields by typing in an empty row.

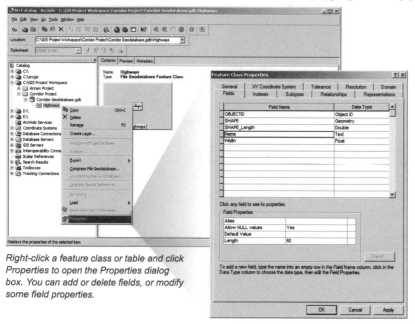

Right-click a feature class or table and click Properties to open the Properties dialog box. You can add or delete fields, or modify some field properties.

You can also delete and add fields when previewing a table in ArcCatalog, as well as when viewing a table in ArcMap (see 'Adding fields and calculating attribute values' in Chapter 5).

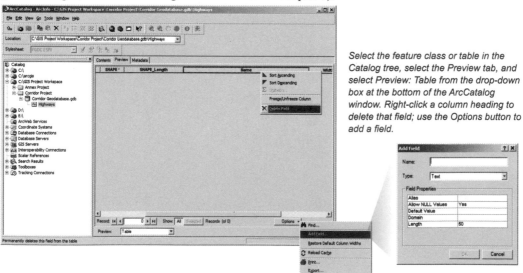

Select the feature class or table in the Catalog tree, select the Preview tab, and select Preview: Table from the drop-down box at the bottom of the ArcCatalog window. Right-click a column heading to delete that field; use the Options button to add a field.

If you've defined many fields and then find—after you've finished creating the feature class or table—that you need to modify the type or length of one or a few fields, you can delete the field and then add a new one. Or, you can create a new feature or class or table and then import the fields from the original one—once you've imported the fields you can modify the ones you need to, up to the point you click the Finish button.

Ensuring spatial data integrity

ArcGIS stores information about a place as layers of data (each represented by a dataset). You need to ensure that the datasets are coincident and register with each other correctly. Adding what's known as a "feature dataset" to your geodatabase ensures that feature classes for the same geographic area have the same coordinate system and therefore register correctly. You also need to ensure that features within a dataset, and between datasets, relate the way the features they're representing do in the real world—for example, that parcels don't overlap. Adding a topology dataset to your geodatabase makes these spatial relationships explicit and ensures they're implemented and maintained.

Creating a feature dataset

Sometimes different datasets that cover the same geographic area are in different coordinate systems and won't register correctly when you display them on a map or combine them when performing geographic analysis. This is often true if you collect existing datasets from various sources. A feature dataset, which contains feature classes and related geodatabase datasets, ensures that all the related datasets are in the same coordinate system and register correctly.

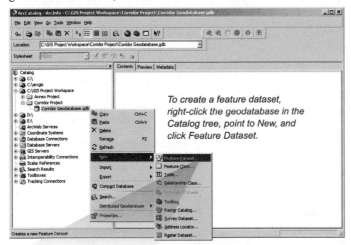

To create a feature dataset, right-click the geodatabase in the Catalog tree, point to New, and click Feature Dataset.

Enter a name for the feature dataset.

As when creating a feature class, you can specify the coordinate system for a feature dataset by selecting a predefined one, importing a coordinate system from another dataset, or creating a custom coordinate system.

Specify a vertical coordinate system if your dataset will include feature classes that have Z values (heights or depths).

Again as when creating a feature class, you specify an XY tolerance to define the distance within which coordinate pairs are considered to be coincident.

Once you've defined the feature dataset, it appears in the geodatabase.

When you define a feature dataset, you specify its spatial reference. This includes its coordinate system and the coordinate domains—the minimum x-, y-, z-, and m-values and their precision. All feature classes in the dataset use the same coordinate system, and all coordinates in all features in all feature classes must fall within the coordinate domains. Any new feature classes you create within the feature dataset are automatically in that coordinate system. Any datasets you want to import to the feature dataset have to be transformed or projected into the coordinate system before you add them. When defining the coordinate system, you can choose a predefined coordinate system, import it from an existing feature dataset, or define a custom coordinate system.

Feature datasets are primarily used for storing feature classes that will participate in a topology, network, or other specialized dataset. These datasets can only be created within a feature dataset, the reason being that all participating feature classes must have the same spatial reference (otherwise, it would be impossible to build the dataset), which the feature dataset ensures.

Getting data into a feature dataset

When you first create a feature dataset, it's empty. There are several ways to add feature classes to the feature dataset. One easy way is to—within ArcCatalog—simply drag and drop a feature class from elsewhere in the geodatabase, or from another geodatabase. Another way to add a feature class is to import it to the feature dataset. Importing lets you modify the incoming feature class, to some extent.

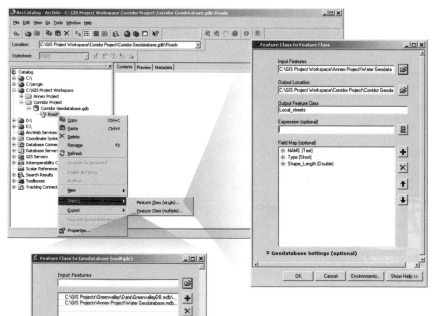

To import data, right-click the feature dataset in the Catalog tree, point to Import, and click Feature Class (single) or (multiple). The (single) option imports one feature class at a time, and lets you specify the input parameters. The (multiple) option lets you import several feature classes at once, but they are imported as-is.

You can also define a new, empty feature class within the feature dataset. The process for defining the feature class is the same as for creating a feature class at the geodatabase level (see 'Creating feature classes and tables' in this chapter).

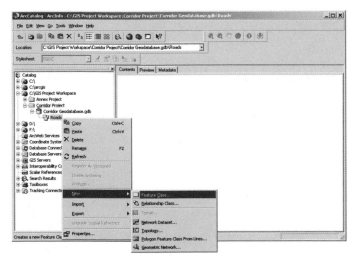

To create a feature class within a feature dataset, right-click the feature dataset, point to New, and click Feature Class.

As you develop the geodatabase, you may add topologies, relationship classes, and specialized datasets to the feature dataset.

Creating a geodatabase topology

Besides referencing the same location on the Earth's surface, datasets for the same place often have spatial relationships with each other. These are relationships you can see when looking at a map and are often intuitively obvious, but they must be made explicit in the GIS. For example, streets must connect at intersections; parcel boundaries cannot overlap; parcels nest within block boundaries; and so on.

A geodatabase topology is a set of rules that specify how points, lines, and polygons share geometry. The rules can apply to features within a single feature class—for example, one topology rule would ensure that adjacent features, such as two counties, will share a common edge, so county boundaries don't overlap. The rules can also apply to features in different feature classes. For example, county boundaries (one feature class) must completely nest within states (another feature class), and share edges along state boundaries.

A topology is created within a feature dataset, and applies to one or more feature classes in the dataset (so if you want to create a topology in your geodatabase, you must first create a feature dataset and add the pertinent feature classes to it). Only feature classes in the same dataset can participate in a topology, but not all the feature classes in a dataset are required to participate in the topology. And a feature class can only participate in one topology at a time.

When you validate a topology, ArcGIS checks the rules you've established. To ensure the rules are not broken, ArcGIS will, if necessary, snap feature vertices together to make them coincident. For example, if two street centerlines are supposed to connect but don't quite meet, ArcGIS will snap the end points of the lines together. Specify a cluster tolerance to control how far features are allowed to move during snapping (the default cluster tolerance is the minimum possible). The cluster tolerance should be small, so only close vertices are snapped together. A typical cluster tolerance is at least an order of magnitude smaller than the accuracy of your data. For example, if your features are accurate to 2 meters, your cluster tolerance should be no more than 0.2 meters.

You'll want the less reliable features to snap to the more reliable ones. Ranks are used to implement this. Vertices of lower-ranking features within the cluster tolerance will be snapped to nearby vertices of higher-ranking features.

To create a topology, right-click the feature dataset, point to New, and click Topology. That opens the New Topology wizard.

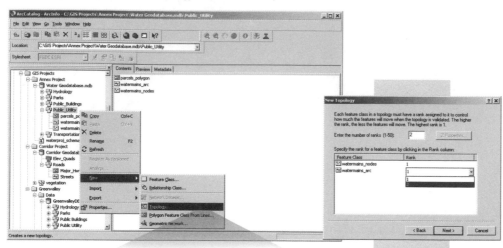

Specify the number of ranks, and use the drop-down menus in the Ranks column to assign each feature class a rank. Features having a lower rank will snap to those having a higher one.

Click Add Rule to add rules—use the drop-down menus on the Add Rule dialog box to construct the rules.

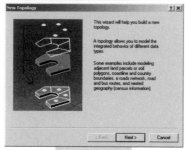

Enter a name for the topology, and specify a cluster tolerance (or accept the default value).

Add all the rules you need to the list. You can save the rule list to use with topologies in other feature datasets and geodatabases.

Select the feature classes that will participate in this topology—you can have more than one topology in a feature dataset, but each feature class can participate in only one topology.

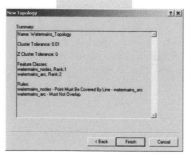

The final panel displays a summary of your topology definition. Click Back to make changes, or Finish to create the topology.

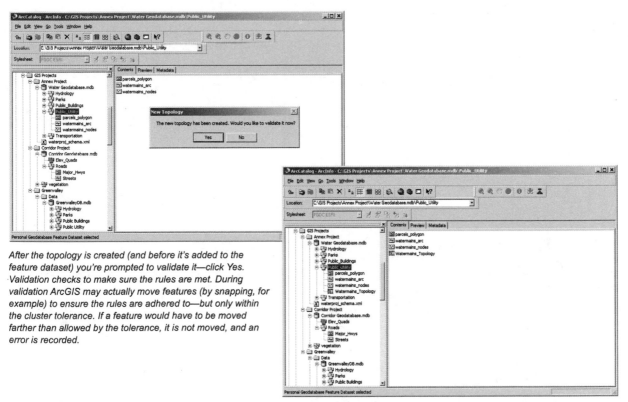

After the topology is created (and before it's added to the feature dataset) you're prompted to validate it—click Yes. Validation checks to make sure the rules are met. During validation ArcGIS may actually move features (by snapping, for example) to ensure the rules are adhered to—but only within the cluster tolerance. If a feature would have to be moved farther than allowed by the tolerance, it is not moved, and an error is recorded.

Once validated, the topology is added to ArcCatalog in the feature dataset.

Validation records errors—that is, instances of rule violations. You can get a list of any errors (or confirm that there aren't any) by accessing the topology's Properties dialog box (see below). You can fix errors by editing them in ArcMap—the Topology toolbar has tools to do this (see Chapter 3, 'Data Compilation and Editing').

Managing a topology

You can view and manage topologies in geodatabases through ArcCatalog—right-click a topology in the Catalog tree and click Properties. New feature classes can be added to a topology at any time, as can new rules. When the rules or other properties of a topology are changed, the topology will need to be validated again.

You can also view a summary of the number of errors in a topology from the Topology Properties dialog box. The summary tells you how many errors exist for each of the topology rules.

Deleting a topology does not delete or modify the participating feature classes themselves; it merely removes the rules governing their spatial relationships. Copying a topology also copies the feature classes that participate in the topology. To rename or delete a feature class that participates in a topology, you must first remove the feature class from the topology. Either that, or delete the topology.

Right-click a topology to access its properties.

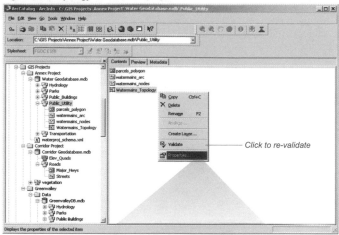

Click to re-validate

Use the General tab to change the name or cluster tolerance.

Use the Feature Classes tab to add or remove feature classes, and to change their rank.

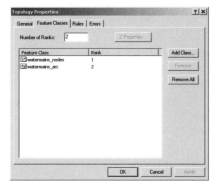

Use the Rules tab to add or remove rules, to save the rule list, or to load saved rules.

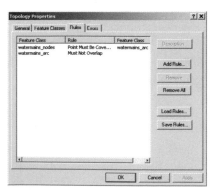

Use the Errors tab to view a summary of topology errors.

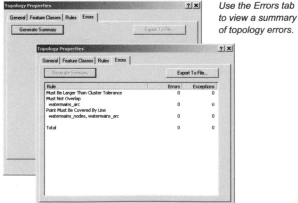

The error summary doesn't automatically appear when you go to the Errors tab. You have to click the Generate Summary button to see the list of errors.

Ensuring attribute data integrity

Attribute data is used throughout ArcGIS—when querying and selecting subsets of data, when symbolizing features on maps, and in a range of geographic analyses. To make sure your queries and maps are correct and your analyses are valid—and that the decisions based on these tools are solid—you need to ensure that the attribute data is as error-free as possible. ArcCatalog includes several tools for minimizing the amount of typing when entering attribute values, helping ensure that attribute data is entered correctly in your geodatabase, whether in a feature class or a standalone table. You can have default values for fields automatically assigned when features are created. You can also create lists of valid values to select from when editing attributes, or ranges of valid numeric values that entered values can be checked against. These are known as domains. And you can create subtypes based on categories within a feature class, each of which can have a different default value or domain. You can assign default values and create domains and subtypes when you first create a feature class or table, or any time thereafter.

Assigning default values to fields

You can assign a default value to one or more fields in a feature class or table, which is useful if many features or records will have the same value for the field. When you're editing in ArcMap and adding new features or records, each feature automatically gets the default value for that field (rather than you having to type it). For example, if you're adding parcels in a new subdivision, the values for some fields will be different for each parcel (such as the address and the owner) but some will be the same—such as the landuse code. You could assign a default landuse code value to that field and all parcels you add will automatically get that code. You can edit and change the assigned value for a particular feature later, if necessary.

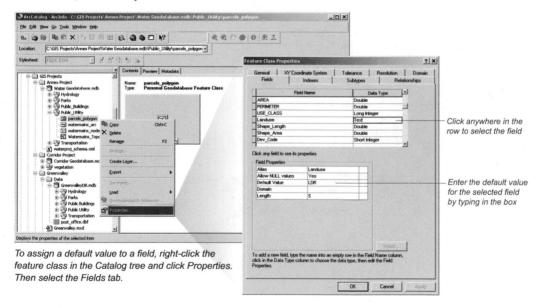

Click anywhere in the row to select the field

Enter the default value for the selected field by typing in the box

To assign a default value to a field, right-click the feature class in the Catalog tree and click Properties. Then select the Fields tab.

To add a new field, type the name into an empty row in the Field Name column, click in the Data Type column to choose the data type, then edit the Field Properties.

Using domains to ensure valid attribute values

For many feature classes and tables, certain fields will have a limited number of possible values. This is often the case for fields that represent categories or classes of data—a parcel can be assigned one of a limited set of landuse codes; only certain pipe diameter values are valid for water mains. Similarly, you may want to specify that continuous numeric values for a field—such as assessed value for parcels—be limited to a range. Using domains ensures only valid values are assigned. (Of course, domains don't ensure a particular parcel was assigned the correct landuse code or a particular water main the correct pipe diameter—only that the assigned value is a valid one.) Domains are essentially a list you create (a table, actually) of each valid code and its description (known as a coded value domain), or, alternately, a range you specify within which numeric values must fall (known as a range domain).

You first create a domain and enter the codes and descriptions, or specify the numeric range. A coded value domain can apply to any type of attribute—text, numeric, date, and so on. The domain type must match the data type you're creating the domain for (if the field is integer, the domain type must also be integer).

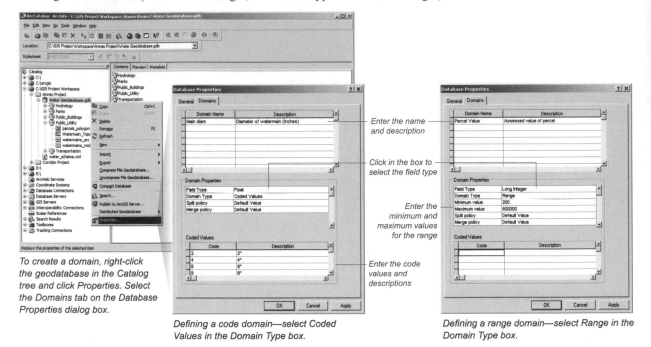

To create a domain, right-click the geodatabase in the Catalog tree and click Properties. Select the Domains tab on the Database Properties dialog box.

Enter the name and description

Click in the box to select the field type

Enter the minimum and maximum values for the range

Enter the code values and descriptions

Defining a code domain—select Coded Values in the Domain Type box.

Defining a range domain—select Range in the Domain Type box.

You then associate the domain with a field in one or more feature classes or tables in the geodatabase.

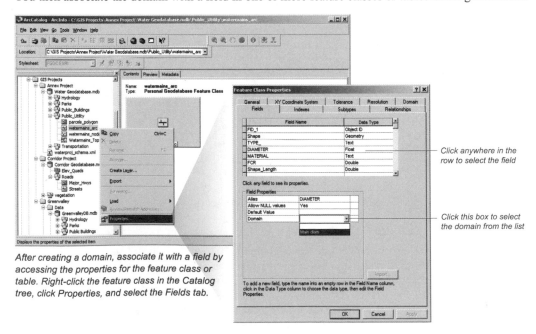

After creating a domain, associate it with a field by accessing the properties for the feature class or table. Right-click the feature class in the Catalog tree, click Properties, and select the Fields tab.

Click anywhere in the row to select the field

Click this box to select the domain from the list

Domains are created at the geodatabase level (for the entire geodatabase rather than for a feature dataset or individual feature class) so they can be assigned to any of the feature classes or tables in the geodatabase. For example, a single paving type domain could be assigned to both a Paving_type attribute in a highways feature class and a Surface_type attribute in a streets feature class. Domains are managed using the Domains property page, which can be accessed from the geodatabase's properties dialog box, or from the Feature Class or Table Properties dialog box. The Domains property page can be used to delete an attribute domain from the geodatabase or modify an existing domain.

Code domains constrain the values you can enter when editing attributes in ArcMap—a drop-down menu lets you choose from the valid attribute values. A range domain doesn't constrain the value that can be entered, but when you validate your edits, any values that are outside the range will generate a warning so you can fix the error (see 'Checking your data for errors' in Chapter 3).

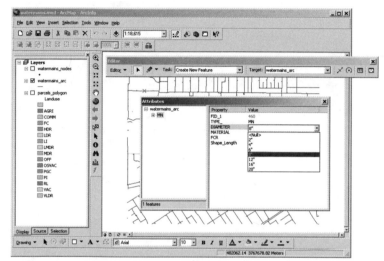

When editing a field with a code domain (in ArcMap), the attribute value is selected from a drop-down list.

Without the domain, values have to be typed in. Not only does the domain save time, it also helps prevent data entry errors.

Using subtypes to assign default values and domains

Subtypes are based on categories or classes within a feature class or table, and are a way of assigning default values and attribute domains without having to create separate feature classes or tables for each category. For example, in a water network, it may be that transmission water mains can have a pressure between 40 and 100 psi, while distribution water mains can have a pressure between 50 and 75 psi. Rather than creating separate feature classes for transmission and distribution water mains, you'd create two subtypes—"transmission mains" and "distribution mains"—within the water mains feature class. You could then assign different range domains for the water pressure field to each. Subtypes can also be used to assign different topology rules to different types of features within a feature class (see the previous section, 'Ensuring spatial data integrity').

The subtype for a feature in a feature class or a record in a table is determined by its subtype code value. The field you're using to define subtypes must be short or long integer. If the values are currently stored as text attributes in the table (as category values often are), you'll need to add an integer field to the table and assign a numeric code to each category value (see 'Adding fields and calculating attribute values' in Chapter 5). For example, if you're creating subtypes for a parcel feature class using a general landuse code, and the categories are "residential," "non-residential," and "undeveloped," you'd need to add a new field to the feature class and assign an integer value to each feature based on its landuse category—say 0, 1, and 2, respectively. You'd then use this new field to create the subtypes.

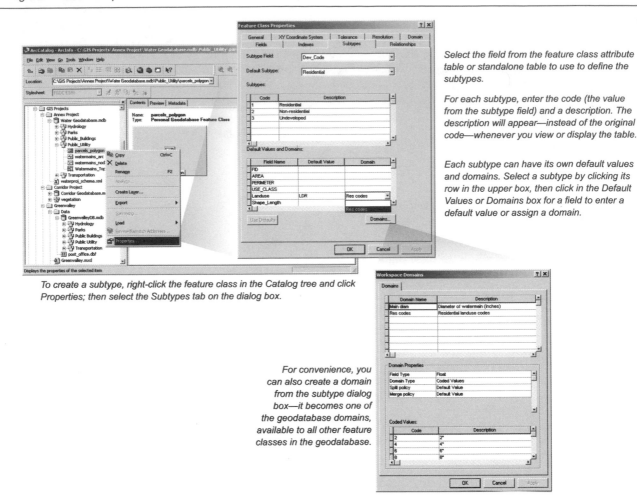

Select the field from the feature class attribute table or standalone table to use to define the subtypes.

For each subtype, enter the code (the value from the subtype field) and a description. The description will appear—instead of the original code—whenever you view or display the table.

Each subtype can have its own default values and domains. Select a subtype by clicking its row in the upper box, then click in the Default Values or Domains box for a field to enter a default value or assign a domain.

To create a subtype, right-click the feature class in the Catalog tree and click Properties; then select the Subtypes tab on the dialog box.

For convenience, you can also create a domain from the subtype dialog box—it becomes one of the geodatabase domains, available to all other feature classes in the geodatabase.

Subtypes can be modified or deleted using the Subtypes tab. To delete an individual subtype, click the box at the beginning of the subtype's row and press the Delete key on your keyboard. To delete all the subtypes, click the Subtype Field drop-down arrow and select <None>.

Once created, subtypes are used in several places in ArcGIS Desktop. When you view the feature class table or standalone table in ArcCatalog or ArcMap, the subtype name appears in the field, rather than the original value the subtype is based on.

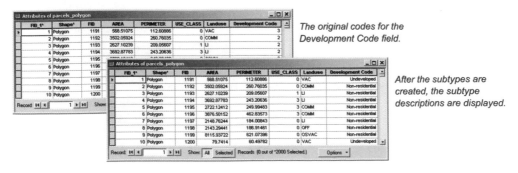

The original codes for the Development Code field.

After the subtypes are created, the subtype descriptions are displayed.

When you preview the feature class in ArcCatalog, the features are symbolized by subtype—normally they're all drawn using a single symbol. Similarly, when you add the feature class to a map in ArcMap, the features are automatically symbolized by subtype.

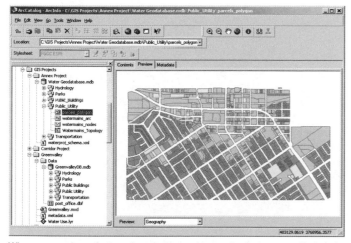

When you preview a feature class that has subtypes, the features are displayed using a different color for each subtype.

When you edit attributes in ArcMap, the subtype names are displayed in the field. Any default values or domains you've defined are active. If you change the subtype, any default values are automatically applied and any domains automatically become available.

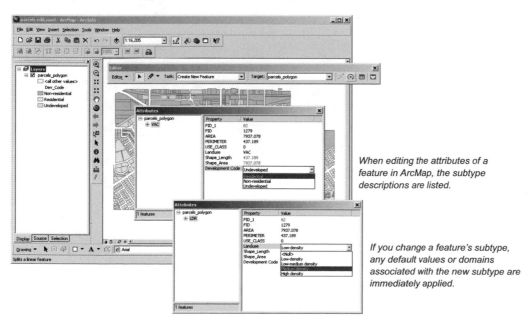

When editing the attributes of a feature in ArcMap, the subtype descriptions are listed.

If you change a feature's subtype, any default values or domains associated with the new subtype are immediately applied.

Building relationships between features and tables

A feature class stores the geometry of geographic features and their attributes. In many cases, you'll be able to store all the descriptive information for the features in the feature class. There may be cases, though where it's more efficient to store information about the features in a separate table, and relate the records in this table to the features in the feature class, using a common field. One way to do this in ArcGIS Desktop is to create a relationship class in your geodatabase. The relationship class defines the relationship between the feature class and the related table, or between two standalone tables.

For example, you may want to store information about the owner for each parcel in a feature class (the owner's mailing address, phone numbers, tax ID, and so on). One person might own several parcels; it would be redundant to store all that information in the feature class for every parcel that the person owns. Conversely, a parcel might be owned by several people; it would be difficult to store their names (let alone their other information) in the record for that parcel—you'd have to have multiple fields (owner1, owner2, owner3, and so on). To solve this dilemma, you'd create a relationship class between the feature class of parcels and a table of owners. Each parcel and each owner is listed once, in their respective tables. A common field in the two tables acts as a key to relate records—in this example, you'd likely use the parcel ID. When you point at a parcel on a map in ArcMap to see who owns it, ArcMap uses the relationship class to select and display the related owner records for that parcel. When you select an owner in the owner table, ArcMap will display all the parcels owned by that person.

Relationship classes are often used to maintain descriptions of category codes. For example, each parcel may have a landuse code, with the detailed description of the code stored in a related table having one record for each code. If you need to change or update a particular code description, you just edit the record in the related table.

Relationship classes are also useful if related tables are maintained and updated separately, or if the attributes you need in a feature class are already stored in another feature class. For example, you may have a feature class of counties, with the health statistics for each county stored in a separate table that is updated monthly. Rather than continuously updating the attributes in the counties feature class, you simply create a relationship class to relate the counties to the health statistics table.

Attribute relationships can also be created using joins and relates in ArcMap (see 'Joining tables' in Chapter 5). These relationships are stored only with the map in which they are created. Relationships created in the geodatabase are available for any map and throughout ArcGIS. Setting up a relationship class in the geodatabase has several other advantages. A relationship class can be set up so when you modify a feature, related features update automatically. This can involve moving or deleting related features, or updating an attribute. For example, you could set up a relationship such that whenever you move a utility pole, attached lines and transformers move with it. By setting rules, a relationship class can restrict the type of relations that are valid. For example, you can specify that a pole may support a maximum of three transformers.

Creating a relationship class

You can create a relationship class at the geodatabase level or the feature dataset level—either way, all the feature classes and tables in the entire geodatabase are available for the relationship; the only difference is where the relationship class will reside. Right-click a geodatabase or feature dataset, point to New, and click Relationship Class.

The wizard will prompt you for a name for the relationship class and the participating feature classes or tables, as well as other properties. You can create a relationship class between a feature class and a standalone table, two feature classes, or two standalone tables in your geodatabase.

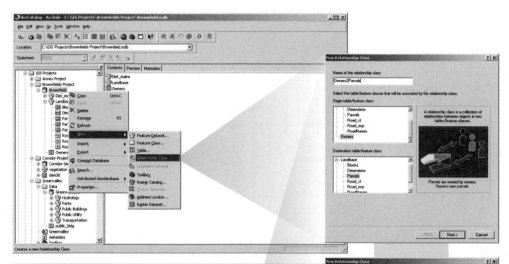

Enter a name for the relationship class, and select the origin and destination feature classes/tables. In general, the destination is the feature class/table you're relating the associated table to. In this example, a table of owners is related to parcels—Owners is the origin and Parcels the destination.

Specify either a simple or composite relationship. In a composite relationship, if a record in the origin is deleted, the related records in the destination are also deleted. In a simple relationship this is not the case.

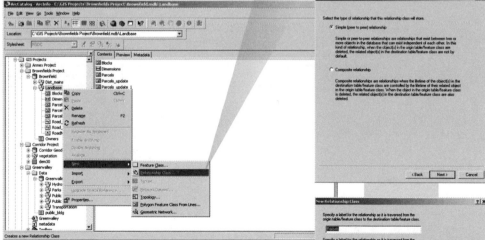

To create a relationship class, right-click a geodatabase or feature dataset in the Catalog tree, point to New, and click Relationship Class. The process is the same either way—the only difference is where the relationship class will be stored (under the geodatabase, or under the feature dataset).

Use messages to enable automatic update of records between the feature classes/tables. You can later set up rules to specify when and how updates will occur (for example, when you move a feature you can have features in a related feature class move with it).

Specify whether one record in the origin relates to only one record in the destination; one record can relate to more than one record in the destination; or multiple records in the origin can relate to multiple records in the destination.

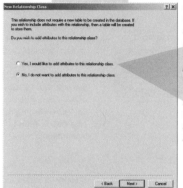

Specify whether the relationship class will have attributes—that is, whether each linked pair of records has associated fields, such as the percentage of a parcel owned by a particular owner. If Yes, an intermediary table is created, and the Next button displays a dialog box in which you define the fields. Each record in the table represents a linked pair of records.

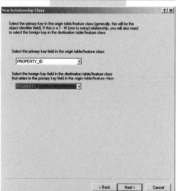

Lastly, specify the fields in the origin and destination feature class/table containing the common values used to relate records. These are known as keys.

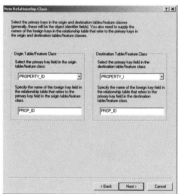

If you specified that the relationship class contain attributes or you specified a many-to-many relate, or both, an intermediary table is created. In addition to the origin and destination keys, you specify the field(s) in the intermediary table that correspond to the origin and destination keys.

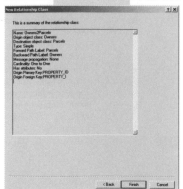

The final panel displays a summary of the options you specified. Click Back to make changes, or Finish to create the relationship class.

On the first panel of the wizard, you choose one feature class/table to be the origin and another to be the destination. An edit made to the origin will affect the destination. For example, in the landuse code example above, you'd set the code table as the origin and the parcel feature class as the destination. Deleting a parcel (a destination object) will have no effect on the code table, and deleting a landuse code (an origin object) will set the value of the code field in the matching parcel records to Null, which is as it should be, because they no longer have a matching code table record. If you set the parcels as the origin, deleting a parcel would set the value for that code to Null in the code table; all other parcels having that code would no longer have a match in the code table.

When you create a relationship class, you specify whether it is simple or composite. In a simple relationship class, if you delete a record in the origin table, the value for the corresponding record in the related table is set to Null. In a composite relationship, destination objects can't exist independently of origin objects, so when the origin is deleted, the related destination objects are also deleted.

You can have origin and destination objects send messages to notify one another when they are changed, allowing related objects to update appropriately. For example, updating an origin can require related destination objects to update. If updating an origin requires related destination objects to update, set the message notification direction to Forward; specify Backward for the reverse. Or, specify Both. Once you've created the relationship, you must then set up rules for the objects that receive the messages so they can respond.

The type of relate—one-to-one, one-to-many, or many-to-many—is known as cardinality. The parcel/owner example earlier describes a many-to-many relate (one or more parcels can relate to one or more owners); the landuse code example is a one-to-many relate (one landuse code relates to many parcels); and the county health statistics example is a one-to-one relate (each county in the feature class has a corresponding record in the health statistics table).

The common fields that relate the feature classes/tables are called keys. The key field in the origin class of a relationship is called the primary key; the key field in the destination class is called the foreign key. It contains values that match those of the primary key field in the origin class. The key fields may have different names but must be of the same data type and contain the same kind of information, such as parcel IDs.

In one-to-one and one-to-many relationships, values in the primary key of the origin class directly relate to values in the foreign key of the destination class. Many-to-many relationships, on the other hand, create an intermediate table to map the associations. When the intermediate table is created, only the fields are generated for you. ArcGIS does not know which origin objects are associated with which destination objects, so you must manually create the rows. Each row associates one origin object with one destination object.

The intermediate table of a many-to-many relationship can optionally serve a second purpose—storing attributes of the relationship itself. For example, in a parcel database you may have a relationship class between parcels and owners, where owners own parcels and parcels are owned by owners. An attribute of each relationship could be the percentage of ownership. If you need to store such attributes, you can add them to the intermediate table when you create the relationship or anytime after. When you're setting up a one-to-one or one-to-many relationship, you may have the same need to store attributes of the relationship. If this is the case, you must specify this when you create the relationship so an intermediate table is created for you.

Specifying the number of allowed linked records

Once you've created the relationship, you can specify rules to refine the cardinality. In a relationship of parcels and buildings, for example, you might specify that each building must be associated with a parcel, or that a parcel can contain a maximum of three buildings. This prevents a user from forgetting to associate a building to a parcel or from associating too many buildings to a parcel when editing data, and ensures the integrity of the relationships between feature classes and tables.

In ArcCatalog, right-click an existing relationship class to display its Relationship Class Properties dialog box and click the Rules tab. If the origin or destination has subtypes, click the subtype you want to apply the rule to. If there are no subtypes, the relationship rule will apply to all features. Check the boxes for the origin and destination cardinality. Set the appropriate Min and Max cardinalities for the rule.

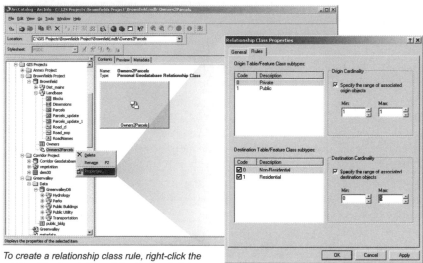

Select the origin subtype to participate in the rule, then select the destination subtype (make sure the box is checked). Then specify the number of allowed linked records. In this one-to-many relate, one private parcel owner can be linked to anywhere from 0 to 5 non-residential properties. Set the Max first, since the Min must be less than the Max.

To create a relationship class rule, right-click the relationship class in the catalog tree, and click Properties, then select the Rules tab on the dialog box.

After you've set up the rules, you can test them in ArcMap with the Validate Features command.

Managing a relationship class

Once you've created the relationship class, it appears in the Catalog tree, and you can inspect—but not change—its properties by right-clicking it and clicking Properties. You can, however, set and change relationship rules on the Rules tab. When you delete a feature class or table in ArcCatalog, if that feature class or table participates in a relationship class, the relationship class is also deleted.

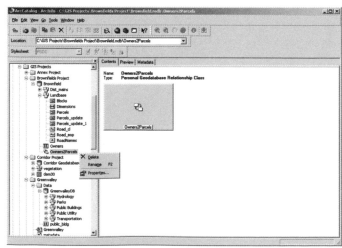

Right-click a relationship class to rename or delete it.

Accessing table relationships in ArcMap

You can use ArcMap to explore the relationships established by the relationship class. When you identify a feature in your map, you can see the features or records related to that feature in the Identify results dialog box.

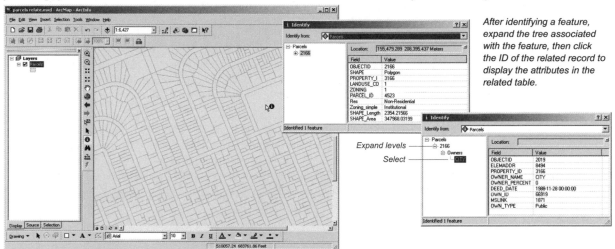

After identifying a feature, expand the tree associated with the feature, then click the ID of the related record to display the attributes in the related table.

Expand levels

Select

When you select one or more rows or features in a table, you can open the related table and select the related objects.

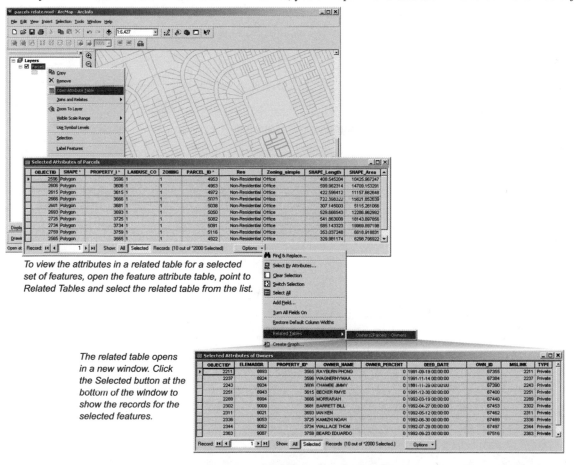

To view the attributes in a related table for a selected set of features, open the feature attribute table, point to Related Tables and select the related table from the list.

The related table opens in a new window. Click the Selected button at the bottom of the window to show the records for the selected features.

Managing raster datasets in a geodatabase

Rasters store geographic data as a continuous grid of cells, each assigned a value. They are most often used for continuous phenomena that can be measured at any location, such as rainfall, elevation, or the concentration of ozone in the air. However, discrete features—such as roads or wells—can also be stored as rasters (the cell value indicates the presence or absence of a feature). Typically, raster datasets are stored in workspaces, along with other files. You can load them into a geodatabase if you want all your data stored in one database. Storing rasters in a geodatabase may also make managing multiple raster datasets easier and more efficient—you can ensure the datasets are in the same coordinate system, for example. Also, storing very large rasters in a geodatabase enables them to display on the screen rapidly. A geodatabase raster is cut up into smaller tiles (referred to as "blocks"). When you zoom in, only the blocks for the current map extent need to be fetched, instead of the entire image.

One way of managing rasters in a geodatabase is to create a raster dataset from one or more existing rasters. This approach is particularly good for combining adjacent rasters and creating a single dataset (such as combining several adjacent elevation surfaces to create a single elevation surface for your study area). The other way to manage rasters in a geodatabase is to create a raster catalog and then load multiple rasters into it. A raster catalog is good for storing and managing individual rasters as a collection, such as storing coincident rasters representing different themes (elevation, slope, soil moisture) for a city or county.

Loading rasters into a geodatabase

There are two ways to create a raster dataset in a geodatabase. One way is to create an empty raster dataset and define its properties, such as cell size and coordinate system, then load one or more rasters into it. You'd typically use this approach when implementing a geodatabase design and populating the geodatabase with data.

To create an empty raster dataset, right-click the geodatabase, point to New, and click Raster Dataset.

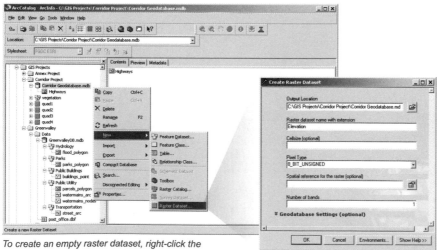

To create an empty raster dataset, right-click the geodatabase name in the Catalog tree, point to New, and click Raster Dataset. Define the properties for the new raster dataset in the dialog box.

You can then load the data—either a single raster, or multiple rasters that you want to "mosaic" into a single dataset. You specify how to handle overlaps, what value to use for "no data," and so on.

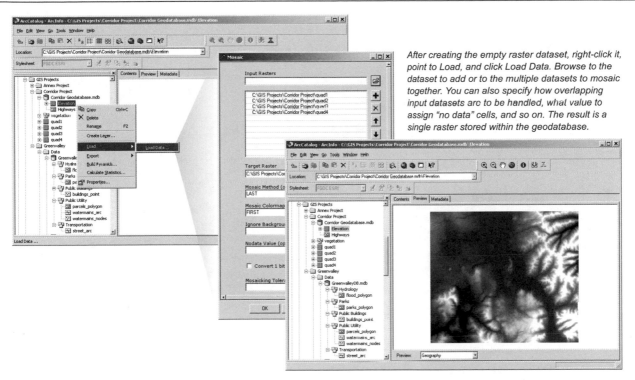

After creating the empty raster dataset, right-click it, point to Load, and click Load Data. Browse to the dataset to add or to the multiple datasets to mosaic together. You can also specify how overlapping input datasets are to be handled, what value to assign "no data" cells, and so on. The result is a single raster stored within the geodatabase.

Another, more ad hoc, approach is to import one or more existing raster datasets directly into the geodatabase. Import assigns the properties of the output raster dataset using the properties of the input rasters, rather than allowing you to define them. There are two options for importing rasters. Both are accessed by right-clicking the geodatabase and clicking Import. If you want to mosaic several adjacent rasters into a single dataset, choose "Raster Datasets (mosaic)." As with loading multiple datasets (described above), you can specify how to handle overlaps, assign "no data" values, and so on.

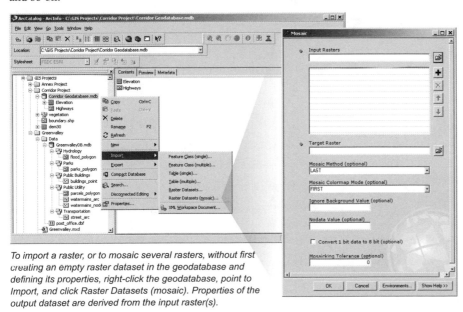

To import a raster, or to mosaic several rasters, without first creating an empty raster dataset in the geodatabase and defining its properties, right-click the geodatabase, point to Import, and click Raster Datasets (mosaic). Properties of the output dataset are derived from the input raster(s).

If you want to import a single raster dataset, or import several datasets at one time but continue to store them as individual datasets (rather than mosaicking them into a single dataset), choose the "Raster Datasets" option.

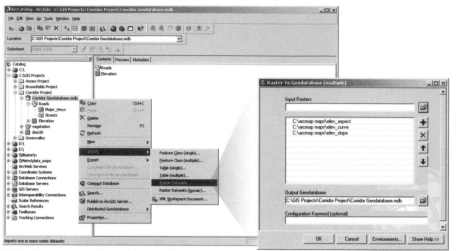

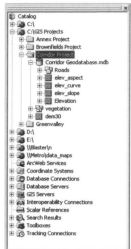

To import one or more rasters into a geodatabase as individual raster datasets, right-click the geodatabase, point to Import, and click Raster Datasets.

The rasters are stored individually in the geodatabase.

Creating a raster catalog

A raster catalog lets you manage a group of individual rasters as a collection. The rasters could be a tiled image—such as all aerial photos for a county—that you want to maintain as separate tiles (rather than mosaicking them into a single dataset); a set of coincident rasters for a location (such as layers for soil type, elevation, rainfall, and so on); a time series for a location (such as urban versus rural landuse for each decade); or any other collection of rasters you want to keep together, such as all the output rasters from a GIS analysis project.

You first create and define the raster catalog. Right-click a geodatabase, point to New, and click Raster Catalog.

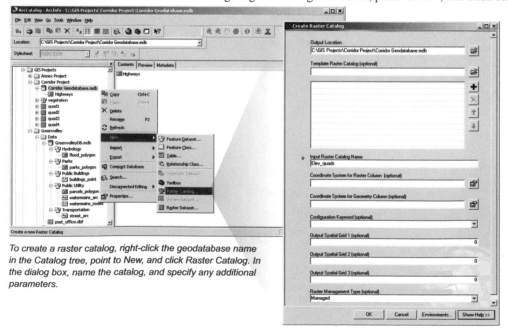

To create a raster catalog, right-click the geodatabase name in the Catalog tree, point to New, and click Raster Catalog. In the dialog box, name the catalog, and specify any additional parameters.

After creating the catalog, you load raster datasets into it.

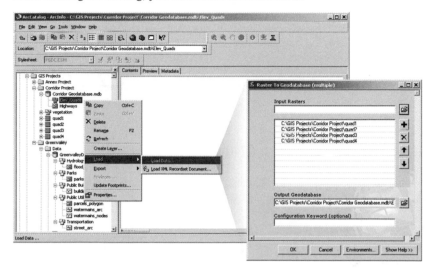

After creating the empty raster catalog, right-click it, point to Load, and click Load Data. Browse to the rasters to add, and add them to the list.

When you create a raster catalog, a table is created that lists each raster. You can display the table by selecting the catalog in the Catalog tree, selecting the Preview tab, and clicking the Table option at the bottom of the window. You can add fields to the table (such as source, creation date, and so on) to track the rasters. Right-click the catalog, click Properties, and select the Fields tab. Then enter the additional fields as you would for any other table (see 'Creating feature classes and tables' earlier in this chapter).

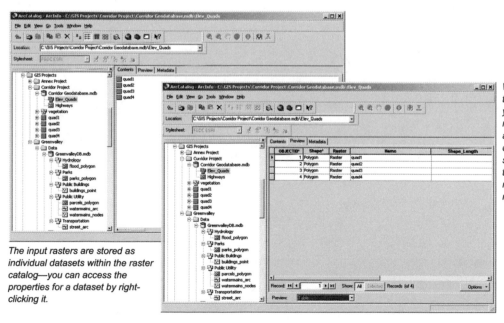

The input rasters are stored as individual datasets within the raster catalog—you can access the properties for a dataset by right-clicking it.

When you preview the table for the raster catalog you can see that each raster dataset is stored as a record in the table. You can add fields to the table, such as the creation date, the source, and so on, to manage the raster datasets more efficiently.

You can also perform searches to query the raster catalog. You might do this to find only rasters of a specific date or having a low percentage of cloud cover on an image. You can search by geography to view only those rasters that coincide with your area of interest. (See 'Searching for data and maps' earlier in this chapter.)

Adding specialized datasets to a geodatabase

In addition to the basic geodatabase data types of feature classes, tables, and rasters, you can extend your geodatabase with datasets that are used for specific applications, such as surface modeling and analysis; modeling the flow of people, goods, or resources over networks; or locating features or incidents along a street or highway network. Usually, these datasets are built from feature classes and tables that already exist in your geodatabase. While this section describes how to define these datasets in your geodatabase, Chapter 3, 'Data Compilation and Editing', contains information on how to create and edit the features that the datasets contain.

Creating a terrain dataset for surface modeling

A terrain dataset is used to model surfaces using TIN structures within a geodatabase (see also 'Creating a TIN surface' in Chapter 5). Terrains are also used to manage massive 3D point collections—for example, billion point LiDAR collections. You define and build the terrain dataset from existing feature classes stored in a feature dataset. You can also specify scales at which to display the terrain at a lower resolution, so it will draw faster.

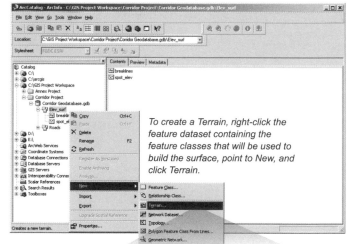

To create a Terrain, right-click the feature dataset containing the feature classes that will be used to build the surface, point to New, and click Terrain.

Select the feature classes that will be used to build the Terrain. These include spot elevations, contour lines, and breaklines (such as streams or graded roadbeds).

Specify the number of pyramid levels. Pyramids are used to draw the Terrain more quickly (but with lower resolution) when zoomed out.

Specify how the feature classes will be used for building the Terrain (or accept the defaults).

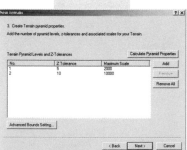

The final panel summarizes the settings—click Finish to build the Terrain (or Back to make changes).

Once the terrain dataset is created, it's added to the feature dataset. You can preview the terrain in ArcCatalog, and view its properties by right-clicking it in the Catalog tree.

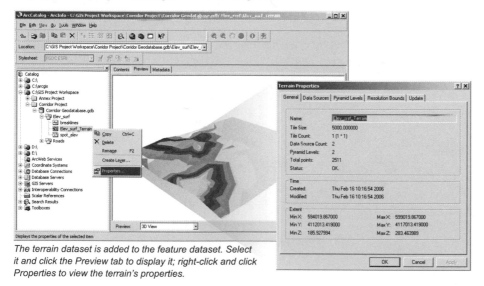

The terrain dataset is added to the feature dataset. Select it and click the Preview tab to display it; right-click and click Properties to view the terrain's properties.

You can display a terrain dataset just as you would a TIN by adding it to a map in ArcMap or to a 3D view in ArcScene. See Chapter 4, 'Mapping and Visualization', for more on displaying surfaces.

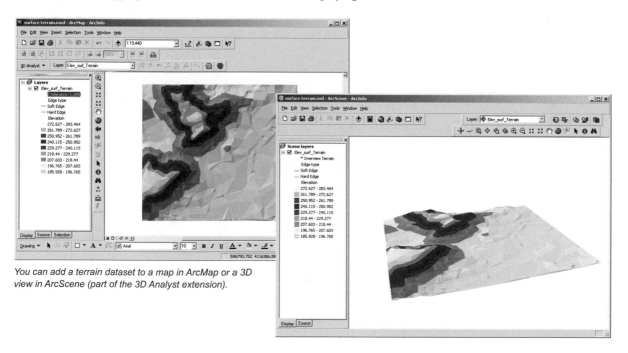

You can add a terrain dataset to a map in ArcMap or a 3D view in ArcScene (part of the 3D Analyst extension).

Creating a network dataset for transportation applications

A network dataset is a collection of edges (any line feature that participates in the network), junctions (where edges connect), and turns, through which you can model navigation and the flow of people, objects, goods, or resources. Each network has a set of navigation properties. These include the cost (such as distance or time) to travel along each edge and to transfer onto another edge; the ability to model one-way, left turn, and other travel restrictions; and the ability to model "multi-modal" networks (modeling trips that use a combination of an automobile, a bus, and walking, for example).

A network dataset uses feature classes as data sources for edges, junctions, and turns. You specify the role each feature class will play in the network along with its navigation properties. The feature classes that participate in a network must be in the same feature dataset, and a feature class can participate in only one network dataset at a time.

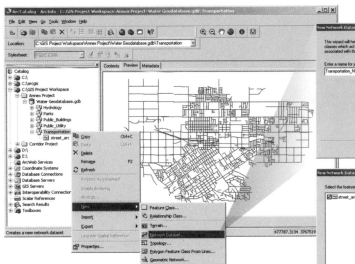

To create a network dataset, right-click the feature dataset containing the network components, point to New, and click Network Dataset.

Enter a name for the network dataset.

Specify which feature classes will be used to build the network. It can be as simple as a single street feature class, with streets forming the edges and intersections forming the junctions. Or it can include multiple modes, such as rail lines, stations, bus routes, bus stops, and so on.

Click the Connectivity button to specify where lines (edges) will connect and network junctions will be created.

Specify—for each feature class—where features in the network can connect. The default is end points, but you can have lines connect to each other at any vertex.

Specify an elevation field if multiple edges meet at a junction, but you want to limit which other edges they connect to—only edges with the same value in the elevation field will be considered connected in the network.

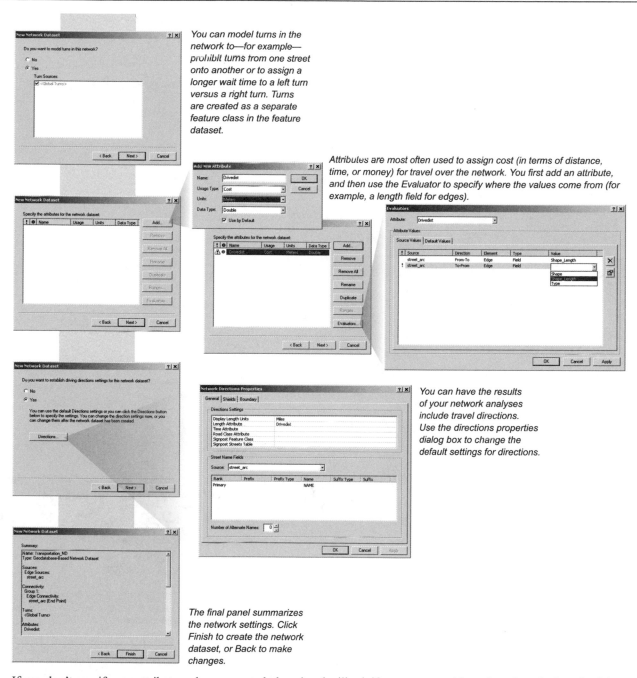

You can model turns in the network to—for example—prohibit turns from one street onto another or to assign a longer wait time to a left turn versus a right turn. Turns are created as a separate feature class in the feature dataset.

Attributes are most often used to assign cost (in terms of distance, time, or money) for travel over the network. You first add an attribute, and then use the Evaluator to specify where the values come from (for example, a length field for edges).

You can have the results of your network analyses include travel directions. Use the directions properties dialog box to change the default settings for directions.

The final panel summarizes the network settings. Click Finish to create the network dataset, or Back to make changes.

If you don't specify any attributes when prompted, the wizard will ask if you want to add one based on the length of the feature. The wizard also recognizes fields with certain names in the feature classes you're building the network from and automatically associates them with the network attributes (if you add a network attribute named "meters" it will automatically be associated with a "meters" field in a line feature class, if it exists).

After the network is created (defined), a prompt appears, asking if you want to build it. (You can always build it later by right-clicking it in ArcCatalog. You might do this if you redefine the network at a later time.)

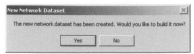

Click Yes when prompted to go ahead and build the network dataset.

The network is added to the feature dataset in which it was created. You can preview it and access its properties by right-clicking the network dataset name in ArcCatalog. The properties dialog box lets you add or remove feature classes or attributes, change the driving direction parameters, and so on. The network junctions are also added as a separate feature class in the feature dataset.

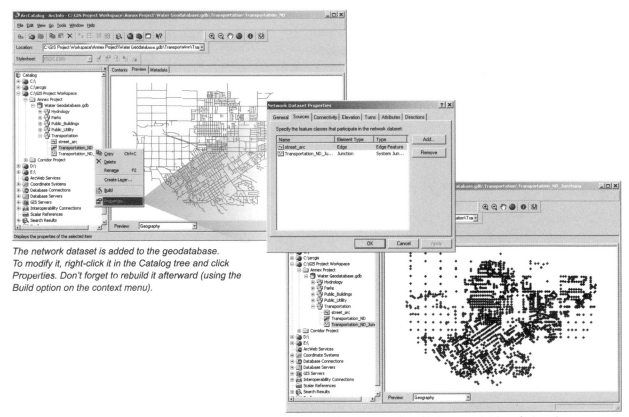

The network dataset is added to the geodatabase. To modify it, right-click it in the Catalog tree and click Properties. Don't forget to rebuild it afterward (using the Build option on the context menu).

The network junctions are also added as a geodatabase feature class.

Once your network is complete, you can add it to a map in ArcMap, and perform network analysis, if the Network Analyst extension is enabled. Open the Network Analyst toolbar using the Toolbars option on the View menu. You can, for example, find the shortest (or quickest) route between stops, define a service area around a facility, or find the closest facility to a location. See 'Creating paths and corridors' and 'Allocating areas to centers' in Chapter 5.

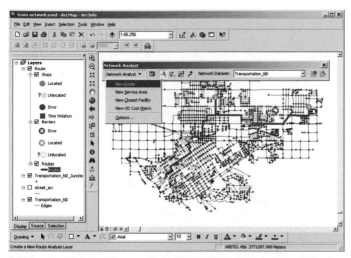

Add the network dataset to a map in ArcMap, and use the tools on the Network Analyst toolbar to perform analysis, such as finding the shortest route between several stops.

Creating a geometric network for utilities applications

A geometric network is a set of connected edge and junction features used to model the flow of electricity, water, gas, stormwater runoff, and so on. Each feature class is assigned a role in the geometric network as a collection of edges or junctions. The connectivity of the network is defined by geometric coincidence—for example, valves (which are held as a point feature class) are connected to the endpoints of pipe segments (stored as line features). If the valve is open, water can flow through it in a specified direction.

Geometric networks are similar to network datasets used for transportation modeling, but have properties that let you perform analysis specific to utilities applications. You can trace upstream or downstream from a location, find all the connected elements, find closed loops, and so on. Geometric networks can be analyzed using the Utility Network Analyst toolbar in ArcMap (see 'Modeling flow' in Chapter 5).

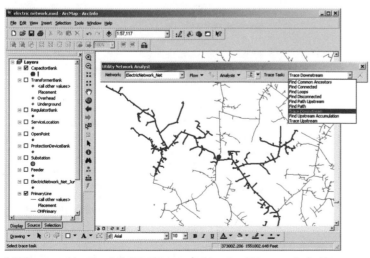

Add the geometric network (in this case, an electric network) to a map in ArcMap, then use the Utility Network Analyst toolbar to trace flow over the network (click Toolbars on the View menu). In this example, the map displays the portions of the network downstream from an outage.

You can build a geometric network from existing feature classes (the most common approach) or define the parameters of the network and load data into it later. Geometric networks are created within a feature dataset so you must have defined and created a feature dataset before creating a geometric network. All feature classes participating in the network must have the same spatial reference, which a feature dataset ensures. Feature classes can belong to only one geometric network at a time.

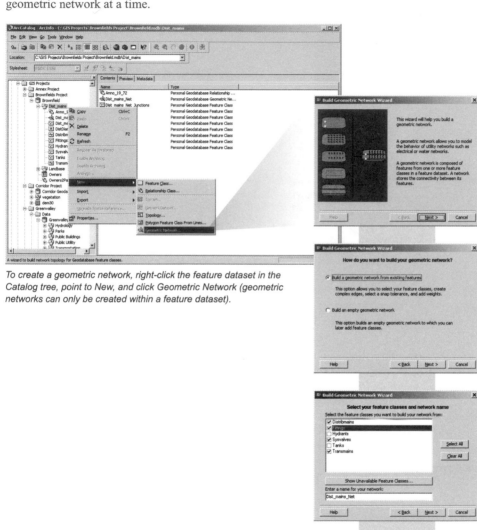

Use the Build Geometric Network Wizard to create a geometric network.

To create a geometric network, right-click the feature dataset in the Catalog tree, point to New, and click Geometric Network (geometric networks can only be created within a feature dataset).

Specify whether you're building a network from existing feature classes, or you're building an empty network that you'll load data into later (in which case the next five panels are skipped).

Select the feature classes that will participate in the network (a feature class can participate in only one network at a time).

The Enabled field (set to either true or false) is added to each feature class in the network to specify whether specific features can participate in tracing flow over the network. The value is initially set to True—you can change this by editing the feature class later. This panel is presented when one or more of the feature classes already has an attribute field called Enabled (it may have previously participated in a network). Specify whether to use or overwrite these values.

Specify whether to build complex edges. If No, line features (edges) will act as simple edges and will connect only at endpoints. If Yes, you can specify which line feature classes will have complex edges and will connect at endpoints or where edges intersect (do this if you want to maintain certain features as single entities, even if they're intersected by other features).

Accept the default to snap features, unless you've already edited all the participating features classes to ensure line ends and junctions are connected.

Specify whether any of the point feature classes in the network represent sources or sinks. You'd include sources and sinks if you'll be modeling flow through the network.

Assign any weights that will be used when modeling flow through the network. These represent the cost of traversing an edge (or junction) in the network. You can then associate weights with fields in the appropriate feature class (by accessing the feature class properties and selecting the Weight Association tab). The values in the field are used as weights.

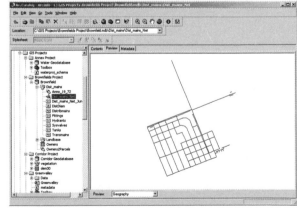

The final panel displays a summary of the options you specified. Click Back to make changes, or Finish to create the geometric network.

The geometric network is added to the feature dataset. To see the list of participating feature classes and their role in the network—along with connectivity rules and weights you've assigned—right-click the geometric network and click Properties.

Creating an address locator for geocoding

A common way of locating geographic entities is to use street addresses. This is often done for tables of customers, students, or any other entities that have an associated street address, such as crimes. The process of assigning coordinates to street addresses is called geocoding. To assist in geocoding, you add an address locator to your geodatabase. A locator is a combination of one of more feature classes containing addressable features, such as address range information for street centerlines, and a set of address styles and parameters that direct the matching process. Each locator dataset is used as the source for matching a single address or a large file of addresses in order to find address locations. See 'Assigning locations using street addresses or routes' in Chapter 3 for more on geocoding.

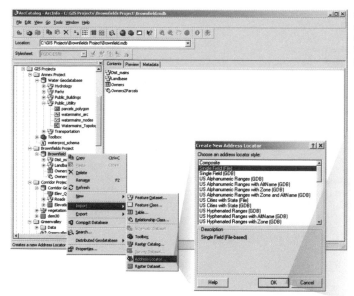

Right-click the geodatabase, point to Import, and click Address Locator. Then pick an address style from the list—styles include basic formats such as the entire address in a single field, to a wide range of standardized formats having multiple address fields.

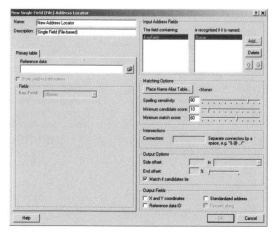

Use the Address Locator dialog box to specify the parameters for address matching, such as field names, intersection separators, and matching rules.

Creating a route dataset for linear referencing

Some GIS applications employ a linear measurement system used to measure distances along linear features, such as along roads, stream lines, and pipelines. One common example is a highway milepost measurement system used by departments of transportation for recording pavement conditions, speed limits, accident locations, and other incidents along highways. Values on the measurement system represent milepost distance from a set location such as a county line, or distance from a reference marker.

Support for these types of applications is referred to as linear referencing. Linear referencing is implemented in ArcGIS using route feature classes, which you build from linear features (such as local streets and highways) that have a common measurement system.

When creating a route feature class, you must define the geometry field's type to be polyline and indicate that it is able to store measure values. You also need to add a route identifier field. This field uniquely identifies each route. There are several ways to create routes in ArcGIS. The simplest is to use the Create Routes Wizard in ArcCatalog. (You can also create a route feature class and then load data into it; use the Linear Referencing tools in ArcToolbox; or create routes interactively in ArcMap. See 'Editing routes and geometric networks' in Chapter 3 for more on linear referencing and on creating routes in ArcMap.)

To use the Create Routes Wizard you first need to add the tool to a toolbar in ArcCatalog.

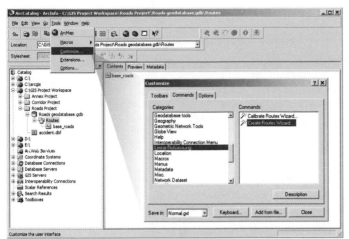

To add the Create Routes Wizard button to a toolbar, click Customize on the Tools menu. Then, on the Commands tab, select Linear Referencing in the Categories list, and drag the tool to a location on the Standard toolbar (or another open toolbar).

You then select the dataset the routes will be created from, such as a roads feature class having route identifiers and milepost measures, and click the tool to open the wizard.

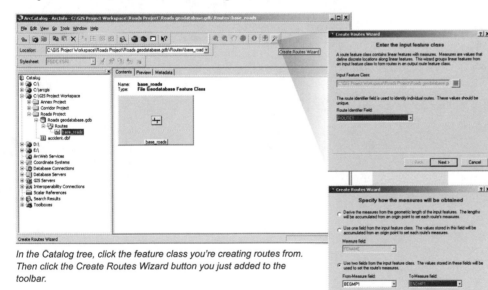

In the Catalog tree, click the feature class you're creating routes from. Then click the Create Routes Wizard button you just added to the toolbar.

The input feature class is automatically entered. From the drop-down list, select the field in the input feature class containing the route identifier for the features (this field has to exist in the input feature class—it's used to assign features to a route).

Specify how the route measures will be derived. You can use the lengths of the features, or use an existing field (or to-from fields) in the input feature class.

Specify whether to create the route as a feature class in a geodatabase, or as a shapefile in a folder.

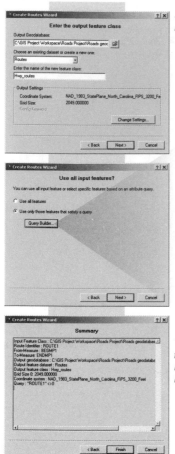

Specify the location and name of the new route.

You can create the route using all features in the input feature class, or use the Query Builder to select a subset of features. You'd use a subset, for example, to exclude features that are not part of a route (as shown here—features with a route ID not equal to 0), or to create routes using only certain route IDs, or to create routes from another selected set (such as a particular road type—only highways, for example).

The final panel summarizes the route parameters. Click Finish to create the route, or Back to make changes.

The route is created as a feature class in the feature dataset. As with any other feature class, you can access its properties by right-clicking it in the Catalog tree.

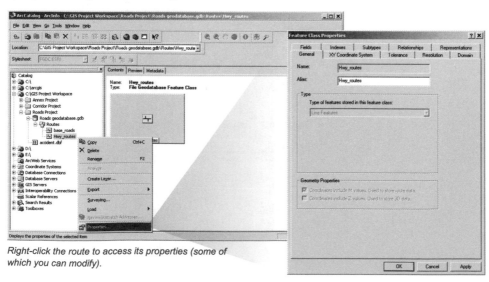

Right-click the route to access its properties (some of which you can modify).

Once the route has been created, you can add it to a map in ArcMap to display and query it—for example, you can point at a location on a route and get the measurement at that point. You can also assign geographic locations to events—such as accidents—that have route measurements rather than street addresses or geographic coordinates. The events can then be displayed on a map. This is a common reason for creating routes. See 'Assigning locations using street addresses or routes' in Chapter 3 for more on adding route events to a map.

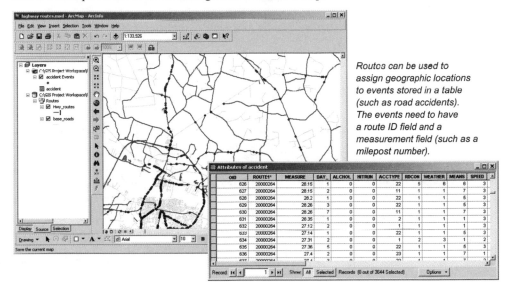

Routes can be used to assign geographic locations to events stored in a table (such as road accidents). The events need to have a route ID field and a measurement field (such as a milepost number).

Maximizing the performance of your database

As you add more and more data to your geodatabase and make changes to the data, the speed with which ArcGIS can search and display the data may suffer. And the size of your geodatabase files may grow. There are several things you can do to make sure your database can access and display your data quickly and efficiently. Creating indexes can help speed up queries. If your database includes raster datasets, you'll want to make sure you've built pyramids for all the rasters, so they'll display faster. Finally you can compact your database from time to time to decrease fragmentation of data on disk and make data searches faster.

Defining or modifying a spatial index

ArcGIS uses spatial indexes to quickly locate features in feature classes. Identifying a feature, selecting features by pointing or dragging a box, and panning and zooming all require ArcMap to use the spatial index to locate features.

Feature classes in a geodatabase use a system of grids as the spatial index. When you zoom to an area in ArcMap, ArcGIS finds the features that fall within the grid cells covering that area and displays only those features—that way it doesn't attempt to draw all the features (even those off the edges of the screen).

A feature class in a personal geodatabase has only one grid. Once a feature class is created in a personal geodatabase, you cannot modify the grid cell size.

A feature class in a file or ArcSDE geodatabase can have up to three grids. The additional grids allow feature classes with features of very different sizes to be queried faster. However, for most feature classes only a single grid is necessary. ArcGIS automatically rebuilds the spatial index after certain operations, to ensure the index is optimal. However, there may be times when you want to manually recalculate the index or assign grid cell sizes of your own— for example, after adding many polygons that are much larger than existing polygons.

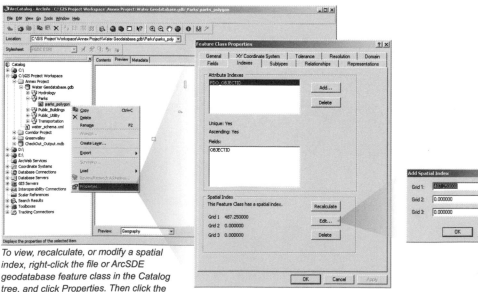

To view, recalculate, or modify a spatial index, right-click the file or ArcSDE geodatabase feature class in the Catalog tree, and click Properties. Then click the Indexes tab on the Feature Class Properties dialog box.

Creating an attribute index

Once you have data in a table or feature class, you can create attribute indexes to speed up queries you make on geodatabase tables and feature classes. It is much faster for the database to use the index to look up a record than to start at the first record and search through the entire table.

Attribute indexes can be created for single or multiple fields in a geodatabase feature class or table by accessing the Properties dialog box in ArcCatalog.

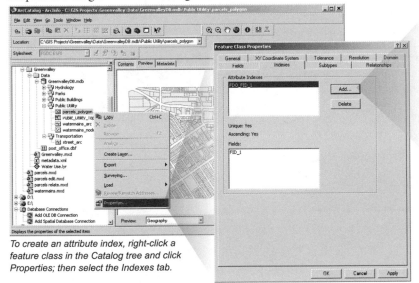

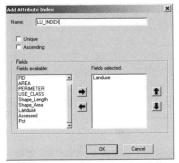

Click the Add button to open the dialog box. Enter a name for the index, then use the arrows to add the fields you want to index to the list. These would be the ones you search or query frequently.

To create an attribute index, right-click a feature class in the Catalog tree and click Properties; then select the Indexes tab.

Creating raster pyramids

Pyramids are reduced resolution representations of your raster dataset used to improve display performance. With pyramids, a lower-resolution copy of the data displays when drawing the entire dataset. Using lower-resolution data allows the dataset to draw quickly, while display quality is not noticeably worse. As you zoom in, higher-resolution data is displayed; performance is maintained because you're drawing successively smaller areas. ArcGIS chooses the most appropriate pyramid level automatically based on the scale of the map.

Pyramids only need to be built once per raster dataset; after that, they will be accessed each time the raster dataset is viewed.

When you display a raster for which pyramids have not been built, you're prompted to build them. It's a good idea to do this. You can also build pyramids for a raster dataset at any time by right-clicking the raster in the Catalog tree and clicking Build Pyramids.

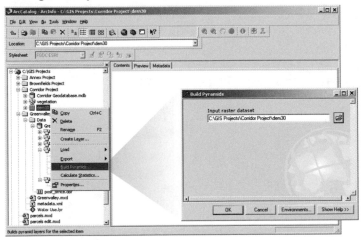

Right-click the raster in the Catalog tree and click Build Pyramids. This opens the Build Pyramids tool—click OK to build the pyramids.

Although you are not able to build pyramids on raster catalogs, it is possible to build pyramids for each raster dataset within the raster catalog.

Compacting and compressing geodatabases

A file geodatabase is stored as a folder of files on disk, while a personal geodatabase is stored in a single Microsoft Access (.mdb) file. When you first add data to either of these geodatabases, the data within each file occupies a continuous space on disk and is accessed efficiently by the software. However, as you delete and add data over time, the data within each file breaks into increasingly smaller, scattered fragments as data is removed and new data is added elsewhere in the file. This causes the software to perform more data-seeking operations within each file, slowing the rate at which the data is accessed. Compacting rearranges how the data is stored in each file, consolidating the data so that it occupies a single, contiguous space. Compacting also reduces the size of each file—it's possible to be able to reduce the size of a geodatabase by half or more. If you frequently add and delete data, you should compact your file or personal geodatabase on a monthly basis. You should also compact a geodatabase after any large-scale change, such as deleting a number of datasets.

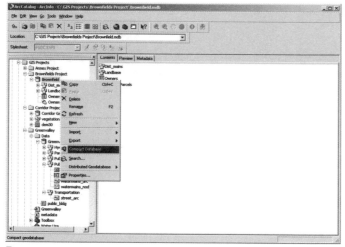

To compact a personal or file geodatabase, right-click the geodatabase and click *Compact Database*.

File geodatabases can also be compressed to make them smaller. Compressing a geodatabase (especially a large one) can yield significant storage savings, which can be helpful when you're pressed for disk space or are trying to fit data onto a CD or DVD.

Once compressed, a dataset looks the same in ArcCatalog and ArcMap as when it was uncompressed. The compressed data is a direct access format, so you do not have to uncompress it each time you access it—ArcGIS reads it directly.

A compressed dataset, however, is read-only and therefore cannot be edited or modified, except for changing its name and modifying attribute indexes and metadata. Compression is best suited for datasets that do not require further editing. If required, a compressed geodatabase can be uncompressed to return it to its original, read–rite format.

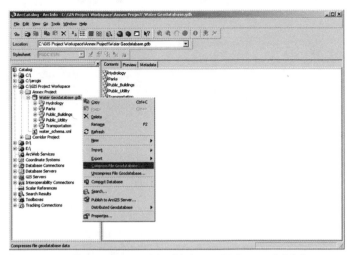

To compress a file geodatabase, right-click the geodatabase and click Compress File Geodatabase.

In addition to compacting or compressing a geodatabase, you should also run the Windows disk defragmenter on an occasional basis to maintain overall file system performance. File and personal geodatabase performance can benefit from this operation just like other types of files can.

The performance of an ArcSDE geodatabase can also become degraded over time as you add and delete features. That's because features that are deleted remain as rows in the geodatabase, but are only marked as "deleted" (so they can be undeleted, if necessary). To remove the deleted rows—and improve performance—you need to compress the database (any deleted rows can no longer be undeleted after the database is compressed).

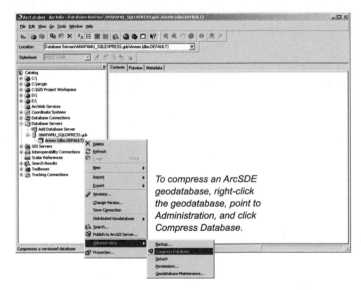

To compress an ArcSDE geodatabase, right-click the geodatabase, point to Administration, and click Compress Database.

Data Compilation and Editing

3

An overview of data compilation and editing

Once you've designed your GIS database, you need to collect the data that it will contain. The data you collect may be the most valuable asset in your GIS, since it underlies all the maps you'll make and analyses you'll undertake. While it's time consuming to collect data from various sources or create the data from raw information—not to mention making sure the data is as accurate and current as possible—the effort will ensure that your data, and the products you create from it, are sound. You may also need to process some of the data you collect—either before or after you put it in your database—to make sure you can use it to make maps and do analysis. You may need to correct or add individual features, add fields, update attribute values, change the coordinate system of a dataset, combine adjacent datasets into a single one, make sure coincident datasets register correctly, and so on.

GIS data sources

There are a variety of ways to collect the data that will go into your GIS database. In the course of your GIS projects—even for a single project—you'll likely use all of them.

Get existing data in an ArcGIS format

GIS data formats that ArcGIS can read directly include geodatabases, shapefiles, and coverages. You might get this from other ArcGIS users, download them from a GIS data clearinghouse, or buy them from a commercial data provider. You can copy this data right into your database in ArcCatalog, add it to a map in ArcMap, or use it for analysis with ArcToolbox tools (although you'll first want to verify the quality and usefulness of the data for your purposes—see 'The process for compiling GIS data' in this section). ArcGIS also recognizes a range of raster data formats (used for digital elevation models, orthophotos, and satellite images) you can load into your database or add to a map.

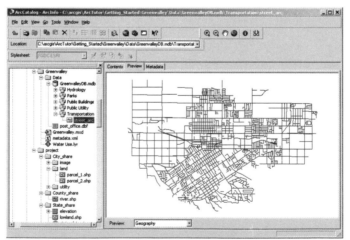

ArcGIS datasets you're likely to acquire include geodatabases, shapefiles, images, layer files, and even map documents, all listed here in ArcCatalog.

Get digital GIS data in another format and import or convert it

While there is a huge amount of data available in an ArcGIS format, you may also come across GIS data that is in another data format. This might be data created in another GIS program, data from a related application such as CAD software, or data in a standard format used by a government agency or other organization (such as the digital line graph, or DLG, format used by the U.S. Geological Survey). ArcGIS includes tools that recognize many standard formats and let you import the data into a geodatabase. You can even create your own tool to import custom formats.

CAD data, including AutoCAD® drawing files
(such as the building footprints, parcels, and
road casings shown here) and MicroStation
design files, can be imported to ArcGIS.

Convert tabular data to GIS data

Some of the data you'll need may be for features that have a geographic location, but have
not yet been assigned geographic coordinates so they can be mapped. Examples include a
table of customers or students with a home address, a table of crimes with a street address
or intersection, or a list of traffic accidents with a milepost marker. ArcGIS includes tools
to read a street address or a measure along a route (such as mileposts), assign geographic
coordinates, and create a feature class or shapefile from the data. You might also receive
data as a list of features with associated coordinates, such as a table of earthquakes with a
latitude/longitude coordinate, or a list of coordinates transmitted by a wolf wearing a GPS
receiver and a radio transmitter. ArcGIS lets you import tables of coordinates—in various
formats—and create a dataset you can store in your database and display on a map.

	OBJECTID	NAME	ADDRESS	ZIP	TYPE	SALES
1	OBJECTID	NAME	ADDRESS	ZIP	TYPE	SALES
2	1	Ace Market	1171 PIEDMONT AVE NE	30309	Store	59811.70
3	2	Andrew's Gasoline	1670 W PEACHTREE ST NE	30309	Service Station	10843.40
4	3	AP Supermarket	455 BEVERLY RD NE	30309	Store	160911.00
5	4	Atlanta Market	241 16TH ST NW	30318	Store	55719.00
6	5	Beans and Stuff	1233 PEACHTREE ST NE	30309	Cafe	73425.10
7	6	Big Sky Groceries	360 FORTUNE ST NE	30312	Store	47896.30
8	7	Breakfast in Atlanta	151 ALDEN AVE NW	30309	Restaurant	33958.90
9	8	Bud's Gas Station	200 CORLEY ST NE	30312	Service Station	29988.20
10	9	Camp Service Station	169 HUNNICUTT ST NW	30313	Service Station	34219.40
11	10	Central Petroleum	1100 CENTER ST NW	30318	Service Station	55130.40
12	11	Charlie Cota Inc.	400 EIGHTH ST NW	30318	Restaurant	45468.80
13	12	City Food Market	501 ETHEL ST NW	30318	Store	55686.90
14	13	Clamerty's	421 SPRING ST NW	30308	Store	56305.90
15	14	Crossroads Theater	120 MEMORIAL DR SE	30312	Movie Theater	30117.70
16	15	Damar Sales	388 7TH ST NE	30308	Service Station	55518.00
17	16	Dan's Taco Emporium	1032 CENTER ST NW	30318	Restaurant	55243.40
18	17	Darby's Market	1001 CENTER ST NW	30318	Store	55369.80
19	18	Dream Ice Cream	77 MILLS ST NW	30308	Restaurant	55260.50
20	19	Eastern Express	150 6TH ST NE	30308	Cafe	55574.10
21	20	Flash in the Pan	101 BAKER ST NW	30308	Restaurant	54649.80
22	21	Food Mart	670 10TH ST NW	30318	Store	90015.50
23	22	Foodmart	20 WILLIAMS ST NW	30303	Store	34185.60
24	23	Gelroy Deli and Cafe	762 ARGONNE AVE NE	30308	Cafe	54812.00
25	24	Henry's Deli and Imports	1250 FRANCIS ST NW	30318	Store	55776.70
26	25	Hometown Plaza	500 RANKIN ST NE	30308	Movie Theater	55251.30
27	26	Hugh's Service Station	299 MILLS ST NW	30313	Service Station	34253.20
28	27	Ivy's	701 JUNIPER ST NE	30308	Restaurant	54922.10
29	28	Lass's Supermarket	191 15TH ST NE	30309	Store	65896.00
30	29	Le Cafe	555 10TH ST NE	30309	Cafe	58652.90

Features stored in tables (such as this Excel table) and having a street address
or other locator can be assigned coordinates and displayed on a map in ArcGIS.

Create GIS data from scratch in ArcGIS

If you haven't been able to get the data you need in a digital format, you can create the datasets. In most cases, you'll draw features right on the screen in ArcGIS, using existing data (such as an aerial photo or satellite image) as a backdrop, guide, and spatial reference. For example, to create a dataset of streets as line features from an aerial photo stored as an image on your computer, you'd display the photo and trace over the streets to create the lines. If the information is on an existing printed map, you can trace over its features on a digitizing tablet to create a GIS dataset. This was the main method of data compilation in the early days of GIS, when most geographic information was in the form of paper maps. Now it's mainly used to fill in holes in your database when the data isn't available from any other source—such as for local historical data. Printed maps and aerial photos can also be scanned and then automatically converted to vector GIS datasets.

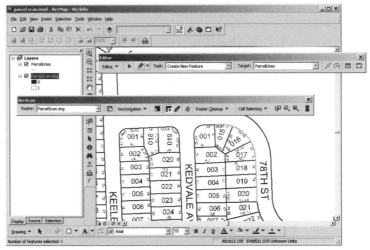

You can create features in ArcGIS by digitizing. In this example, the ArcScan for ArcGIS extension is used in an ArcMap edit session to create features (blue line) by tracing over a scanned parcel map.

Make new data from existing GIS data

Some of the data you'll require can be constructed or derived from datasets you've already loaded into your database. This might be a specialized dataset built from a collection of other features, such as a transportation network constructed from streets, highways, intersections, bus stops, and so on. Or, it may be a dataset you derive by processing an existing dataset—you might clip streams for your study area out of a larger dataset of streams, or you might process an elevation surface to create a raster dataset of slope steepness (see Chapter 5, 'Geographic Analysis', for more on processing datasets to create new ones).

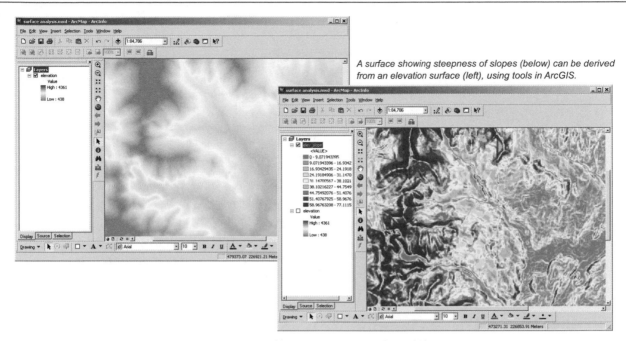

A surface showing steepness of slopes (below) can be derived from an elevation surface (left), using tools in ArcGIS.

The process for compiling GIS data

Compiling and editing GIS data is a loosely structured process that includes a number of tasks. You may not perform these tasks in just this order, but you'll want to make sure you've at least considered each of these points. You may also find that while building the database your various datasets will be at various stages in the process. And you may also find you'll have to revisit earlier tasks as new data is available. Keeping a GIS (or any) database current is an ongoing process. Developing a system to track your datasets and where they are in the process will be very beneficial (metadata can help with this, or even a spreadsheet).

Set up a workspace structure and database design

Before collecting data, you need to know what data to collect. Your database design process will result in a list of required datasets. Having the workspace structure or geodatabase in place will allow you to keep the data organized as you compile it. The section 'An overview of geographic data management' in Chapter 2 includes a discussion of how to set up a workspace structure and design a GIS database.

Once you've completed the database design, it's a good idea to list—for all the required datasets—where the data is going to come from, if you know. That will help focus your search. For example, you may already know that some of the data you need is only on printed maps that you'll need to scan or digitize. You may be aware of some GIS datasets available from a local agency or that you will need to buy from a commercial provider. For other datasets, you may not know if they already exist—either in digital form or on paper—so you'll have to initiate a search.

Search for existing data

Once you know what data you need, you need to find it and collect it one place. If you don't already know that it exists and where it is, you will need to search for it. There are several places where you can start your search.

ESRI Data & Maps

The ESRI Data & Maps CDs and DVDs contain basic global and national level data for parts of the world, such as hydrography, transportation networks, administrative boundaries, and demographic information (see the appendix in this book). These datasets are useful if you're working at a national or global scale. However, you may need more specialized data (such as vegetation types, air quality readings, or health statistics), or more detailed data (a coastline dataset, for example, is often very generalized for display on a national map), especially if you're working at a local or regional scale.

GIS data clearinghouses

There are several global and national GIS data clearinghouses set up on the internet (for example, www.geodata.gov). You can search by data theme or by location, or both. Some of the data is free, while other data you have to purchase. Again, the key is finding data that is detailed enough for your needs. Many states and regions have set up clearinghouses for local data. Data that you download or obtain may have restrictions on its use. You'll want to check this for all data you obtain, but especially data you download from a clearinghouse.

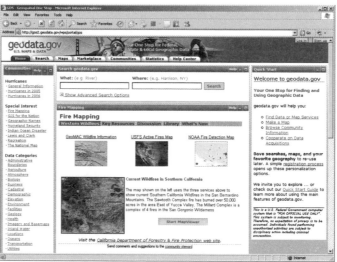

geodata.gov is a U.S. government clearinghouse where you can search for, and download, data and maps.

Local or regional agencies

Many local government agencies are willing to share their GIS data if you contact them directly. Some data you may have to purchase, usually at a relatively low price that covers the distribution costs. Once you start building your own GIS datasets you may find that agencies are willing to exchange data they have for data they need. A good way to find data is through local and regional ESRI user groups, many of whom hold regular meetings.

Commercial data providers

There are many companies that sell GIS data. Sometimes this is public domain data that a company has updated or corrected with newer or more accurate information (streets are a good example); or sometimes the company has compiled information from various sources in one dataset and used it to create new information, such as retail lifestyle categories for ZIP Codes. They may also process the data or use models to make predictions, such as projected population growth for counties. Some data you can buy is from companies that go out and collect raw data, such as satellite imagery or aerial photography. Commercial sources can be found at some of the clearinghouses, in GIS magazines and other publications, at GIS conferences, and by searching on the internet.

Regardless of the source, you'll want to make sure you get information about the data:

- The coordinate system it's in

- The date it was collected, and when it was updated

- For attributes, the descriptions of category codes and the units of measurement for numeric fields

- The resolution of the data (the appropriate scale at which it can be displayed)

- The owner of the data (if not the provider) and any restrictions on its use

This is usually in the metadata documentation that either comes with the data or is available at the clearinghouse. But in some cases you'll get data without documentation, so make sure the provider gives you at least these basic details.

Import or convert existing datasets, as necessary

In many cases, the data you obtain will already be in one of the formats ArcGIS can directly read and use (a geodatabase, a shapefile, an ArcInfo coverage, or a supported raster format). However, you'll probably get at least some data that is another GIS format, some other digital format, in a table with a geographic locator (such as a street address), or otherwise needing to be converted or imported before you can add it to your database and use it with ArcGIS.

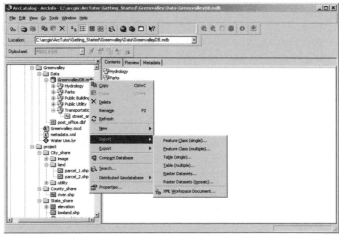

Use ArcCatalog to import datasets.

Create additional datasets

Once you've collected all the available data, you may still be missing some datasets you need. If there is source data—such as an existing printed map—you can digitize it. If not, you may have to collect the data in the field, or pay someone to do it. Or, you may have to substitute other available data that may not be your first choice (for example, lower resolution satellite imagery). Or, do without.

Since similar data is often available from different sources, there will be decisions—and trade-offs—along the way. You may have to decide between obtaining an existing GIS dataset that is out of date (and either updating it or using as is), and digitizing a recent map to have the latest information. The first option is faster and less expensive, but you may end up with lower quality data.

Make sure the datasets are integrated

The next step is to make sure you can use all the data for its intended purposes. To do this, you need to make sure the various datasets you've obtained from various sources fit together. First, you'll want to make sure the datasets can all be displayed in the same geographic space. While they don't have to all be in the same coordinate system, they at least have to have a spatial reference defined so ArcMap can display them together on a map (ArcMap will project data on the fly). ArcGIS data should already have a spatial reference defined; if you've imported data, you'll have to define it. However, it's usually a good idea—at least for a database you're building for the long haul—to put all the data in the same coordinate system. It will minimize registration problems between datasets, and you won't have to worry about it as you're making maps and doing analysis.

Then you'll want to make sure that the features in different coincident layers match up as closely as possible—for example, you don't want street centerlines stored in one dataset to cross over any parcels stored in another dataset. Even if the features are in the same coordinate system, the data may have been collected by different agencies at different times and at different resolutions (or with varying quality control). Usually, you'll have more confidence in the accuracy of one of the datasets. You'll use this one as the control, and adjust the other datasets to match it. In the end, you may have to edit and move individual features, but adjusting one dataset to another can at least get the features close to the right location.

Finally, to make sure the data covers your area of interest, you may need to match tiled datasets to build a continuous dataset for your study area. This is often the case for national databases stored in quadrangle sheets, such as hydrology or elevation data. Conversely, if you have a dataset that covers a large area, you may want to clip out the portion that pertains to your study area (clipping data is covered in Chapter 5—see 'Extracting a portion of a dataset').

Make sure the data has all the attributes you need

During the database design process, you identified and listed all the attributes each dataset should have. The attributes will at least partially drive your search for data—if there are choices, you'll want to use the dataset that has more of the attributes you need.

If you collected data from another source, you'll likely need to add attribute fields and assign values—for example, assigning your own paving codes to a street dataset you bought. If you're creating the data yourself, adding attributes is a major part of the process.

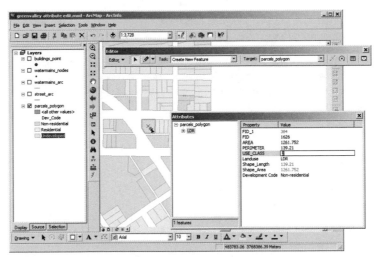

*Attribute editing is done in ArcMap. You can update the attributes of existing
features, or enter the attribute values for newly created ones.*

Make sure the data is as correct as possible

It goes without saying that you'll want your database to be as error-free and up-to-date
as possible, within your time and money constraints. The better your data, the better your
maps and analyses, and the better the decisions based on them. The goal, of course, is to
have your data reflect as accurately as possible what's actually on the ground. You'll likely
spend some time editing both individual features and their associated attributes. You'll
move features to the correct location or change their shape, connect features that need to
be connected, add missing features and delete ones that no longer exist (or shouldn't have
been there in the first place). ArcGIS has tools to check for errors and validate any edits
you've made. Part of this involves checking the data against any topology or attribute rules
you set up when you designed your geodatabase (see 'Ensuring spatial data integrity' and
'Ensuring attribute data integrity' in Chapter 2). As mentioned before, keeping a database
current and accurate is an ongoing process.

Create any extended or derived datasets

Once you're confident in the quality of your data, you'll create any extended or derived
datasets you need in your database. These might be datasets constructed from existing
features, such as a bus route built from streets and bus stops, or a water system built from
pipes, junctions, and pumps. You might also use geoprocessing tools to derive new datasets,
such as creating a slope or hillshade surface from an elevation raster, or building watershed
boundaries from an elevation raster and a streams dataset.

Document the data

Documenting your data is necessary so anyone in your organization who uses the data
will know what they're dealing with. And it will be invaluable when you revisit the data at
some point in the future. It's also critical if you end up sharing your data with other users,
or publishing it on the internet. Documenting data is more efficient if you do it as you go
along, working with each dataset. The metadata tools in ArcCatalog make it relatively
easy (see 'Documenting your database with metadata' in Chapter 2). While metadata
documentation can be extensive, you should include at least the basic pieces of information
listed above under 'Search data sources for existing data'.

Collecting, importing, and converting GIS data

A lot of data is available in a format ArcGIS can use directly (shapefiles, geodatabases, coverages, rasters, and some CAD data). This is especially true of basemap data such as hydrology, street networks, elevation, administrative boundaries, and so on. You may get data, though, that is not yet in a format ArcGIS can use. Or, you may want to convert ArcGIS data to another format to share with other GIS users. ArcGIS Desktop lets you import or export a wide range of both feature and raster data.

Collecting data in an ArcGIS format

You can add data to a map—or use it in an analysis—from any source or workspace you've connected to if it's already in ArcGIS format (see 'Finding and connecting to data' in Chapter 2). You may want to copy the data into your own workspace. Use the copy and paste functions in ArcCatalog to copy data to the location you want. The data can only be copied to an appropriate destination location (the Paste function will be grayed out if you can't copy the data to that location). Alternatively, you can click and drag datasets in the Catalog tree. Shapefiles, geodatabases, tables, and images can be copied from one folder to another. Feature classes can be copied from one geodatabase to another.

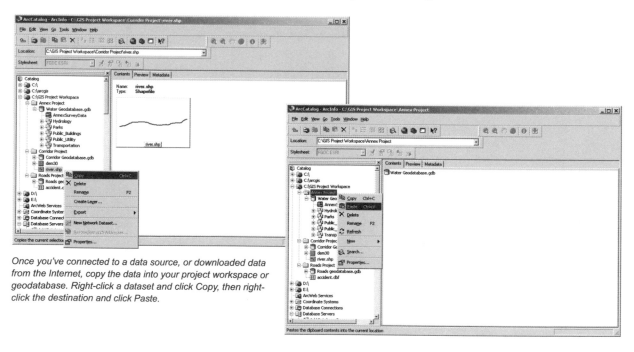

Once you've connected to a data source, or downloaded data from the Internet, copy the data into your project workspace or geodatabase. Right-click a dataset and click Copy, then right-click the destination and click Paste.

Shapefiles, tables, and images can't be directly copied into a geodatabase, but rather must be imported. Conversely, data held in a geodatabase can't be copied to a folder, but must be exported to another format (for example, you'd export a geodatabase feature class to a shapefile).

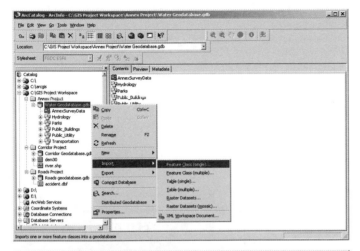

Right-click a geodatabase to import a shapefile (use the Feature Class option), table, or raster. The "multiple" options let you create a list of datasets to import at one time.

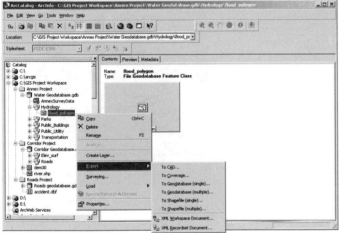

Right-click a feature class or other geodatabase dataset to export it to a format outside the geodatabase (or to another geodatabase). You can also export shapefiles, tables, and rasters to other formats by right-clicking them in the Catalog tree.

ArcToolbox contains a number of tools that also perform these (plus other) import and export operations to convert ArcGIS and related data between formats. For example, you may want to convert a dataset of soil type polygons to a raster dataset to use in analysis. The tools are particularly useful for converting data within a script or model.

The Conversion Tools toolbox contains toolsets for converting between a variety of feature and raster formats.

Compiling GIS data in other formats

ArcGIS Desktop lets you work directly with a number of other, non-ESRI geographic data formats. You can add a wide range of image formats to your ArcCatalog workspaces and can add the data to a map in ArcMap to display it. These include common raster formats such as DEM (used for digital elevation models), various ERDAS® formats (used for satellite images), and MrSID® (a compressed raster format often used for very large datasets), as well as common graphic formats including BMP, TIFF, JPEG, and GIF. A complete list can be found in the 'Data Support in ArcGIS' section of the Desktop Help.

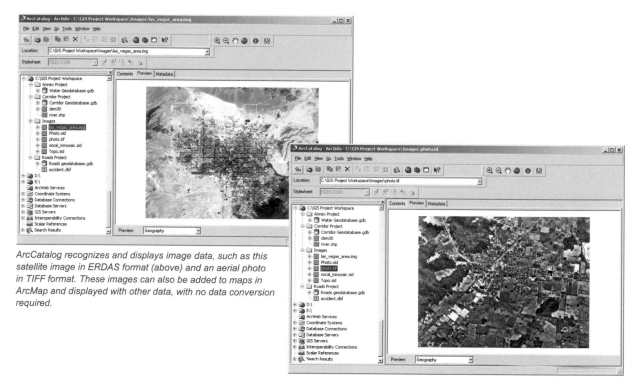

ArcCatalog recognizes and displays image data, such as this satellite image in ERDAS format (above) and an aerial photo in TIFF format. These images can also be added to maps in ArcMap and displayed with other data, with no data conversion required.

Similarly, ArcGIS Desktop recognizes several common CAD formats, including AutoCAD DXF and DWG formats, and MicroStation® DGN formats. You can manage the CAD drawing in ArcCatalog, display it on a map in ArcMap, or use it with many of the tools in the toolbox for analysis or other geoprocessing tasks (however, it can't be edited in ArcGIS unless you import it into a geodatabase feature class or shapefile). Each layer in the drawing is displayed as a separate layer in ArcGIS Desktop (even though they're part of a single entity—the CAD drawing). In some cases, you may want to convert a single layer in the drawing to an ArcGIS dataset (shapefile or feature class)—you may only need that layer for your maps or you may need to edit it for use in analysis. Right-click the layer in the Catalog tree, point to Export, then click the format you want to export to (geodatabase feature class or shapefile). Alternatively, you can use the conversion tools in ArcToolbox.

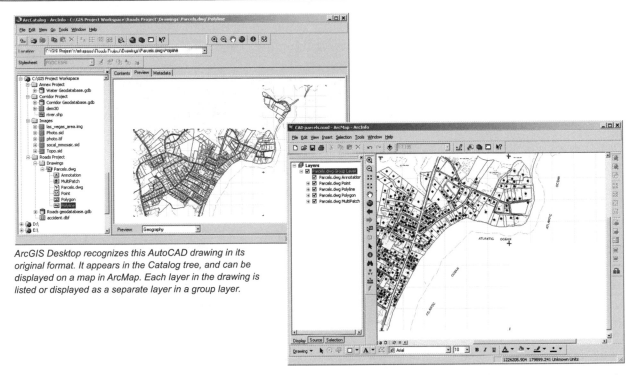

ArcGIS Desktop recognizes this AutoCAD drawing in its
original format. It appears in the Catalog tree, and can be
displayed on a map in ArcMap. Each layer in the drawing is
listed or displayed as a separate layer in a group layer.

ArcGIS supports other feature data formats through the ArcGIS Data Interoperability extension. The Quick Import and
Quick Export tools in the Data Interoperability toolbox in ArcToolbox allow you to import data to a geodatabase feature
class from a wide range of vector formats, including DLG, MIF, MGE, and many others. The Data Interoperability
extension also allows you to create custom converters.

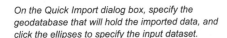

On the Quick Import dialog box, specify the
geodatabase that will hold the imported data, and
click the ellipses to specify the input dataset.

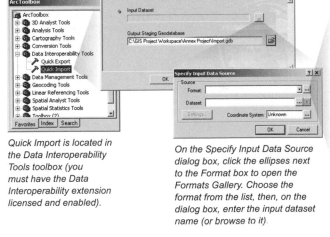

Quick Import is located in
the Data Interoperability
Tools toolbox (you
must have the Data
Interoperability extension
licensed and enabled).

On the Specify Input Data Source
dialog box, click the ellipses next
to the Format box to open the
Formats Gallery. Choose the
format from the list, then, on the
dialog box, enter the input dataset
name (or browse to it).

Compiling raw coordinate data

Some GIS data may be in tabular or list form, but have geographic coordinates associated with the features. Often this is data that has been directly captured in the field using GPS or another device. GPS units calculate their position using signals from satellites (and sometimes base stations). If you have a table of point features with associated x,y coordinates, you can import the data to a layer in ArcMap, and then create a dataset by exporting the layer (see 'Adding data to a map' in Chapter 4). You can also stream coordinate data directly to ArcMap via a GPS connected to a laptop computer or Tablet PC running ArcGIS Desktop. By capturing the streamed coordinates in a log, you can save them as point or line features in a geodatabase feature class or shapefile.

Use the GPS toolbar in ArcMap to input data directly from a GPS unit (click View, point to Toolbars, and click GPS).

The GPS Position window shows you your real-time position, altitude, speed, and heading using the GPS input.

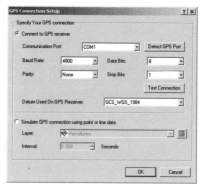

Use the GPS Connection Setup dialog box to specify the communication parameters for the GPS receiver.

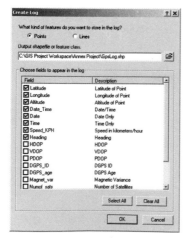

When you create a new log, you specify which fields to include—these will become the initial fields for the shapefile or feature class.

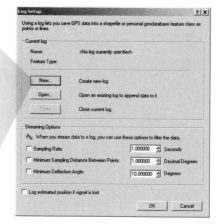

Use the Log Setup dialog box to create a new log to capture GPS data points as a shapefile or geodatabase feature class. You can specify the streaming options, such as how often to capture coordinates, or a minimum sampling distance.

Assigning locations using street addresses or routes

ArcGIS includes tools to read a street address or a measure along a route, assign coordinates, and create a geodatabase feature class or shapefile from the data. The process of assigning coordinates using an address is called geocoding. Geocoding is mostly used to assign locations on a map to a table of features that have a street address, such as customers, students, businesses, or even crime scenes. Linear referencing is the process of assigning locations to features—usually events, such as accidents—along a route dataset, using measurements such as distance from mileposts.

Geocoding street addresses

To geocode a table of addresses, you need reference data (usually a dataset of streets with address ranges for each block). The reference data is used to create an address locator that can be used to match the addresses (see 'Adding specialized datasets to a geodatabase' in Chapter 2).

This table of customers includes a street address that can be used to assign coordinates and create point features. The features can then be displayed on a map or used in analysis.

This dataset of streets has been prepared for use in geocoding. The elements of the address have been placed in separate fields, and include the address range for each street segment for the left and right sides of the street, the prefix direction, prefix type, the name itself, the street type, suffix direction, and the ZIP Code on both the left and the right side of the street. All these elements are used to find as close a match as possible for each street address in the customer table.

An address locator specifies the reference data to use, as well as parameters and queries that direct the matching process. For each address in the table, ArcGIS attempts to find the best match against the reference street features stored in the address locator. When it finds a match, it assigns coordinates to a new feature in the output dataset. The coordinates locate the feature to the correct side of the street and in the best estimated location based on the street number and the range of addresses for that street segment. So an address of 150 W Elm St. would be located halfway along the 100–200 block of West Elm Street.

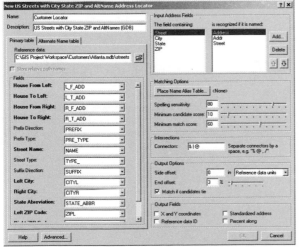

The Address Locator specifies the reference data (street dataset) and the names of the fields in the dataset containing the various address elements. It also lets you set the matching options and additional output fields in the output dataset. Address locators can be created in a folder (workspace) or within a geodatabase, and can be used with shapefiles or feature classes.

You can geocode in either ArcCatalog or ArcMap. Right-click the table containing the addresses in the Catalog tree (ArcCatalog) or the table of contents (ArcMap).

To geocode in ArcCatalog, in the Catalog tree right-click the table containing the addresses, then specify the address locator to use.

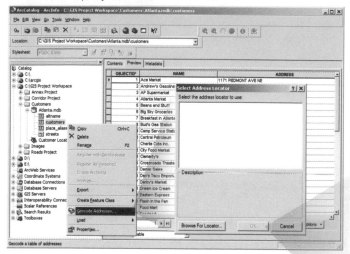

In the dialog box, specify the field in the table that contains the street address (if it's a standard name—such as ADDRESS—it will be selected automatically). Also specify the name and location of the output dataset that will be created. Click OK when you're ready to geocode the addresses.

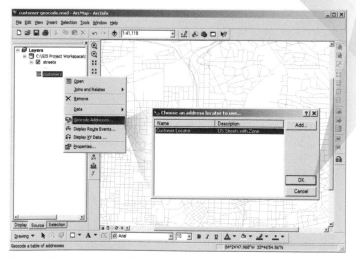

To geocode addresses in ArcMap, add the table containing the addresses to be geocoded, and the streets (optional) to your map. Right-click the table (select the Source tab to see it in the table of contents) and click Geocode Addresses. Use the Add button on the dialog box to specify the address locator to use.

Use the Geocoding Options dialog box to temporarily override the settings in the address locator, if necessary.

There may be more than one possible match for an address. Each potential matching street candidate is assigned a score based on how closely it matches the address, and the address is then matched to the candidate with the best score. The more complete the addresses in the table (with correct prefixes, street types, name spellings, and so on) and the more accurate your streets dataset, the better the results. After running a first pass you have the option of relaxing the parameters and re-geocoding the addresses that didn't match, or matching addresses interactively.

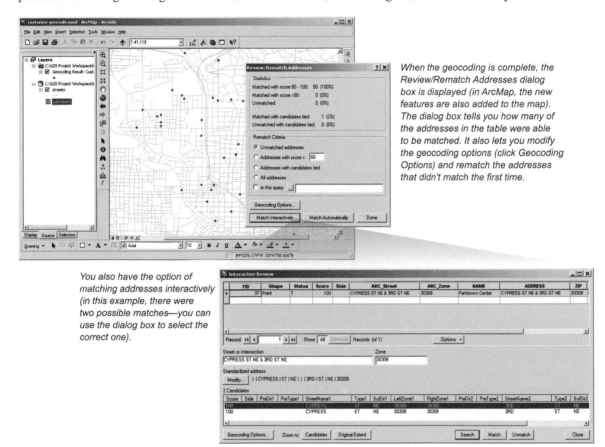

When the geocoding is complete, the Review/Rematch Addresses dialog box is displayed (in ArcMap, the new features are also added to the map). The dialog box tells you how many of the addresses in the table were able to be matched. It also lets you modify the geocoding options (click Geocoding Options) and rematch the addresses that didn't match the first time.

You also have the option of matching addresses interactively (in this example, there were two possible matches—you can use the dialog box to select the correct one).

You can also rematch addresses later, in either ArcMap or ArcCatalog. To rematch in ArcMap use the Tools menu, or right-click the results in the table of contents.

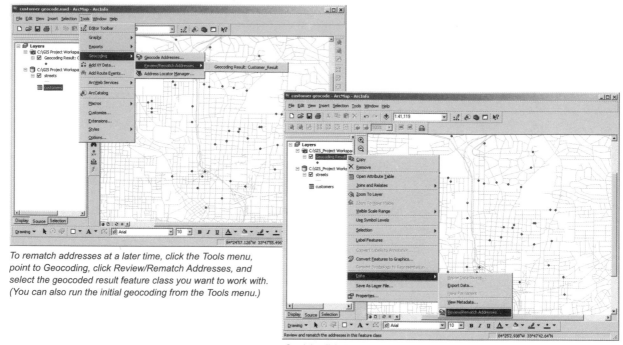

To rematch addresses at a later time, click the Tools menu, point to Geocoding, click Review/Rematch Addresses, and select the geocoded result feature class you want to work with. (You can also run the initial geocoding from the Tools menu.)

Or, right-click the result in the table of contents, point to Data, and click Review/ Rematch Addresses (as shown above).

To rematch addresses in ArcCatalog, right-click the output dataset in the Catalog tree. The Geocoding tools in ArcToolbox also allow you to perform all the geocoding tasks, from creating an address locator, through geocoding and rematching addresses.

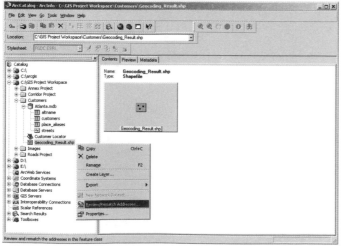

To rematch the addresses in ArcCatalog, right-click the output dataset in the Catalog tree and click Review/Rematch Addresses.

The Geocoding Tools toolbox contains tools for geocoding addresses.

Linear referencing

If you have a route dataset you've built from other features (streets, intersections, and so on) you can add data from an existing table that contains measurements along the route (see 'Adding specialized datasets to a geodatabase' in Chapter 2 for more on creating route datasets). The records in the table are referred to as events. The measurements are used to locate the events and display them on a map. Events can be points (such as accident locations) or lines (such as sections of highway with poor paving condition). Departments of transportation, for example, often create and maintain such event tables. The measures can be distance from the beginning of the route or markers along the route, such as milepost numbers. Route events are added to a map in ArcMap. You can then symbolize or query the events as you would any other features.

Point event tables must contain the route ID of each event (which route it's associated with) and a measure along the route, such as the distance from the start of the route. Before adding the events, add the route dataset and the event table to the map.

To add route events to a map, select Add Route Events on the Tools menu.

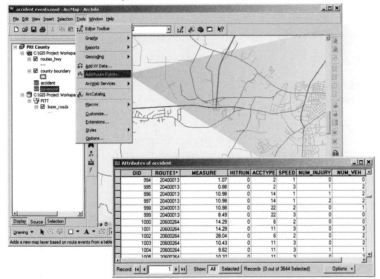

A point event table contains the route ID, the measure along the route, and any other attributes associated with the event—in this example, the events are automobile accidents that occurred along highways.

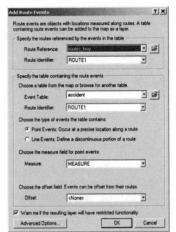

In the dialog box, specify the route dataset and field containing the route ID. Then specify the event table and the fields containing the route ID and route measure.

Once added, the route events are stored with the map document. To save the events as permanent features, export them to a dataset.

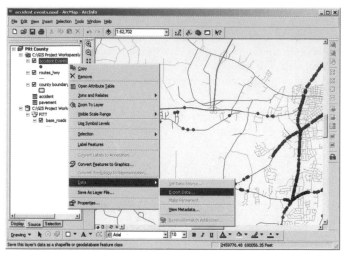

The events (accidents) are added as points on the map, along the routes. To save them as features in a dataset, right-click the events layer in the table of contents, point to Data, and click Export Data.

Line events must have fields containing the start point and an end point, in addition to the route ID. In the example below, the start and end points are represented by a "from milepost" field and a "to milepost" field.

Events can also be added by right-clicking the event table in the table of contents and clicking Display Route Events.

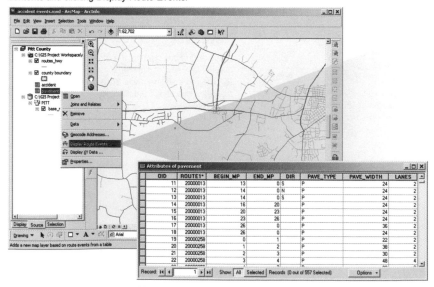

Line event tables must contain fields for the start and end points (milepost markers, in this example), as well as the route ID.

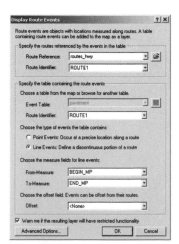

To add line events, specify Line Events as the type, and enter the fields containing the start and end points.

The line events are added to the map as a new layer. Export the events to save them as a dataset.

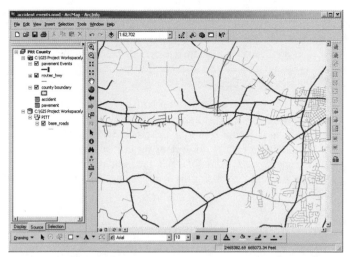

The route events (representing sections of highway with poor paving condition, in this example) are added to the map.

The Make Route Event Layer tool in the Linear Referencing Tools toolbox performs the same function as the Add Route Events tool in ArcMap. It's useful for assigning locations to events within a script or model. The Linear Referencing toolbox contains a number of other tools for working with routes and route events.

Make Route Event Layer is found in the Linear Referencing toolbox in ArcToolbox.

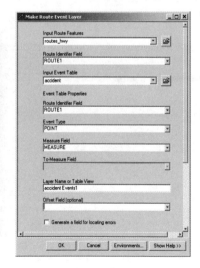

Starting and managing an edit session

At some point in building and maintaining your database, you'll need either to correct errors you discover in the data or update the existing data with newer information. For example, you may need to modify the shape of a road that's recently been surveyed, or update a parcel that's been split. You do this by editing the geographic features interactively in ArcMap. Many of the same editing tools are also used for creating new features—either in a new, empty dataset or in a dataset containing features, such as adding a new subdivision to a parcel dataset.

The editing tools and settings are located on the Editor toolbar—you need to open the toolbar in ArcMap before editing. You use the toolbar to start an edit session, add or modify features, save your edits, and end the session. During the edit session, other ArcMap functions are still available—adding layers to the map, zooming, panning, changing symbology of features, and so on. The only difference is that layers are available for editing, as long as the edit session is open. As you edit the data, even though the data appears as a layer in ArcMap, you're actually editing the underlying data source. After you close the edit session the layers can no longer be modified until the next time you open an edit session.

Starting the edit session

Once you have added the data you want to edit to a map in ArcMap, you'll open the Editor toolbar and start an edit session.

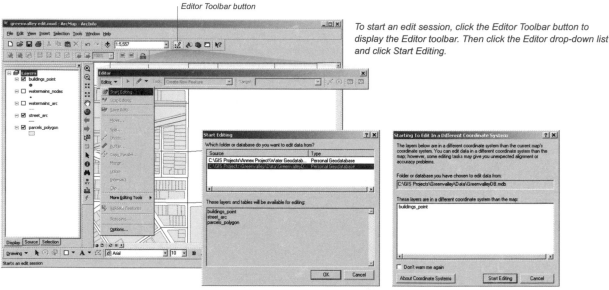

To start an edit session, click the Editor Toolbar button to display the Editor toolbar. Then click the Editor drop-down list and click Start Editing.

You might see one or both of these windows when you start editing. You'll see the one on the left if the datasets you've added to ArcMap reside in different geodatabases or folders. You can only edit the data in one workspace (geodatabase or folder) at a time (you can still display and snap to all the layers on the map). You'll see the window on the right if the coordinate system of any of the datasets you're editing is undefined or does not match that of the map (defined by default as the coordinate system of the first dataset you add to the map).

Next you'll choose the workspace and data frame (if more than one) containing the datasets you want to edit, and choose the target layer (the one you'll be working on) using the Target drop-down list—you can switch between targets during a single edit session. You'll probably also want to set the snapping environment, to make sure new (or modified) features snap to existing ones—this ensures features connect to each other correctly.

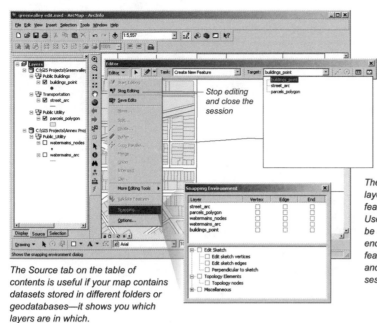

Use the Target drop-down list to select the dataset to which the edits will be applied (the list contains only those datasets in the geodatabase or folder you specified). You can switch between layers during an edit

The Snapping Environment dialog box lets you specify which layers can be snapped to as you're creating or modifying features. All the layers on the map are available for snapping. Use the check boxes to specify for each whether features can be snapped to vertices, edges (lines or polygon borders), or end points of existing features. Features will snap to existing features in the same layer or another layer. You can access and change the snapping settings anytime during an edit session.

The Source tab on the table of contents is useful if your map contains datasets stored in different folders or geodatabases—it shows you which layers are in which.

During the edit session, you can use the Undo button (on the Standard toolbar) to undo your last action. Use the Editor drop-down menu to save your edits. Just saving a map document does not save the edits to the features—you need to specifically save the edits in your edit session. You can choose to quit an edit session without saving your changes.

Managing the edit session

ArcMap includes several options for making your edit session more efficient. Open a magnifier window to get a closer view of a small area without changing the map extent. Click and drag the window over the area you want to magnify.

To open a magnifier window, click Magnifier on the Window menu.

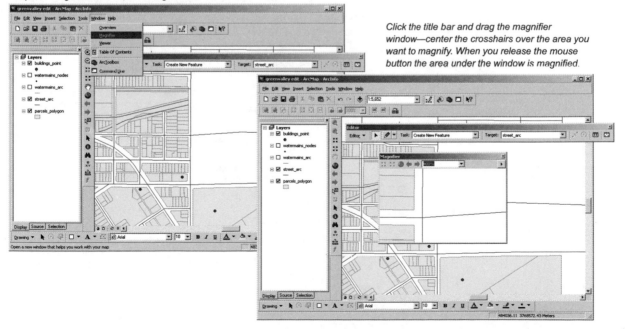

Click the title bar and drag the magnifier window—center the crosshairs over the area you want to magnify. When you release the mouse button the area under the window is magnified.

When you release the mouse button, the area under the window is magnified, centered on the crosshair. You can move the magnifier window and drag it while holding on to the same sketch or modification already in progress. Use the drop-down menu to change the magnification level. You can also set the window to magnify as you drag it—select Update While Dragging from the pull-right menu. In this mode, the magnifier window is like moving a magnifying glass over the map.

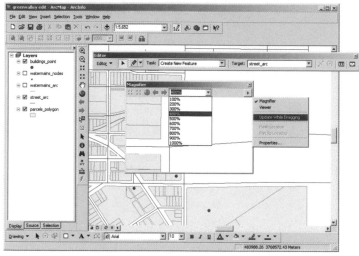

Use the drop-down menu to change the magnification. Click Update While Dragging to use the magnifier window like a magnifying glass.

Many editing functions have keyboard shortcuts associated with them, including those on the context menus. These can minimize the use of your mouse and speed up your edits. For example, with the Sketch tool active, you can press the F6 key to quickly enter the coordinate location of the point or vertex you want to place. See 'Getting started with editing' in the Desktop Help for a list of keyboard shortcuts. Sometimes you may need to enter lengths or other measurements in units different from your map units. In many dialog boxes throughout the editing environment that require you to enter a distance value, you can specify values in a different unit of measure by simply typing a unit abbreviation after the number. For example, if your map units are feet, by default, ArcMap will assume any distance values you enter are in feet. However, you can simply add "m" after your input value so ArcMap knows you the value you entered is actually in meters.

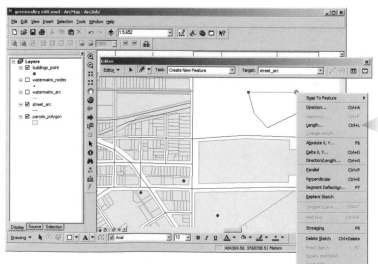

If you need to enter distances in a measurement unit other than the one the map is in, simply type an abbreviation for the unit after the distance value. In this example, the map units are meters, and the distance is entered in feet (ft.). ArcMap does the conversion on-the-fly.

The options for adding segments and vertices can also be accessed using keyboard shortcuts (such as Ctrl+L to enter a length). Shortcuts can be more efficient than using the menu, especially if you're entering many vertices by typing angles and distances.

Click Options on the Editor drop-down menu to access settings for the edit session. You can set the snapping tolerance, specify the symbol to use to highlight selected features, or customize the Tasks list, and so on.

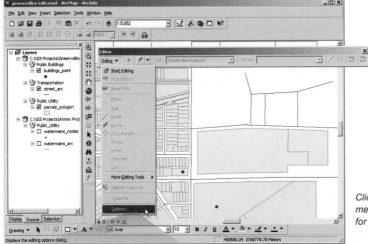

Click Options on the Editor menu to access the settings for the edit session.

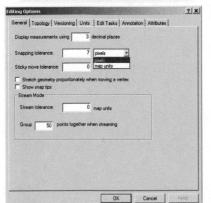

The General tab lets you specify the snapping tolerance, in pixels or map units. Make the tolerance larger if you're having trouble snapping to any feature; make it smaller if you're having trouble snapping to the correct feature.

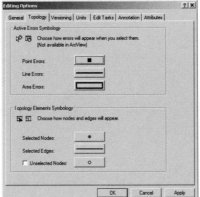

The Topology tab lets you specify the symbol to use for selected topology elements—click a symbol on the tab and use the Symbol Selector dialog box to change the color and size of the symbol (see Chapter 4 for more on map symbols).

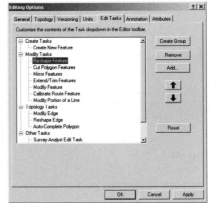

The Edit Tasks tab lets you rearrange or remove tasks from the Task list on the Editor toolbar.

If you specify a sticky tolerance distance (on the General tab), when you move a selected feature, the feature will stay put until the cursor has moved the specified distance—this helps you avoid inadvertently moving a feature.

Creating and modifying features

There are many different editing tasks you'll need to perform, and there are often several ways to complete the same task. This section presents a few of the most common ways to create new features, modify the shape of an existing feature, or reposition features. See the Desktop Help for additional tasks and a full discussion of editing options.

Creating features

To create either point, line, or polygon features you set the Task to Create New Features. The type of feature you're editing is determined by the Target layer—the dataset you're creating the new feature within.

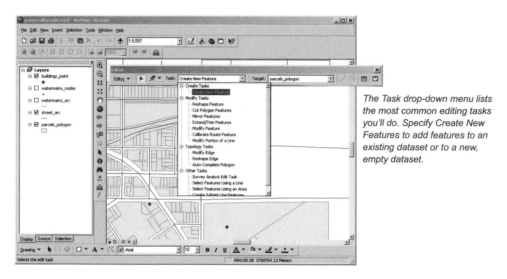

The Task drop-down menu lists the most common editing tasks you'll do. Specify Create New Features to add features to an existing dataset or to a new, empty dataset.

For point features, you'll click the Sketch tool on the toolbar, and then click on the map to enter the location of the point.

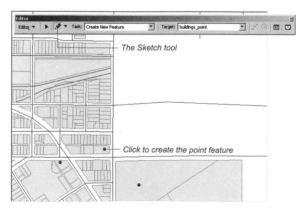

To create a point feature, click the Sketch tool, then click where you want to place the point.

The point feature you created is the currently selected feature—right-click it for options.

Creating line and polygon features involves creating a "sketch" which is a temporary representation of the feature showing the segments and vertices. When you create the vertices in a sketch (typically, by clicking with your mouse), the segments between vertices are added for you automatically. Once you're satisfied with the shape of the sketch, you need to finish the sketch to complete the feature's geometry and actually create the feature. There are several ways that you can finish a sketch, including double-clicking with your mouse, choosing the command from a context menu, and using a keyboard shortcut (F2). There are also a variety of options for entering vertices, in addition to clicking with the mouse.

To add a line feature, click the Sketch tool, then click the location of the start point. Click to add each vertex and define the shape of the line. The segments between vertices are drawn automatically. The last vertex you added is shown in red.

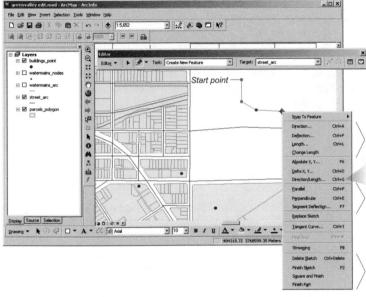

Right-click while adding vertices to a line or polygon and you get options for adding the next segment or vertex, as well as for finishing (or deleting) the line. The same menu can be displayed for point features, but most of the options are not available.

These options let you add a segment or vertex by entering a distance, angle, x,y coordinate pair, and so on. Type the values, then press the Enter key to add the vertex.

These options let you add a segment parallel or perpendicular to a selected feature.

Use these options to delete the current sketch or finish it and create the feature.

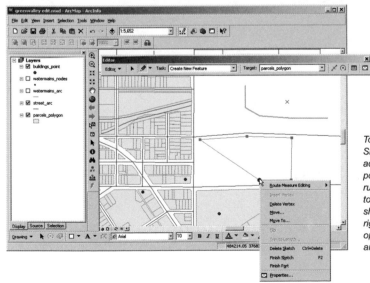

To create a polygon feature, click the Sketch tool, click a starting point, and add vertices to define the shape of the polygon. As you add vertices, a segment rubberbands from the last vertex added to the start point to maintain the closed shape. When creating polygons or lines, right-clicking a vertex will display more options. To finish the polygon, right-click and click Finish Sketch, or just double-click.

In addition to the Sketch tool, other tools are available from the Editor toolbar to add point features or line vertices and segments using arcs, distance, and so on. You can switch tools at any time while creating a sketch.

The Sketch tool lets you add a point or vertex by clicking a location. The drop-down menu next to the tool displays the Sketch Tool Palette, which lets you select other tools for creating points and vertices.

The tools let you create curved segments; create a segment by tracing over an existing feature (with an optional offset distance—useful for creating parallel lines); place a vertex at the midpoint of a line you draw, or at the intersection of two lines; or create a vertex at a given distance and direction.

Modifying the shape of a feature

To modify the shape of a feature, the feature must be currently selected—use the Edit tool to select the feature. To modify the shape by moving a vertex, set the Task to Modify Feature. (Double-clicking a feature selects it and sets the Task to Modify Feature so you can start editing vertices—one of many editing shortcuts.)

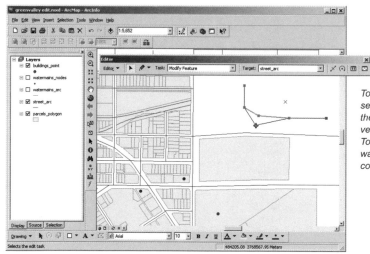

To move or delete a vertex, use the Edit tool to select the feature you want to modify, and set the task to Modify Feature. Click and drag a vertex to move it, or right-click it and click Delete. To insert a vertex, place the cursor where you want to add the vertex, right-click to display the context menu, and click Insert Vertex.

You can also reshape a line or polygon using a sketch. Set the Task to Reshape Feature. Make sure the first and last segments of the sketch intersect the feature you're reshaping. Vertices will be added where the sketch intersects the feature, and the sketch segments you draw will replace the segment(s) of the feature between these vertices.

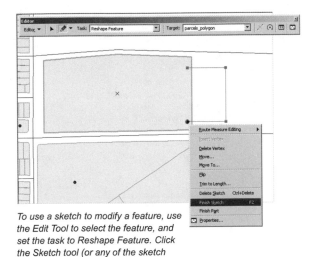

To use a sketch to modify a feature, use the Edit Tool to select the feature, and set the task to Reshape Feature. Click the Sketch tool (or any of the sketch options) and add vertices, making sure the first and last segments intersect the feature you're reshaping.

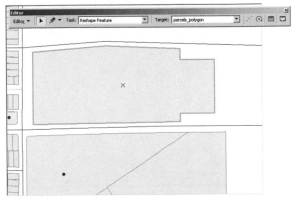

When you click Finish Sketch, the segments you drew are added to reshape the feature.

Changing the position of a feature

To move, copy, delete or rotate a feature, first select it using the Edit tool. To move it, click and drag it to a new location. To copy a feature, right-click it and select Copy, then right-click again and click Paste (or use the Windows standard Ctrl+C and Ctrl+V). The copy is placed on top of the original feature, but is currently selected—drag it to a new location. To delete a selected feature, right-click and click Delete, or press the Delete key on your keyboard. To rotate a selected feature, click the Rotate tool on the Editor toolbar. Then click and drag the cursor—the feature rotates around its center.

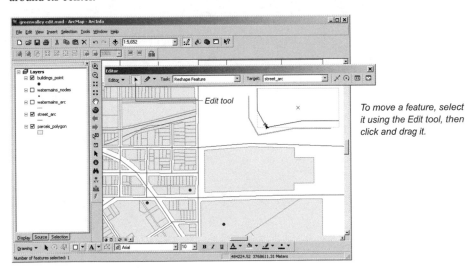

To move a feature, select it using the Edit tool, then click and drag it.

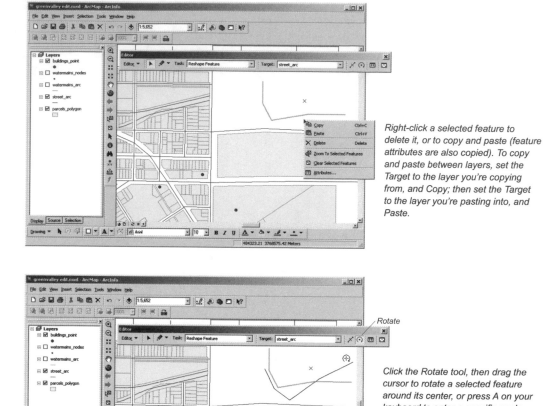

Right-click a selected feature to delete it, or to copy and paste (feature attributes are also copied). To copy and paste between layers, set the Target to the layer you're copying from, and Copy; then set the Target to the layer you're pasting into, and Paste.

Click the Rotate tool, then drag the cursor to rotate a selected feature around its center, or press A on your keyboard to enter a specific angle.

You can drag a box to select multiple features, or hold the Shift key while clicking. You can then move, copy, or delete the selected features.

Editing connected features

Whether you're creating features in a new dataset or adding features to an existing one, at some point you'll likely need to edit lines that connect (or should connect)—such as connecting a new road to an existing one—or to create adjacent polygons that share a border—such as parcels or administrative boundaries. You might also need to move a shared vertex or border, thereby moving or reshaping the connected features. You perform these tasks in an edit session in ArcMap.

Connecting line features

To add a line that connects two existing lines, you snap the end points of the new line to the existing lines (either at a vertex or anywhere along the edge). You may also need to split the existing lines where the new line connects, to create intersections (for example, if you'll be using a dataset of streets for routing delivery trucks).

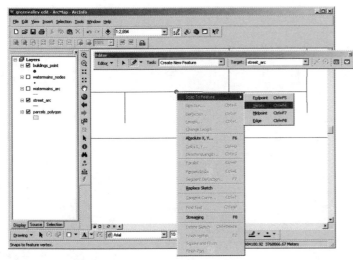

Make sure the task is set to Create New Feature and the Sketch tool is active. This end of the line connects to a vertex on the existing line—move the cursor over (or near) the vertex, right-click, point to Snap To Feature, and click Vertex.

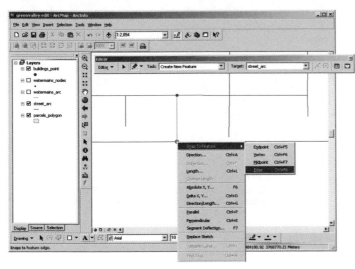

The other end of the new line connects to an existing line where there is no vertex. Place the cursor over the line, right-click, point to Snap to Feature, and specify Edge as the feature to snap to. (Alternatively, you could set the snapping environment to Vertex and Edge for the streets layer; then the new line will snap automatically, which is more efficient if you're adding many lines.)

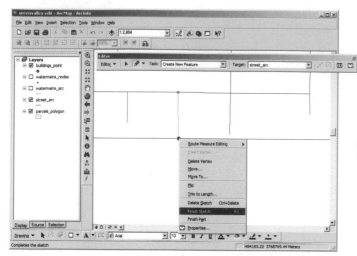

Right-click the vertex you added and click Finish Sketch to finish the new line.

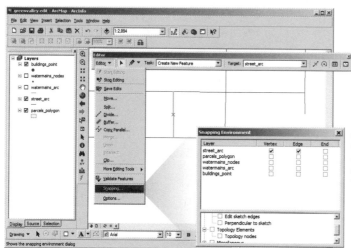

Next you'll split the existing line where you connected. First, set snapping to Vertex and Edge for the streets layer. That will ensure the line gets split at the right place—right at the vertex where the new line connects.

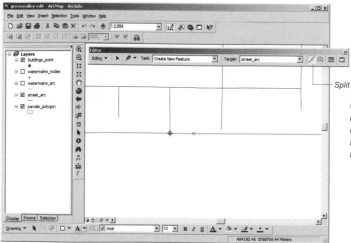

Split

Click the Split tool on the toolbar, place the cursor over the vertex, and click to split the line. (You could also have split the line first, then specified Endpoint when using Snap To Feature to add the new line.)

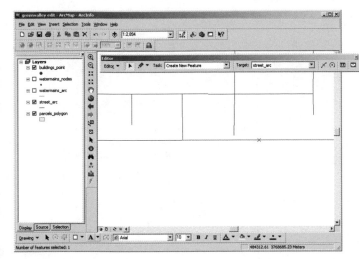

When you select the line on the right, you can see that the original line has indeed been split. You'd split the first line that the new line connects to in a similar manner.

Extending a line

You can extend a line to connect to another line. One way to do this is using the Extend tool on the Advanced Editing toolbar.

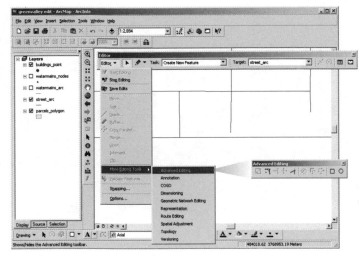

Click the Editor drop-down list, point to More Editing Tools, and click Advanced Editing.

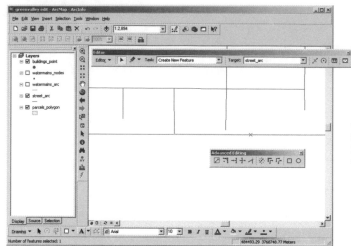

Select the line you want to extend the other lines to, using the Edit tool on the Editor toolbar. When you do, the tools on the Advanced Editing toolbar become available.

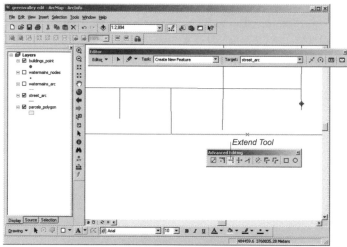

Click the Extend Tool button, and click the line you want to extend.

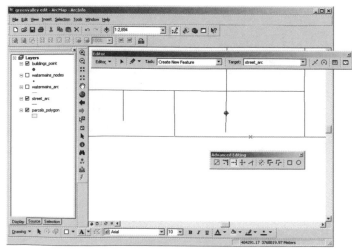

The line extends and snaps to the selected line. Point to any other lines you want to extend (you can keep extending lines as long as the Extend tool is active). To stop, select another tool, or select the Edit tool (on the Editor toolbar).

Creating an adjacent polygon

To add a polygon adjacent to an existing polygon, you simply make sure the sketch for the new polygon crosses the existing polygon at least twice.

Make sure the task is set to Auto-Complete Polygon, and set snapping to Vertex for the polygon layer you're editing.

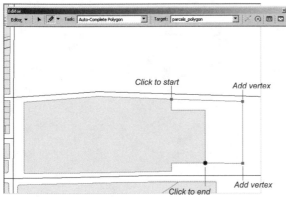

Click the Sketch tool and click the vertex on the existing polygon where you want the new polygon to connect. Continue adding vertices using the Sketch tool (or any of the other options for adding vertices), then click a vertex on the existing polygon to close the new polygon. Double-click the vertex to finish the sketch (or right-click and click Finish Sketch).

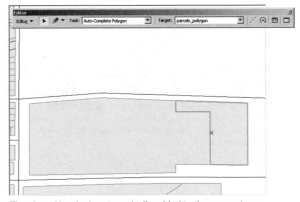

The shared border is automatically added to the new polygon to complete it.

Editing features that share a vertex or border

If you want to move a vertex at which two or more features connect and have them all adjust accordingly, you need to establish a topology. A topology makes explicit the connection between features. This allows you to move a vertex to which several lines connect (known as a node) and have all the line end points move with the node—without the topology, moving the vertex would move only the end point of the selected line while the endpoints of the other lines remained in place. One way to establish a topology is within a geodatabase, usually as part of the geodatabase building process, as described in Chapter 2 (see 'Ensuring spatial data integrity'). A geodatabase topology is stored with the data and is in effect on any map the data is added to. Sometimes—even if a geodatabase topology doesn't exist for a dataset—you want to be able to make a topological edit for that dataset. If a geodatabase topology has not been defined for the dataset, you can create what is known as a "map topology" in ArcMap. The map topology is stored only with the current map—not with the data.

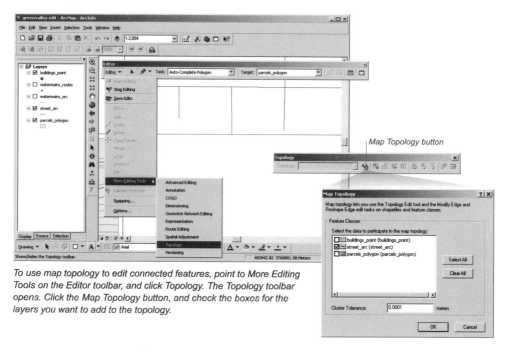

To use map topology to edit connected features, point to More Editing Tools on the Editor toolbar, and click Topology. The Topology toolbar opens. Click the Map Topology button, and check the boxes for the layers you want to add to the topology.

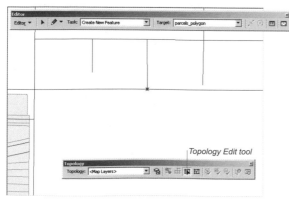

Click the Topology Edit tool on the Topology toolbar, then click the node you want to move, to select it.

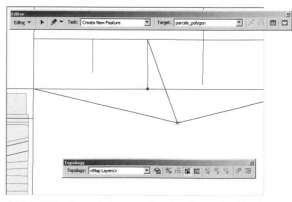

Click and drag the node to its new location. The end points of the connected lines move with the node, but the other vertices of the lines stay put.

If the dataset you're editing does have a geodatabase topology defined, you add the topology to your map, and then use the tools on the Topology toolbar to edit the connected features. Editing connected features in a geodatabase topology is the same as for a map topology—for lines connected at a node, click the Edit Topology tool, select a node, and drag it to its new location.

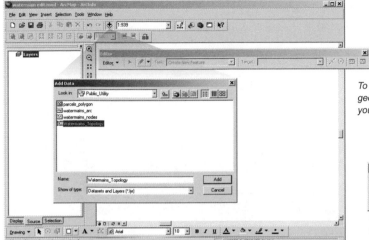

To edit connected features using a geodatabase topology, add the topology to your map.

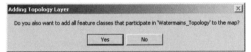

You'll be prompted to add to the map the feature classes that participate in the topology—click Yes.

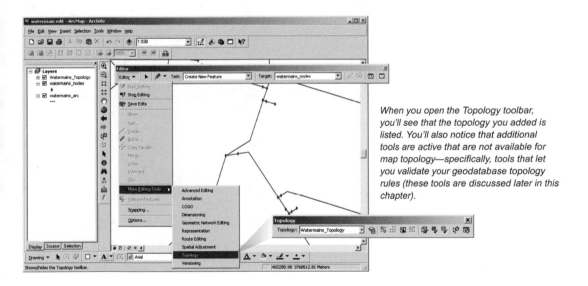

When you open the Topology toolbar, you'll see that the topology you added is listed. You'll also notice that additional tools are active that are not available for map topology—specifically, tools that let you validate your geodatabase topology rules (these tools are discussed later in this chapter).

You also use the Topology Edit tool to move or reshape a shared boundary between two polygons that participate in a topology (either a map or geodatabase topology). While the shared boundary looks like a single line, that line is, in fact, stored with each polygon. If you moved the boundary without having created a topology, only one of the lines would move, creating either a gap or an overlap.

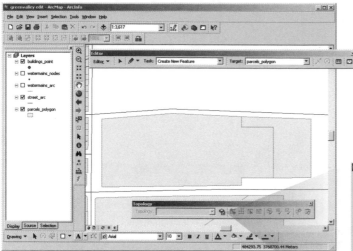

Add the geodatabase topology to the map, or use the Map Topology button on the Topology toolbar to make sure topology is turned on for the polygon layer.

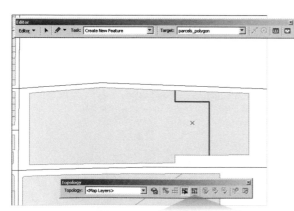

Click the Topology Edit tool and select the border you want to modify. The Show Shared Features button displays a list of features that share the border. Click a feature on the list to flash it on the map and confirm it's the one you want to edit (the check boxes determine which features participate in topology edits).

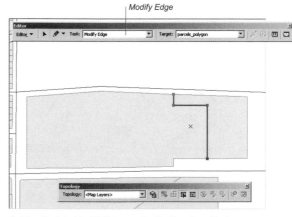

Set the Task to Modify Edge under the Topology Tasks group; or just double-click the selected border—the Task is automatically set to Modify Edge. Once the task is set, the vertices for the shared border are visible.

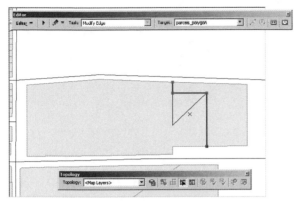

Click a vertex and drag it to a new position. You can also reshape a shared border—using a sketch—by setting the task to Reshape Edge.

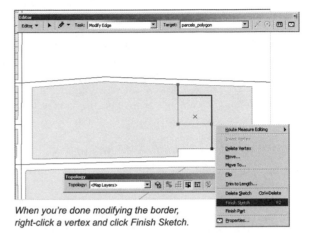

When you're done modifying the border, right-click a vertex and click Finish Sketch.

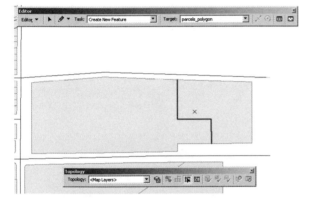

When you finish the sketch, the new shared border is displayed.

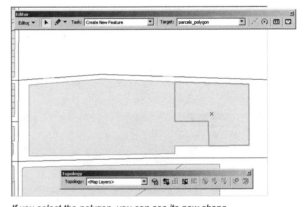

If you select the polygon, you can see its new shape.

You can use map topologies and geodatabase topologies concurrently. The active topologies appear in the drop-down list on the Topology toolbar; you can switch between them during an edit session.

Creating features from a printed or scanned map

You'll likely obtain most of your GIS data already in an ArcGIS format, or by importing it or interactively creating it on-screen. However, in some cases, the data you need may only be available on an image, such as an orthophoto, satellite image, or scanned map. While the image is in raster data format (pixels), what you may want to create are vector features—points, lines, or polygons. ArcGIS contains tools for tracing over an image on-screen to create geographic features—a process known as digitizing. In other cases, you may need to create features in the GIS from a printed map. You can digitize the map using a digitizing tablet, or scan the map and automatically create geographic features. These tasks are all performed in ArcMap.

Digitizing over a background image

You can use a scanned map or drawing, aerial photo, orthophotograph, or satellite image as a background in ArcMap, and create features (such as streams, roads, or building footprints) by tracing over the objects in the image. Some aerial photos and satellite images are already spatially referenced—that is, the extent of the image in geographic space is known. If this is the case, you can simply use the editing tools described in the previous sections to trace over the image and create features—the new features will be stored in x,y coordinates in geographic space.

On the other hand, if the image is in page or screen units—likely the case for a scanned map or drawing—you need to place it in geographic space (see 'GIS data concepts' in Chapter 2). This is known as georeferencing, and is performed by associating locations on the image (control points) with the corresponding coordinates in geographic space. You can type the coordinates (if known) or create a link between a control point on the image and the corresponding location on an existing spatially referenced dataset. There is a range of situations you might encounter when georeferencing an image. Here's the process if the image has control points marked on it, the control points are labeled with their x,y coordinates, and the coordinates are in the same coordinate system as the existing dataset.

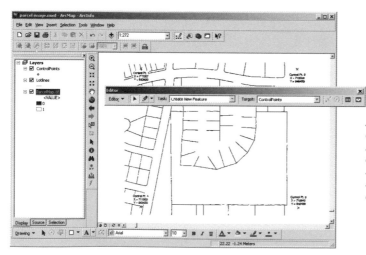

Add the image to the map, along with the dataset you'll be adding features to. If you zoom to the image (right-click it in the table of contents and click Zoom To Layer), you won't see the existing features, since the image is still in page units, and the features are in map units.

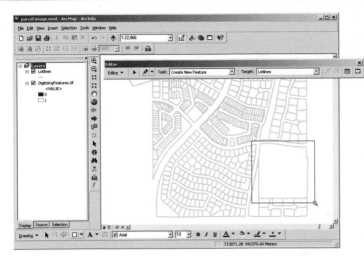

Now zoom to the location on the existing parcels layer corresponding to the location of the image.

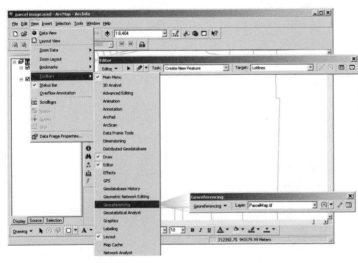

To add links and transform the image, you'll use the Georeferencing toolbar. Click the View menu, point to Toolbars, and click Georeferencing.

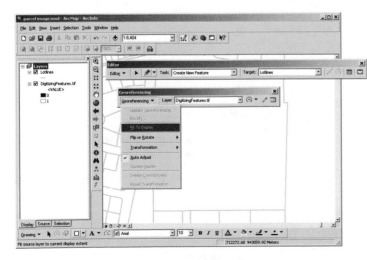

Use Fit To Display to show the image in roughly the same location as the existing features—that will make it easier to work as you add links.

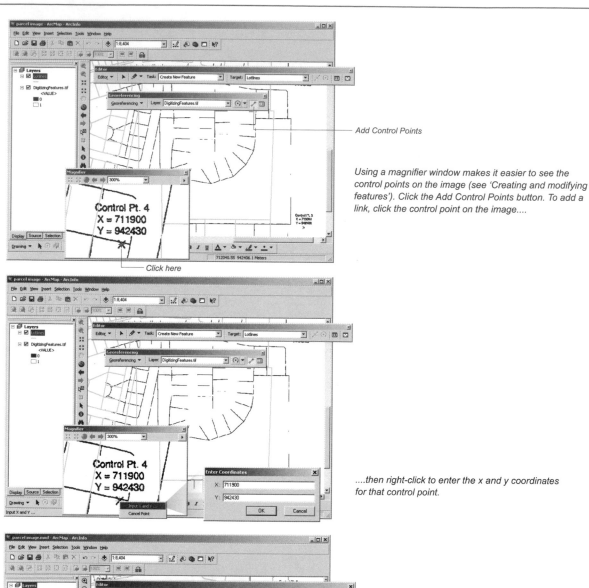

Add Control Points

Using a magnifier window makes it easier to see the control points on the image (see 'Creating and modifying features'). Click the Add Control Points button. To add a link, click the control point on the image....

Click here

....then right-click to enter the x and y coordinates for that control point.

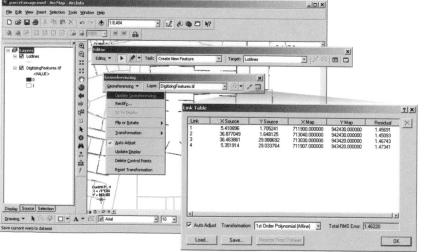

The image adjusts as you add links. To review the links you've created, click the View Link Table button. You can remove errant links by selecting them in the table and clicking the X button. When you're satisfied with the registration of the image to the existing features, click Update Georeferencing on the Georeferencing drop-down menu.

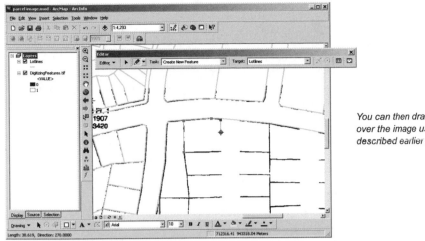

You can then draw the new features by tracing over the image using any of the editing tools described earlier in the chapter.

If the coordinates on the image are in a different coordinate system than the existing dataset, you'd create a new point feature class or shapefile in that coordinate system, create the control points as point features in this new dataset at the x,y locations indicated on the image, and then project the dataset to the coordinate system you're using. You'd then be able to link the control points on the image to the control point feature class in the correct coordinate system and transform the image. You'd click the control point on the image, as shown below, then—rather than entering the x,y coordinates to create the link—you'd click the corresponding control point feature.

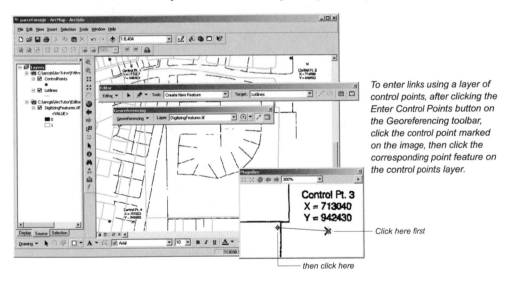

To enter links using a layer of control points, after clicking the Enter Control Points button on the Georeferencing toolbar, click the control point marked on the image, then click the corresponding point feature on the control points layer.

In some cases there may be control points on the image, but no coordinates indicated. Hopefully, the control points will be at recognizable features, such as street intersections, or the peak of a hill. You'd then find the corresponding features in your dataset, create the links, and transform the image. If there are no control points on the image, you'll have to try to identify features on the image that you can link to corresponding features on a dataset you have. Streets and street intersections—if any—are good candidates.

Digitizing from a printed map

To digitize directly from a printed map, you use a digitizing table connected to your computer. ArcGIS converts positions on the table surface into digital x,y coordinates as you trace them with a handheld puck (a pen or mouse-like device). As with creating features interactively or on-screen digitizing, you use a digitizing table within an edit session. With a digitizing table installed, the Digitizer tab is available on the Editing Options dialog box. The digitizing puck is initially in mouse mode—you can click menus and buttons on the computer screen. You can still use a mouse connected to your computer as you normally would, as well—having the digitizing table in mouse mode just allows you to access the ArcMap interface using the digitizing puck. Set the Enabled option to put the digitizing table in "digitize" mode.

The first step is to register the map—which is in page units on the digitizing table—to geographic space. Your map must have control points drawn on it for which you know the x,y coordinates. To register the map, you enter the point on the digitizing tablet, then type in the x,y coordinates for that point.

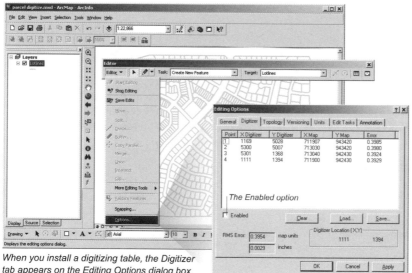

To register a map, click a control point on the map—the location (in page units) will appear. Type the corresponding geographic x,y coordinate values in the X Map and Y Map columns; an RMS error for that control point will appear. As you add points, a cumulative RMS error is displayed.

When you install a digitizing table, the Digitizer tab appears on the Editing Options dialog box. Check the Enabled box to set the digitizer to "digitize" mode.

After you've entered the control points and their coordinates, ArcMap displays an error report. The error report includes two error calculations: a point-by-point error and a root mean square (RMS) error. The point-by-point error represents the distance deviation between the transformation of each input control point and the corresponding point in map coordinates. The RMS error is an average of those deviations.

ArcMap reports the point-by-point error in current map units. The RMS error is reported in both current map units and digitizer inches. If the RMS error is too high, you can re-enter the appropriate control points. To maintain highly accurate data, your RMS error should be less than 0.004 digitizer units (often inches or centimeters) or the equivalent scaled distance in map units—the ground units in which the coordinates are stored. For less accurate data, the value can be as high as 0.008 digitizer units.

To start digitizing features, select the Sketch tool on the Editor toolbar. Since you're creating the features by tracing, the other options for entering vertices are unavailable (such as creating a curve or entering a direction and distance). You can, however, use snapping to have vertices you enter snap to existing features displayed on the screen. To digitize, you trace over the printed map, by either clicking points on the puck (point mode) or by simply moving the puck over the feature you want to digitize—without clicking—and having ArcMap automatically add vertices (stream mode). The stream tolerance specifies the distance interval between vertices added in stream mode. You can also specify that points be grouped when added—when you undo or delete the previous entry, the whole group of points will be deleted (not just the last one entered). That way you don't have to delete the points individually to erase a line segment.

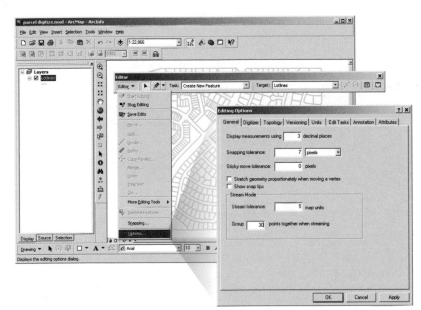

To use the digitizer in stream mode, first click the General tab on the Editing Options dialog box, and enter a stream tolerance (in map units) and the number of points to group.

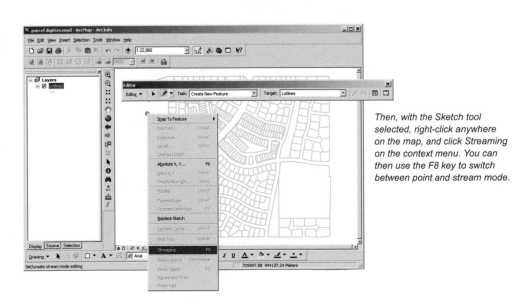

Then, with the Sketch tool selected, right-click anywhere on the map, and click Streaming on the context menu. You can then use the F8 key to switch between point and stream mode.

Creating features using vectorization

Vectorization is another method of digitizing features. The ArcScan for ArcGIS extension enables you to automatically create features from a scanned image you've added to your map. As with digitizing, you create features within an edit session. You need a dataset (feature class or shapefile) to create features within. It can be a new, empty dataset, or a dataset with existing features that you're adding more features to.

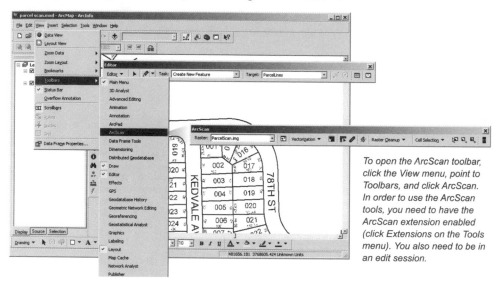

To open the ArcScan toolbar, click the View menu, point to Toolbars, and click ArcScan. In order to use the ArcScan tools, you need to have the ArcScan extension enabled (click Extensions on the Tools menu). You also need to be in an edit session.

You can vectorize the image either by tracing or by using automatic "batch" vectorization. You'd trace if the image is of poorer quality or has lots of text or extraneous pixels that might end up as features you don't want. If your image is fairly clean, you can remove any unwanted pixels (either by painting over them or by selecting and deleting) and then create the vector lines (or polygons) using automatic vectorization.

With either method, the first step is to set the snapping environment to make sure the lines you create snap to the pixels in the image. When using ArcScan, snapping is specified in two places—on the Raster Snapping Options dialog box, and on the Snapping Environment dialog box.

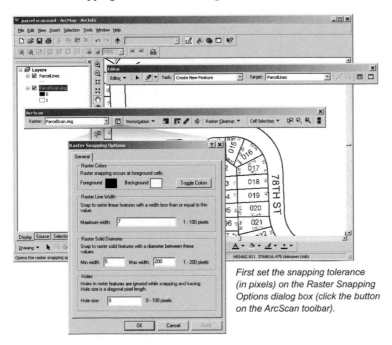

First set the snapping tolerance (in pixels) on the Raster Snapping Options dialog box (click the button on the ArcScan toolbar).

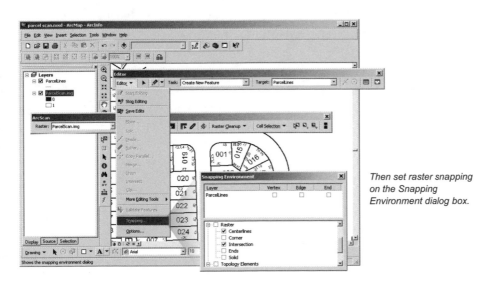

Then set raster snapping on the Snapping Environment dialog box.

To trace over the lines on the image, use the Trace tool on the ArcScan toolbar. The Editor toolbar must also be displayed, and an edit session must be open—click Start Editing on the Editor toolbar, and select the Target dataset to create the features within.

Click the Trace tool, then click on a raster line to start tracing; as you click along the line, vertices are added. Right-click and click Finish Sketch to create the vector line.

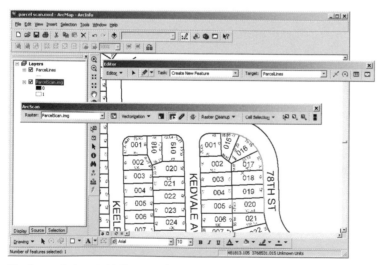

The line you just created is the currently selected feature, and you can continue to edit it using any of the other editing tools. Or, continue tracing with the Trace tool.

To use automatic vectorization, you'll first want to remove any extraneous pixels, such as text or other graphics on the image.

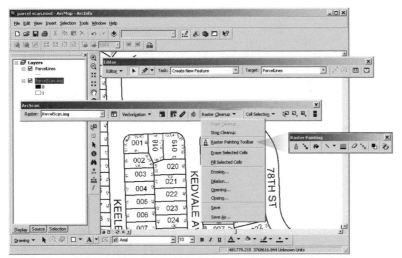

Use the Raster Painting tools to interactively delete unwanted pixels, such as text.

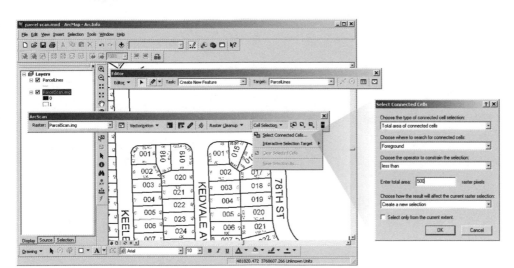

Or, use Cell Selection to create a query statement that selects all the unwanted cells at one time. Then use the Erase Selected Cells option on the Raster Cleanup menu to delete the cells.

Then preview the vectorization, and use the Generate Features option to create the lines or polygons.

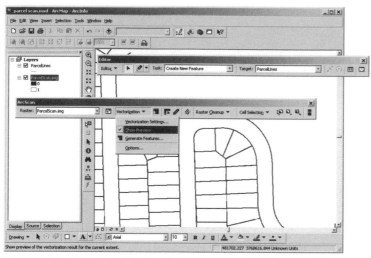

You can preview the vectorization to make sure you removed all the unwanted cells. Use the Generate Features option to perform the vectorization and create the features.

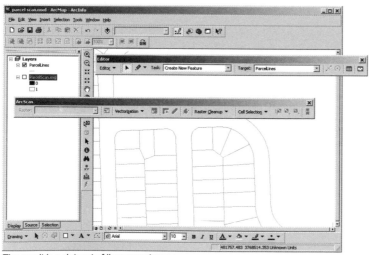

The result is a dataset of lines or polygons.

Adding and editing attribute data

Attributes store descriptive information for geographic features. They're used to symbolize and label features on a map, to create reports and graphs, and for analysis. A large part of data compilation involves adding attribute values to features either in a new dataset you're creating or updating the values in an existing dataset. You use the same tools for both—all within ArcMap. You can enter specific values, or calculate values using a mathematical expression. If necessary, you can also add fields to a table while editing.

Using the Attributes dialog box

The Attributes dialog box is designed for quickly adding or editing one or more attributes for features. It is available within an edit session, and is accessed from the Editor toolbar (see 'Creating and modifying features' earlier in this chapter). Click the Attributes button to open the dialog box. The box is initially empty, until you select a feature (or features) to edit, using the Edit tool on the toolbar.

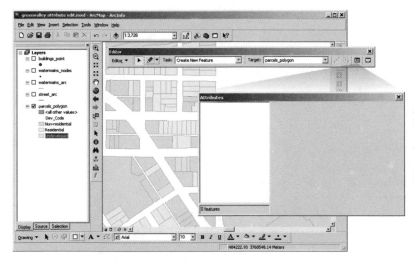

To edit attributes using the Attributes dialog box, open the Editing toolbar, start an edit session, and click the Attributes button on the toolbar. The box is empty until you select a feature, or features, to edit.

The selected features are listed in the left panel; click a feature to display and edit its attributes in the right panel.

When you select a feature (using the Edit tool on the Editing toolbar), its attributes appear in the box. Select and type over a value to change it (grayed-out attributes are controlled by ArcGIS and can't be edited). When you select an attribute for which domains or subtypes have been defined, a drop-down list allows you to select the value.

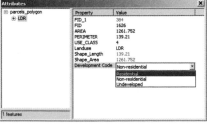

To select several features and display them in the box simultaneously, press the Shift key while selecting, or drag a box using the Edit tool. When you click a feature in the list, it flashes red on the map.

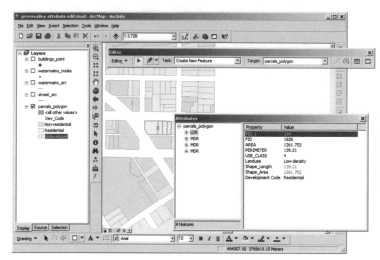

To select several features and add them to the dialog box, press the Shift key while selecting. Click a feature in the list (left panel) to view and edit its attributes.

To assign a value to all the selected features, click the layer name at the top of the list. You can then click the Value field next to the attribute and enter the value—all the features in the list will be assigned this value.

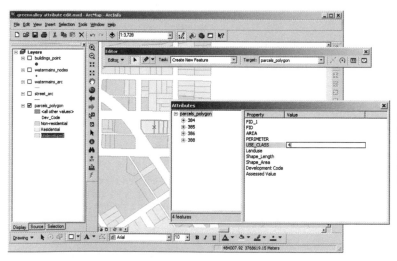

To assign the same attribute value to all the selected features, click the layer name. The values column is blank, but when you click next to an attribute, you can enter the value.

Use the Fields tab on the Layer Properties dialog box to set the Primary Display Field—features are listed by the values in that field (you'll usually use a name or unique identifier). Right-click a feature in the list to flash it on the map or zoom to it.

Use the Fields tab on the Layer Properties dialog box to specify which attribute to use to identify features in the Attributes dialog box. Select the attribute values that will appear in the list using the Primary Display Field drop-down list.

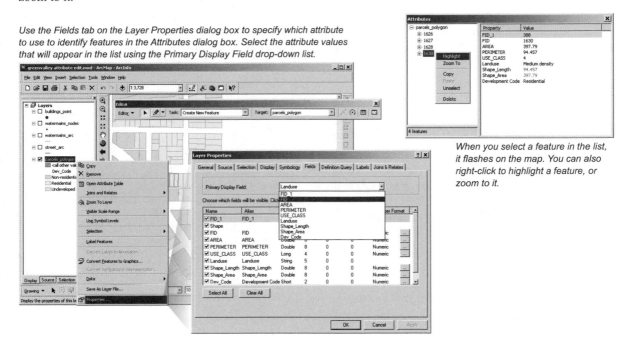

When you select a feature in the list, it flashes on the map. You can also right-click to highlight a feature, or zoom to it.

If you're adding attribute values for newly created features, the values for each field are set to <Null>, except for fields for which default values have been defined or fields calculated and maintained by ArcGIS (shown in gray in the dialog box). Type over the <Null> to enter a valid value. Use the drop-down menus to assign values to fields for which domains or subtypes have been defined.

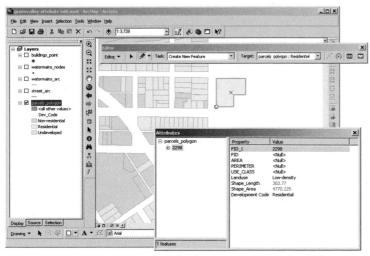

Select and type over a <Null> value setting to change the value.

Domain values and subtypes are available from drop-down menus when you click in the Value column for that attribute.

Using an attribute table to add or edit attributes

You can also assign values using the attribute table for a layer (to open the table, right-click the layer in the table of contents and click Open Attribute Table). When viewing a table outside an edit session, the column headings have a gray background. If the table is open during an edit session, the fields available for editing have a white background for the column heading, while the fields maintained by ArcGIS and which can't be edited maintain a gray column heading. Also, the editing icon (pencil) appears at the bottom of the table, next to the Options button, to indicate an edit session is open. To edit a value, simply click the value you want to change in the table and type over it.

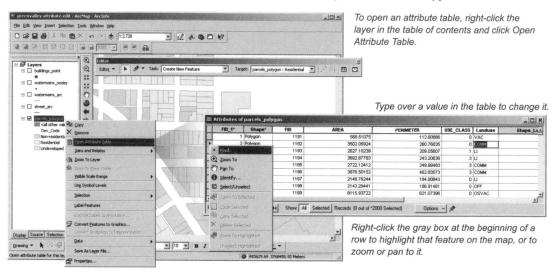

To open an attribute table, right-click the layer in the table of contents and click Open Attribute Table.

Type over a value in the table to change it.

Right-click the gray box at the beginning of a row to highlight that feature on the map, or to zoom or pan to it.

An advantage of using the attribute table is that you can calculate values for multiple features at one time—either for all features, or a selected set. (The Show Selected button at the bottom of the table window displays only the selected features, if any, making it easier to see the features you're calculating values for.) To do this, you create an expression using a combination of constants, mathematical or logical operators, and values in other fields in the table. For example, you might calculate the value per square foot of parcels by dividing the assessed value of each by its area. Right-click the field column heading and use the Field Calculator to create the expression and calculate the values (the value you're calculating can be of any type—numeric, text, and so on).

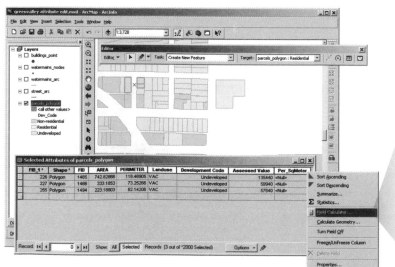

To calculate values for all features (or a selected set) for a field, right-click the column heading for the field and open the Field Calculator. Complete the expression in the lower box.

You can edit values in the attribute table outside an edit session, but only by using the Field Calculator—not by entering individual values in a column. When you calculate values outside an edit session you'll get a warning message telling you the Undo button is unavailable.

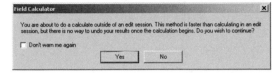

When you use the Field Calculator outside of an edit session, you'll receive this warning message. If you want to undo your edits, you'll need to recalculate new values, or delete the field and add it again.

Use the Fields tab on the Layer Properties dialog box to control which fields appear in the table (this is useful if the table contains many fields, and you're only editing one or a few of them).

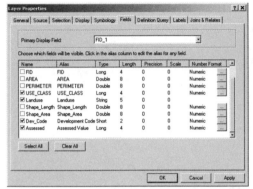

Before, all fields are visible in the table.

After setting the visible fields, only the specified fields are displayed.

To open the Layer Properties dialog box, right-click a layer in the table of contents, and click Properties. On the Fields tab, select the fields you want to be visible in the table.

You can also hide a field by right-clicking the column heading and clicking Turn Field Off. To show the field again, check it on the Layer Properties dialog box, or click Options on the table and click Turn All Fields On (this will, of course, show all hidden fields).

Hide a field from the table by right-clicking the column heading and clicking Turn Field Off.

Editing attributes for datasets having table relationships

If you're editing an attribute table that has a related table (that is, a relationship class has been defined—see 'Building relationships between features and tables' in Chapter 2), you can access and edit the records in the related table from the original table. For example, if you have a table of landowners that is related to a parcel feature class, you can select a parcel feature, use the relationship class to find the owner of that parcel, then edit the attributes in the owner table. You can edit a related table using either the Attributes dialog box or the attribute table.

Some relationship classes have rules that control how features can be related. After you edit related geodatabase features or tables that have relationship rules, you can validate your edits to check that the related objects still conform to the relationship rules (see 'Checking your data for errors' in this chapter).

To edit a related table using the Attributes dialog box, click the plus sign next to a feature to list any related tables.

When you click the related table for a feature, the related record is displayed. You can edit the values as you would for the feature attribute table.

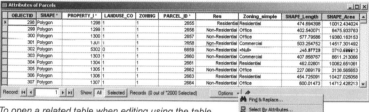

To open a related table when editing using the table window, click Options, point to Related Tables, and click the name of the related table you want to edit.

The related table opens; you can edit the values as you would in the feature attribute table—by entering a value in a column, or right-clicking a column heading and using the Field Calculator.

Adding fields to a table

If you need to add a field to the table, use the Options menu. You cannot do this while in an edit session (if necessary, save your edits, stop editing, add the field, and then restart the edit session). See also 'Adding fields and calculating attribute values' in Chapter 5.

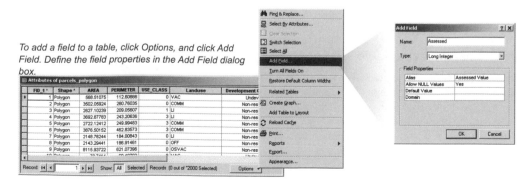

To add a field to a table, click Options, and click Add Field. Define the field properties in the Add Field dialog box.

Creating and editing annotation

ArcGIS provides several options for displaying text on a map to describe particular features or add general information to the map. One simple option is to use map labels which are created from feature attribute values and are placed automatically (see 'Labeling features' in Chapter 4). Another option is to create annotation. With annotation, the position, text string, and display properties of text can all be edited. Using annotation allows you to select and position individual pieces of text. This provides flexibility in the appearance and placement of your map text. Annotation can be stored with a specific map ("map document annotation") or stored in a geodatabase, enabling the same map text to be placed on different maps ("geodatabase annotation").

Editing map document annotation

Map document annotation can be quickly created by converting labels on your map (see 'Labeling features' in Chapter 4). It is stored in the map in which it was created. You edit map annotation using the tools on the Draw toolbar, as you would other graphics (you can use these same tools to create map document annotation). To edit an individual annotation, select it using the Select Elements tool. You can then drag it to a new position or rotate it using the Rotate tool. Press the Delete key to delete the annotation, or right-click and click Delete.

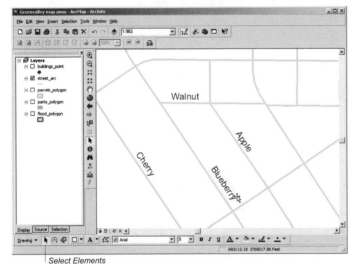

Select map annotation using the Select Elements tool.

Select Elements

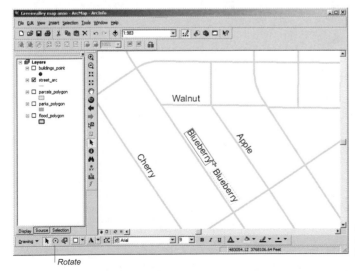

Drag selected map annotation to reposition it. Use the Rotate tool to rotate it around its center point.

Rotate

To change the font, size, or color of the annotation, use the tools on the Draw toolbar.

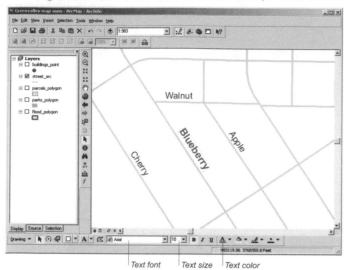

Text font   Text size   Text color

Right-clicking displays additional options.

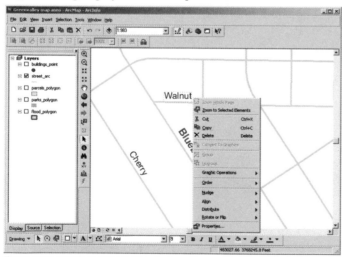

Right-click a selected annotation to display editing options.

Creating and editing geodatabase annotation

Geodatabase annotation is stored as a feature class in a geodatabase. Because of this, it can be added to different maps and accessed by anyone in your organization who has access to the geodatabase. Geodatabase annotation also has a wider range of editing options than does map annotation.

There are two types of geodatabase annotation—standard and feature linked. Standard annotation is independent of features in the geodatabase. For example, you might have a piece of standard annotation that labels a mountain range or a neighborhood in a city—the annotation simply marks the general area on the map. Feature-linked annotation is associated with the feature it is describing. The text reflects the value of a field or fields from the feature to which it's linked—if an attribute value is updated, the linked annotation is also updated. You might use feature-linked annotation to identify particular features like streets, buildings, or rivers. If you move, copy, or delete a feature, the annotation is moved, copied, or deleted with it. In addition, with feature-linked annotation, as you create new features annotation will be created automatically.

A quick way to create geodatabase annotation is to convert existing labels on a map in ArcMap, the same way you would when creating map document annotation. By default, the annotation is feature linked (since you're creating it from labels associated with the features) but you can uncheck the box to make it standard annotation. When you create geodatabase annotation you specify a reference scale. This is the map scale at which the annotation will appear at its assigned font size (the size will increase when you zoom in and decrease when you zoom out on the map).

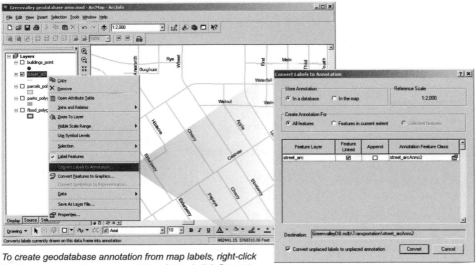

On the dialog box, select the option to store annotation in a database. By default, annotation is feature linked. The annotation feature class will be created in the same geodatabase or feature dataset as the feature class you're creating annotation from.

To create geodatabase annotation from map labels, right-click the layer you want to create annotation for and click Convert Labels to Annotation. You'll first want to make sure the labels are the size you want for the scale they're displayed at (this becomes the reference scale).

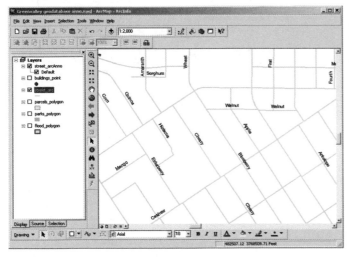

The annotation is added as a new layer to the map (it initially looks the same as the labels it was created from, but you can now select and edit individual text).

Another way of creating geodatabase annotation is to create an empty feature class, in ArcCatalog, and then create annotation within the feature class using ArcMap. You'd use this method when creating a structure for your geodatabase as part of the geodatabase design process as described in Chapter 2. Creating an annotation feature class is described on the next page.

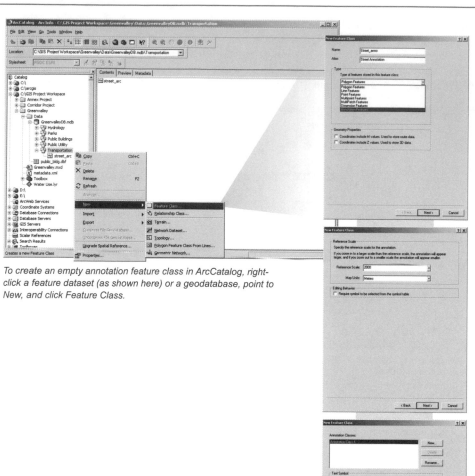

To create an empty annotation feature class in ArcCatalog, right-click a feature dataset (as shown here) or a geodatabase, point to New, and click Feature Class.

Enter a name and (optionally) an alias for the feature class. From the drop-down list, specify the type as Annotation Features.

Specify the reference scale for the annotation.

You can specify more than one class for the annotation—you might create one class for major roads and another for local streets if the annotation symbols will be different for each class. You also specify the symbol for each class here.

The new annotation feature class (Street_anno) appears in the Catalog tree, in the feature dataset it was created in. At this point, there are no annotation features—you need to edit the feature class in ArcMap to add them.

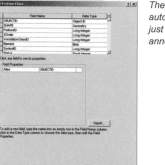

The required fields are automatically created, so just click Finish to create the annotation feature class.

After you specify the feature class type as annotation, you're given the option of making it feature linked, and specifying the feature class to link it to. If you do create feature-linked annotation, you'll be given additional options for specifying editing behavior and annotation placement. If you create annotation at the geodatabase level you'll be presented with additional panels prompting you to specify the coordinate system for the annotation, and the x,y tolerance. And if you're creating annotation in a file or ArcSDE geodatabase, you'll be given the option of entering a configuration keyword. See 'Creating feature classes and tables' in Chapter 2 for more on these settings.

You edit geodatabase annotation in an edit session in ArcMap (see 'Starting and managing an edit session' earlier in this chapter). Once you've added the annotation feature class to your map, open the Editor toolbar and start the edit session. You can use the Editor toolbar to perform some basic editing on existing annotation. Use the Edit tool to select the annotation to edit. You can then drag to move it, or use the Rotate tool to rotate it. As with any edit session, the Undo and Redo buttons are active.

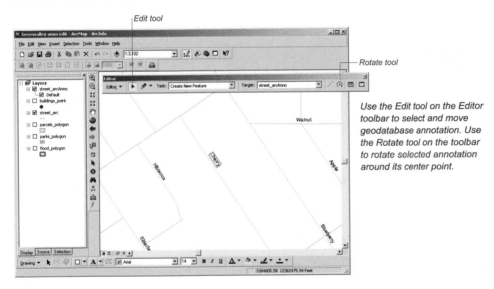

Use the Edit tool on the Editor toolbar to select and move geodatabase annotation. Use the Rotate tool on the toolbar to rotate selected annotation around its center point.

Right-click the annotation to display more options, including Copy and Delete. Click the Attributes option (or click the Attributes button on the toolbar) to change the appearance of the annotation, or to change the text (by typing in the box).

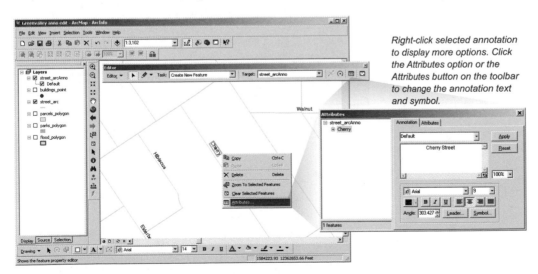

Right-click selected annotation to display more options. Click the Attributes option or the Attributes button on the toolbar to change the annotation text and symbol.

For additional editing options, or to create new annotation, open the Annotation toolbar from the Editor drop-down list. Point to More Editing Tools, and click Annotation.

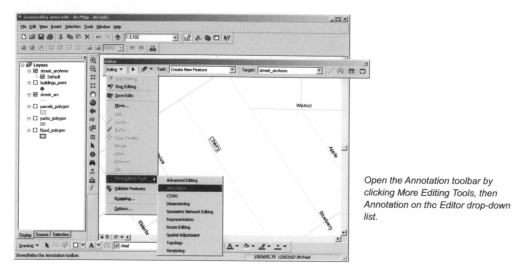

Open the Annotation toolbar by clicking More Editing Tools, then Annotation on the Editor drop-down list.

When you select annotation using the Edit Annotation tool on the Annotation toolbar, a blue box (known as the bounding box) appears around the annotation. The box provides several options for interactively editing the annotation. Click and drag the lower left or lower right corner of the box to rotate the annotation (the annotation pivots around the opposite corner).

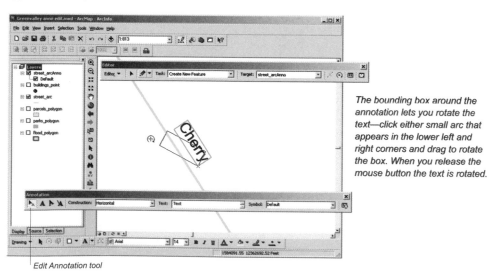

The bounding box around the annotation lets you rotate the text—click either small arc that appears in the lower left and right corners and drag to rotate the box. When you release the mouse button the text is rotated.

Edit Annotation tool

Click the red triangle at the top of the box and drag the cursor up or down to interactively increase or decrease the text size. Click the crosshair in the center of the box and drag the cursor to move the text.

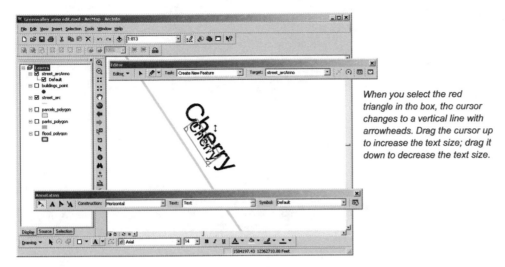

When you select the red triangle in the box, the cursor changes to a vertical line with arrowheads. Drag the cursor up to increase the text size; drag it down to decrease the text size.

Right-click to display more options, including changing the curvature of the annotation—you can change it from straight (that is, straight-line at any angle) to horizontal or curved, for example.

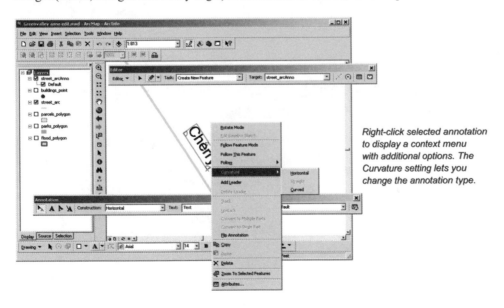

Right-click selected annotation to display a context menu with additional options. The Curvature setting lets you change the annotation type.

To create new annotation, first make sure the Target on the Editor toolbar is set to the layer to receive the annotation. Then select the Construction type from the drop-down list on the Annotation toolbar.

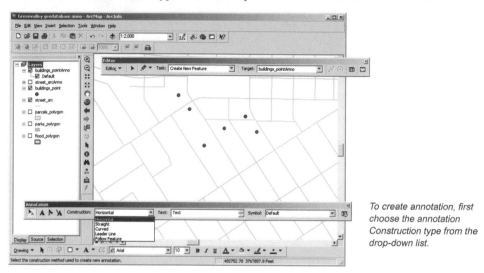

To create annotation, first choose the annotation Construction type from the drop-down list.

Type the annotation text in the Text box, then click the Sketch tool on the Editor toolbar and place the annotation on the map. Each time you click, annotation is placed on the map (so you can place the same annotation text in multiple locations). To stop placing annotation, click any tool on the Editor toolbar or on the Annotation toolbar.

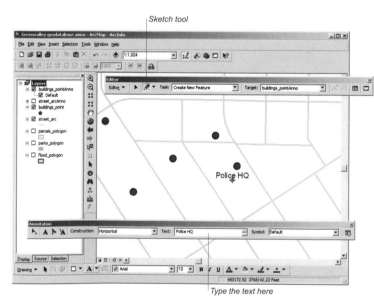

Type the text for the annotation in the Text box, then select the Sketch tool. Use the cursor to place the annotation in the correct location—the text is previewed as you drag it. For Horizontal annotation, the text is placed when you click the cursor. You can continue placing the same annotation text in other locations.

For Horizontal, Straight, and Leader Line you can also click the appropriate button at the left end of the Annotation toolbar to place the annotation.

Each type of construction works slightly differently. When placing Straight annotation, click to place the center point, then drag around the center point to the desired angle, and click again to place the annotation. Curved annotation lets you enter the vertices of a line along which the annotation will be placed. For the Follow Feature construction, click a feature the annotation will be parallel to, then click again to locate the annotation along that feature.

For Leader Line, click the location of the leader line end point, then drag to place the annotation—the leader line stretches to the annotation as you drag it.

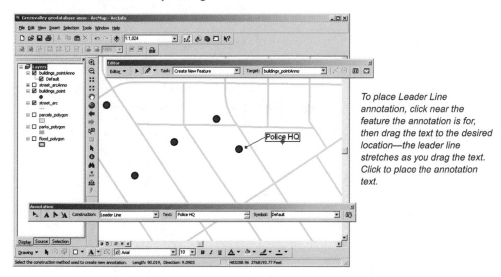

To place Leader Line annotation, click near the feature the annotation is for, then drag the text to the desired location—the leader line stretches as you drag the text. Click to place the annotation text.

The text symbol used for the annotation is one of the symbols specified when you created the annotation feature class. Right-click an annotation to change the text symbol or leader line for that specific annotation. These symbols are stored in what's known as the annotation symbol collection.

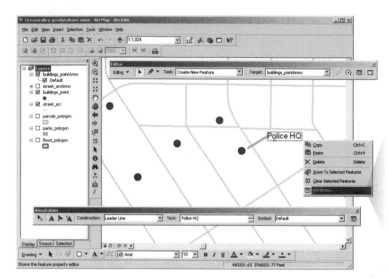

To modify the symbol for a particular piece of annotation, select the annotation using the Edit tool on the Editor toolbar, right-click, and click Attributes. Choose another symbol from the symbol collection using the drop-down list in the Attributes dialog box or use the buttons to change the font, size, and so on. Click the Leader button to modify the leader line.

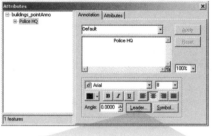

Click the Symbol button on the Editor dialog box to open the Symbol Selector and specify the leader line color and thickness.

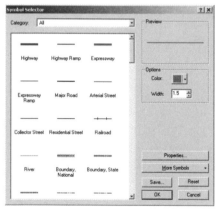

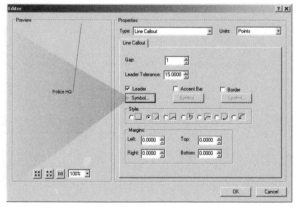

Use the Editor box to set the gap between the leader line and the text, the leader line type, and other options.

You set the symbol for leader line annotation—along with other properties of the annotation—on the Annotation tab of the Attributes dialog box (existing leader line annotation won't change).

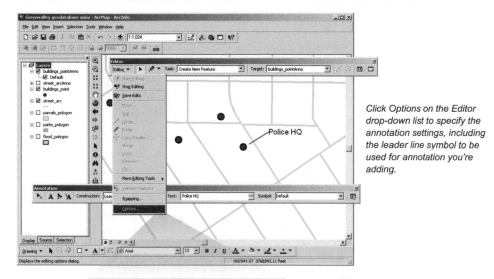

Click Options on the Editor drop-down list to specify the annotation settings, including the leader line symbol to be used for annotation you're adding.

On the Annotation tab, click the Leader button to open the Editor dialog box and set the leader line properties for leader line annotation you add.

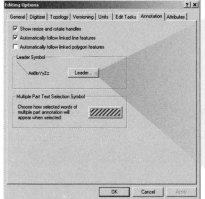

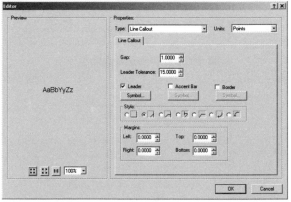

You can add new annotation symbols to the symbol collection at any time in ArcCatalog. Right-click the annotation feature class in the Catalog tree and click Properties. Then click New on the Annotation tab.

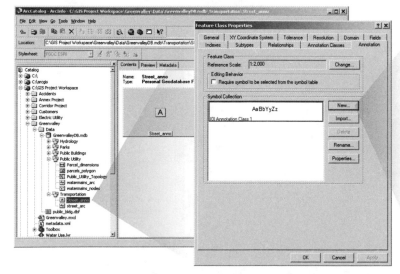

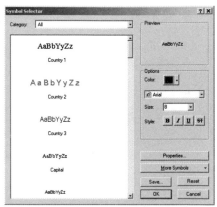

Use the Symbol Selector to choose a new text symbol to add to the annotation symbol collection.

Creating and editing dimensions

Dimension features are a specialized type of geodatabase annotation for showing lengths or distances on a map. A dimension may indicate the length of a side of a building or land parcel, or it may indicate the distance between two features, such as a fire hydrant and the corner of a building. Dimension features are stored in dimension feature classes in a geodatabase. You need to create a dimension feature class before creating the dimension features themselves.

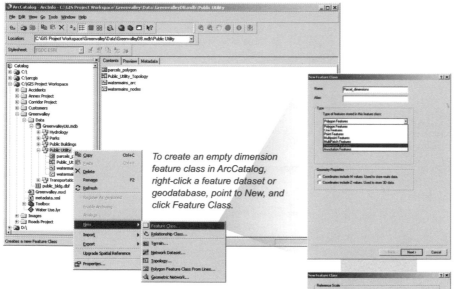

To create an empty dimension feature class in ArcCatalog, right-click a feature dataset or geodatabase, point to New, and click Feature Class.

Enter a name and (optionally) an alias for the feature class. From the drop-down list, specify the type as Dimension Features.

Specify the reference scale for the dimensions. This is the map scale at which the dimensions will appear at their assigned font size (the size will increase when you zoom in and decrease when you zoom out on the map). Also specify whether to accept the default style, create one, or import one from an existing dimensions feature class.

If you're creating a file or ArcSDE geodatabase, at this point you'll be given the option of entering a configuration keyword (see 'Creating feature classes and tables' in Chapter 2).

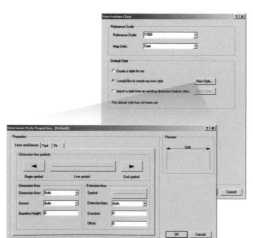

If you select the option to create a style, click the New Style button on the wizard panel to open the Dimension Style Properties dialog box. Specify the symbols and spacing for the dimension and extension lines, the dimension text symbol, and so on.

The required fields are automatically created, so just click Finish to create the dimensions feature class. It is added as a new feature class in the feature dataset you created it in. (You can also create dimension feature classes at the geodatabase level.)

Dimension features are added to a dimension feature class in ArcMap, within an edit session. First, add the dimensions feature class to your map, along with the features for which you're adding dimensions (the parcels, streets, buildings, or other features). Then open the Editor toolbar, and start an edit session. Specify the Task as Create New Feature, and specify the Target layer as the dimensions feature class; you'll also want to set the snapping environment to the vertices of the features you're dimensioning. Then open the Dimensioning toolbar which contains tools for creating dimension features.

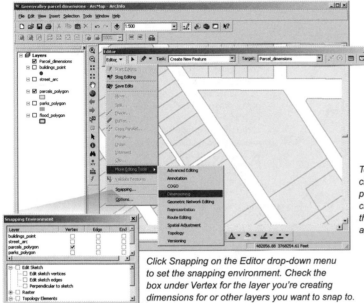

To open the Dimensioning toolbar, click the Editor drop-down menu, point to More Editing Tools, and click Dimensioning. The options on the toolbar are active only during an edit session.

Click Snapping on the Editor drop-down menu to set the snapping environment. Check the box under Vertex for the layer you're creating dimensions for or other layers you want to snap to.

Use the Construction drop-down list on the Dimensioning toolbar to specify the dimension type.

Specify the type of dimension from the Construction drop-down list.

The dimension features are based on points that you input with the Sketch tool. An "aligned" dimension, for example, requires three points: the start point, the end point, and an offset point. Select the Sketch tool on the Editor toolbar, then enter the points on the map to create the dimension. As you move the mouse, you will see that the new dimension dynamically draws itself with the cursor location as the end dimension point. When you click the final point, the dimension position and text are fixed.

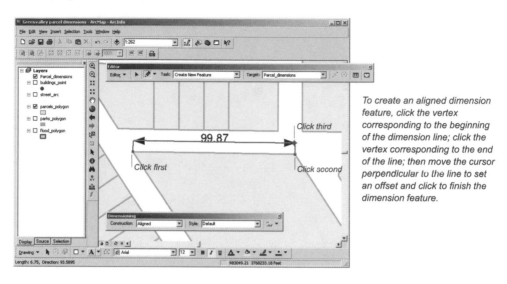

To create an aligned dimension feature, click the vertex corresponding to the beginning of the dimension line; click the vertex corresponding to the end of the line; then move the cursor perpendicular to the line to set an offset and click to finish the dimension feature.

You can create aligned, simple aligned, horizontal linear, vertical linear, or rotated linear dimension features.

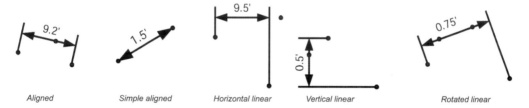

| Aligned | Simple aligned | Horizontal linear | Vertical linear | Rotated linear |

There are several tools on the toolbar that allow you to create new dimension features from a selected feature (these are available from the Autodimension palette). You select the dimension type, then select the feature—the dimension is created automatically.

If more than one style is defined for the dimension feature class, select the one to use from the drop-down menu on the Dimensioning toolbar. To override the current dimension style for a particular dimension feature, right-click the feature and click Attributes. The dialog box lets you change the dimension style.

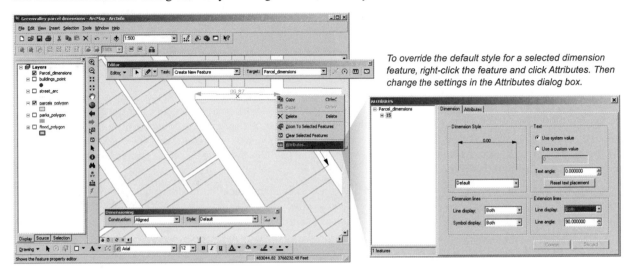

To override the default style for a selected dimension feature, right-click the feature and click Attributes. Then change the settings in the Attributes dialog box.

You can add more styles at any time in ArcCatalog (except when the dimensions are being edited in an edit session in ArcMap). Right-click the dimension feature class in the Catalog tree, and click Properties. On the Dimensions tab, click New to open the Dimension Style Properties dialog box, and define the properties of the new style.

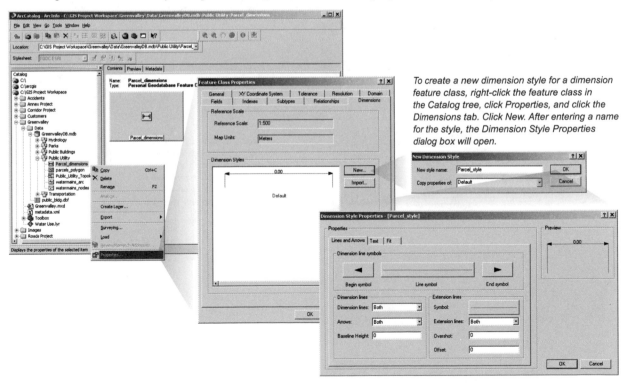

To create a new dimension style for a dimension feature class, right-click the feature class in the Catalog tree, click Properties, and click the Dimensions tab. Click New. After entering a name for the style, the Dimension Style Properties dialog box will open.

Editing routes and geometric networks

Routes and geometric networks are collections of line features and junctions, or intersections, used to represent transportation and utility networks. You create both types of datasets using ArcCatalog (see 'Adding specialized datasets to a geodatabase' in Chapter 2). ArcMap contains tools for interactively editing the datasets to add or delete features.

Editing a route dataset

Routes are collections of linear features built from existing features such as roads or pipelines. They're often used to manage subsections of an existing line dataset—for example, to indicate different pavement conditions along stretches of a highway. They are also used to assign geographic locations to events stored in a table (see 'Assigning locations using street addresses or routes' earlier in this chapter). You can modify an existing route dataset—or add features to an empty dataset you created in ArcCatalog—using tools in ArcMap. Routes are edited within an edit session, using tools on the Editor toolbar and the Route Editing toolbar.

First, add the route dataset to your map. Then open the Editor toolbar and click Start Editing on the Editor drop-down menu. Set the Target layer to be the route dataset. You can use the Edit tool to select a route, then right-click to delete the route or click Attributes to modify its attributes (such as the route ID).

If you're adding features to the route (as opposed to merely deleting them or modifying their properties) you'll want to also add the dataset containing the base features (such as a streets dataset). Set the Task to Create New Feature. Then open the Route Editing toolbar—point to More Editing Tools on the Editor drop-down menu, and click Route Editing.

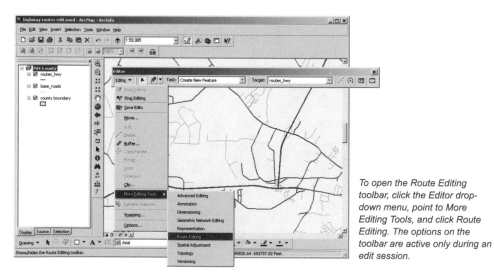

To open the Route Editing toolbar, click the Editor drop-down menu, point to More Editing Tools, and click Route Editing. The options on the toolbar are active only during an edit session.

To create a new route, select the base features that will comprise the route using the Edit tool on the Editor toolbar. Press and hold the Shift key to select multiple features. Once you've selected all the features to include in the route, click the Make Route button on the Route Editing toolbar.

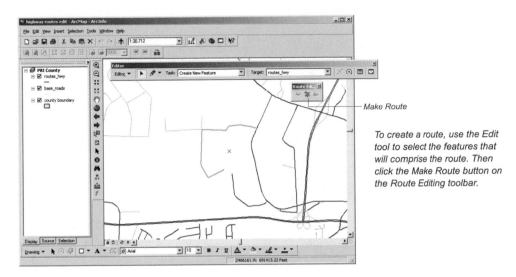

Make Route

To create a route, use the Edit tool to select the features that will comprise the route. Then click the Make Route button on the Route Editing toolbar.

In the Make Route dialog box, specify the start point of the route (where the measuring will start from) and how the distance will be obtained (the default is to use the distances calculated from the geometry of the features in the route). An easy way to specify the start point is to simply click on the map. First, click the arrow button in the dialog box.

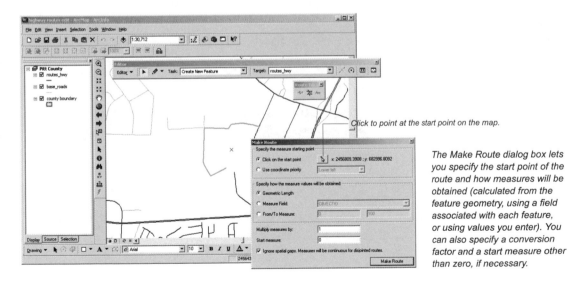

Click to point at the start point on the map.

The Make Route dialog box lets you specify the start point of the route and how measures will be obtained (calculated from the feature geometry, using a field associated with each feature, or using values you enter). You can also specify a conversion factor and a start measure other than zero, if necessary.

You're prompted to click near the end point of the selected base feature that defines the start of the route. When you move the cursor near the point on the map, it will snap to the point.

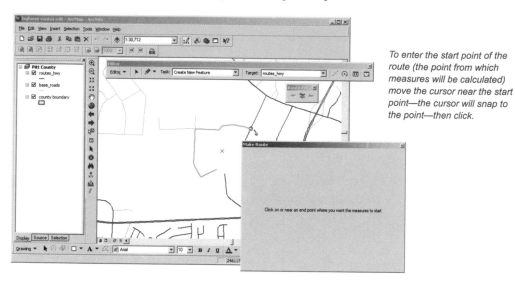

To enter the start point of the route (the point from which measures will be calculated) move the cursor near the start point—the cursor will snap to the point—then click.

After you've specified the start point, the dialog box reappears. Set any other parameters in the dialog box (or accept the defaults) and click Make Route at the bottom of the dialog box.

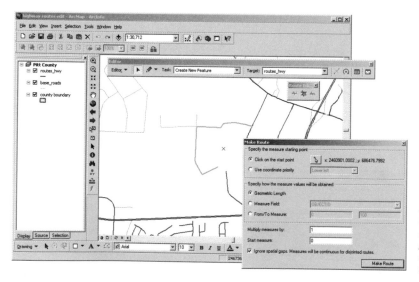

After setting the start point, the Make Route dialog box reappears—set any other parameters, then click the Make Route button on the dialog box to create the route.

Once the new route has been created in the target feature class, the selected set of input linear features will become unselected and the new route will become selected. This is so you can set the attributes, such as the route identifier. The route identifier is used when locating events along the route— each event in the event table includes the route identifier so it can be assigned to the correct route. To assign the route identifier (and any other attributes), right-click the selected route and click Attributes. Type in the box next to the route identifier field to assign the route identifier.

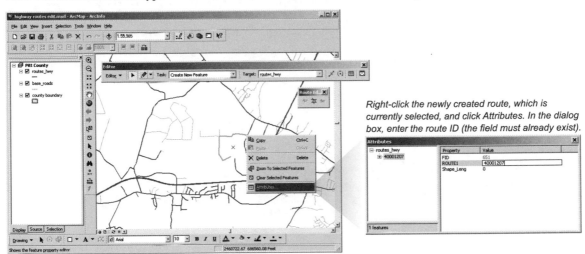

Right-click the newly created route, which is currently selected, and click Attributes. In the dialog box, enter the route ID (the field must already exist).

The Linear Referencing toolbox in ArcToolbox contains tools for building routes and locating events. The Create Routes tool, for example, lets you create a route dataset. The tools are useful when building routes and locating events within a script or model, but they can also be used on their own.

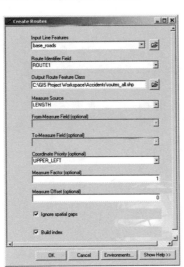

The Create Routes tool in the Linear Referencing toolbox lets you create routes from a set of base features by entering the input and output datasets, along with other parameters, in a dialog box.

Editing a geometric network

Geometric networks are used to represent utility networks such as electrical networks or water systems. They are built in ArcCatalog, using existing features—for example, transmission lines, capacitors, transformers, and so on, for an electrical network (see 'Adding specialized datasets to a geodatabase' in Chapter 2). A defining characteristic of a geometric network is that it stores and maintains the connectivity between the various features in the network.

Geometric networks are edited in an edit session in ArcMap. Add the network to your map (when you do, all the feature classes that comprise the network are added to the map). You can delete features or modify the attributes for a feature in the network as you would any other feature. Select the feature using the Edit tool on the Editor toolbar. Right-click to delete or copy it (keeping in mind that deleting a feature may impact the connectivity of the network). Click Attributes to modify its attribute values.

Because the connectivity between features in the network is inherent, when you move a feature, the features to which it is connected move with it to maintain the connectivity.

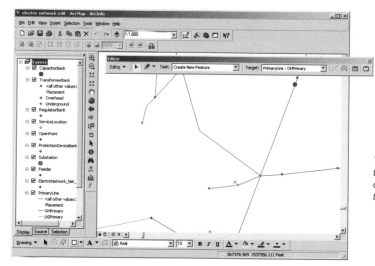

To edit a geometric network, open the Editor toolbar, and click Start Editing on the Editor drop-down menu. Use the Edit tool on the toolbar to select the feature to work with.

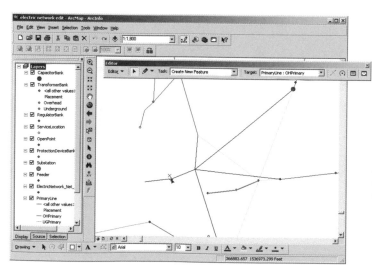

When you drag to move a feature, the junction at which the feature connects to other features moves with it, and the connected features stretch accordingly.

There may be cases where you need to move a feature without changing the position of features it's connected to (for example, to move the position of a transmission line without moving the position of the pole it's connected to). To do this, you need to first disconnect the feature. Open the Geometric Network Editing toolbar from the Editor drop-down menu. Then select the feature to disconnect—using the Edit tool on the Editor toolbar—and click the Disconnect button.

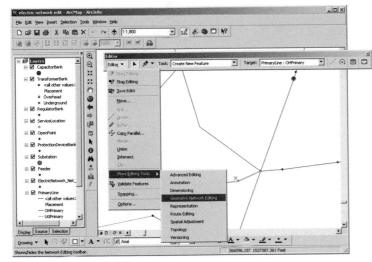

To disconnect a feature from the network, open the Geometric Network Editing toolbar (click the Editor drop-down menu and point to More Editing Tools).

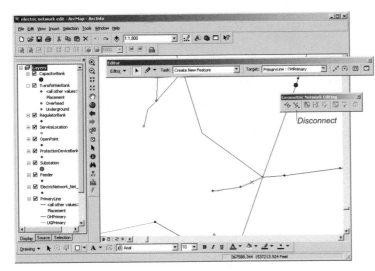

With the feature selected, click the Disconnect button on the toolbar.

Now when you move the feature, the connected features stay put. To reconnect the feature to the network, snap an end to a feature on the network, and click the Connect button on the toolbar.

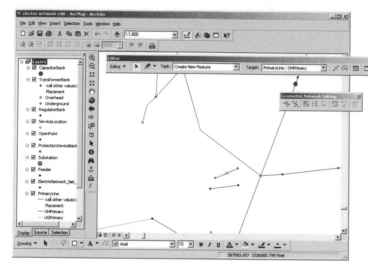

When you move the disconnected feature, it floats free of the network.

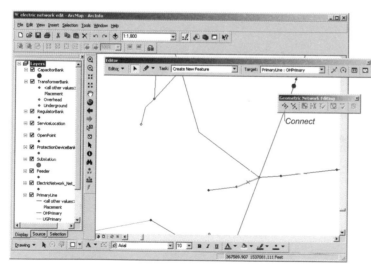

To reconnect a feature to the network (or connect a new feature), snap the feature to an existing network edge or junction, and click the Connect button on the toolbar.

When adding a feature to a geometric network, you'll want to set the snapping environment so that all layers in the network have snapping on. That will ensure new features snap to existing ones, thus maintaining network connectivity.

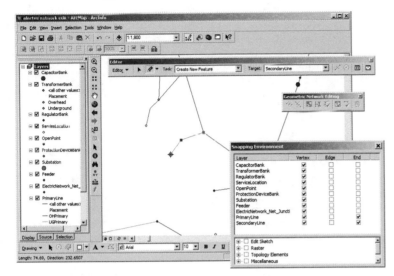

When adding features to a geometric network, set snapping on for the network layers. Point features should have Vertex checked; line features should have Vertex and End checked (as well as Edge, if required).

Checking your data for errors

ArcGIS Desktop contains several tools to help you check for errors in your geodatabase that may have been introduced during editing or when importing data. These validation tools work within an edit session in ArcMap (see 'Starting and managing an edit session' earlier in this chapter for a discussion of starting an edit session). The Validate Features tool checks for invalid values for subtypes or attribute domains, as well as invalid relationship classes and broken network connectivity. The Topology toolbar lets you check and verify any topology rules you've established for specific datasets.

Validating attribute values

The Validate Features tool on the Editor toolbar checks the values of domains and subtypes to make sure they're valid (see 'Ensuring attribute data integrity' in Chapter 2 for a discussion of creating domains and subtypes). When editing subtypes and coded value domains using the Attributes dialog box, a drop-down menu lets you select from a list of valid values to ensure that acceptable values are entered (see 'Adding and editing attribute data' earlier in this chapter). However, it may be the case that there are attribute values in a field that pre-date the creation of the coded value domain or subtype. Also, values entered using the field calculator in the table window are not restricted to those defined in the coded value domain or subtype, so errors may creep in if values are entered using this method. For range domains, the values that can be entered—using either the Attributes dialog box or the field calculator in the table window—are not restricted when you enter them, so, again, errors may occur. The Validate Features tool finds any invalid domain or subtype values that occur in the table, for the selected feature(s), and displays a message.

After starting an edit session, use the Edit tool to select the feature(s) to be validated. Then click the Editor drop-down menu and click Validate Features. If a single feature is selected, the message indicates the nature of the problem.

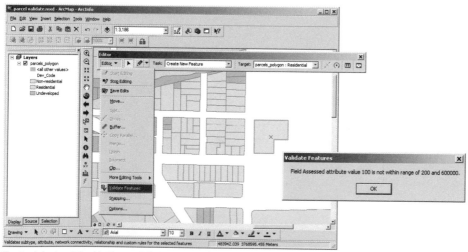

To check for invalid subtypes or attribute domain values, open an edit session
and use the Edit tool to select the feature to check. Then select Validate
Features on the Editor drop-down menu. A message is displayed indicating the
error. If there are no errors, the message indicates that all features are valid.

Right-click the feature to open its attribute dialog box and correct the value.

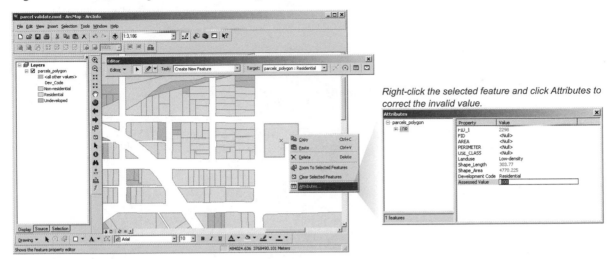

Right-click the selected feature and click Attributes to correct the invalid value.

If more than one feature is selected, the message tells you how many features have invalid values; only those features remain selected. Select one of these features and run Validate Features again to get an explanation of why the feature is invalid (or just open the Attributes dialog box for the feature and see for yourself).

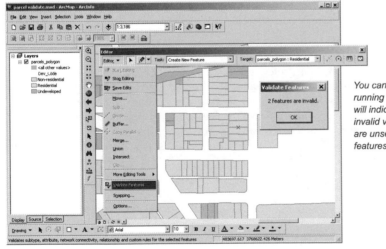

You can select multiple features before running Validate Features. The message will indicate how many features have invalid values. Features with no errors are unselected, leaving selected only the features having invalid values.

To open the Attributes dialog box, click the Attributes button on the toolbar, or right-click one of the selected features and click Attributes. The selected features are listed in the left panel; click a feature in the list to display and edit its attributes.

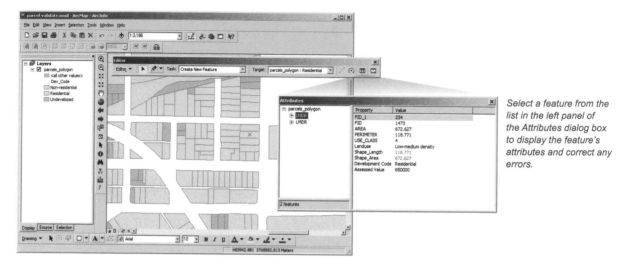

Select a feature from the list in the left panel of the Attributes dialog box to display the feature's attributes and correct any errors.

Validate Features checks for the different types of errors sequentially, so if a feature has errors of more than one type it will generate a message if you run it again. For example, if a feature has an invalid subtype and an invalid domain value, it will generate an error when the invalid subtype is encountered. If you fix the error and re-run Validate Features, a message will be generated when the invalid domain value is encountered.

Validating relationship classes and network connectivity

Validate Features will check to make sure any relationship class rules you've set up in your geodatabase are not broken. For example, in an electric network, there may be a relationship class between substations and feeders, with a rule that a substation cannot have more than two feeders. Validate Features will check to ensure there are no violations of the rule (a substation has no more than two feeders associated with it). Select the feature or features to validate, then click Validate Features on the Editor drop-down menu. Validate Features displays a message indicating that all features are valid, or that it has found a rule that has been broken, and the cause. In this case, the tables or features would have to be edited to modify the relationships between the features.

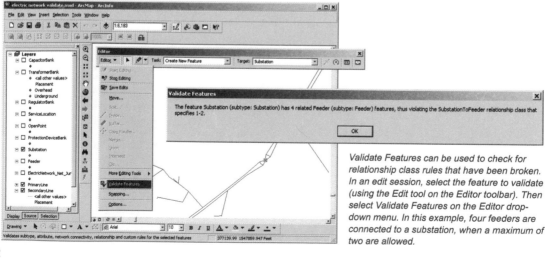

Validate Features can be used to check for relationship class rules that have been broken. In an edit session, select the feature to validate (using the Edit tool on the Editor toolbar). Then select Validate Features on the Editor drop-down menu. In this example, four feeders are connected to a substation, when a maximum of two are allowed.

Similarly, Validate Features will evaluate connectivity for a geometric network. In an electric network, for example, a substation might be able to connect only to a primary line. If a substation is added and connected to a secondary line, running the Validate Features tool will reveal this, and display a message. To correct the error, the feature would have to be deleted or moved to connect to a different—primary—line.

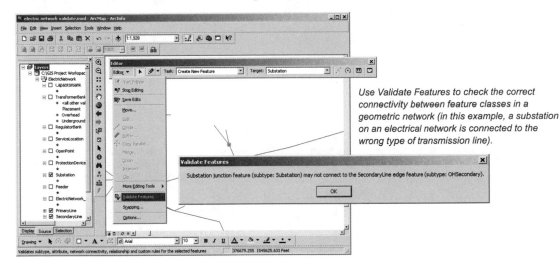

Use Validate Features to check the correct connectivity between feature classes in a geometric network (in this example, a substation on an electrical network is connected to the wrong type of transmission line).

Validating topology rules

A topology is a set of rules that define the spatial relationships between features. The rules ensure, for example, that parcels don't overlap or that census tracts completely nest within counties. If you've made edits to a feature that participates in a topology, you need to validate the topology to identify any violations of the rules that have been defined for the topology.

ArcMap includes tools for validating geodatabase topology. (The tools are not available for map topology. For more on geodatabase topology see 'Ensuring spatial data integrity' in Chapter 2. For more on map topology, see 'Editing connected features' in this chapter.)

Topology validation occurs within an edit session in ArcMap, using the Topology toolbar. After starting an edit session, click the Editor drop-down menu, point to More Editing Tools, and click Topology.

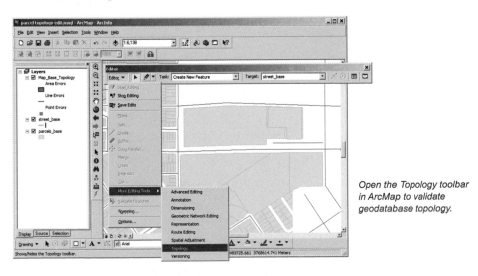

Open the Topology toolbar in ArcMap to validate geodatabase topology.

If there is more than one geodatabase topology on your map, use the drop-down list to select the one you want to validate.

The toolbar includes three buttons that let you validate topology—they vary only in the extent of features they will validate. You can validate feature topology within a selected area on the map, within the current extent of your map, or the entire topology. When you click one of the three Validate Topology buttons, ArcMap checks the features against the topology rules in the geodatabase. Any features that violate the rules are highlighted in red on the map. After validating, use the Error Inspector to list the errors—click the button on the toolbar to open the Error Inspector window. Use the drop-down list to specify which errors to search for and list (based on the rule that's been broken), or select Errors from all rules. Then click the Search Now button on the window.

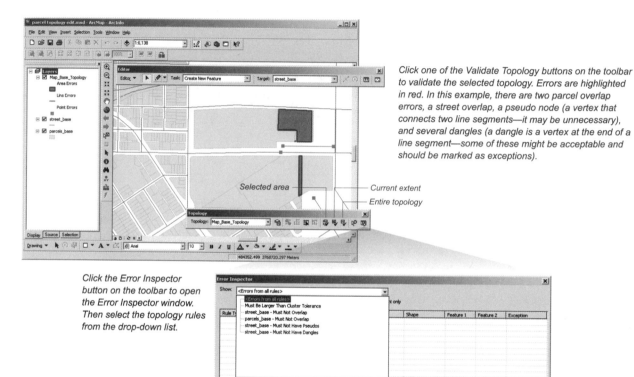

Click one of the Validate Topology buttons on the toolbar to validate the selected topology. Errors are highlighted in red. In this example, there are two parcel overlap errors, a street overlap, a pseudo node (a vertex that connects two line segments—it may be unnecessary), and several dangles (a dangle is a vertex at the end of a line segment—some of these might be acceptable and should be marked as exceptions).

Click the Error Inspector button on the toolbar to open the Error Inspector window. Then select the topology rules from the drop-down list.

When you select an error in the list, the corresponding feature is highlighted in black on the map. You can use the Error Inspector to manage the errors—you can sort the errors by any of the fields in the table so you can work with all the errors of a given type. You can also limit the errors shown in the table to errors of a given type, errors that occur in the currently visible map extent, or errors that have been marked as exceptions (that is, are acceptable, even though they violate a topology rule).

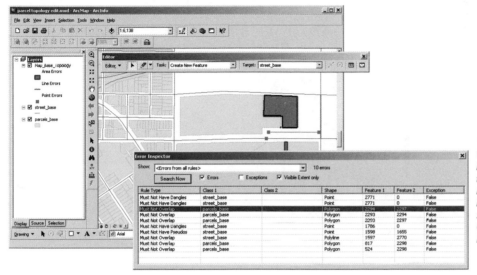

When you select an error in the Error Inspector table, the corresponding feature is highlighted on the map, in black. Right-click a row to zoom or pan to that feature. Click a column heading to sort by that column.

Once you identify errors, use the tools on the Topology toolbar to fix them. In many cases, you can use the Fix Topology Error tool on the toolbar to resolve errors. When you use the tool to select a feature that has an error, and then right-click, applicable predefined fixes are displayed in the context menu. For example, if the error is an overlapping polygon, the Merge fix is available. If you click Merge, you can select which of the overlapping polygons will be merged into the other. The same menu is displayed when you select and right-click an error in the Error Inspector window.

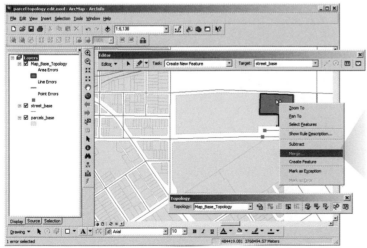

Click the Fix Topology Error tool on the toolbar, then right-click a selected feature on the map. You can zoom or pan to the feature, or select a fix—in this example, selecting Merge lets you pick the duplicate line to delete.

You can also use ArcCatalog to validate an entire topology. It's a good idea to do this when you first build the topology in ArcCatalog (see 'Ensuring spatial data integrity' in Chapter 2). Right-click the topology in the Catalog tree, and click Validate. Errors will be displayed when you click the Preview tab.

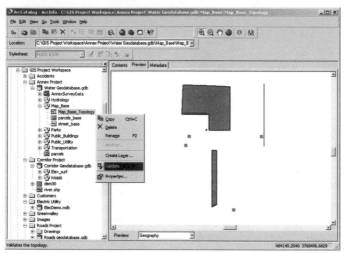

After validation, topology errors appear in ArcCatalog when you select the Preview tab.

When you open a map that contains the topology, in ArcMap, any errors ArcCatalog identified will be highlighted in red.

Defining coordinate systems and projecting datasets

The spatial reference for a feature class describes its coordinate system—for example, geographic, UTM, or State Plane—its spatial domain extent, its resolution, and its tolerance. When you're building your geodatabase, you assign the spatial reference when you create feature classes and feature datasets (see 'Creating feature classes and tables' and 'Ensuring spatial data integrity' in Chapter 2). If you've received data from an outside source, the data may have a spatial reference, but it may not yet be defined in ArcGIS. Or, the dataset may be in a different map projection than the rest of your data. ArcGIS includes tools to define coordinate systems and to project datasets to other map projections.

To see if a dataset has a defined coordinate system, right-click the dataset in the Catalog tree and click Properties, then select the XY Coordinate System tab. If the coordinate system is undefined, the name will say Unknown (or Assumed Geographic if the coordinates are in degrees of latitude and longitude), and the Details box will be empty. If the spatial reference is not included in the documentation that accompanied the dataset, you'll need to contact the source and get the spatial reference information.

You define a coordinate system by selecting a predefined coordinate system, importing one from another dataset, or defining the parameters for the coordinate system yourself to create a new one. You can do this in ArcCatalog (as shown on the next page) or using the Define Projection tool in ArcToolbox.

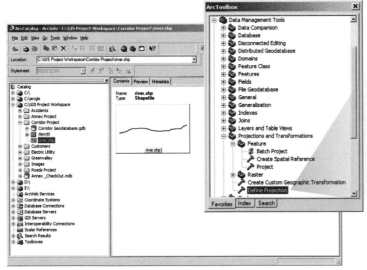
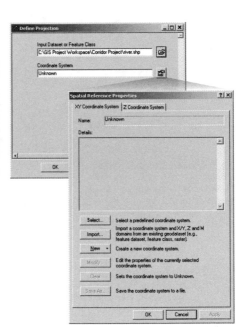

The Define Projection tool in the Projections and Transformations toolset lets you define a dataset's coordinate system. On the Define Projection dialog box, enter the input dataset and click the button next to the Coordinate System box to open the Spatial Reference Properties dialog box. The options for assigning a coordinate system are the same as when using ArcCatalog.

To assign the coordinate system for a dataset in ArcCatalog, right-click the dataset in the Catalog tree and click Properties.

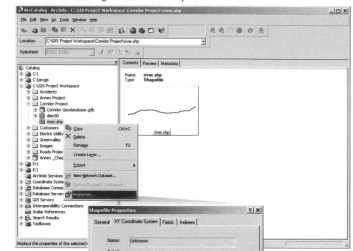

On the Properties dialog box, select the XY Coordinate System tab to display the options for assigning a coordinate system to the dataset.

The Import option lets you assign the coordinate system by using the coordinate system of an existing dataset.

The Select option lets you choose a predefined coordinate system—either projected or geographic.

The New option lets you enter parameters to create a custom projected or geographic coordinate system.

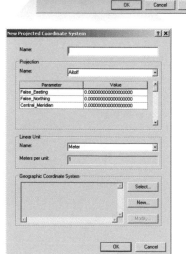

Defining a coordinate system does not change the coordinates of the data—it merely makes the coordinate system known to ArcGIS. If you need to change a dataset's coordinate system to a different one—for example, to be consistent with the rest of your geodatabase—use the Project tool. This may be the case if you receive data from another agency or other source that doesn't use the same coordinate system you're using for your geodatabase. Feature classes stored in a geodatabase feature dataset must have the same map projection as the feature dataset (see 'Ensuring spatial data integrity' in Chapter 2).

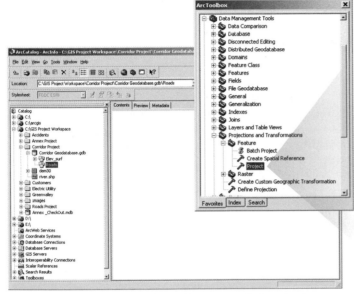

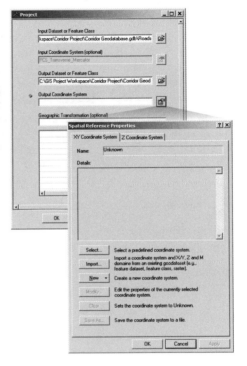

The Project tool lets you convert a dataset from one coordinate system to another (the coordinate system for the dataset you're converting must already be defined). The options for assigning the coordinate system to convert to are the same as when defining a coordinate system—select from a predefined one, import one from an existing dataset, or define a custom one. You can also modify the existing one, or select or import one and then modify it. When projecting a dataset, a new dataset is created in the new coordinate system.

The Projections and Transformations toolset contains additional tools for defining, projecting, and spatially adjusting rasters.

The Raster toolset under Projections and Transformations (in the Data Management toolbox) contains tools for projecting and adjusting raster datasets.

Adjusting and integrating datasets

Inconsistencies between GIS datasets obtained from different sources sometimes require you to perform additional work to integrate new data with the rest of your data. Some data may be distorted or rotated with respect to your base data and need to be transformed or "rubber sheeted" (stretched or warped) to match the base data. Or you may need to make sure features at edges of map sheets match up before the datasets are appended. You may want to transfer attribute values from one feature to another (often used to assign values to new features or to replace values with more accurate or current ones). This work is often in preparation for combining adjacent datasets to create a continuous dataset.

Transforming, rubber sheeting, and edge matching datasets

ArcGIS includes a number of tools that let you match up features in different datasets with each other. This is often needed when you've imported data from another source, such as a CAD drawing, or if you need to combine adjacent map sheets. The transform operation rotates and scales features to a set of control points; the rubber sheet operation stretches and warps features; and edge match lets you ensure that features meet up across map sheet edges. These are collectively known as spatial adjustment operations.

Spatial adjustment is done within an edit session in ArcMap. Open the Editor toolbar and start an edit session (see 'Starting and managing an edit session' earlier in this chapter). Spatial adjustment tools are located on the Spatial Adjustment toolbar—click the Editor drop-down menu, point to More Editing Tools, and click Spatial Adjustment.

Once you open the Spatial Adjustment toolbar, the process is essentially the same for transforming, rubber sheeting, and edge matching. The steps are:

1 Set the snapping environment for adding links

2 Specify the features to be adjusted

3 Specify the adjustment method

4 Create links between the features you're adjusting and the target features

5 Preview the adjustment

6 Adjust the features

The following example of transforming parcels to a new location shows these basic steps. The new parcels (shown in purple) need to be rotated and scaled to fit into the empty plot along the right edge of the map.

Set the snapping environment from the Editor drop-down menu. In this case, snapping is set for vertices for the new parcels and the existing parcels—this will make it easy to snap links to the corresponding vertex in each layer. Then open the Spatial Adjustment toolbar.

Set the snapping environment for the datasets you'll be creating links between.

On the Editor drop-down menu, point to More Editing Tools, and click Spatial Adjustment.

Next specify the layers that will participate in the adjustment (in this example two layers will be transformed at the same time—the NewBuildings layer and the NewParcels layer). Then set the spatial adjustment method.

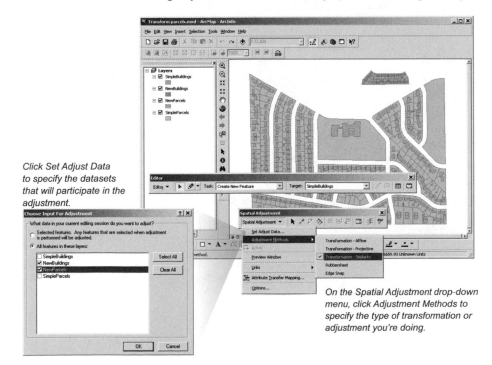

Click Set Adjust Data to specify the datasets that will participate in the adjustment.

On the Spatial Adjustment drop-down menu, click Adjustment Methods to specify the type of transformation or adjustment you're doing.

The next step is to add a link from a vertex on the source layer (the one you're transforming) to the corresponding vertex on the destination layer. You'll likely want to add at least four links to ensure a successful transformation.

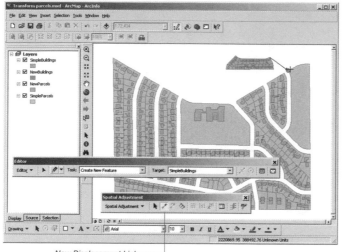

Click the New Displacement Link button on the Spatial Adjustment toolbar, then click the from point and to point to create each link.

New Displacement Link

To preview the result, open the Adjustment Preview window. You can also open the Link Table to display a list of the links. The table shows you the accuracy of the transformation (as indicated by the RMS error—the lower, the better). You can also delete errant links here, and then click the Add Link button to replace them with the correct link, if necessary.

Click Preview Window on the drop-down menu to open a window showing how the result of the adjustment will look. You can use the zoom and pan tools—either in the preview window or the map—to get a closer look.

Click the View Link Table button on the toolbar to display the list of links. Right-click a link to flash it on the map, zoom or pan to it, or delete it.

If the preview looks good and the links are accurate, click Adjust on the Spatial Adjustment drop-down menu to go ahead and transform the features.

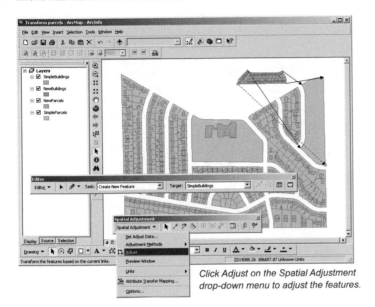

Click Adjust on the Spatial Adjustment drop-down menu to adjust the features.

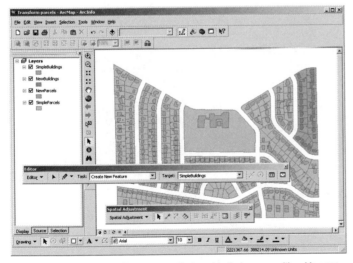

When you click Adjust, the features are displayed in their new position. You can use the Undo button on the Standard toolbar, if necessary.

To rubber sheet one set of features to match another, set the Spatial Adjustment method to Rubbersheet. You can also set the rubber sheeting method. Use Natural Neighbor when you have a few links, widely spread. The Linear method works best when you have many links, uniformly placed.

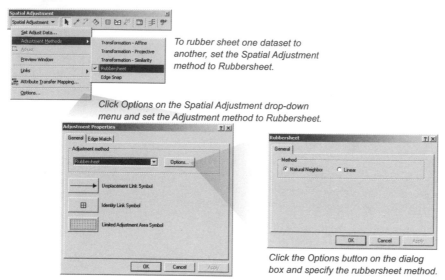

To rubber sheet one dataset to another, set the Spatial Adjustment method to Rubbersheet.

Click Options on the Spatial Adjustment drop-down menu and set the Adjustment method to Rubbersheet.

Click the Options button on the dialog box and specify the rubbersheet method.

To edge match features in two adjacent map sheets, set the Spatial Adjustment method to Edge Snap. Then open the Adjustment Properties dialog box to specify (on the Edge Match tab) which features will snap to which—the features in the source layer will snap to those in the target layer. You can also specify (on the General tab) the edge match method—Smooth (the default), or Line. The Line option moves only the last vertex on each line that's being adjusted; the Smooth option adjusts the entire line, providing a smoother effect along the matched edge.

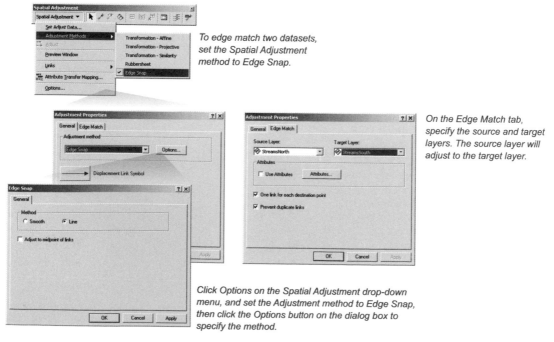

To edge match two datasets, set the Spatial Adjustment method to Edge Snap.

On the Edge Match tab, specify the source and target layers. The source layer will adjust to the target layer.

Click Options on the Spatial Adjustment drop-down menu, and set the Adjustment method to Edge Snap, then click the Options button on the dialog box to specify the method.

To create the links for edge matching, click the Edge Match tool on the Spatial Adjustment toolbar, and draw a rectangle that encompasses the edge to be matched — the links will be created automatically. You'll want to zoom to areas where features are bunched together to make sure the links are linking the correct features (use the link table to delete any incorrect links, then add them manually using the New Displacement Link button). You also need to select the features that will be matched—use the Edit tool on the Editor toolbar to draw a rectangle encompassing the edge to select the corresponding features in both layers.

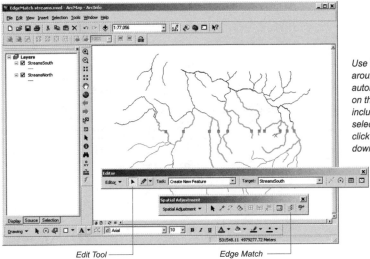

Use the Edge Match tool to draw a rectangle around the area to match—the links are automatically created. Then use the Edit tool on the Editor toolbar to select the features to include in the edge matching process—the selected features are highlighted. When you click Adjust from the Spatial Adjustment drop-down menu, the features are matched.

Edit Tool ————

Edge Match ————

Copying attributes from one feature to another

The Attribute Transfer tool, also on the Spatial Adjustment toolbar, lets you copy the attribute values from a feature in one dataset to a feature in another dataset. You'd do this, for example, to add street names and types to a new dataset of streets that extends existing streets before combining the datasets.

First, set the snapping environment, using the Editor drop-down menu (for line features, set the snapping to Edge). Then click Attribute Transfer Mapping on the Spatial Adjustment toolbar. In the dialog box, specify the source layer (the layer the attributes will be copied from) and the target layer. Select a source field in the left panel then the corresponding target field in the right panel, and add them to the list (this lets you copy attributes even if the fields aren't named the same). Include only those fields for which you want attribute values transferred.

By identifying the target feature (in red, left) before transferring attributes, you can see it has no values for Name and Type.

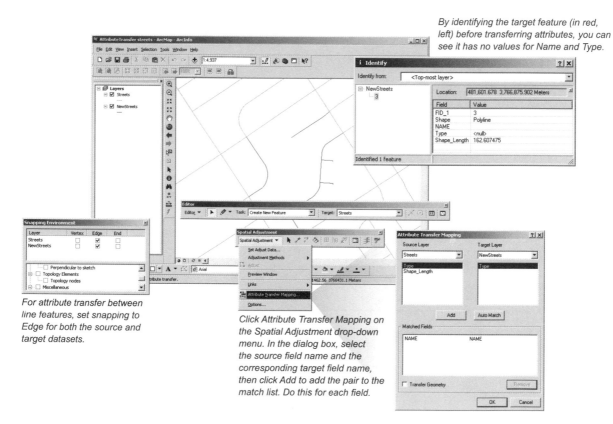

For attribute transfer between line features, set snapping to Edge for both the source and target datasets.

Click Attribute Transfer Mapping on the Spatial Adjustment drop-down menu. In the dialog box, select the source field name and the corresponding target field name, then click Add to add the pair to the match list. Do this for each field.

To copy the attributes, click Attribute Transfer on the Spatial Adjustment toolbar. Then, on the map, click a location on a source layer feature, and then click the target feature to receive the attribute values. The values are immediately copied to the target.

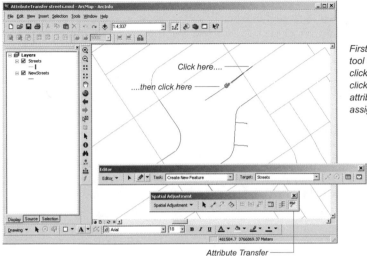

First click the Attribute Transfer tool on the toolbar (below). Next, click the source feature, then click the target feature—the attribute values are immediately assigned to the target.

After transferring attributes, the target feature has the same Name and Type values as the source feature.

Attribute Transfer

Combining datasets into a single dataset

Often, the ultimate goal of spatial adjustment and attribute transfer is to combine datasets containing the same type of feature to create a single dataset that covers your entire area of interest. For example, you may have edge matched a set of hydrology map sheets that need to be appended to create a continuous dataset. Or, you may have rubber sheeted datasets of new streets and parcels that fill a previously undeveloped area and want to drop them into the existing datasets. The Merge and Append tools in ArcToolbox are used for this. The Merge tool combines all the input datasets you specify into a single, new dataset. Append is similar, except it adds the datasets you specify to an existing dataset. In both cases, the types of features must be the same in all input datasets (all points or all lines, for example).

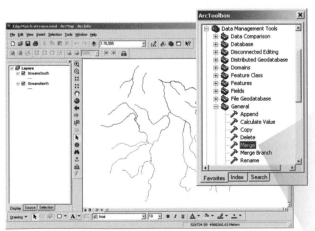

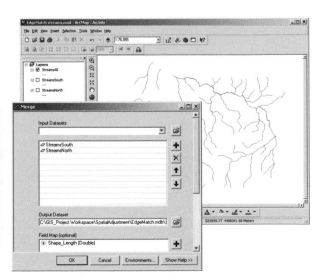

The Merge tool, located in the General toolset (Data Management toolbox) lets you combine two or more datasets of the same type into a single dataset. Specify the input datasets, and the name and location of the output dataset.

Editing multiuser and distributed geodatabases

Many organizations need to maintain large geodatabases that require frequent or continuous updating, such as a city's parcel database. This often entails having several people editing the database concurrently. When you start an edit session to edit a file geodatabase or personal geodatabase, or a workspace containing shapefiles, no one else can edit that data while your edit session is active (as soon as you stop the edit session, the data is available for others to edit). The entire geodatabase or workspace is said to be "locked" during editing. An ArcSDE geodatabase, on the other hand, can be edited by several people at the same time. This is one of the main reasons for using ArcSDE. ArcSDE accesses data stored in a DBMS, such as Oracle, SQL Server, DB2, or Informix (see 'An overview of geographic data management' and 'Creating a geodatabase' in Chapter 2 for more on creating an ArcSDE geodatabase).

There are several approaches to using ArcSDE to enable multiuser editing. One approach allows editors to work on the same dataset at the same time, but if an individual feature is edited by one editor, it is locked for editing—no other editors can change it, until the first editor saves the edits.

Another approach allows editors to work on the same dataset and even the same features simultaneously—when the last editor saves edits, any conflicts are listed (if one editor moved a point to new location, and another editor moved the same point to a different location, for example). The conflict then needs to be reconciled before the final edits can be saved in the geodatabase.

A third approach is to create a different view—or version—of the geodatabase for each editor, and let them work on their version independently. When an editor finishes edits and posts them to the main—or published—geodatabase, any conflicts are listed and can be reconciled. A version is simply a view of a geodatabase, rather than a copy of the data in it—no matter how many versions of the geodatabase you create, there is still only a single copy of the geodatabase. Each version lists or displays all the datasets in the geodatabase.

Versioning has a number of other advantages: you can create multiple versions of a geodatabase for sub-tasks or different phases of a project that can be edited separately from the original database, without having to create and track separate copies of the data (this is especially useful for very large geodatabases). You can create archive versions of a database to preserve a snapshot of the geodatabase at a given time. Versioning also allows you to perform editing operations that span several days or weeks—for example, adding all the parcels in a new subdivision. The editor maintains the edits in progress in a separate version and can continue to make changes and updates; when complete, the edits are posted to the published geodatabase (this process is referred to as a "long transaction").

A fourth approach is to create full copies of a geodatabase—known as replicas—which can be stored and edited separately. The replicas are then synchronized to make sure all the geodatabases are the same, and everyone is working with the same data. Using replicas may be efficient when the editing is done at multiple office locations or in the field, or when different departments or organizations are responsible for updating one portion of the geodatabase.

The approach you use depends on the size and requirements of your database and the nature of the GIS work your organization does. In practice, you may end up combining some or all of these approaches. You might, for example, create replicas, and then create versions from each replica, some of which are set up for multi-user editing, and some not.

The 'Geodatabases and ArcSDE' topic in the Desktop Help system includes various multiuser editing scenarios.

There are two mechanisms at play when you set up an ArcSDE geodatabase for multi-user editing: there can be multiple versions of a geodatabase; and each individual dataset in a geodatabase can be registered to allow several people to edit that dataset simultaneously.

- An ArcSDE geodatabase can have a single version or multiple versions. When you create an ArcSDE geodatabase, a version is created named Default, so every ArcSDE geodatabase has at least one version. This version often represents the "published" geodatabase. If necessary, you can then create additional, named versions from the Default version (or from other versions you create). Usually, you maintain and update the Default version over time by posting changes to it from other versions. You can also edit the Default version directly, just like any other version. But unlike other versions, it can't be deleted.

- Each dataset in an ArcSDE geodatabase can be registered as "versioned," or not. Registering a dataset as versioned allows two or more editors to edit and modify the same feature at the same time. If a dataset is not registered as versioned, several editors can still edit the dataset simultaneously, but an edited feature is locked until the editor who modified it saves the edit. With nonversioned data there are no possibilities for edit conflicts since a modified feature must be saved before another editor can modify it. Once you register a dataset as versioned, it is registered for all versions of the geodatabase you create (recall that there is only one copy of the dataset in the geodatabase, so any settings for a dataset apply across versions). You can edit versioned and nonversioned datasets in the same geodatabase, based on your requirements. If you need to edit feature classes that participate in a topology or a geometric network, you need to register the datasets as versioned in order to edit them. Registering a dataset as versioned also allows it to be enabled for archiving. The date and time of each edit, or series of edits, is stored with the dataset, which then lets you view the state of the geodatabase on any given date (see the Desktop Help for more on geodatabase archiving).

Depending on the multiuser editing scenario you establish, you might implement one or both of these mechanisms. For example, you might edit the default version of the geodatabase, with all of the datasets in the geodatabase registered as versioned (you might do this if you only need to maintain a single version of the geodatabase, but need to have several people editing it).

Editing an ArcSDE geodatabase using nonversioned data

Your organization may not need multiple versions of a geodatabase, but rather only the ability to have several people editing the geodatabase concurrently, for occasional edits. One way to do this is to set up the geodatabase for multi-user editing using the default version with nonversioned data. With this approach, the source data is edited directly and you don't have to manage separate versions of the geodatabase.

To edit using nonversioned data, first make sure the data is not registered as versioned (this is, in fact, the default when data is imported to, or created in, an ArcSDE geodatabase). In ArcCatalog, right-click the feature class or standalone table in the Catalog tree and click Properties. In the Versioning section on the General tab, make sure the dataset is listed as not currently versioned.

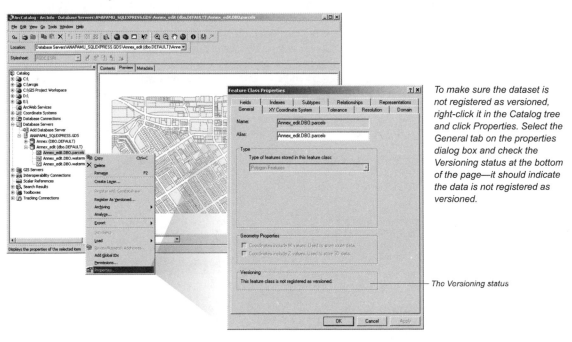

To make sure the dataset is not registered as versioned, right-click it in the Catalog tree and click Properties. Select the General tab on the properties dialog box and check the Versioning status at the bottom of the page—it should indicate the data is not registered as versioned.

— The Versioning status

When you're ready to start editing in ArcMap, display the Editing Options dialog box and uncheck the Edit a Version check box (this box is checked on by default). Then edit the data using any of the edit tools, as you would any other dataset.

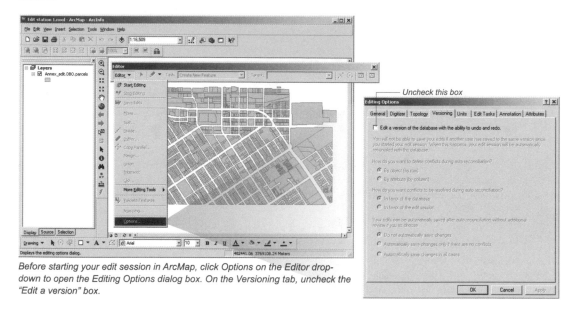

Before starting your edit session in ArcMap, click Options on the Editor drop-down to open the Editing Options dialog box. On the Versioning tab, uncheck the "Edit a version" box.

Usually this approach is used to allow people to edit different portions of a dataset at the same time (note that ArcSDE Personal Edition allows only one editor at a time, in any case). When one editor completes an operation (completing a polygon, for example), the feature locks. The feature remains locked until this editor either saves the edits or quits the edit session without saving. While the feature is locked, the other editors' edit operations on the feature are blocked, and the hourglass cursor displays in their ArcMap edit sessions. The hourglass continues to display until either the lock is released or the request for the lock times out (a setting in the underlying DBMS, if supported). Different DBMSs handle these locking issues in slightly different ways. Because of this data locking, you can edit simple data only—points, lines, polygons, annotation, and relationships. You cannot edit feature classes in a topology or geometric networks with this approach. (That's because when you edit a feature in a network or topology, not all the features in the network or topology are locked—there is the potential for other editors to edit another part of the network or topology in a way that conflicts with your edits.)

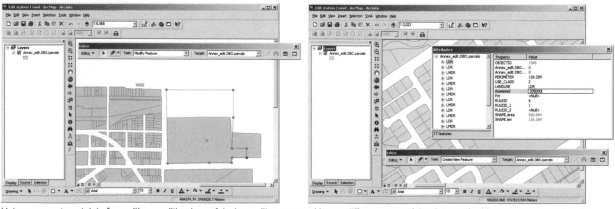

Using nonversioned data for multiuser editing is useful when editors are working on different parts of the dataset. In this example, one editor is updating parcel boundaries on one section of the city (left) while another editor is updating parcel attributes in another part of the city (right).

Editing using versioned data

Using versioned data allows two or more editors to edit the same features at the same time, without feature locking. It also allows multiuser editing of topologies or geometric networks. To edit versioned data, you "register as versioned" each individual dataset that will be edited. In ArcCatalog, right-click the dataset in the Catalog tree, and click Register As Versioned. You're presented with a window that gives you the option of moving the edits to base. This option is applicable when you're editing multiple geodatabase versions (as discussed later in this section) rather than just the default version, as you are here—leave it unchecked.

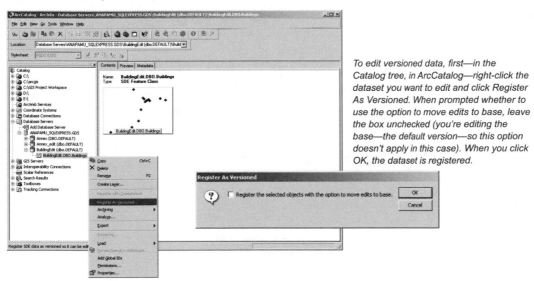

To edit versioned data, first—in the Catalog tree, in ArcCatalog—right-click the dataset you want to edit and click Register As Versioned. When prompted whether to use the option to move edits to base, leave the box unchecked (you're editing the base—the default version—so this option doesn't apply in this case). When you click OK, the dataset is registered.

Now when you check the Versioning status on the properties dialog box, the dataset is listed as registered as versioned (notice also that the Register As Versioned option on the context menu is now unavailable).

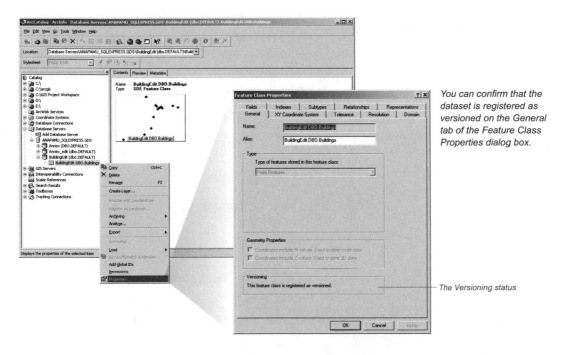

You can confirm that the dataset is registered as versioned on the General tab of the Feature Class Properties dialog box.

— *The Versioning status*

251

When you're ready to start your edit session in ArcMap, you need to make sure the Edit a Version option is checked on the Versioning tab of the Editing Options dialog box (this is the opposite of using nonversioned data).

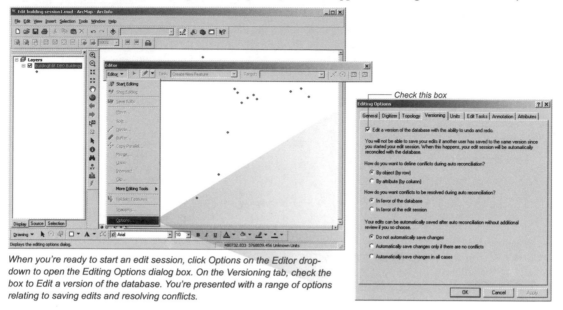

When you're ready to start an edit session, click Options on the Editor drop-down to open the Editing Options dialog box. On the Versioning tab, check the box to Edit a version of the database. You're presented with a range of options relating to saving edits and resolving conflicts.

When you register a dataset as versioned, a couple of tables (known as delta tables) are created to store the changes to the dataset—one for additions and one for deletions. ArcGIS uses an ID (known as a State ID) for each version to keep track of which changes belong to which version. When an edit is made in a version, the change is tagged with that version's State ID when it's stored in the delta table. When the editors save their edits, the changes are posted to the geodatabase, but all the changes continue to be maintained in the delta tables. The delta tables can get quite large over time, so you need to compress the geodatabase on a regular basis (see 'Maximizing the performance of your database' in Chapter 2).

Two or more editors concurrently editing the same feature or features can edit without any locking during their respective edit sessions—it's as if they're editing their own version. (In fact, they are editing temporary, unnamed versions created from the Default version that are discarded at the end of the edit session.) When the editor saves his or her edits, the edits are saved in the Default version.

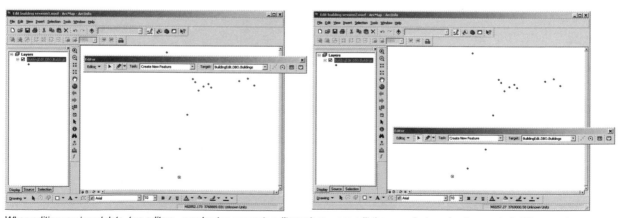

When editing versioned data, two editors—running two separate edit sessions—can edit the same feature simultaneously. In this example, the editor running the edit session on the left has moved a point feature to the lower center of the map (blue dot). The editor on the right has moved the same feature to a location farther to the left. They each see their own version of the dataset. If one of the editors saves the edit, when the other editor saves the edit there will be a conflict.

In a perfect world, and with good planning and editing procedures, none of the edits made by different editors would conflict with each other. Editors working on the dataset concurrently will either work on different sets of features in different parts of the geographic area, or will work sequentially, with one editor entering more recent information; or perhaps one editor will edit the geometry of features while another will edit the attributes. However, with several editors working on the same data at the same time, there is the potential for edits made on the same feature by two (or more) editors to conflict with each other. For example, suppose two people are editing a feature class of points representing building locations, and one moves a point to one location and the other editor moves the same point to a different location. The first editor then saves edits. When the second editor saves edits, the Conflicts window will appear, indicating a conflict in the edits. Click the Conflict Display button to open a panel that lets you view the conflicting edit—the previously saved edit (the pre-reconcile edit) is shown on the left while the current edit (the one that's causing the conflict) is shown on the right.

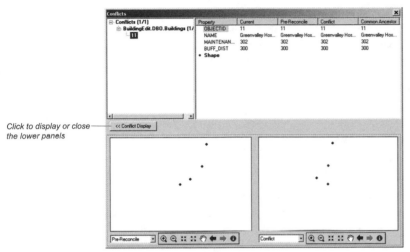

Click to display or close the lower panels

If there are conflicts between edits, the Conflicts window will appear when the second editor saves the edits. Use the Conflict Display button to display panels showing the two edited versions. Select a conflict in the left panel to display the details.

Right-click the feature listed in the left panel, or any of the rows in the right panel, to display additional display options. You can also select a solution to the conflict—use the pre-reconcile edit, use the conflict edit, or discard them both and go back to the location of the feature before either of the edits (the common ancestor).

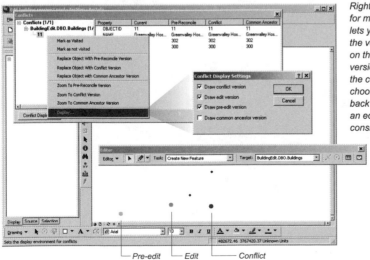

Right-click a conflict in either panel for more options. The Display option lets you show any combination of the versions of the edited feature on the current map—the original version, the previously saved edit, or the conflict edit. The list also lets you choose a solution (or, you can go back and edit one of the versions in an edit session so the versions are consistent).

Pre-edit — Edit — Conflict

Creating and editing multiple geodatabase versions

If you have several editors working over multiple edit sessions (days, weeks, or longer), or if you want to edit subprojects or phases of a project separately while leaving the published geodatabase intact, you can create multiple versions of a geodatabase. There are a number of issues to consider when deciding whether, and how, to create multiple versions, including:

- How to structure the versions, whether parallel (such as when having multiple editors work on the same database), sequential (such as when editing phases of a project), or hierarchical (such as when editing several subprojects)

- How to resolve edit conflicts between versions

- Which version to post edits to, and how often

You'll base these decisions on the editing procedures and workflows you've established.

The Default version is created when you create an ArcSDE geodatabase. The first derived version you create is from this Default version. You can create additional versions from the Default version or from any of the versions you create. You could, for example, create versions corresponding to phases of a project—the version for the next phase would be created from the version for the previous phase.

You create new geodatabase versions with ArcCatalog or ArcMap. When you create a version, you specify its name, an optional description, and the version's permission. You set the permission to ensure only those users who need to edit the data have access to it, thus providing a level of quality assurance and security. The options are:

- Private—the owner may view the version and modify available datasets.

- Public—anyone may view the version and modify available datasets.

- Protected—anyone may view the version, but only the owner may modify available datasets.

To create a geodatabase version in ArcCatalog, right-click a geodatabase in the Catalog tree and click Versions to open the Version Manager dialog box. Then right-click the version from which you want to derive the new version, and click New.

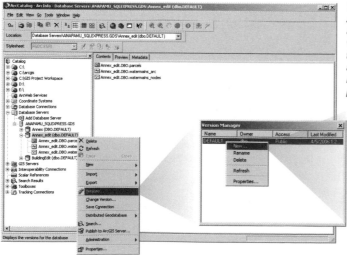

To create versions of an ArcSDE geodatabase using ArcCatalog, right-click the geodatabase in the Catalog tree and click Versions. In the Version Manager, select the existing version from which the new version will be created (initially there is only one—the default version). Right-click the version and click New. Then, in the dialog box, enter the name of the new version and (optionally) a description. Then specify the permission to assign to the version.

Creating a version does not change which version is currently displayed in the Catalog tree (only one version is displayed at a time). When you open the Version Manager, you can see all the versions—for which you have permission—that have been created for that geodatabase.

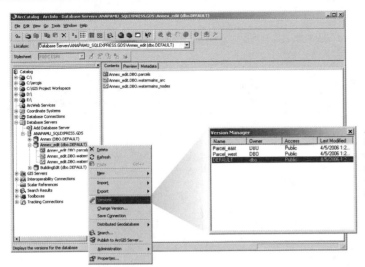

After creating a new version,
the previous version will still be
displayed in the tree. Right-click the
geodatabase and click Versions to
see a list of all the versions for that
geodatabase.

To display and work with a different version in the Catalog tree, right-click the geodatabase and click Change Versions. Then select the version to display from the list that appears. (You can think of viewing versions like viewing pages lined up exactly behind each other—when you change to a page, that page is brought to the front so you can view and work with it. The other pages are still there, lined up behind the front page.)

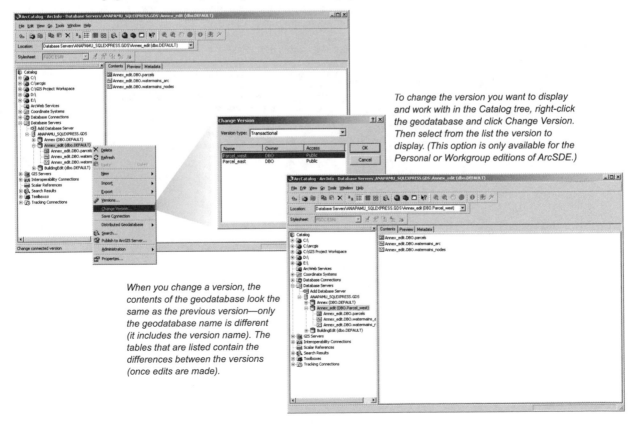

To change the version you want to display
and work with in the Catalog tree, right-click
the geodatabase and click Change Version.
Then select from the list the version to
display. (This option is only available for the
Personal or Workgroup editions of ArcSDE.)

When you change a version, the
contents of the geodatabase look the
same as the previous version—only
the geodatabase name is different
(it includes the version name). The
tables that are listed contain the
differences between the versions
(once edits are made).

To alter the permission of a version (or change its description), right-click the version and click Properties.

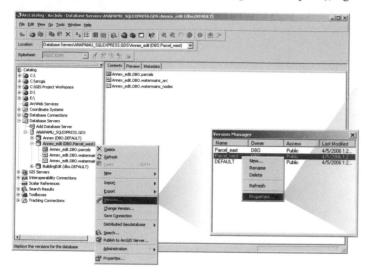 

To change the description or permissions for a version, open the Version Manager, right-click the version you want to modify, and click Properties.

To display a version in ArcMap, you add data to your map just like you would add any other data. The data initially added comes from the version specified in the database connection properties dialog box. You can then switch to the version you want to display and edit. (Alternatively, you can display the version you want to work with in ArcCatalog, and then drag and drop the datasets from that version onto your map in ArcMap.)

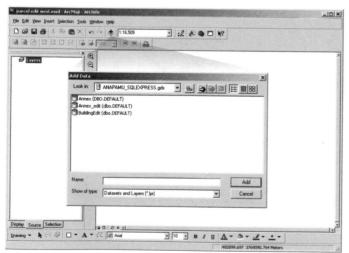

When you add data from a geodatabase with versions in ArcMap, the version you're currently connected to is displayed in the Add Data dialog box (double-click the geodatabase to display the datasets). You can then change to another version after adding the data. If you add data by dragging from ArcCatalog, you can add any dataset from the currently displayed version in the Catalog tree.

To change versions, click the Source tab at the bottom of the table of contents, right-click the geodatabase, and click Change Versions. Then select the version to display. When you switch from one version to another, all datasets present in the map change to be those in the version to which you've switched.

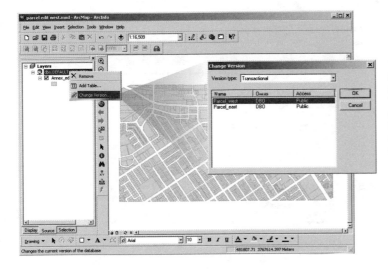

To change versions in ArcMap, first select the Source tab at the bottom of the table of contents. Then right-click the geodatabase in the table of contents, and click Change Versions. In the dialog box, select the version you want to change to.

The Versioning toolbar in ArcMap also lets you manage versions. On the Editor drop-down menu, click More Editing Tools, and click Versioning (you don't need to be in an active edit session to do this). You can also open the toolbar from the View menu (click Toolbars and click Versioning).

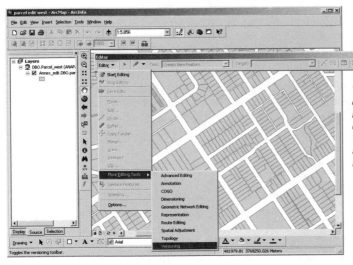

To open the Versioning toolbar, click More Editing Tools on the Editor drop-down menu, and click Versioning. Or, click the View menu, point to Toolbars, and click Versioning (at the bottom of the list).

From the toolbar you can manage existing versions, create new ones, or change versions (if the geodatabase is currently selected on the Source tab; otherwise, this button is unavailable).

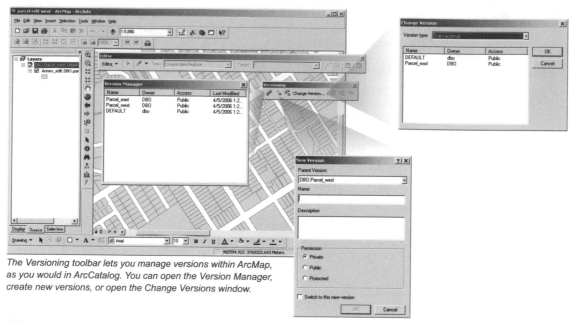

The Versioning toolbar lets you manage versions within ArcMap, as you would in ArcCatalog. You can open the Version Manager, create new versions, or open the Change Versions window.

When editing a geodatabase version, you can edit a versioned or nonversioned dataset, as described above (once a dataset is registered as versioned, it will have that status across all geodatabase versions). When you register data as versioned, you have the option to "move edits to base" (you'd choose to move edits to base if the updates need to be shared with other applications that access your RDBMS). If you register with the option to move edits to base, edits to the Default version save to the base tables (the tables containing the actual datasets), while edits to all other versions save to the delta tables but are moved to the base tables when you post to the default version. If you don't use this option, all edits save to the delta tables—including those made to the Default version. When you create a second (or third) version of the geodatabase, new delta tables are not created—rather all changes for all versions go into the same set of delta tables, and are tracked by version, using the State ID.

When editing versioned data with multiple versions, the concepts are basically the same as when editors are editing a single version. However with multiple versions, when editors save their edits, the edits are saved only in their version. When they've finished the edits, they reconcile them with other versions, at which point any conflicts are revealed and can be reviewed.

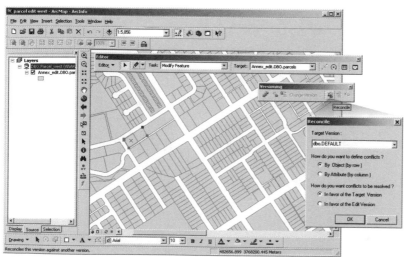

After making edits, click the Reconcile button to see if your edits conflict with any others that have been made to the target version. You can opt to use the edit currently in the target version, or use the one in the edit version that you're working with.

Once the edits are reconciled, the editor can post them to the target database (often the default version). Posting cannot be undone, since you are applying changes to a version you are not currently editing. This process allows editors to conduct ongoing edits over several edit sessions (so-called "long transactions") without having to save the edits in the published database until all the edits are done. Reconciling, resolving conflicts, and posting edits are all done from the Versioning toolbar.

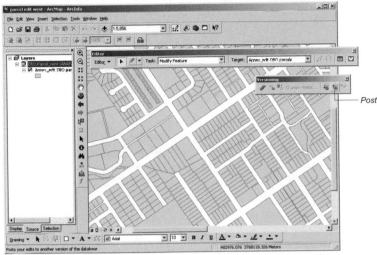

— Post

*Once any conflicting edits are reconciled, click the Post button to save the edits
in the target version (usually the Default version).*

After posting, you can continue to make edits and then reconcile and post edits again, as necessary. Once editing is completed, the version can be deleted, if it's no longer needed—open the Version Manager, right-click the version, and click Delete. You can delete a version provided all the versions derived from it are first deleted. Only the version's owner (or the ArcSDE administrator) can delete a version.

ArcToolbox also contains a number of tools for creating and managing geodatabase versions and versioned datasets. These can be used in scripts and models to automate data management tasks.

*The Versions toolset in the Data
Management toolbox contains tools
for creating and managing versioned
geodatabases and datasets.*

Creating geodatabase replicas for distributed editing

Creating geodatabase replicas allows you to create copies of data across two or more geodatabases, make changes to the geodatabases separately, and then synchronize the changes so the geodatabases remain consistent with each other. As you might imagine, creating, synchronizing, and managing replicas is a fairly involved process that requires planning, preparation of the data, and coordination between the sites that will maintain the replicas. There are also a number of options for the type of replicas to create and methods for synchronization. The Desktop Help includes a full discussion of tasks and steps for using replicas.

When you create a replica, you're creating a relationship between two geodatabases. The replica in the geodatabase from which the data originated is referred to as the "parent" replica. The replica in the geodatabase where the data is copied to is referred to as the "child" replica. Three types of replicas allow you to control whether the parent replica, the child replica, or both replicas have the ability to send and receive changes: check out/check in replicas; one way replicas; and two way replicas.

A check out/check in replica allows for one-time synchronization. Changes can only be sent from the child replica to the parent replica. Parent replicas must be ArcSDE geodatabases while child replicas can be ArcSDE, file or personal geodatabases. Check out/check in replication is useful for field editing where an area of the geodatabase is replicated, edited in the field, and synchronized with the parent replica. If additional field edits are required, another child replica must be created.

A one way replica allows changes to be sent multiple times, but only from the parent replica to the child replica. The data on the parent is editable, but the data on the child is considered read-only (any edits to the child replica are overwritten during synchronization if they conflict with edits to the parent replica).

Two way replicas allows changes to be sent multiple times from the parent replica to the child replica or from the child replica to the parent replica. If the same feature is edited in both geodatabases it is detected as a conflict when the replicas are synchronized. You can choose a reconcile policy during synchronization to define how conflicts are processed.

The first step in preparing data for replication is to make sure the datasets you would like to replicate are registered as versioned (see the discussion earlier in this section). For one way and two way replication, each replicated dataset will also need to have a Global ID column. A Global ID column is a field which cannot be edited that contains a unique identifier for each row (feature) in a dataset. (Global ID fields are not necessary for check out/check in replication because the Object ID that each feature in a dataset has is sufficient to maintain feature identity during one-time synchronization.) To add Global IDs, use the Add Global IDs command in ArcCatalog.

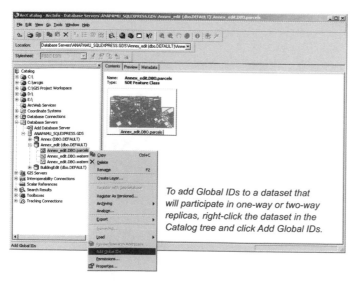

To add Global IDs to a dataset that will participate in one-way or two-way replicas, right-click the dataset in the Catalog tree and click Add Global IDs.

Replicas are created in ArcMap, using the Distributed Geodatabase toolbar. When you click the Create Replica button, a wizard opens to lead you through the process.

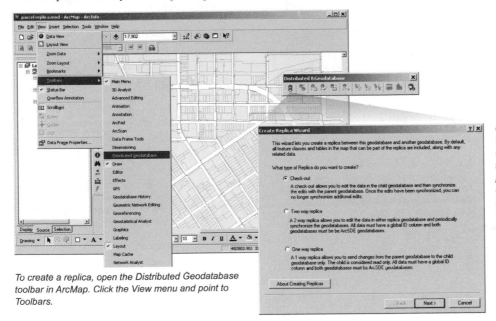

To create a replica, open the Distributed Geodatabase toolbar in ArcMap. Click the View menu and point to Toolbars.

Open the Create Replica Wizard from the Distributed Geodatabase toolbar. Specify the type of replica on the first panel (Check out/Check in, one way, or two way). Then on the second and third panels, specify the name of the replica and where it will be stored, and the actions to take after the replica is created (for example, you can have the wizard create a new map containing the replica).

Synchronizing replicas—after changes are made—is also done from the Distributed Geodatabase toolbar. Clicking the Synchronize Changes button opens a wizard that leads you through the process. You specify the two geodatabases to synchronize, the direction changes will be sent (if you're synchronizing a two-way replica), and how to handle edit conflicts.

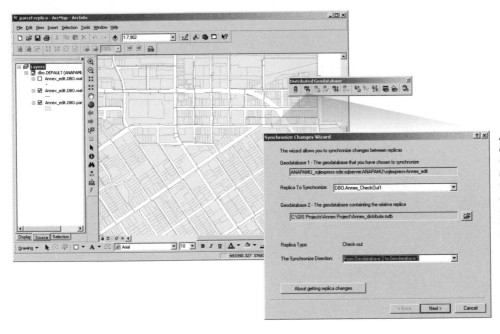

After the replica has been edited, open the Synchronize Changes Wizard from the toolbar to synchronize edits with the parent replica or any other replicas. The Distributed Geodatabase toolbar contains additional tools for managing replicas.

Replicas can also be synchronized and managed in ArcCatalog. Right-click the geodatabase containing the replica and click Distributed Geodatabase. ArcToolbox also contains a full set of tools for creating, synchronizing, and managing replicas. These are located in the Distributed Geodatabase toolset in the Data Management toolbox.

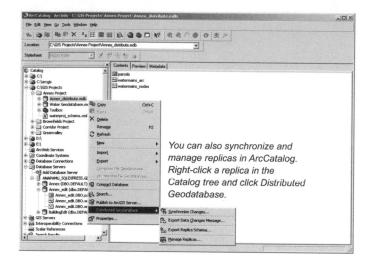

You can also synchronize and manage replicas in ArcCatalog. Right-click a replica in the Catalog tree and click Distributed Geodatabase.

The Distributed Geodatabase toolset in the Data Management toolbox contains tools for creating, synchronizing, and managing replicas.

Mapping and Visualization

An overview of mapping and visualization

Maps are the primary means for communicating geographic information. ArcMap is the primary application in ArcGIS for making maps. ArcMap is where you display and query datasets, where you display the output from your geographic analysis, and where you create finished maps for printing or for publishing over a network or on the internet.

Beyond maps, storing geographic data in digital format on a computer gives you other ways of displaying information, such as perspective views, globe views, and animations. ArcScene and ArcGlobe™—included with the ArcGIS 3D Analyst extension—allow you to create perspective and globe views. The animation toolbar in ArcMap, ArcScene, and ArcGlobe allows you to capture a sequence of maps or views and play them back as an animation. The Tracking Analyst extension provides advanced capabilities for displaying and animating temporal data.

The process for creating a map in ArcMap

As with other GIS tasks, creating a map—whether for simple display of your data or for creating a finished cartographic product for publication—is a process. Before creating your map, you'll want to give some thought to the purpose of the map and its design:

- Who is the audience for the map? Are you making the map for your own use or to share with a few peers, or will it be presented to a larger group of people? Is the audience professional, or the general public?

- What geographic area, or areas, does the map need to show? What is the map scale? Do you need to include a reference map showing a larger area? The map area (or extent) and the scale will help determine how much detail to show on the map.

- Are there standard symbols or colors that are required (often the case in particular industries)?

- How will the map be displayed or distributed? Will it be in a PowerPoint® presentation, in a printed report, displayed on a wall, or distributed over the internet? The size and media will determine how much additional information is required—such as legends, titles, labels, and so on.

These are just some of the issues you'll want to consider. Several resources for learning more about map design and production are listed in the appendix.

There are a few basic steps used to create almost all maps. For a specific map, you may skip some of these, or you may perform additional, more advanced tasks. Making a map is often an iterative process, so you may not always follow the steps in this order.

Open ArcMap

When you open ArcMap (from ArcCatalog or from the ArcGIS program group on the Start menu), you're prompted to create a new map or open an existing one. The table of contents is initially empty except for a default data frame (named Layers), and the display window is blank.

A new, empty map

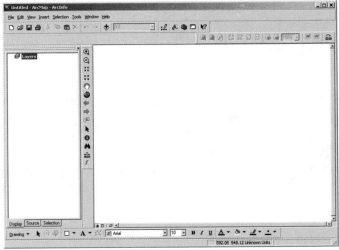

When creating a new map, you add GIS data to this empty map. The data can be:

- stored locally on your computer, either on disk or on a CD/DVD
- from a shared database or GIS server you connect to
- on the Internet

In any case, the data must be in a format ArcMap can read directly, such as a geodatabase feature class, a shapefile, or a compatible raster format (see 'An overview of data compilation and editing' in Chapter 3).

Find and connect to GIS data

The next step is to find the data (from whichever source) and set up a connection to it, if necessary. ArcCatalog provides an efficient way of doing this, since you can quickly see and preview large amounts of GIS data (See 'Finding and connecting to data' in Chapter 2). You can also search for data from within ArcMap.

Add data to your map

After you've found the data you want, you add it by dragging it from ArcCatalog, or by browsing to it in the ArcMap Add Data dialog box. You can also add data directly from the Internet—either from the Geography Network, or by entering the URL of a site containing geographic data.

Search for, preview, and connect to data in ArcCatalog, then drag the dataset to ArcMap.....

....or search for and add data in ArcMap, using the Add Data button....

....or add data directly from the Internet.

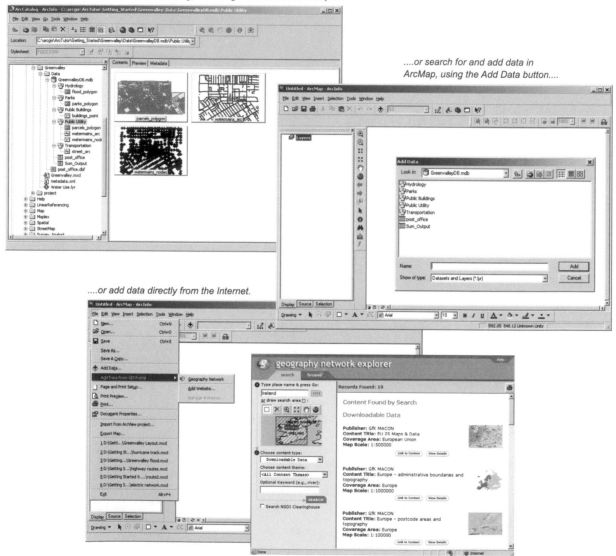

Reset the map extent

By default, the map display is set to the extent and coordinate system of the first dataset you add. Depending on the extent of the individual datasets, and the order in which you add them to the map, you may need to change the map extent for the display window to show the area you're interested in. Two quick ways to do this are to use the navigation tools to zoom and pan, or to zoom to a specific layer. You can also set a fixed map scale or extent.

Navigation tools

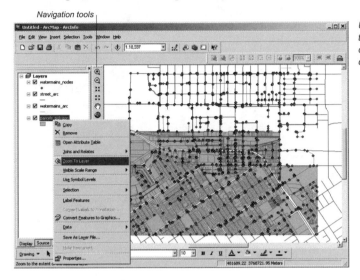

Use the navigation tools to zoom and pan, or right-click a layer in the table of contents to zoom to it.

Modify the map display

You may also want to change the layer drawing order, set transparencies, or give layers more descriptive names (only the layer in the map is renamed, not the underlying dataset).

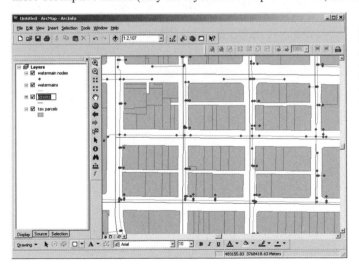

Type over a layer name in the table of contents to rename it; drag layers up or down in the table of contents to change the drawing order; double-click a layer name and select the Display tab to set the transparency.

Assign symbols

When data is added to the map to create a layer, a default symbol is assigned. The next step is often to change the symbols to make the map easier to read or to assign symbols based on attribute values (categories or class ranges).

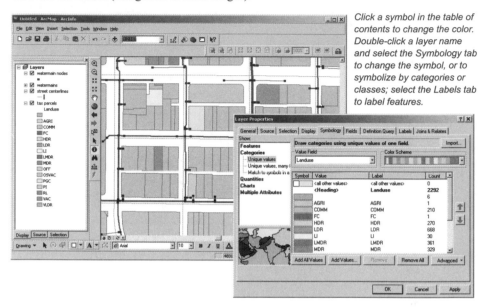

Click a symbol in the table of contents to change the color. Double-click a layer name and select the Symbology tab to change the symbol, or to symbolize by categories or classes; select the Labels tab to label features.

If you're creating a map to use for interactive query or to display the inputs and outputs from an analysis, you'll likely use simple symbols that make the map easy to read on the computer screen. If you're creating a map for publication, you'll likely spend more time on assigning symbols—perhaps using a set of standard symbols or even creating custom symbols—to ensure the map effectively presents all the information you want to convey to the readers. In any case, you'll want to choose symbols with some thought for how they represent the layers and how they appear with each other.

Create labels and graphic objects

You may also want to label features with descriptive information, or add graphic objects to highlight aspects of the map.

For a simple map being used to display data, basic map labels or graphic text will suffice to identify features. If you're creating a map for publication, you'll probably want to create annotation, which lets you place and edit each text string individually (see 'Creating and editing annotation' in Chapter 3).

Organize the data

Data is added to the active data frame (there is only one to begin with, but you can insert more). Use additional data frames to group datasets or to create multiple data views on a single map (especially useful for published maps).

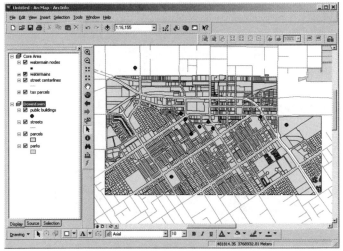

Use the Insert menu to add data frames. Right-click a layer name to copy or delete it.

If you're making a map to explore and query your data, at this point the process is pretty much complete. You'll likely continue to work with the map—possibly changing data classification schemes, removing or adding datasets as necessary, performing queries, making measurements, summarizing attribute values, creating charts and reports, and so on.

If you're making a map for publication, you'll undertake a few additional steps.

Create a map layout

The first step in creating a map for publication is to create a map layout on the page. To do this you switch to layout view, which shows you how the data frames will appear on the page. You can move and resize data frames, and add new ones to show multiple data views on a single page.

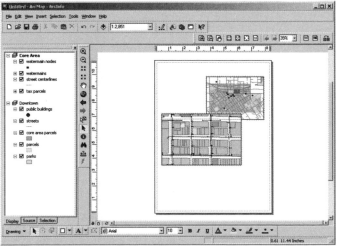

Use the View menu to switch to Layout View. Then select a data frame on the page to move or resize it.

In fact, if you know your map is for publication, it's a good idea to have a sense of the layout you want before you start creating the map. You'll want to at least set up the page size and orientation (on the File menu). And, while you can insert new data frames and move layers around after you've added data to your map, it's more efficient to create all the data frames up front and place the data in the appropriate data frame as you add it to the map.

Add map elements

Finally, you'll add map elements to the page, such as legends, titles, neatlines, scalebars, and north arrows. You might also add charts, reports, text blocks, and logos. Once you've arranged the various elements, you're ready to print the map or publish it to the Internet.

Use the Insert menu to add legends, titles, and so on. To move an element on the page, select and drag it.

**Visualization—
other ways of
looking at GIS data**

Visualizations, such as perspective views, animated fly-overs and globe views, and time-series animations, can be an effective way of presenting information, especially to audiences not accustomed to reading specialized maps.

Perspective views are created using the ArcScene application in ArcGIS 3D Analyst. 3D Analyst allows you to navigate through the scene interactively as well as capture and store animated fly-throughs. For realism, 3D symbols, such as trees or light poles, can be added to the scene.

Use an elevation surface—or any other surface with z values—to create a base for the perspective view. Then drape other layers on top.

ArcScene also lets you extrude features to create, for example, a 3D model of buildings in a city, or a perspective view of a thematic map.

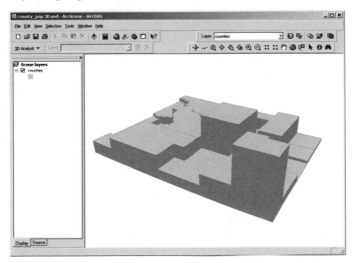

ArcScene lets you extrude features to create 3D maps—in this case, showing the relative population of each county.

Globe views are created using the ArcGlobe application, included in ArcGIS 3D Analyst. A key feature of ArcGlobe is the ability to reveal more detailed layers of information as you zoom in. As with ArcScene, you can work interactively—rotating the globe, zooming in and out—and capture the navigation path as an animation.

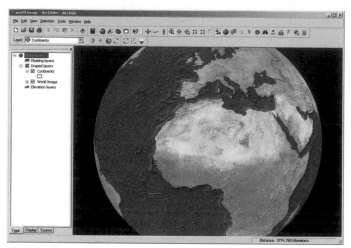

The default view in ArcGlobe includes a shaded relief image of the earth. Add your own local, regional, or global layers.

Maps in ArcMap can also be used to make animations. The Animation toolbar lets you capture a series of increasingly zoomed in views, or create an animation that pans across a region. Time-series data can be viewed using the Animation toolbar or using Tracking Analyst. You can step through the data, or create, store, and replay animations. You might animate the path of a storm over several days, for example, or the population growth in each county over several decades.

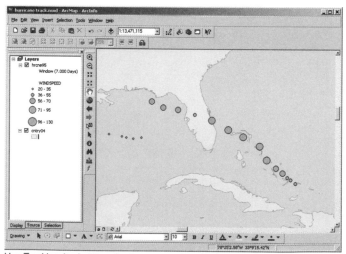

Use Tracking Analyst to animate movement or change over time—in this case, the path and strength of a storm.

Adding data to a map

There are several ways to add a dataset to a map—drag it from ArcCatalog, use the ArcMap Add Data dialog box to browse to it, add data directly from the Internet, or add a table of features that have fields containing geographic coordinates. When you add a dataset, it becomes a layer on the map. Once you've added a layer you can display the dataset and its associated attributes. A layer references the underlying dataset, so on a single map you can have multiple layers created from the same data, each drawn with different symbols or representing different attributes—for example, one layer of census tracts showing population and another layer of the same tracts showing median income.

Dragging and dropping from ArcCatalog

You can drag data from any folder or connection that appears in ArcCatalog (in either the tree view or in the Contents panel) and drop it onto the display window or table of contents in ArcMap. The data is added as a layer on the map. See 'Finding and connecting to data' in Chapter 2.

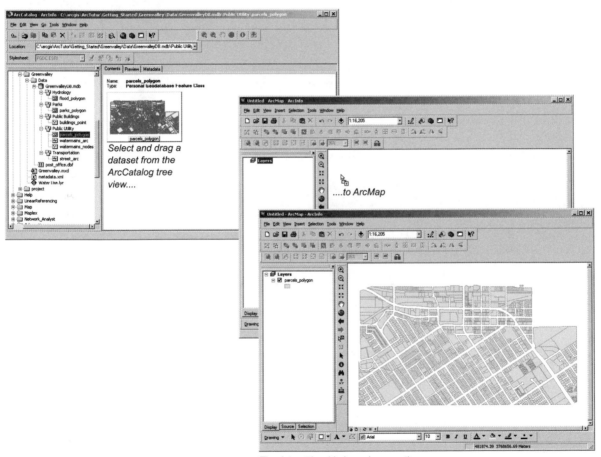

Select and drag a dataset from the ArcCatalog tree view....

....to ArcMap

The dataset is added as a layer on the map.

If you're adding data to an existing map, you can drag it to a specific position in the table of contents so it draws on top of (or beneath) other layers.

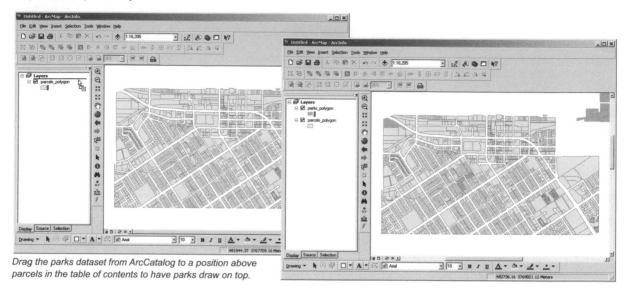

Drag the parks dataset from ArcCatalog to a position above parcels in the table of contents to have parks draw on top.

Adding data from a folder or other connection

In ArcMap, use Add Data on the File menu, or the Add Data button, to locate and add data to the map—any connections you have established show up on the list. You can also add a new connection, as well as display the thumbnails for the datasets or a list with dataset details such as file type. In other words, the Add Data dialog box is like a mini-ArcCatalog.

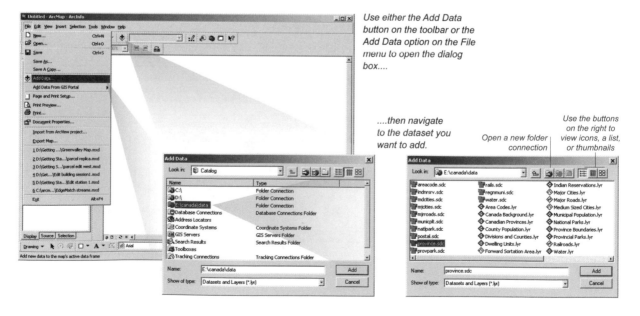

Use either the Add Data button on the toolbar or the Add Data option on the File menu to open the dialog box....

....then navigate to the dataset you want to add.

Open a new folder connection

Use the buttons on the right to view icons, a list, or thumbnails

Adding data directly from the internet

To add data directly from the Internet, use Add Data from GIS Portal on the File menu. If you know the URL of a metadata server, such as a regional GIS data clearinghouse, you can enter it and go directly there to access available data. Or, you can go to the Geography Network and search or browse for data to add to your map. Much of the data is free; some requires a fee to download.

Select Add Data from GIS Portal on the File menu to go directly to the Geography Network or to enter the address of a Web site.

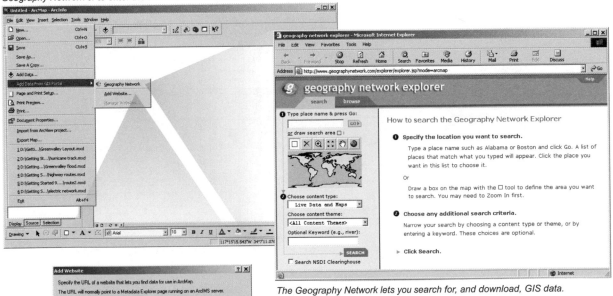

The Geography Network lets you search for, and download, GIS data.

Enter the URL of an ArcIMS metadata service, such as a regional GIS data clearinghouse.

Adding x,y coordinate data

To add data from a table of locations, such as data collected with a GPS unit, use Add XY Data on the Tools menu. Each location must have associated x and y coordinates stored in separate fields, as well as a unique identifier.

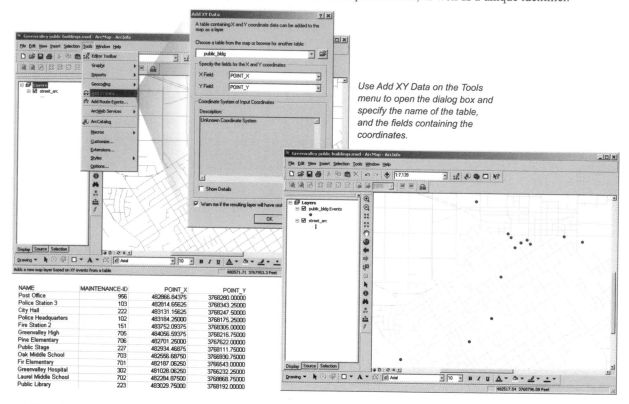

Use Add XY Data on the Tools menu to open the dialog box and specify the name of the table, and the fields containing the coordinates.

NAME	MAINTENANCE-ID	POINT_X	POINT_Y
Post Office	956	482866.84375	3768280.00000
Police Station 3	103	482814.65625	3768343.25000
City Hall	222	483131.15625	3768247.50000
Police Headquarters	102	483184.25000	3768175.25000
Fire Station 2	151	483752.09375	3768305.00000
Greenvalley High	705	484056.59375	3768216.75000
Pine Elementary	706	482701.25000	3767622.00000
Public Stage	227	482934.46875	3768111.75000
Oak Middle School	703	482556.68750	3766930.75000
Fir Elementary	701	482187.06250	3766543.00000
Greenvalley Hospital	302	481028.06250	3766232.25000
Laurel Middle School	702	482284.87500	3768868.75000
Public Library	223	483029.75000	3768192.00000

Adding datasets having different coordinate systems

The coordinate system for the data frame you're adding layers to is that of the first layer added, by default, but you can also set the coordinate system manually. If you're adding data from various sources, rather than data stored in a single geodatabase, the coordinate system of the dataset might not match that of the data frame. If a spatial reference is defined for a dataset you're adding, ArcMap projects the layer on the fly (the spatial reference of the underlying data is not modified). If a dataset does not have the same underlying geographic coordinate system as the data frame or if the dataset you're adding does not have a spatial reference defined, warnings are displayed. See 'Defining coordinate systems and projecting datasets' in Chapter 3 for a discussion of assigning a spatial reference to a dataset.

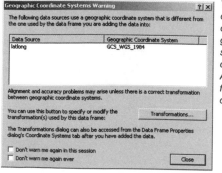

This warning means the dataset you're adding does not have the same geographic coordinate system as the other data in the data frame— ArcMap projects it on the fly, but it may not register correctly.

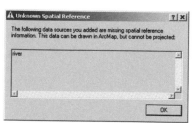

This warning means the dataset you're adding does not have a spatial reference defined—if it is, in fact, in the same coordinate system, it will correctly register; otherwise, it may not.

Working with layers

When you add a dataset to a map, a layer is created. In the course of making your maps, you'll add and remove layers, turn them on and off, change the drawing order, and so on, to display exactly the data you need to see and work with.

Controlling what's drawn on the map

You use the table of contents to control how the layers are displayed. Use the check boxes to turn layers on and off. Use the + and - signs to display or hide a layer's legend. When you add data to create a layer, the layer is assigned a position on the table of contents based on its data type. For example, lines are added above polygons, and points are added above lines.

New layers are positioned above existing layers of the same type. The order in the table of contents determines the drawing order on the map—a layer draws on top of layers listed below it in the table of contents and under layers above it.) Change the drawing order by clicking a layer name in the table of contents and dragging it to a new position.

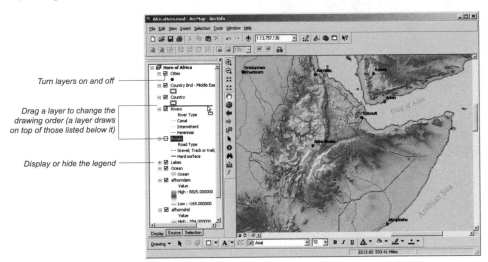

Turn layers on and off

Drag a layer to change the drawing order (a layer draws on top of those listed below it)

Display or hide the legend

Managing data layers

The table of contents is also where you rename, copy, or remove layers from the map. Since a layer points to an underlying dataset, if the dataset is moved or deleted, the link is broken and the layer can't be drawn on the map (a red exclamation mark next to a layer in the table of contents indicates this). Use the layer's properties dialog box to reset the source (right-click the layer name and click Properties at the bottom of the context menu) or click the exclamation mark. The properties dialog box also lets you access all of a layer's properties, including how it's symbolized, which features are displayed, and so on. It can also be opened by double-clicking a layer name.

Layers can be copied as layers on the same map, saved as layer files to be added to other maps, or exported to new datasets (you'd do this to create a new dataset containing a selected set of features in a layer, to be used in analysis). To save a layer file, or export it, right-click the layer name to display the context menu.

Right-click a layer name and click Copy; then right-click the data frame and click Paste Layer(s).

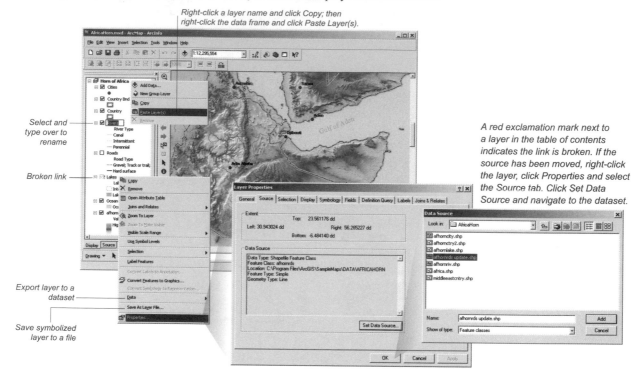

Select and type over to rename

Broken link

Export layer to a dataset

Save symbolized layer to a file

A red exclamation mark next to a layer in the table of contents indicates the link is broken. If the source has been moved, right-click the layer, click Properties and select the Source tab. Click Set Data Source and navigate to the dataset.

Individual layers within a data frame can be grouped by creating what's known as a group layer. The layers can then be managed as a unit. When you turn the group layer on, all the layers in it are displayed. Group layers are especially useful if there are many layers on your map, or if you have layers that are always displayed together on maps. Using group layers is also an efficient way to share data and maps. A group layer can be copied or saved as a file—all the layers in the group are saved or copied together. To create a group layer, right-click a data frame name in the table of contents and click New Group Layer. You then drag individual layers under the group layer, or copy and paste them.

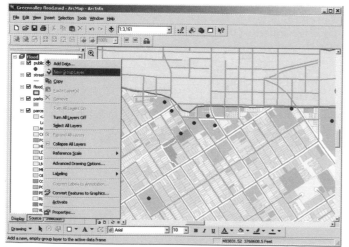

To create a group layer, right-click the data frame name in the table of contents and click New Group Layer. Then drag or add layers under the group layer. Click the group layer check box to turn all the layers on or off. If the group is on, individual layers under it can be turned off; if the group is off, the layers under it will not be displayed.

Setting the map extent and scale

The map extent and scale determine the geographic area that is displayed on the map. ArcMap includes a number of ways to set the map extent. You can zoom in and out and pan the display, step through or save extents.

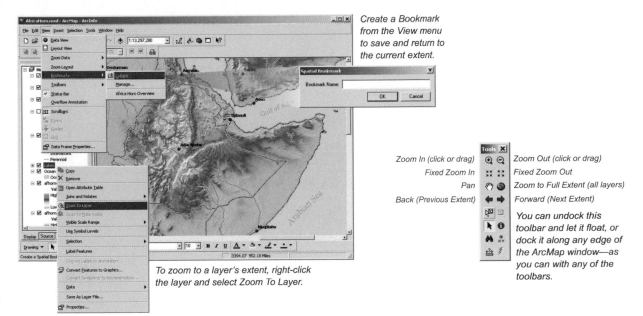

Create a Bookmark from the View menu to save and return to the current extent.

To zoom to a layer's extent, right-click the layer and select Zoom To Layer.

Zoom In (click or drag) / Zoom Out (click or drag)
Fixed Zoom In / Fixed Zoom Out
Pan / Zoom to Full Extent (all layers)
Back (Previous Extent) / Forward (Next Extent)

You can undock this toolbar and let it float, or dock it along any edge of the ArcMap window—as you can with any of the toolbars.

The My Places option on the Tools menu lets you create a list of frequently visited locations that you can zoom or pan to. The places can be created from the current map extent or from a selected feature (or features). Unlike bookmarks, which are stored with the current map document, your My Places list can be accessed from any ArcMap map document, ArcScene view, or ArcGlobe view.

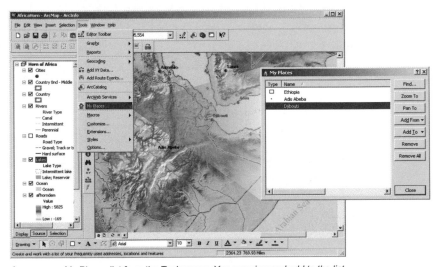

Access your My Places list from the Tools menu. You can view and add to the list from any map, scene, or view.

By default, the full extent of the first dataset you add to a data frame becomes the initial extent of the map display (for that data frame). If you add a dataset that extends beyond that initial extent, only features within the extent will be visible (use the Full Extent tool to zoom out to the extent of all layers).

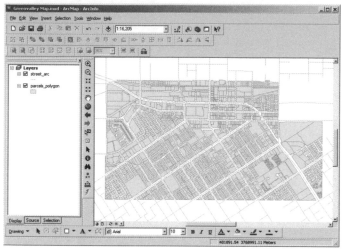

The display is set to the extent of the parcel layer. The streets layer extends beyond this extent.

The current map scale is displayed in the scale box at the top of the ArcMap window. To specify a map scale, type the scale in the scale box—the map display is adjusted to the new scale. The drop-down list lets you pick from standard map scales; any scale you type in is added to the top of the list so you can quickly get back to it. You can also customize the list by adding or removing scales. You often set a particular map scale when creating a map for printing or publication.

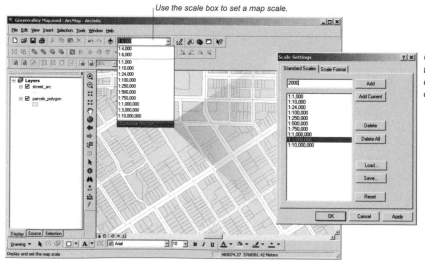

Use the scale box to set a map scale.

Click Customize This List to remove scales from the drop-down list or add your own scales to it.

You can also control the scale at which layers are displayed—some layers (usually more detailed ones) can be set to display only when you're zoomed in to a small area.

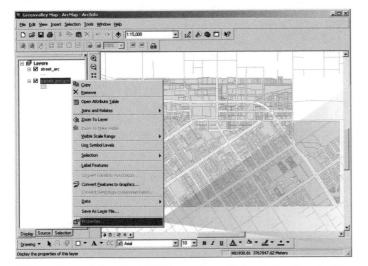

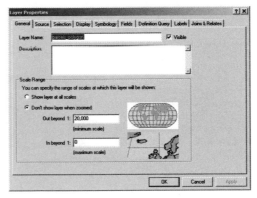

With a minimum scale set to 1:20,000, parcels are displayed when the extent is zoomed in to 1:15,000 (above) but aren't displayed when the extent is zoomed out to 1:40,000 (below). A small scalebar appears under the grayed-out check box for the layer to indicate the layer is outside the visible scale range.

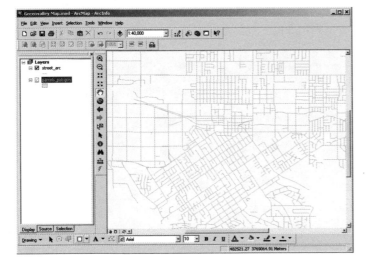

To view the data at several scales at once, use a Magnifier/Viewer window. In Magnifier mode, the window magnifies whatever it is over when you drag and release the window's title bar (in Update While Dragging mode it acts as a magnifying glass as you move the window over the display). In Viewer mode, the window takes a snapshot of whatever it is over. When you drag the window, the snapshot stays in it, so you can view one area or scale while continuing to zoom and pan in the main display window. A Viewer window allows you to pan or zoom, display the full extent of the map, or display the previous extent (or next extent). It's essentially a free-floating display window. You can open as many of these windows as you want.

An overview window shows you the location of the current extent within the full extent of the data frame.

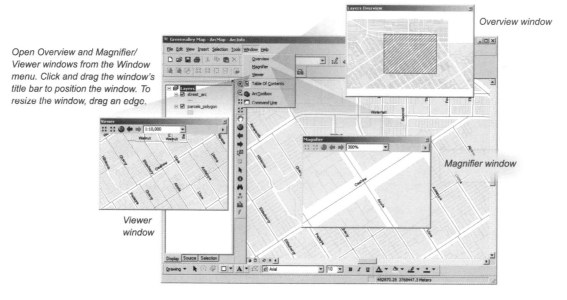

Overview window

Open Overview and Magnifier/ Viewer windows from the Window menu. Click and drag the window's title bar to position the window. To resize the window, drag an edge.

Magnifier window

Viewer window

You can toggle a window between Magnifier and Viewer mode by clicking the menu button on the window.

Click the menu button on a Viewer window to flash the location in the main display window. Use the Pan tool on the Tools toolbar to pan within the viewer window; then use Pan To Location to pan to that area in the main display window.

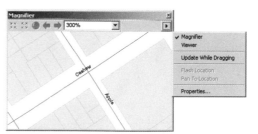

Click the menu button on a Magnifier window to switch to Update While Dragging mode. You can also switch a window between Magnifier and Viewer mode.

Identifying and locating features

Maps in a GIS are sometimes referred to as "smart maps" because—unlike paper maps—you have the ability to point at something on the map and get information about it (specifically, all the information about the feature stored in the layer's attribute table). Conversely, you may know something about a feature, such as its name, but not know where it is on the map—you want to enter the feature's name and locate it on the map. ArcMap includes several tools for identifying and locating features.

Identifying a feature on a map

Use the Identify tool to point at a feature on the map and display its attribute values. The information appears in the Identify Results box. Once you've identified a feature you can click it in the Identify box and it will flash on the map. Hold down the Shift key while clicking a feature to add it to the list of identified features (otherwise it will replace the previous feature), or drag the cursor to create a box around the features you want to identify.

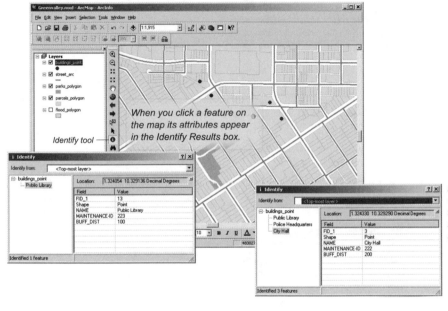

When you click a feature on the map its attributes appear in the Identify Results box.

Identify tool

Press and hold the Shift or Ctrl key while clicking features to add them to the results box. You can also add several features at once by dragging to create a box around them.

You control which layers to identify features from—choose all layers, a subset, or a specific layer (the topmost layer in the table of contents is the default).

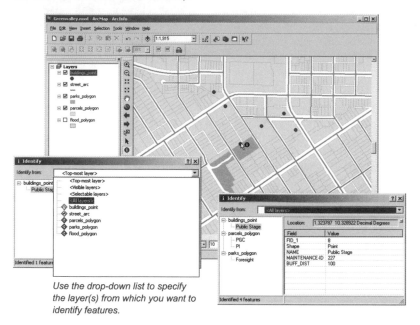

Use the drop-down list to specify the layer(s) from which you want to identify features.

By default, all the attribute values for the identified feature are listed. The fields listed in the box can be controlled using the Fields tab (uncheck the fields you don't want displayed).

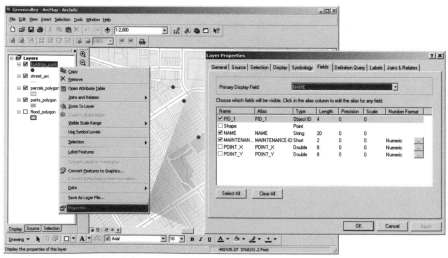

The Fields tab on the Layer Properties dialog box lets you specify which fields will appear in the results box.

If you're having trouble picking the feature you want, change the Selection tolerance—choose Options from the Selection menu (setting a larger selection tolerance will select features farther from the cursor).

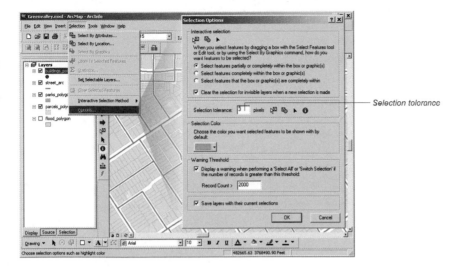

Selection tolerance

Identifying a feature using MapTips

A quick way to identify features is to use MapTips. When MapTips is turned on for a layer, placing the cursor over a feature displays the feature's name (or other attribute). If MapTips is on, the tip will also appear when you use the Identify tool—you can make sure you have the right feature before clicking it to display the additional attributes.

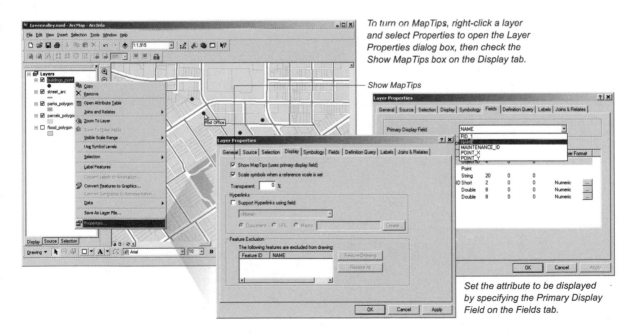

To turn on MapTips, right-click a layer and select Properties to open the Layer Properties dialog box, then check the Show MapTips box on the Display tab.

Show MapTips

Set the attribute to be displayed by specifying the Primary Display Field on the Fields tab.

Locating a feature by searching

Use Find on the Edit menu (or the Find tool on the Tools toolbar) to locate a feature by typing an attribute value. Once you've found the feature you want, you can flash it on the map or zoom to it.

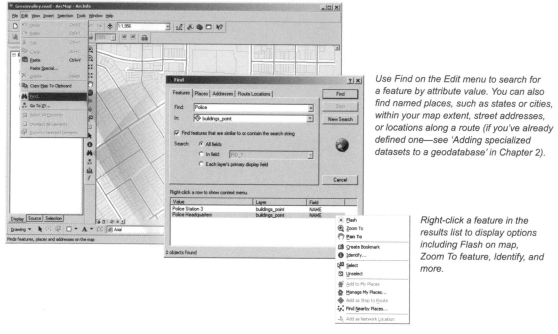

Use Find on the Edit menu to search for a feature by attribute value. You can also find named places, such as states or cities, within your map extent, street addresses, or locations along a route (if you've already defined one—see 'Adding specialized datasets to a geodatabase' in Chapter 2).

Right-click a feature in the results list to display options including Flash on map, Zoom To feature, Identify, and more.

Locating features via an attribute table

There may be instances when you prefer to locate a feature (or several features) on a map by scanning through a layer's attribute table—to find several features by name or ID, for example. Once you've found a feature in the table, right-click the gray box at the beginning of the row to flash that feature on the map. You can also zoom or pan to the feature, or display the Identify window.

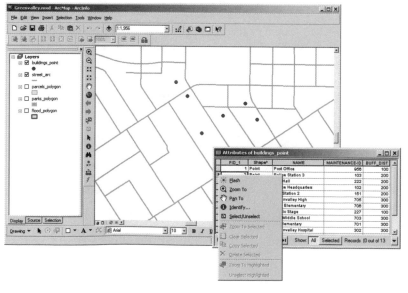

To use an attribute table to locate a feature on the map, right-click the gray box at the beginning of the feature's row, and select an option from the menu.

To locate a feature and have it stay highlighted on the map, select it in the layer's attribute table. Click the gray box (or right-click and click Select/Unselect). To select multiple features and highlight them, press the Ctrl key while clicking the gray box next to each feature's record in the table.

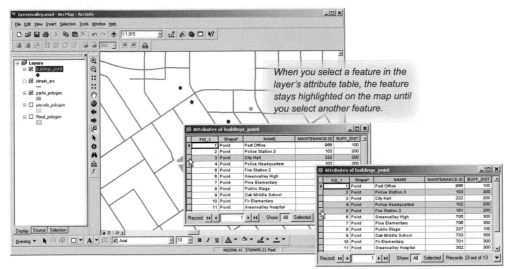

When you select a feature in the layer's attribute table, the feature stays highlighted on the map until you select another feature.

Press and hold the Ctrl key while clicking to select multiple features and highlight them.

With this method, you're actually creating a selected set, so when you're done highlighting features you'll want to clear the selection (see 'Selecting a subset of features' and 'Working with a selected set' in Chapter 5 for more on feature selection).

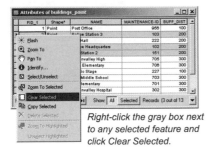

Right-click the gray box next to any selected feature and click Clear Selected.

Symbolizing data

Specifying the symbols you use to draw features on a map lets you ensure that the map is easy to read and conveys the information you want. For some audiences, standard symbols are immediately recognizable. Different feature and attribute types are drawn using different types of symbols—points with marker symbols of a specific size and color, lines with symbols of a specific width, pattern, and color. Areas can be drawn using an outline, or filled with a pattern or color.

Assigning symbols to layers

When you add a layer to a map, ArcGIS assigns a default symbol—all features in the layer are drawn using the same symbol. To change the symbol, right-click the layer name and click Properties to display the Layer Properties dialog box. Then choose the Symbology tab. (You can also get to the Layer Properties dialog box by double-clicking the layer name in the table of contents.) Pick a method of symbolizing the features, then specify the symbol(s).

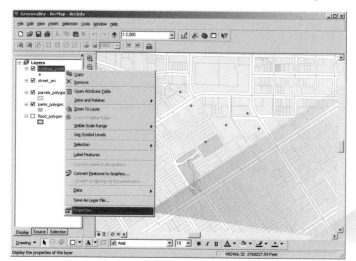

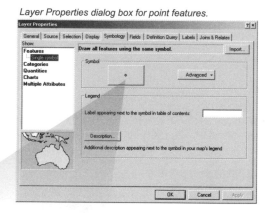

Layer Properties dialog box for point features.

Select a predefined symbol from this panel in the Symbol Selector dialog box.

The Symbol Property Editor lets you modify all the properties of the symbol. You also use this dialog box to create custom symbols.

Use these options to modify basic properties of the current symbol.

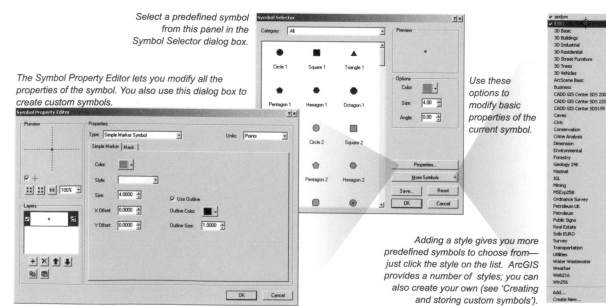

Adding a style gives you more predefined symbols to choose from— just click the style on the list. ArcGIS provides a number of styles; you can also create your own (see 'Creating and storing custom symbols').

You can also draw features using symbols based on the attribute values of the features—for example, roads of type "Highway" would be drawn using a wider line symbol than roads of type "Local" (see the next section, 'Using attributes to symbolize features').

Raster datasets that represent categories, such as vegetation types, are initially displayed using a default color for each category. Raster datasets that represent continuous values, such as elevation, are initially displayed using a grayscale color ramp, with lower values drawn in darker shades. If the raster is a multiband image, such as a satellite image, it draws in its defined RGB values. As with feature datasets, these symbols can be changed via the layer properties.

The specific options in the Layer Properties dialog box depend on the type of data you're symbolizing and the method you're using.

Layer Properties for line data

Layer Properties for polygon data

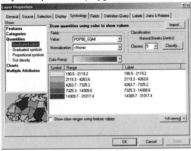

Layer Properties for raster data with continuous values

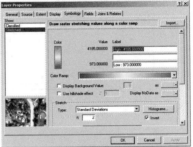

The symbol specifications are stored with the map, so once you've saved the map, the data will be symbolized the same way the next time you open the map. You can also store symbol specifications to use on other maps—see 'Saving and reusing symbol definitions' later in this chapter.

Shortcuts

Clicking a symbol in the table of contents lets you specify symbols directly, without opening the Layer Properties dialog box.

Symbol Type	Left-click opens…			Right-click opens…
◆ Marker — Line ■ Area Fill				
	Corresponding Symbol Selector Dialog			Color Palette
■ Classified or categorized raster	Color Selector dialog			Color Palette
■ Stretched raster	Select Color Ramp dialog			

Assigning symbols using cartographic representations

Assigning symbols to map layers in ArcMap lets you to portray features using basic properties such as color, line width, pattern, and so on. Sometimes, though, you'll need to depict the features—and the relationships between them—in a more realistic way. For example, you might want to create a transportation map showing overpasses, bridges, and tunnels. On a map of voting districts you might want to more clearly portray adjacent boundaries, rather than simply showing a single shared line. Or, on a map of building locations, you might want to rotate the building symbols (representing point locations) to face the street they're on. Cartographic representations allow you to do this.

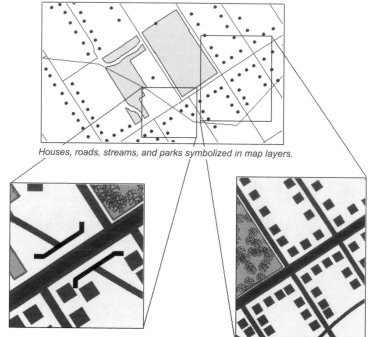

Houses, roads, streams, and parks symbolized in map layers.

Using cartographic representations for the various feature classes, bridge symbols are added around road symbols where streams and major roads intersect—with stream lines ending at the bridge—and small squares are placed at house locations and are oriented along the roads they face.

A cartographic representation is a set of rules, overrides, and graphical edits that allow you to represent geographic features cartographically without having to change the shape or location of the underlying data (which is, after all, an accurate representation of the features in geographic space). For example, if a road runs parallel to a river, it may be that at the map scale you're using, the two lines appear to touch or cross. You can use a cartographic representation rule to ensure that the road is offset from the river when drawn on the map (without having to actually move the location of the road or the river, which could affect other maps or any geographic query or analysis you perform).

Cartographic representations in ArcMap also include a series of tools to perform graphical edits directly in the GIS without having to export the cartography to a graphics package—for example, removing a portion of a line that obscures another feature. Cartographers refer to this as "map finishing and editing."

Cartographic representations are created within a geodatabase. They are stored as columns in the feature class attribute table and in system tables in the geodatabase. A quick way to create a cartographic representation is to convert the symbology for an existing layer on a map. Once you've converted the symbology, you can edit the representation, if necessary.

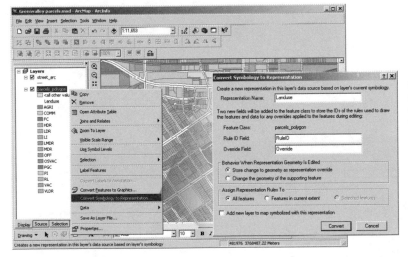

To create a feature representation for a feature class from existing map symbology, right-click the feature class in the table of contents and click Convert Symbology to Representation.

You can store multiple representations of the same feature class. For example, you could have one representation of parcels for a local zoning map and another representation for a general plan map. You select the representation you want after you add the feature class to a map (using the Symbology tab on the Layer Properties dialog box). This approach eliminates having to create and store several layer files for a feature class, each having different symbology.

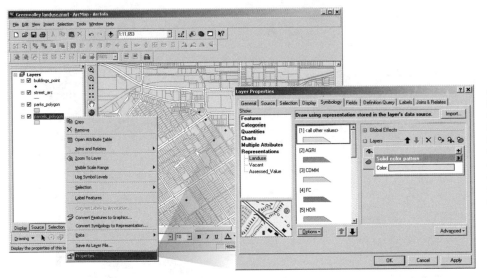

After adding a feature class to a map, open the Layer Properties dialog box and select the Symbology tab. Any defined feature representations will appear under the Representations heading—select the one you want to use. You can also modify the representation here.

Cartographic representations are useful if you create maps for publication—especially if the same feature classes are displayed using different symbology on different maps. Anyone in your organization who has access to the geodatabase also has access to the symbology for a feature class.

You can also create a representation directly in a feature class, using ArcCatalog. This method also gives you the option of importing the symbology from an existing layer file.

Using attributes to symbolize features

When you add a dataset to a map, ArcMap draws all the features using the same symbol. Often you'll want to draw the data symbolized by an attribute value (almost always the case for contiguous areas). The symbol used to draw each feature (the marker size, line width, or area color fill, for example) is determined by the value of a feature for a particular attribute.

Displaying quantities using a classification scheme

Many numerical attribute values can reflect measurements—for example, population counts or percentages, measurements of rainfall, and so on. Such values can be classified into ranges of values, and each range assigned a symbol for display purposes. When you specify the attribute value to use, a default classification is assigned. You can modify the classification scheme, the number of ranges, and the class breaks.

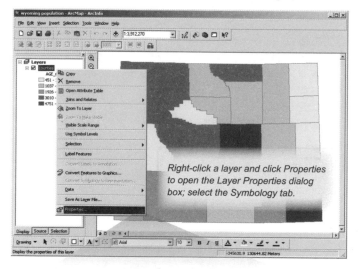

Right-click a layer and click Properties to open the Layer Properties dialog box; select the Symbology tab.

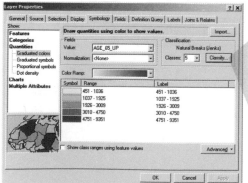

Choose a symbol type under Quantities—when you specify a field containing the numeric values, ArcMap assigns a default classification.

Specify a classification scheme and number of classes, and ArcMap will set the class breaks for you.

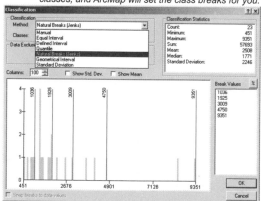

Drag the class break lines on the histogram to set breaks manually, or type the break values in the box on the right.

Select a color ramp from the drop-down menu, or set the color of a class by double-clicking it to display the Symbol Selector.

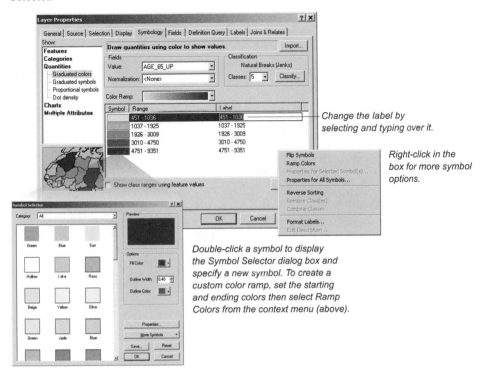

Change the label by selecting and typing over it.

Right-click in the box for more symbol options.

Double-click a symbol to display the Symbol Selector dialog box and specify a new symbol. To create a custom color ramp, set the starting and ending colors then select Ramp Colors from the context menu (above).

Normalize your data to account for differences between features. Normalization divides the values of one attribute by those of another to create a ratio. For example, if you're mapping counties that vary in size, you might normalize the population by the area of each county (to map density of people per square mile), or normalize the number of seniors by the total population of each county to map the percentage of seniors in each.

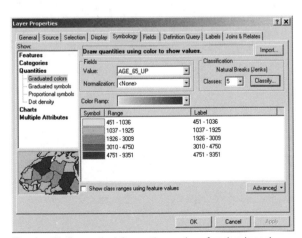

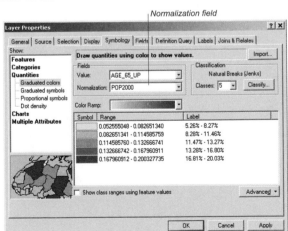

Normalization field

The classification on the left uses the number of seniors in each county. The classification to the right normalizes the number of seniors by the total population of the county to map the percentage of seniors in each county.

293

Displaying categorical data using unique symbols

When symbolizing using categories, a unique symbol is assigned to each value—all features with that category value are drawn using the symbol—for example, all agricultural parcels green, all commercial parcels yellow, and so on. Pick a color scheme from the drop-down menu, or assign colors to each category by double-clicking a color to display the color palette.

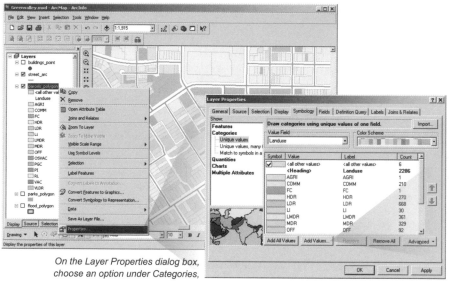

On the Layer Properties dialog box, choose an option under Categories, then specify a Value Field.

Use the Add All Values button to symbolize all categories.

Use the Add Values button to display a list from which you can choose values— any values not listed will be drawn using the <all other values> symbol.

Using charts to compare quantities

Symbolizing each feature with a chart is a way of comparing two or more quantities (bar charts) or showing quantities that are proportions of a whole (pie charts). For example, a dataset of counties might have fields for age groups—under 5, 5–17, 18–21, and so on—containing the number of people in each group. You could use these fields to create pie charts showing the relative number of people in each age group, for each county.

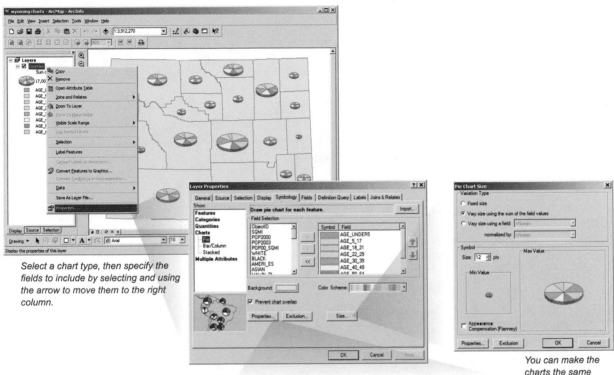

Select a chart type, then specify the fields to include by selecting and using the arrow to move them to the right column.

You can make the charts the same size, or vary the size based on a value, such as the sum of values for a field.

Here's where you modify the graphic properties of the chart, such as the outline color and thickness.

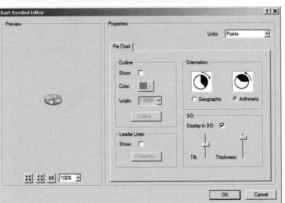

Saving and reusing symbol definitions

Once you've assigned symbols to a layer, there's a distinct possibility you'll want to apply the same symbols to the same features on another map, or to similar features on the same or a different map. For example, you may want to symbolize rivers the same way on all the maps you create. ArcMap provides several ways to save and reuse the symbol definitions so you don't have to reassign the symbols each time you display the features.

Saving a map layer as a layer file

The symbol definitions for a layer are stored with the map—the layer will be drawn with these symbols the next time you open the map. To display the same set of features with the same symbols on a different map, save the layer as a layer file. This creates a file with a .lyr extension. The file references the source data and contains the symbol definitions.

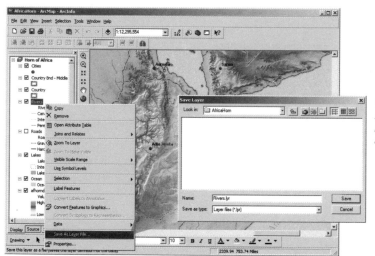

To save the layer—as symbolized—to add to other maps, right-click the layer name and select Save As Layer File.

You can then add the layer file to a new map as with any other data source. Layer files are indicated by a distinctive icon.

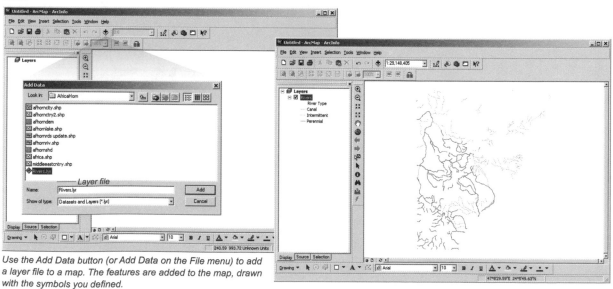

Use the Add Data button (or Add Data on the File menu) to add a layer file to a map. The features are added to the map, drawn with the symbols you defined.

Importing symbol definitions from a layer or layer file

You can also assign the symbols to similar features from a different dataset, on the same or another map. This is useful if you want to symbolize the same type of features for a different geographic area (whereas adding a layer file is useful for adding the same set of features to different maps). The field and attribute values you're using to symbolize the features have to correspond to the ones in the layer file.

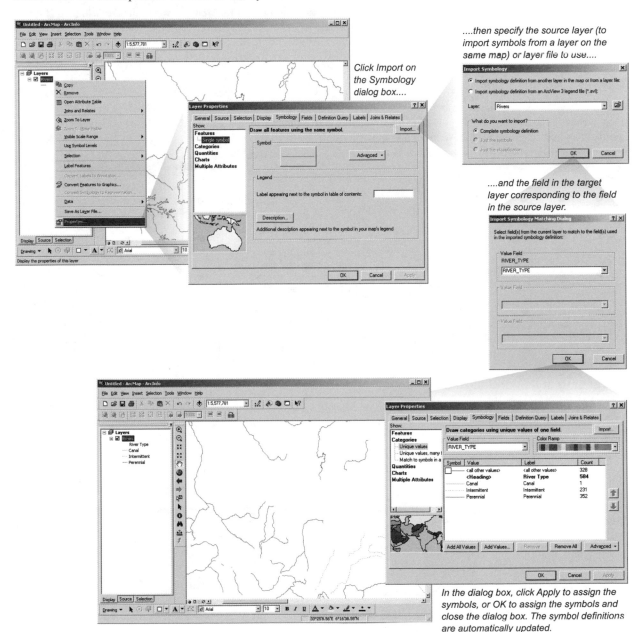

Click Import on the Symbology dialog box....

....then specify the source layer (to import symbols from a layer on the same map) or layer file to use....

....and the field in the target layer corresponding to the field in the source layer.

In the dialog box, click Apply to assign the symbols, or OK to assign the symbols and close the dialog box. The symbol definitions are automatically updated.

If the symbol definitions are for features that have been classified or categorized, the classes or categories will also be imported and applied.

Creating and storing custom symbols

ArcMap contains a wide variety of symbols, including sets of symbols used in specific industries. However, there may be cases when you need to use symbols that aren't provided with ArcMap. You can modify existing symbols as you create a map, and save them, or you can design and create symbols from scratch.

Symbols in ArcMap are stored in what are known as style files. When you start ArcMap two of these are loaded automatically—a set of basic symbols called ESRI.style, and a personal style file (stored in Documents\Settings). The personal style file is initially empty. You can load additional styles provided with ArcMap (see 'Symbolizing data' earlier in this chapter).

Saving a modified symbol

A quick way to create custom symbols is to modify existing symbols and save them in your personal style file. They then appear in the symbol palette with the other symbols that are currently loaded. You'd do this if you want to keep the symbols and use them with other features and other maps.

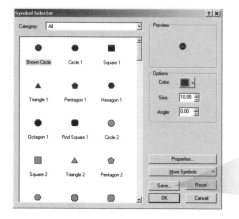

When you modify the current symbol and save it (with a name) it appears in the symbol palette and is stored in your personal style.

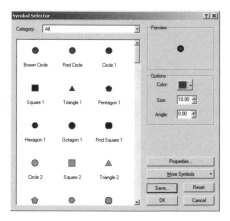

Accessing styles and stored symbols

Style files are accessed and managed using the Style Manager. Here's where you can edit, copy, and delete symbols. You can move the symbols in your personal style into another style file, or you can create a new style and move symbols into it. A style organizes each symbol type (marker, line, text, and so on) in a different folder.

The specific properties you can set depend on the type of symbol. Here are some examples of the properties for several symbol types.

Color ramp editor

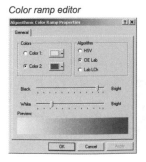

Color editor

Scalebar editor

Text editor

The Style Manager is accessed from the Tools menu. The left panel displays the folders for the currently loaded styles; the right panel displays the individual symbols for the selected style and folder.

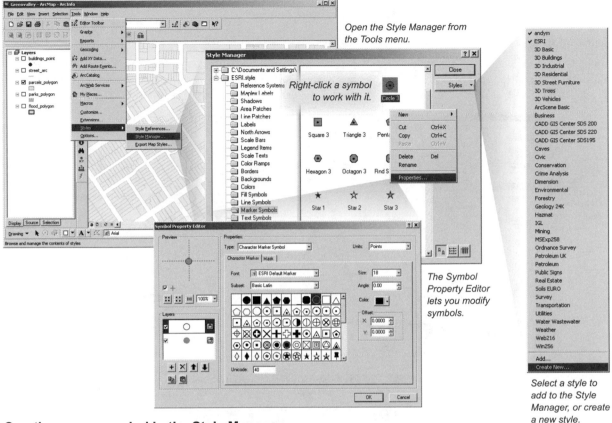

Open the Style Manager from the Tools menu.

Right-click a symbol to work with it.

The Symbol Property Editor lets you modify symbols.

Select a style to add to the Style Manager, or create a new style.

Creating a new symbol in the Style Manager

The Style Manager also lets you create symbols from scratch. Since ArcMap includes many symbols, you may only need to do this if you use very specific, unique, or very complex symbols. Even then, in many cases it's more efficient to start with an existing symbol and modify it. You can, if necessary, create new symbols from picture files (bitmaps or EMFs) or from characters in any font installed on your computer (set the Type to picture or character, respectively).

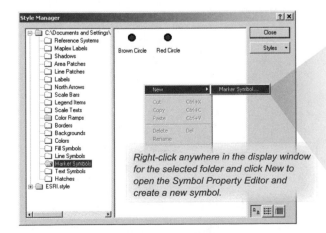

Right-click anywhere in the display window for the selected folder and click New to open the Symbol Property Editor and create a new symbol.

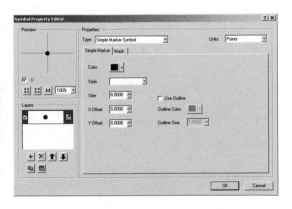

Labeling features

Feature labels make your map easier to read and understand. Labels range from simple text you add to a map as you explore your data to highly stylized labels used in cartographic production.

Using map labels

A map label is any value stored in a layer's attribute table and rendered as text on a map. A quick way to display labels is using the Label Features option on a layer's context menu—a default field, placement, and font are used. Use the Labels tab on the Layer Properties dialog box to access all the label settings for that layer.

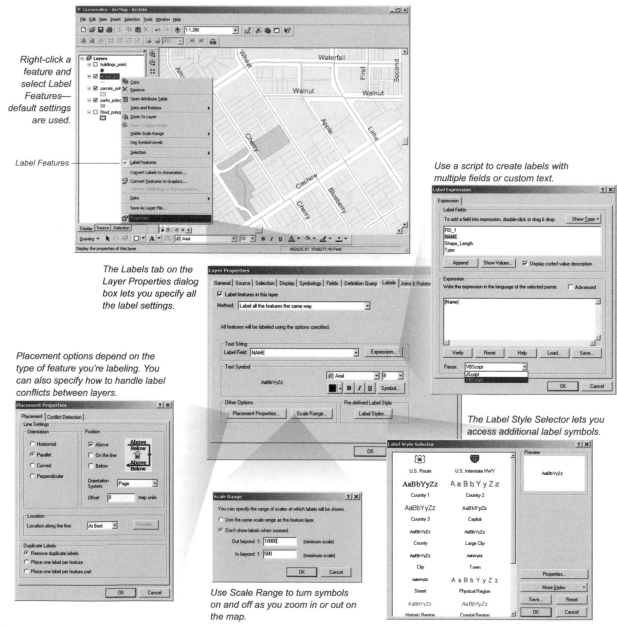

Right-click a feature and select Label Features— default settings are used.

Label Features

Use a script to create labels with multiple fields or custom text.

The Labels tab on the Layer Properties dialog box lets you specify all the label settings.

Placement options depend on the type of feature you're labeling. You can also specify how to handle label conflicts between layers.

The Label Style Selector lets you access additional label symbols.

Use Scale Range to turn symbols on and off as you zoom in or out on the map.

All features in the layer are labeled using the same text font, size, and color. (By default, labels don't draw if they would overlap.)

While you can change the text symbol for all the features, you can't modify the symbol, text, or position of individual labels. You can, however, define categories of features within a layer and label each category differently—major roads could have a large label and minor roads a small one. You can also use this method to label only certain categories (for example, only major roads).

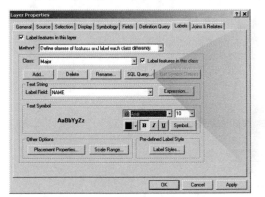

When you select "Define classes" as the method, additional options are available.

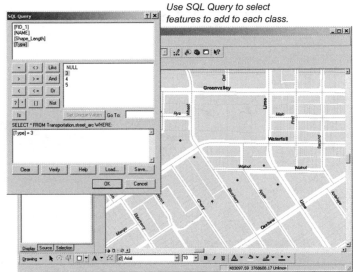

Use SQL Query to select features to add to each class.

To label an individual feature with its name or other attribute use graphic text—specifically, the Label tool (see the next section 'Drawing graphics on a map'). This tool is useful for labeling one feature, or a few. It also lets you use a different text symbol for each.

Managing labels on multiple layers

While you can manage each layer's labels from the table of contents, the Label Manager lets you modify the label settings for the various layers within a data frame from a single dialog box. It also includes options for managing label placement by giving labels for certain layers higher priority or greater weight (labels with a higher weight take precedence over those with a lower weight).

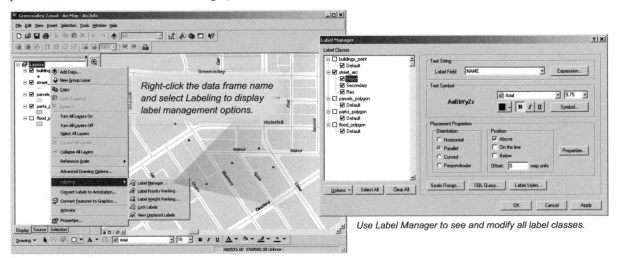

Right-click the data frame name and select Labeling to display label management options.

Use Label Manager to see and modify all label classes.

These options are also available from the Labeling toolbar (click the View menu, point to Toolbars, and click Labeling).

The Labeling toolbar

Labels will remain the same size as you zoom in or out on the map. If you want the labels to get larger or smaller as you change the map scale, set a reference scale for the data frame. The reference scale specifies the map scale at which the size of the labels on the map matches the defined size of the labels in page units, such as points. Typically, you'll set a map scale (or interactively zoom) to show your area of interest, set the reference scale, and create the labels using an appropriate text size for the current display. When you zoom in or out, the label text size will increase or decrease, accordingly.

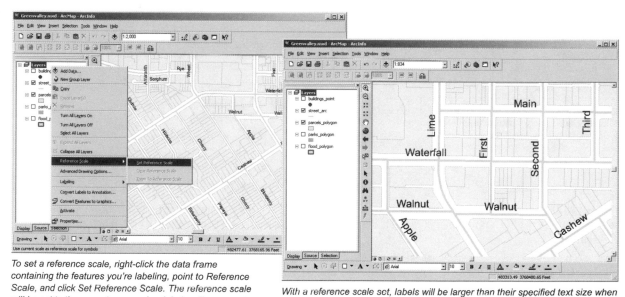

To set a reference scale, right-click the data frame containing the features you're labeling, point to Reference Scale, and click Set Reference Scale. The reference scale will be set to the current map scale—labels will appear at their specified text size at this scale.

With a reference scale set, labels will be larger than their specified text size when you zoom in, and smaller when you zoom out beyond the reference scale.

Advanced label placement using Maplex

The Maplex for ArcGIS extension enhances cartographic design with a sophisticated set of rules that automatically modify labels so they can be placed correctly. Maplex can save time by automating much of the work of manual label placement. The text placement rules include positioning, label fitting, and conflict resolution. You can also create rules for text stacking, font reduction, curving, and abbreviation. These rules are useful when you're creating complex maps for publication that include many features and numerous levels of labeling. They're accessed via the Label Manager and Layer Properties dialog boxes.

Maplex is included with an ArcInfo license. Once the extension is enabled (see The ArcGIS Desktop framework in Chapter 1), select the Maplex labeling engine (the default is the ESRI standard labeling engine).

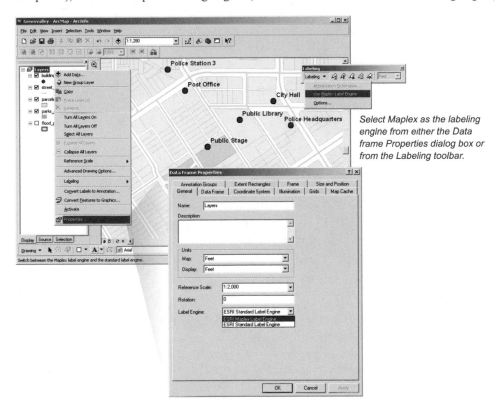

Select Maplex as the labeling engine from either the Data frame Properties dialog box or from the Labeling toolbar.

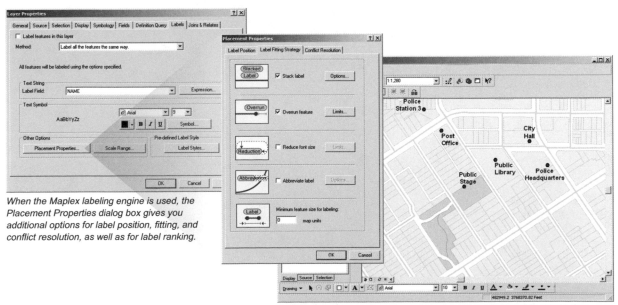

When the Maplex labeling engine is used, the Placement Properties dialog box gives you additional options for label position, fitting, and conflict resolution, as well as for label ranking.

In this example, rules have been defined to stack labels and to ensure they don't overlap streets.

Using annotation to label features

Annotation allows you to place and edit text individually. This is useful if you need to control the exact positions of labels. A quick way to create annotation for all features in a layer is to convert existing map labels using the Convert Labels to Annotation option on a layer's context menu. You can then select and work with the individual text strings. Annotation automatically scales with the features as you zoom in or out (a reference scale is set—using the current map scale—when you convert labels to annotation).

Right-click a layer in the table of contents and select Convert Labels to Annotation.

The Label tool described above is also a way of quickly creating annotation for individual features (as opposed to all features at once).

Map document annotation is stored only with the particular map in which it is created. If the annotation will be used on different maps, create geodatabase annotation. The annotation is stored as a separate feature class in the geodatabase and can be accessed by many users (see 'Creating and editing annotation' in Chapter 3).

Drawing graphics on a map

Adding graphics to your map can clarify the information that the map conveys. For example, you might add circles on top of the data on your map to draw attention to particular features, outline a study area with a polygon, or add lines that point to potential locations for new stores. Graphics are saved in the map document.

Using the Draw toolbar

Graphics are created using symbols—markers, lines, fills, colors, and text—that you access from the Draw toolbar. By default the Draw toolbar appears at the bottom of the ArcMap window. As with all toolbars, you can move and dock it anywhere on the window, or let it float.

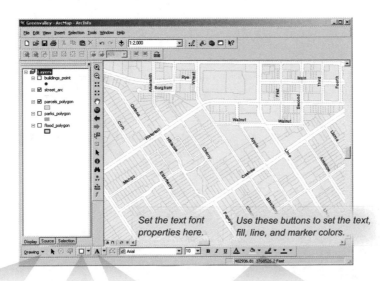

Set the text font properties here.

Use these buttons to set the text, fill, line, and marker colors.

The Drawing menu lets you arrange selected graphics and set default graphic symbol properties.

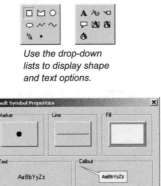

Use the drop-down lists to display shape and text options.

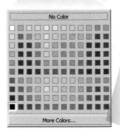

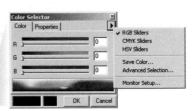

Specify a custom color. Click the menu button to change the color model.

Drawing shapes and text

The tools on the Draw toolbar for creating shapes and text work just like tools in a drawing program.

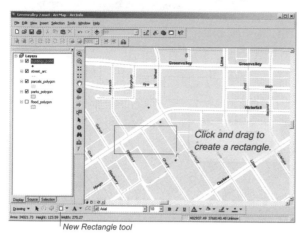

Click and drag to create a rectangle.

New Rectangle tool

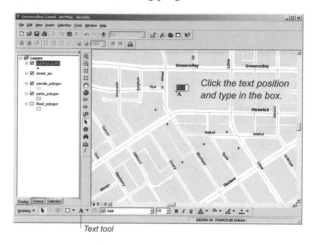

Click the text position and type in the box.

Text tool

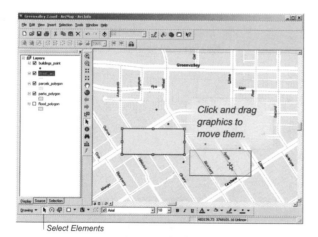

Click and drag graphics to move them.

Select Elements

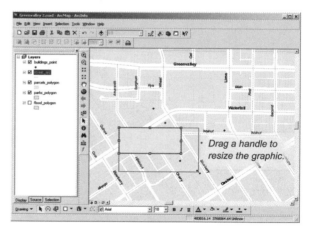

Drag a handle to resize the graphic.

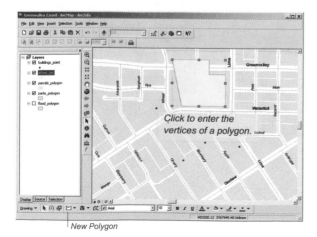

Click to enter the vertices of a polygon.

New Polygon

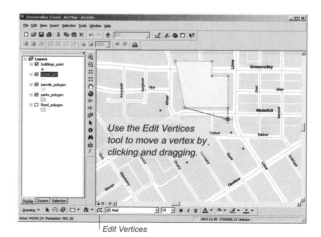

Use the Edit Vertices tool to move a vertex by clicking and dragging.

Edit Vertices

The text drop-down menu provides a variety of options for placing text.

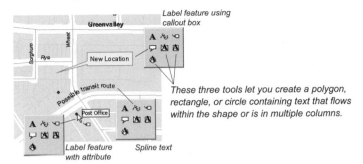

Label feature using
callout box

New Location

These three tools let you create a polygon,
rectangle, or circle containing text that flows
within the shape or is in multiple columns.

Label feature   Spline text
with attribute

Any shapes or text you draw while in Data view are drawn in geographic space—they move and scale with the geographic data as you pan and zoom. They appear in both Data and Layout view. Any shapes or text you draw while in Layout view are drawn in page space—they move and scale as you pan and zoom on the layout page. They're stored with the layout and appear only in Layout view.

You can add graphics to a data frame (in geographic space) while in Layout view by clicking the Focus Data Frame button on the Layout toolbar (you can also double-click the data frame on the page or right-click and click Focus Data Frame).

Modifying a graphic

Each graphic object has a context menu that lets you work with the object. Right-click the object to display the menu. Use the Properties option to modify the object's symbology.

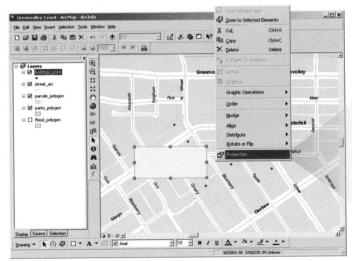

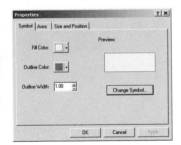

Right-click any graphic shape or text to display more options. Choose Properties to set the color, font and position. (You can also double-click the graphic to open the Properties dialog box.)

Creating graphics from features

An alternative way to create graphics is to convert features to graphic objects. You'd do this if, for example, you want to highlight a particular feature but don't need or want to create a new layer containing only that feature. You'd select the feature, convert it to a graphic, and modify its properties to assign a new symbol and color.

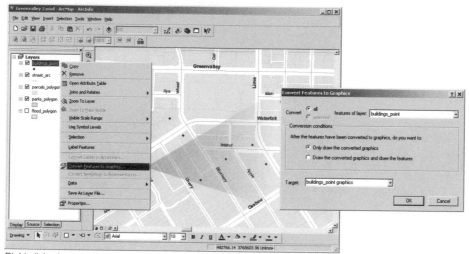

Right-click a layer and select Convert Features to Graphics to turn geographic features into graphic objects.

Creating a map layout

Map layouts are used to compose a finished map for printing or publication. When you create a layout, you arrange the various map elements—the geographic data itself (contained in a data frame), as well as explanatory information, such as titles, legends, scalebars, and so on. The ultimate goal is to present the necessary information as simply and clearly as possible.

Working in Layout View

Layout View shows you how the map page will look, and lets you display rulers and grids to help you arrange the map elements (see the next section, 'Adding and arranging map elements'). Select Layout View on the View menu. The buttons at the bottom of the ArcMap window also let you switch between Data and Layout view.

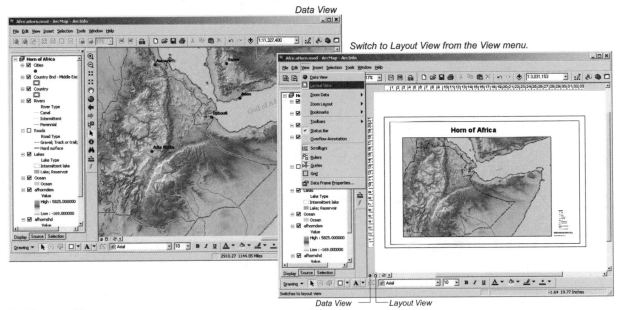

Data View

Switch to Layout View from the View menu.

Data View — *Layout View*

Setting up the page

The page setup defines the size and orientation of the final map, the printer you'll be using, and other settings.

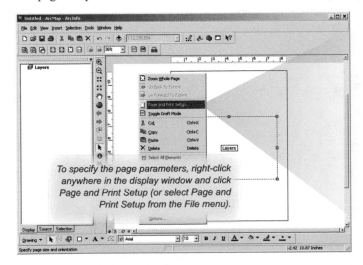

To specify the page parameters, right-click anywhere in the display window and click Page and Print Setup (or select Page and Print Setup from the File menu).

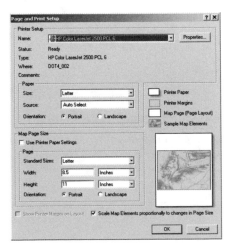

Navigating the layout

Layout View has its own set of navigation tools that work on the page, contained on the Layout toolbar. They are distinguished from the data navigation tools by the page icon. You can work with the data in the data frame in Layout View just as you would in Data View—any changes you make in the Data View are reflected in Layout View. However, it's often easier to switch to Data View to work with the data and then switch back to Layout View to work with the page layout.

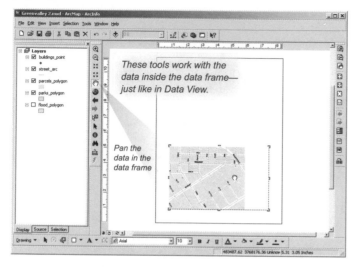

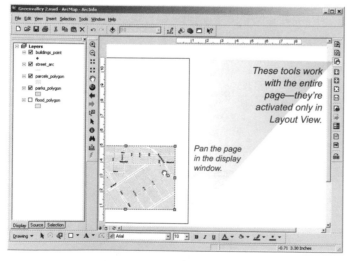

Layout toolbar

Working with multiple data frames

Multiple data frames are often used to display an area of interest in one frame and a reference map showing the location of the area in another frame—in this case, the data frames have different map scales and extents. Multiple data frames are also used to show different views of the same geographic area—in this case, the data frames have the same scale and extent.

Add new data frames to a map from the Insert menu. A quick way to make a map showing different views of the same area is to copy and paste a data frame, then modify how the data is displayed in each frame.

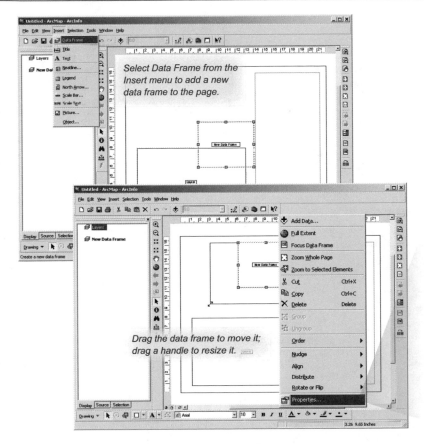

Select Data Frame from the Insert menu to add a new data frame to the page.

Drag the data frame to move it; drag a handle to resize it.

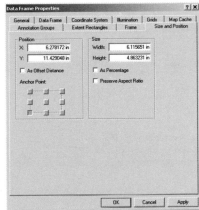

Right-click the data frame and select Properties to explicitly set the size and position.

When working with multiple data frames, many operations, such as creating a legend, apply to the active frame. The data frame that's currently active has a dotted line around it and its name is bold in the table of contents. Click a data frame on the map, using the Select tool, to make it active. Or, right-click the name in the table of contents and click Activate.

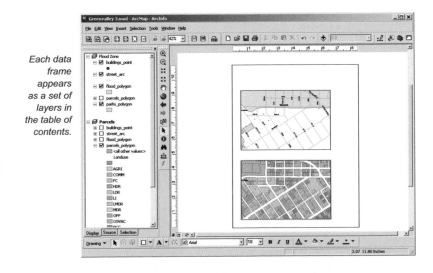

Each data frame appears as a set of layers in the table of contents.

Using map templates

Once you compose your map, you can save the layout as a template. That's useful if you make sets of maps showing the same information for different areas, such as a book of parcel maps for a city. The template stores the layout (data frame arrangement, map elements, and so on) as well as any data layers on the map (so your template can include base layers you want to appear on every map). When you start a new map by opening a template, ArcMap reproduces the template as a new map document and keeps the original template document intact. Map templates have a file extension of .mxt to distinguish them from map documents (.mxd).

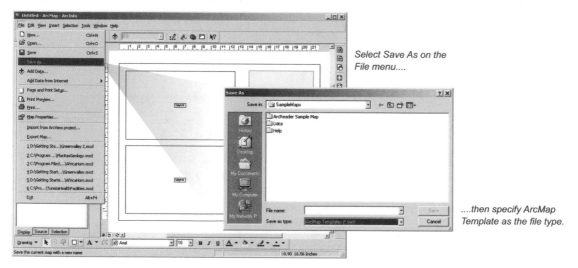

Select Save As on the
File menu....

....then specify ArcMap
Template as the file type.

ArcMap also provides a number of standard map templates. You can select one of these when you open a new map.

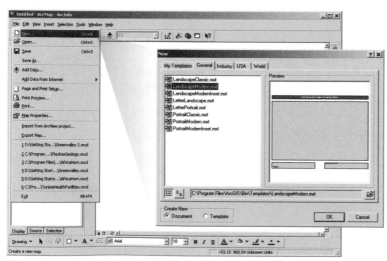

When you open a new map you have a choice of predefined templates.

Adding and arranging map elements

Map elements explain the information on your map to the map reader. They can also make the map easier to read. The goal in adding and arranging map elements is to create a map that's attractive and easy to understand. Too much information or too many boxes and other elements just obscures the information you're trying to convey.

Map elements are essentially graphic objects—some more complex than others—so they can be moved and re-sized like any other graphics. You can modify how they're drawn using the properties dialog box for the element or—in some cases—using the tools on the Draw toolbar. Titles, text, and neatlines are simply graphics. Legends, scalebars, and north arrows—while composed of graphic objects—are derived from the geographic data in the data frame. Any changes to the data that is displayed will be reflected in these map elements.

Map elements are added to the page in layout view, using the Insert menu.

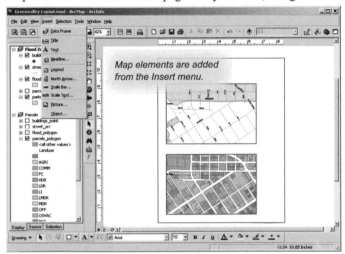

Map elements are added from the Insert menu.

Adding titles, text, and legends

Titles and text appear on the layout as soon as you choose the option on the Insert menu. You can then modify the text using the tools on the Draw toolbar. If wizards are enabled in your ArcGIS installation, the Legend Wizard will appear when you insert a legend (to enable wizards, click the Tools menu, click Options, and—on the General tab—check the box to turn Wizard Mode on). The wizard steps you through setting up the legend. Otherwise, a default legend will appear on the layout immediately, and you can use the Properties option to change its settings (right-click the legend).

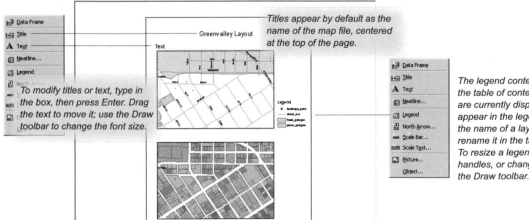

Titles appear by default as the name of the map file, centered at the top of the page.

To modify titles or text, type in the box, then press Enter. Drag the text to move it; use the Draw toolbar to change the font size.

The legend content comes from the table of contents—layers that are currently displayed on the map appear in the legend; to change the name of a layer in the legend, rename it in the table of contents. To resize a legend, drag one of its handles, or change the text size on the Draw toolbar.

Adding scalebars, north arrows, and neatlines

When you insert a scalebar, scale text, north arrow, or neatline from the Insert menu, a symbol selector dialog box appears. When you select the element you want and click OK, it's added to the page. As with any other symbol you can customize north arrows and scalebars (click the Properties button on the dialog box).

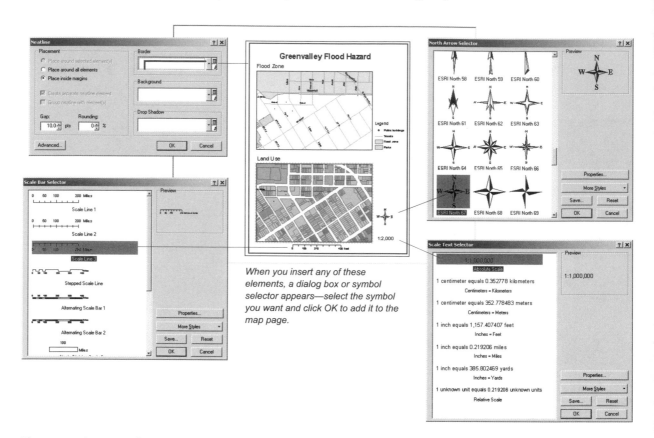

When you insert any of these elements, a dialog box or symbol selector appears—select the symbol you want and click OK to add it to the map page.

If your map has more than one data frame, when you add a scalebar or north arrow that map element relates to the active data frame (different data frames on a single map can have different scales and orientations).

The Insert menu also lets you add picture files, such as a photo, a scanned image, or a bitmap logo, or embedded objects, such as a Microsoft Word document. You can double-click the object to open its application—any changes to the object are automatically reflected on the map page.

Modifying map elements

Click and drag an element to move it, use the handles to re-size an element. Right-click any selected element to display its Properties dialog box. You can also use the tools on the Draw toolbar to modify the selected element—select a neatline or box and use the Draw tools to change the fill or outline.

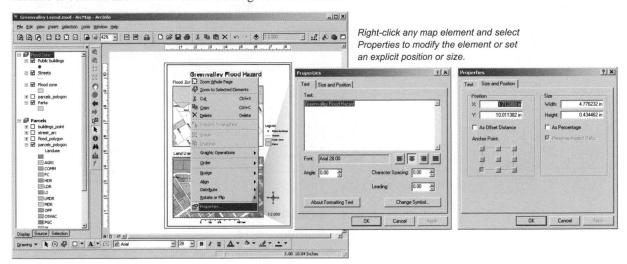

Right-click any map element and select Properties to modify the element or set an explicit position or size.

Aligning elements

To align elements, select the elements, then use the Align option on the Drawing menu. Or right-click the selected elements and use the options on the menu that appears.

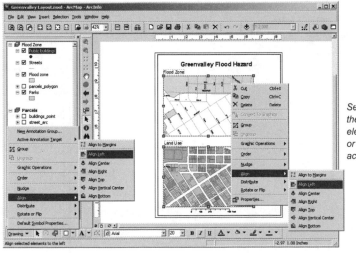

Select one or more elements, then right-click a selected element to access the options; or open the Drawing menu to access the same options.

Using grids and guidelines

You can set up a grid or guidelines to make sure elements line up. You can use these purely as visual aids, or have the elements snap to the grid, guidelines, or the ruler.

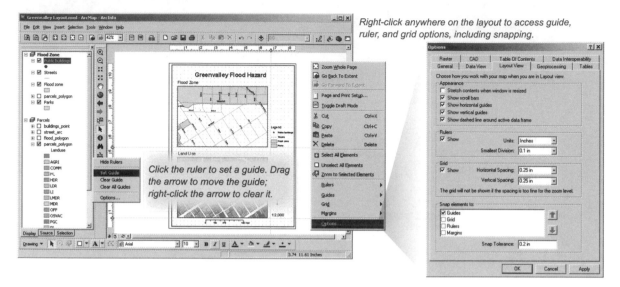

Right-click anywhere on the layout to access guide, ruler, and grid options, including snapping.

Click the ruler to set a guide. Drag the arrow to move the guide; right-click the arrow to clear it.

Navigating the layout

As you work with the map elements, you'll likely want to zoom in and out, and pan across the page. Use the special page navigation tools—rather than the data navigation tools—when moving around the page. These are located on the Layout toolbar.

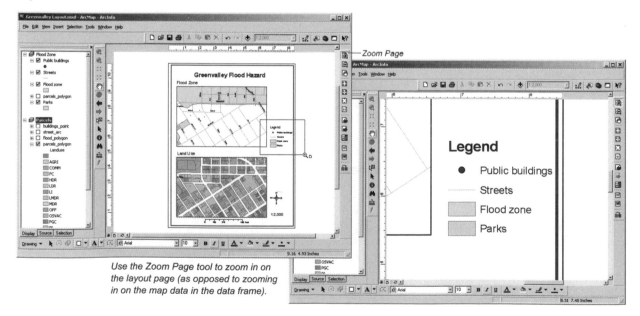

Use the Zoom Page tool to zoom in on the layout page (as opposed to zooming in on the map data in the data frame).

Using draft mode

Draft mode displays the map elements (except for text) as empty boxes containing the name of the element, so the display refreshes faster. Using draft mode for arranging elements may be easier and faster—at least for an initial layout—especially if your map is complex. Draft mode also provides a schematic view of your layout.

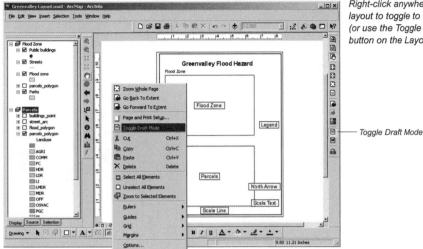

Right-click anywhere on the layout to toggle to draft mode (or use the Toggle Draft Mode button on the Layout toolbar).

Toggle Draft Mode

Creating a graph

Graphs are created from within ArcMap, and are derived from values stored in a layer's attribute table (or other table that has been added to the map). Graphs provide a visual summary of attribute values and can add useful information to your map.

Using the Graph Wizard to create a graph

Create a new graph from the Tools menu or open a table and use the Options button.

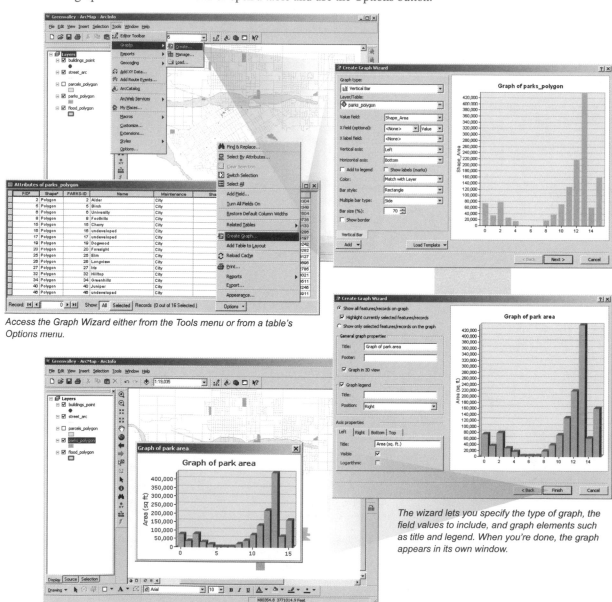

Access the Graph Wizard either from the Tools menu or from a table's Options menu.

The wizard lets you specify the type of graph, the field values to include, and graph elements such as title and legend. When you're done, the graph appears in its own window.

Adding a graph to a layout

Once you've created a graph, you can add it to your map layout (you can also print, save, or export the graph to a graphics file). Access these options by right-clicking the graph window title bar.

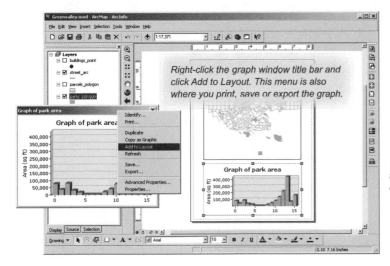

You can move and resize the graph just like any other map element.

Modifying a graph

To modify an existing graph, right-click the graph window title bar and select Properties, or Advanced Properties.

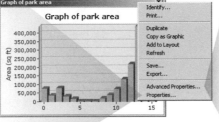

Right-click the graph window title bar and select Properties, or Advanced Properties.

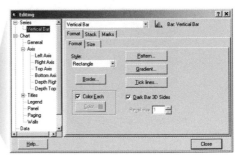

Use Advanced Properties to access all the properties of the graph.

Properties is the same as the Graph Wizard, only presented as a dialog box with two tabs.

Managing graphs

The Graph Manager lets you access the graphs associated with a map. Click Tools, point to Graphs, and click Manage.

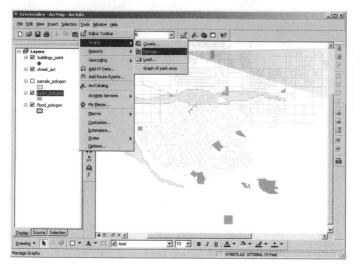

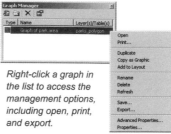

Right-click a graph in the list to access the management options, including open, print, and export.

Creating a report

Reports in ArcMap let you list—and optionally summarize—data contained in tables. As with graphs, they are derived from the fields in a layer's attribute table or other table that has been added to a map. ArcGIS Desktop also includes Crystal Reports® for creating presentation-quality reports.

Creating a basic report in ArcMap

The basic process for creating a report is to specify fields to include from a table, using the Fields tab on the Report Properties dialog box.

Access the Report Properties dialog box from either the Tools menu or from a table's Options menu.

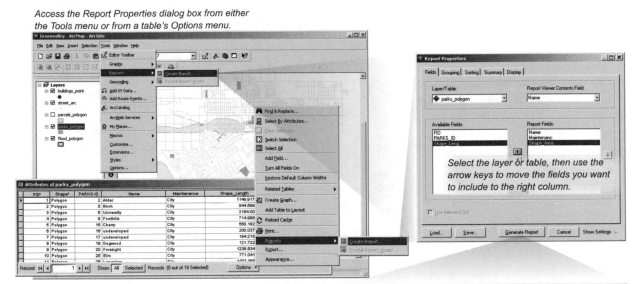

Select the layer or table, then use the arrow keys to move the fields you want to include to the right column.

When you click Generate Report, the report is displayed in the Report Viewer window.

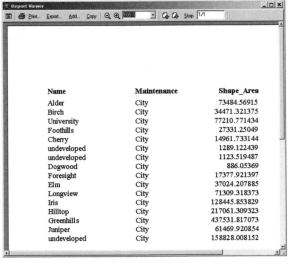

Name	Maintenance	Shape_Area
Alder	City	73484.56915
Birch	City	34471.321375
University	City	77210.771434
Foothills	City	27331.25049
Cherry	City	14961.733144
undeveloped	City	1289.122439
undeveloped	City	1123.519487
Dogwood	City	886.05369
Foresight	City	17377.921397
Elm	City	37024.207885
Longview	City	71309.318373
Iris	City	128445.853829
Hilltop	City	217061.309323
Greenhills	City	437531.817073
Juniper	City	61469.920854
undeveloped	City	158828.008152

Once the report is generated, you can print or export the report, or add it to your map layout.

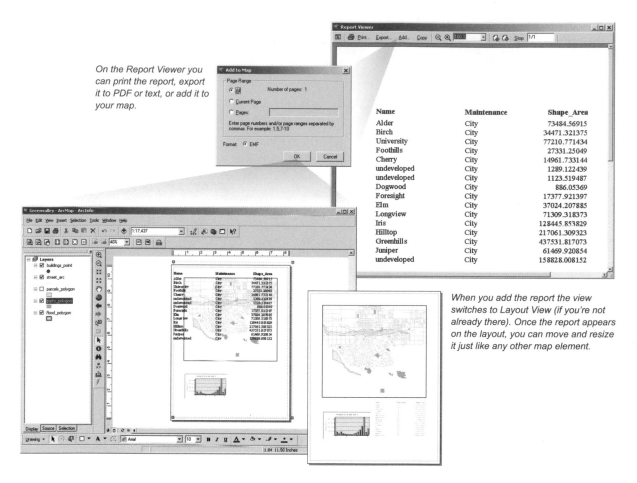

On the Report Viewer you can print the report, export it to PDF or text, or add it to your map.

When you add the report the view switches to Layout View (if you're not already there). Once the report appears on the layout, you can move and resize it just like any other map element.

Use the tabs on the Report Properties dialog box to customize the report.

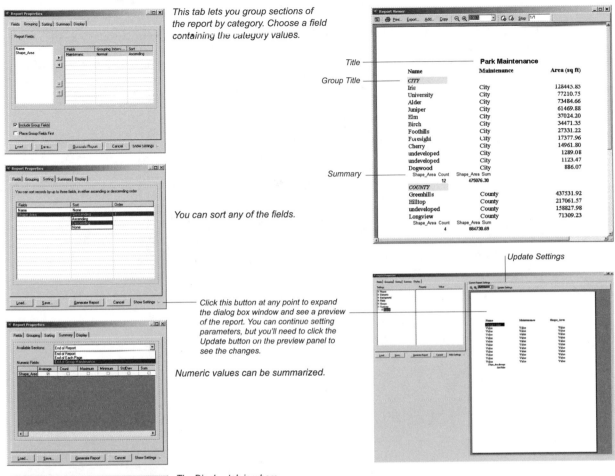

This tab lets you group sections of the report by category. Choose a field containing the category values.

You can sort any of the fields.

Click this button at any point to expand the dialog box window and see a preview of the report. You can continue setting parameters, but you'll need to click the Update button on the preview panel to see the changes.

Numeric values can be summarized.

The Display tab is where you set the parameters for how the report will look. Click in a Value box to change a setting.

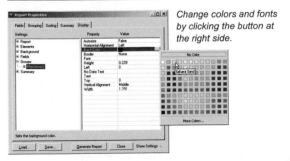

Change colors and fonts by clicking the button at the right side.

Using Crystal Reports

The report tool included with ArcMap is meant for creating basic reports that can be added to a map layout. You can optionally install Crystal Reports for creating presentation-quality reports (however these reports exist as files outside ArcMap and can't be added to a map layout). The Crystal Reports wizard (if installed) is available from the Reports option on the Tools menu in ArcMap.

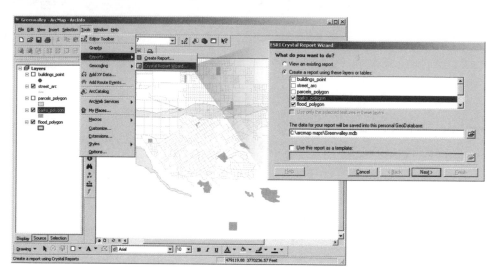

Creating relief maps and perspective views

Shaded relief maps and perspective views are useful for visualizing features that have height above or depth below the earth's surface. The tools to create these maps and views are included in the ArcGIS Spatial Analyst and ArcGIS 3D Analyst extension products.

Creating a shaded relief map

Shaded relief maps are usually derived from raster elevation surfaces, such as a digital elevation model. You create a hillshade view from the surface using tools in the Spatial Analyst or 3D Analyst extensions (available via ArcToolbox). The appearance of the hillshade layer depends on settings such as azimuth, altitude, and z-factor (the Hillshade tool provides default settings). You then display other layers on top of the hillshade—the classic shaded relief map uses an elevation layer symbolized using a color ramp and displayed using a transparency setting.

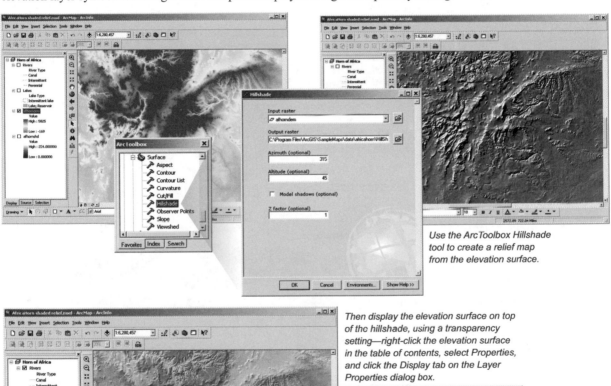

Use the ArcToolbox Hillshade tool to create a relief map from the elevation surface.

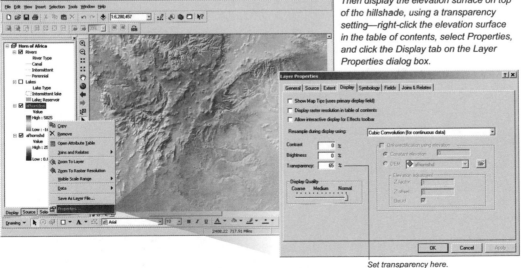

Then display the elevation surface on top of the hillshade, using a transparency setting—right-click the elevation surface in the table of contents, select Properties, and click the Display tab on the Layer Properties dialog box.

Set transparency here.

325

Creating a perspective view

Perspective views are created in the ArcScene application provided with the 3D Analyst extension (available from the ArcGIS program group on the Start menu, if 3D Analyst is installed). You add datasets to a blank scene, similar to creating a map in ArcMap. To add a third dimension to the display, you specify an attribute associated with each feature that can be used as (or to calculate) a height or depth for the feature (known as a z value). Z can be a height or depth measurement—such as an elevation on the earth's surface, the height of a building, or the depth of a pipeline—or it can be a quantity, such as the population of each county.

Terrain views require an elevation surface, upon which other layers can be draped. These additional layers don't require z values—rather their elevations are established with reference to the underlying elevation surface.

When creating the view, you choose the viewer's angle and altitude, as well as the vertical exaggeration and illumination (3D Analyst provides default settings). Once you've created the initial view, you can navigate by panning, rotating and changing the altitude, and zooming in or out, to create the view you want.

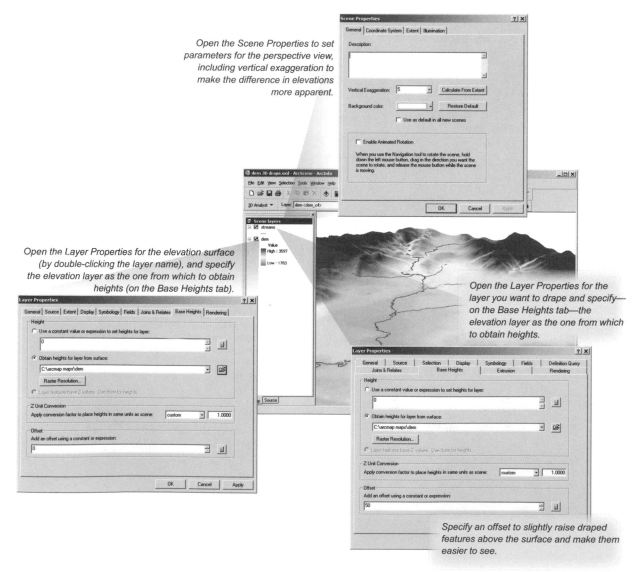

Open the Scene Properties to set parameters for the perspective view, including vertical exaggeration to make the difference in elevations more apparent.

Open the Layer Properties for the elevation surface (by double-clicking the layer name), and specify the elevation layer as the one from which to obtain heights (on the Base Heights tab).

Open the Layer Properties for the layer you want to drape and specify— on the Base Heights tab—the elevation layer as the one from which to obtain heights.

Specify an offset to slightly raise draped features above the surface and make them easier to see.

You can create 3D maps by extruding features, such as counties extruded by population or building footprints extruded using building height. The attribute values are used as relative heights in the view. You can also combine perspective views with extruded features (to show buildings on a hillside, for example).

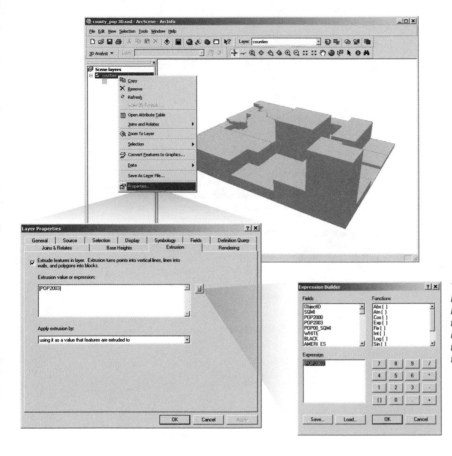

To extrude features open the Layer Properties dialog box and—on the Extrusion tab—make sure the box at the top is checked. Then enter the field name in the box. Or click the Calculator button to open the Expression Builder and pick a field name or create an expression.

Creating dynamic views and animations

Dynamic views and animations are great presentation tools—especially when presenting geographic information to audiences not used to working with complex maps. Globe views are useful for providing context for your area of interest, as well as for presenting global geographic phenomena. The ArcGIS 3D Analyst extension contains two applications that let you create dynamic views and animations—ArcScene and ArcGlobe. Both applications are available from the ArcGIS program group on the Start menu, if the 3D Analyst extension is installed. You can also create animated maps in ArcMap to show a changing view of your data.

Navigating ArcScene and ArcGlobe

Once you've created a view in ArcScene (see 'Creating relief maps and perspective views'), use the Navigate button to change the viewing angle and altitude, or use the Fly Over tool to move continuously through the scene.

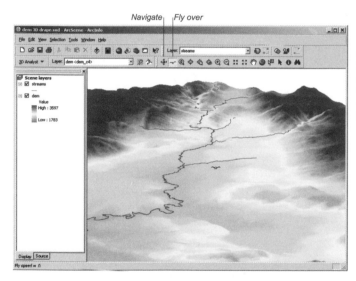

Navigate | Fly over

The Navigate button lets you change the viewing angle and altitude—hold down the left mouse button, and drag the cursor. In fly mode, click anywhere on the scene to start moving; left-click to speed up, right-click to slow down. The Fly speed indicator in the lower left corner of the window gives you a reference.

In ArcGlobe, a shaded relief image of the earth's surface appears by default when you first open the application. The additional layers you place on the globe can cover any geographic extent—they don't have to be global. ArcGlobe has two navigation modes you toggle between. In globe mode the navigation tools let you spin the globe to view different portions of the earth's surface. In surface mode, you navigate across the surface, similar to navigating a view in ArcScene. ArcGlobe also lets you walk through the landscape, as well as fly over it.

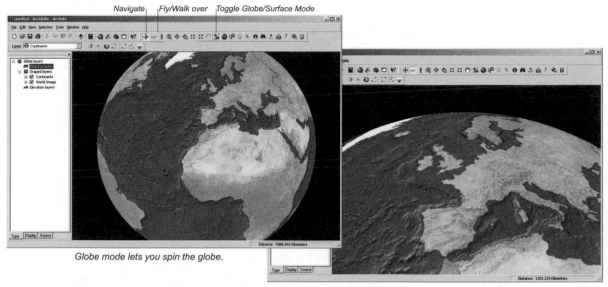

Globe mode lets you spin the globe.

Surface mode lets you travel over the surface.

Capturing a navigation path as an animation

ArcScene and ArcGlobe let you record the path of your navigation and play it back as an animation. You do this using the Animation toolbar (click the View menu, then select Toolbars and select Animation). Press Record, then start navigating through the scene as described above. The navigation is recorded as you move through the view or spin the globe. Press the Escape button on the keyboard to stop navigating, then click the Stop button on the Animation Controls to stop recording. Click Play to replay the animation.

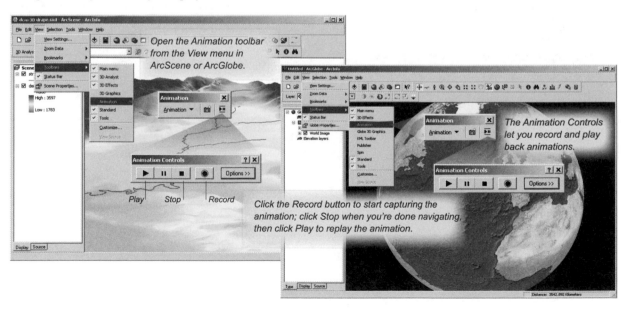

Open the Animation toolbar from the View menu in ArcScene or ArcGlobe.

The Animation Controls let you record and play back animations.

Play Stop Record

Click the Record button to start capturing the animation; click Stop when you're done navigating, then click Play to replay the animation.

Creating an animation by capturing individual views

You can use the Animation toolbar to create an animation in ArcMap, ArcScene, or ArcGlobe by capturing a "snapshot" of each static view (the map, scene, or globe view) in a sequence (these are known as keyframes). You then play back the captured frames—the interim frames are automatically filled in to create an animation. You'd use this method to animate panning across or zooming into a map.

Use the navigation tools to set up a scene, then click Capture on the Animation toolbar to create a keyframe. When you're done capturing frames, use Play on the Animation Controls toolbar to play the animation (zooming on a topographic map draped over a surface, in this example).

You'd also use it to capture a series of static views in a scene or globe view (rather than capturing a navigation as described earlier), and then play them back. This would let you animate, for example, changing layers on a globe—from shaded relief, through country boundaries, to population density.

You can also animate changes to the map, scene, or globe display—for example, you might gradually increase the transparency of one layer to reveal a layer beneath. To do this, you create the keyframes by setting the display parameters and then creating a frame. Click Create Keyframe on the Animation drop-down menu. Set the Type to Map Layer (ArcMap), Layer (ArcScene), or Globe Layer (ArcGlobe) and select the layer you'll be animating (the Source object). Then click New to create a new track. Set the layer properties for the first frame (for example, you might change the transparency or symbology in the Layer Properties dialog box), and enter a name for the frame. Then click Create. Change the layer settings, enter a name for the next frame, and click Create again. Repeat this process for each frame; click Close when you're done.

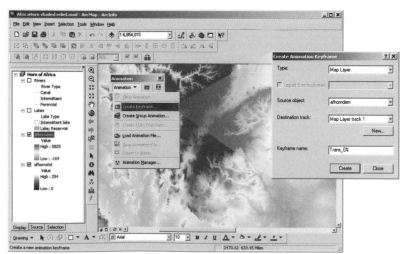

Use Create Keyframe to animate changes in the properties of a layer (such as symbology or transparency settings). Click the New button to create a new track; then change the layer display settings and name each keyframe before creating the frame. All the frames will be contained in the track.

When you play the animation, the interim frames are created. In this example, the transparency of the elevation layer increases to reveal the hillshade layer beneath, creating a shaded relief map.

To animate a sequence of layers, add the layers to the map and select Create Group Animation on the Animation drop-down menu. When you play the animation, the layers will display in sequence (from top to bottom in the table of contents). You'd do this, for example, to create an animation of the locations of different types of crimes in a city, by police beat.

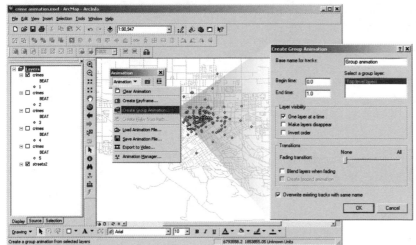

Use Create Group Animation to animate a sequence of layers on your map.

Saving and modifying an animation

The animation is only active during the current ArcMap, ArcScene, or ArcGlobe session, unless you save it. You can reload a saved animation to run in another session. Use the Animation Manager to edit animations (to remove unneeded keyframes, for example). You can also export an animation to a video file (.avi or .mov) that can be played in other software programs.

Use the Animation drop-down menu on the toolbar to Save an animation (or load a saved one).

Save

The Animation Manager lets you edit the animation.

Creating a time series animation

ArcGIS Desktop lets you dynamically display—and create animations for—data that has a time element. You can animate the path of a feature that moves through space over time (such as a vehicle or a storm), the occurrence of events or phenomena over a period of time in a region (such as earthquakes, or crimes), or the change in static features over time (such as counties that increase or decrease in population each year). Time series animations can be created using the Animation toolbar in ArcMap, ArcScene, or ArcGlobe. The ArcGIS Tracking Analyst extension provides additional options for displaying and animating temporal data.

Creating a time series animation using the Animation toolbar

Any layers you've added to a map in ArcMap, a scene in ArcScene, or a globe view in ArcGlobe can be animated using the Animation toolbar, provided they include a field defined as Date field type or containing date and/or time data as a text string in one of several standard formats. Open the Animation toolbar from the View menu (point to Toolbars, and click Animation). You first create a new track containing a start keyframe and an end keyframe.

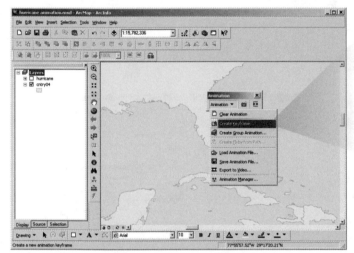

To create a time-based animation using the Animation toolbar, click Create Keyframe on the Animation drop-down menu. Then create a new track and the start and end keyframes.

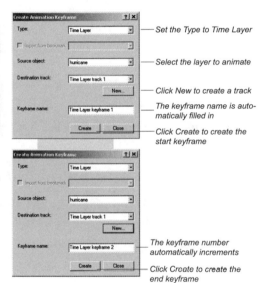

— Set the Type to Time Layer

— Select the layer to animate

— Click New to create a track

— The keyframe name is automatically filled in

— Click Create to create the start keyframe

— The keyframe number automatically increments

— Click Create to create the end keyframe

Next you modify the track properties to specify the field containing the date/time data, specify the format (if the data is stored as a text string), and calculate the time values for the keyframes (this is the range for the automation). You can then modify the keyframe properties to control the playback.

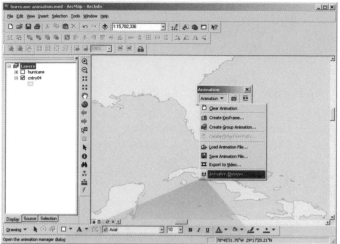

Use the Animation Manager to specify the settings for the animation. On the Tracks tab, select the newly created Time Layer track. Then click Properties.

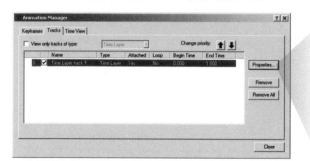

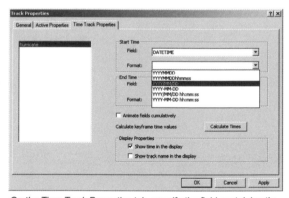

On the Time Track Properties tab, specify the field containing the date/time data. Use the drop-down menu to specify the format of the data (if the field is defined as a Date type, you don't need to specify the format). Then click Calculate Times.

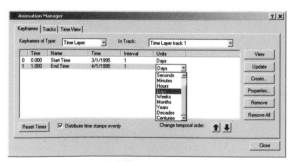

On the Keyframes tab, alter the time interval and units to use, based on your date/time field values. Use the default start and end times, or alter them to shorten the animation time.

To display the animation, use the Animation Controls dialog box or the Time View tab slider in the Animation Manager. Use the options on the Animation drop-down menu to save the animation or export it to a movie file (.avi or .mov) you can play in a media player.

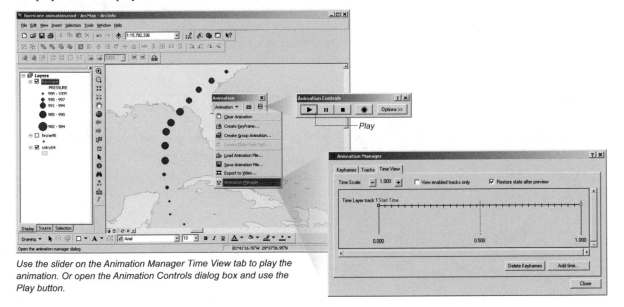

Use the slider on the Animation Manager Time View tab to play the animation. Or open the Animation Controls dialog box and use the Play button.

Creating an animation using Tracking Analyst

The ArcGIS Tracking Analyst extension allows you to display temporal data dynamically or capture an animation. Tracking Analyst accepts a wide range of date/time formats. It also has advanced options for symbolizing temporal data, viewing animations, and interacting with temporal data (for example, it will capture a live data feed to track objects in real time). The Tracking Analyst—if enabled—is accessed from inside ArcMap, via the Tracking Analyst toolbar. You load a dataset containing a time element to create a temporal dataset using the Add Data button on the Tracking Analyst toolbar.

Use the Add button on the Tracking Analyst toolbar to open the Add Temporal Data Wizard.

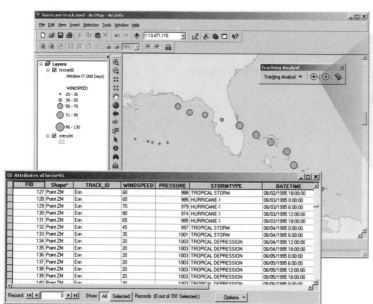

Any geographic data having a date and/or time stamp can be used with Tracking Analyst.

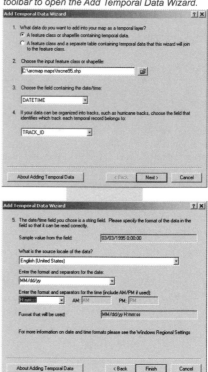

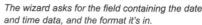

The wizard asks for the field containing the date and time data, and the format it's in.

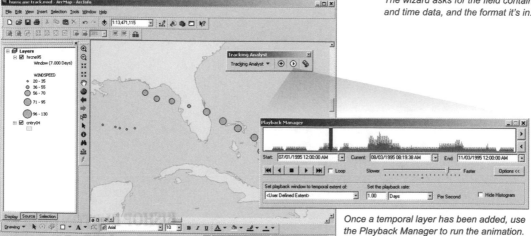

Once a temporal layer has been added, use the Playback Manager to run the animation.

There are a number of options for displaying the data—you can animate the time series, drag the red bar to manually step through the frames, or pick a specific date from the calendar to see the conditions on that day and time.

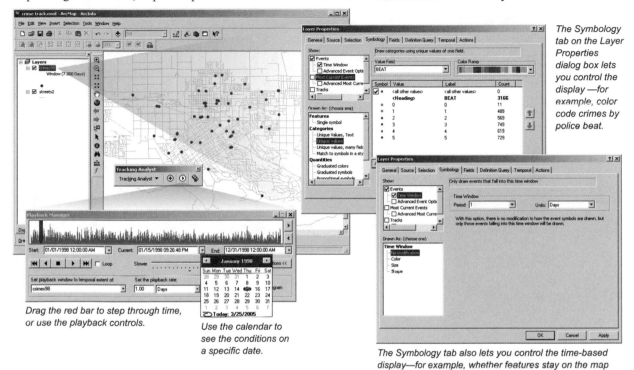

The Symbology tab on the Layer Properties dialog box lets you control the display —for example, color code crimes by police beat.

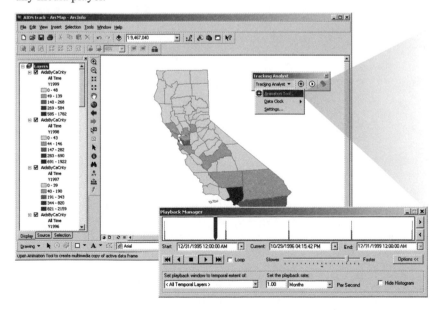

Drag the red bar to step through time, or use the playback controls.

Use the calendar to see the conditions on a specific date.

The Symbology tab also lets you control the time-based display—for example, whether features stay on the map as the animation plays, or only appear during a brief time window.

Use the Animation tool to create and save an animation. Animations are saved as a movie file that can be played using any media player.

Open Animation Tool from the Tracking Analyst toolbar to generate an animation and save it as a movie file that can be played in any media player.

Geographic Analysis

An overview of analysis in ArcGIS Desktop

GIS analysis covers a wide range of tasks and applications, from simply calculating values for a new field in a table, to modeling complex processes such as the flow of water over terrain or using statistics to perform spatial pattern analysis. The ultimate goal of analysis is to get more information from your data to make better decisions.

ArcGIS Desktop lets you perform geographic and spatial analyses on a variety of datasets: tables, feature classes, rasters, terrains, TINs, network datasets, and geometric networks. The tools to perform these analyses are found in several toolboxes in ArcToolbox, as well as on specialized toolbars in ArcMap and in several ArcGIS Desktop extension products—ArcGIS Spatial Analyst, ArcGIS 3D Analyst, and ArcGIS Network Analyst.

Types of GIS analysis

The GIS analysis functions in ArcGIS Desktop can be grouped into several fundamental types of operations: tabular analysis, data extraction, overlay analysis, distance analysis, surface creation and analysis, and statistical analysis.

Tabular analysis

Tabular analysis includes basic functions such as sorting or finding the frequency of values, modifying tables by adding and calculating new fields, and establishing and managing relationships between tables.

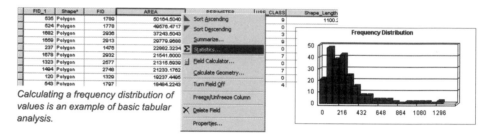

Calculating a frequency distribution of values is an example of basic tabular analysis.

Data extraction

Data extraction is a component of most analyses. It includes extracting a subset of features for analysis or clipping a study area out of a larger dataset, as well as dissolving or generalizing to create fewer, larger features from many small ones.

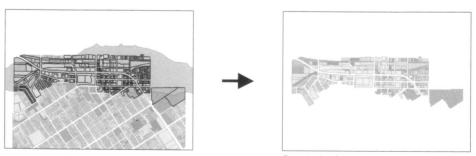

Parcels that fall completely or partially within the flood zone have been selected and saved as a new layer.

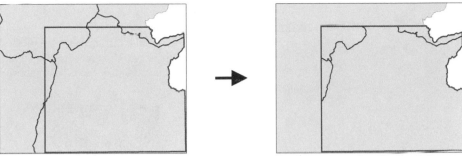

Roads have been clipped by the study area boundary to create a new dataset of roads that fall within the study area.

Overlay analysis

Overlay analysis allows you to combine layers that share a geographic extent (or at least overlap) to create a new layer that has the attributes of the input layers. This lets you find relationships between features on different layers. You can, for example, identify features that meet some combination of criteria—to site a new facility or subdivision you might overlay layers of slope, vegetation, and soils, and then select locations that are on level terrain, not forested, and on buildable soils.

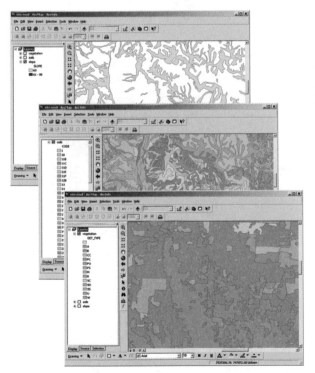

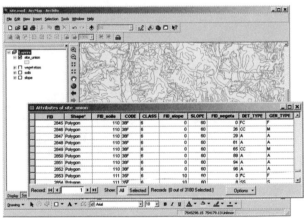

Use overlay to append fields from multiple layers to find features meeting specific criteria.

Distance analysis

ArcGIS Desktop includes a variety of distance analysis functions that allow you to measure the distance between features, find the features within a given distance of other features (buffer), create a continuous surface of distances from a set of features (such as distance from roads or streams), or find the optimum path over a network of linear features (streets or pipelines) or over terrain.

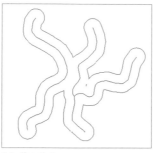

A buffer of streams

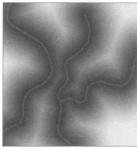

A surface of distance from streams

The shortest path between three stops on a street network

Surface creation and analysis

Surface creation functions let you create a surface of spatially continuous values from a set of sample measurements or observations (interpolation, or density), or create derived layers from a surface (slope, aspect, contours, or a hillshade view). Surface analysis functions include specialized tools for predicting the flow and dispersion of water or other materials over a surface, calculating volumes (such as cut and fill), performing visibility analysis, or calculating the amount of solar radiation received at each location.

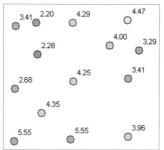

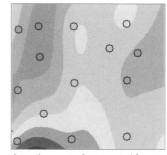

A continuous surface created from a set of sample point values.

A surface of road density—darker orange indicates higher density.

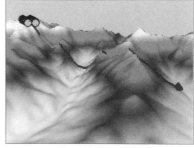

Line-of-sight analysis—green indicates areas visible from the observer point.

Statistical analysis

Statistical analysis ranges from tabular statistics, such as finding the mean or standard deviation of a set of values in a table, to functions that measure the characteristics of a distribution of geographic features (such as the center or directional trend), to spatial statistical tools that identify patterns formed by features (or their associated attribute values) and let you determine the probability the pattern did not occur by chance.

Summary statistics have been calculated for each landuse class showing the number of parcels in that class, the size of the smallest and largest parcel, the average parcel size, and the total area in the class.

The standard deviational ellipse for burglaries (showing the directional trend)

The map on the right shows statistically significant clusters of census tracts with many senior citizens (orange) or few (blue), calculated from the percentage of seniors in each tract (shown in the map on the left).

ArcGIS Desktop analysis tools

ArcGIS Desktop provides a range of tools to perform analysis operations. The tools described in this chapter are some of the most commonly used—there are many more tools available. Many of the tools are generic and can be applied to any application or industry. Some are more application specific (such as functions for analyzing groundwater movement).

Most tools for analyzing vector (feature) data are provided with ArcGIS Desktop (if you have an ArcInfo license). Most tools for analyzing surfaces (rasters and TINs) are included in several different ArcGIS Desktop extension products.

Tools for analyzing features

ArcMap functions for analyzing feature data include tabular analysis, available from the menus associated with table views, and some data extraction functions, available from the Selection menu. ArcToolbox functions include tabular analysis, data extraction, feature overlay analysis, feature distance analysis, and statistical analysis.

The Utility Network Analyst toolbar—included in ArcMap—allows you to trace flow over electric, water, or other utility networks. You can trace upstream or downstream, find loops, find connected features, and so on.

Network Analyst, an extension product, provides functionality for distance analysis along connected linear features such as in transportation networks.

Tools for analyzing surfaces

Three ArcGIS Desktop extension products—Spatial Analyst, 3D Analyst, and Geostatistical Analyst—provide tools for creating and analyzing surfaces. While they include some overlapping functionality, they were each developed to meet the needs of analysts requiring specific capabilities for their application.

Spatial Analyst includes tools for analyzing the relationships between rasters. These can be rasters representing surfaces of continuous values (such as elevation, slope, temperature, or precipitation), or rasters representing contiguous areas (such as soil types, vegetation types, land cover, or geology). Along with tools for managing and processing rasters, Spatial Analyst includes functions for raster data extraction, overlay analysis, and distance analysis, as well as for surface creation and analysis.

3D Analyst provides functionality for surface creation and analysis. 3D Analyst also includes visualization tools for creating perspective and globe views (see 'Creating relief maps and perspective views' and 'Creating dynamic views and animations' in Chapter 4).

Geostatistical Analyst provides advanced functionality for creating continuous surfaces from a set of sample points. It also includes tools for interactive data exploration to aid in the selection of appropriate interpolation parameters. These are accessed from the Geostatistical Analyst toolbar in ArcMap. The Geostatistical Analyst toolbox (in ArcToolbox) contains a set of geostatistics tools that can be used in scripts or models.

This table summarizes some common types of GIS analysis and where the specific functionality is located in ArcGIS Desktop.

	ArcMap	ArcToolbox Tools	Network Analyst Extension	Spatial Analyst Extension	3D Analyst Extension	Geostatistical Analyst Extension
Tabular Analysis	Sort field Summarize by other field(s) Field summary statistics	Value frequency Field summary statistics				
Data Extraction	Interactive feature selection Select features by attribute Select features by location	Clip/Split features Update features Select features by attribute		Extract raster cells by attribute or geometry Extract raster cell values to point features		
Overlay Analysis		Feature overlay		Combine rasters Raster overlay Cross-tabulated areas		
Distance Analysis	Measure distance tool Select features within distance Utility network trace	Buffer features Point-to-feature distance Allocation	Shortest/Least-cost path and allocation over a transportation network	Euclidean and cost distance Shortest and least-cost path and allocation over a surface		
Surface Creation and Analysis				Surface interpolation Surface density Surface analysis	Surface interpolation TIN creation Surface analysis 3D visualization	Advanced surface interpolation (kriging) Predictive surfaces
Statistical Analysis		Geographic center/dispersion Pattern/Cluster analysis Directional trend analysis		Raster cell, neighborhood, zonal, and multivariate statistics		Exploratory spatial data analysis

In many cases, you'll combine different types of analysis to perform more complex analyses. A suitability analysis, for example, may involve distance analysis and surface creation to generate input layers, data extraction to clip out the study area, tabular analysis to reclassify feature values, overlay analysis to combine layers, and data extraction to select polygons meeting the criteria and to dissolve the selected polygons to create the final areas.

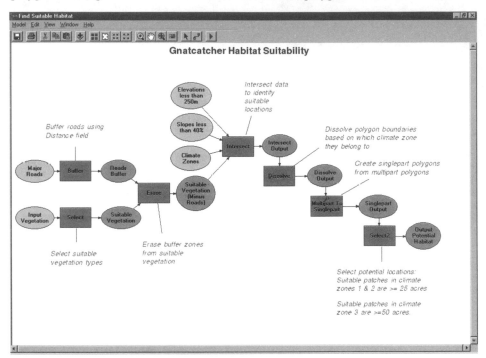

An example of a suitability model, built using the ModelBuilder interface

Models and scripts are often used to automate the analysis process. You can easily change the parameters of the analysis by opening a tool in the model or editing the script. You can then rerun the analysis without having to run all the individual tools. Models and scripts are also a good way to document, store, and share your analysis methods.

The underlying engine for analysis is geoprocessing. Broadly, geoprocessing involves applying a function, or set of functions, to existing data to get new data. Most of the geoprocessing functions in ArcGIS Desktop are provided through tools in ArcToolbox. Some functions appear as menu options in ArcMap. Accessing and using geoprocessing functions—including building models and scripts—is discussed in the section 'The ArcGIS Desktop framework' in Chapter 1.

The GIS analysis process

GIS analysis is a process that follows a basic set of steps. The actual methods you use can be simple or complex, from selecting features having a given value to building a model to combine many layers of data. For simple methods, such as a selection to extract features from a dataset, you might intuitively implement the process as a single operation, rather than as distinct steps.

Frame the question

You start an analysis by figuring out what information you need. This is often in the form of a question. Where were most of the burglaries last month? How much forest is in each watershed? Which parcels are within 500 feet of this liquor store? Being as specific as possible about the question you're trying to answer will help you decide how to approach the analysis, which method to use, and how to present the results.

Other factors that influence the analysis are how it will be used and who will use it. You might simply be exploring the data on your own to get a better understanding of how a place developed or how things behave; or you may need to present results—to policy makers or the public for discussion, for scientific review, or in a courtroom setting. In the latter cases, your methods need to be more rigorous, and the results more focused.

Prepare your data

The type of data and features you're working with helps determine the specific method you use (for example, your forest and watershed data might be stored as polygons, or rasters). Conversely, if you need to use a specific method to get the level of information you require, you might need to obtain additional data. You have to know what you have (the type of features and attributes), and what you need to get or create. Creating new data may simply mean calculating new values in the data table or obtaining new layers. Understanding the data that goes into the analysis will help you interpret the results.

Choose a method

There are almost always two or three ways of getting the information you need. Often, one method is quicker and gives you more approximate information. Others may require more detailed data and more processing time and effort, but provide more exact results. For example, you can find parcels within 500 feet of a school as the crow flies—by simply creating a buffer—or within 500 feet walking along streets and paths (a more involved network analysis). You decide which method to use based on your original question and how the results of the analysis will be used.

Process the data

Once you've selected a method, you perform the necessary steps in the GIS. This often involves running several functions in sequence. For example, to find the amount of forest in each watershed, you might extract the area of interest from the forest layer, convert it from raster to polygons, overlay it with the watershed boundaries, then do tabular analysis to calculate the total forest in each watershed. In the case of statistical analysis, you'll also want to calculate the statistical significance of your initial results.

Investigate and analyze the results

Looking at and questioning the results help you decide whether the information is valid or useful, or whether you should rerun the analysis using different parameters or even a different method. GIS makes it relatively easy to make these changes and create new output. You can compare the results from different analyses and see which method provides the most accurate information.

Working with tabular data

An important part of analysis is working with the data in tables. These can be standalone tables, or attribute tables associated with feature or raster data. You may want information about the values in a table for its own sake or in preparation for other analysis. For example, you'd want to identify any outliers (extreme high or low values) before creating a surface or performing pattern analysis, since outliers can skew the results of your analysis.

Exploring tables in ArcMap

To sort a field or summarize the values by another field, open the table in ArcMap and right-click the field name.

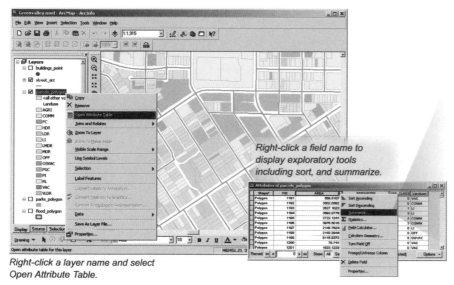

Right-click a field name to display exploratory tools including sort, and summarize.

Right-click a layer name and select Open Attribute Table.

The Summarize dialog box lets you get summary statistics for one field by other fields—for example, total area of each landuse type. The results are saved in a new table and added to the map.

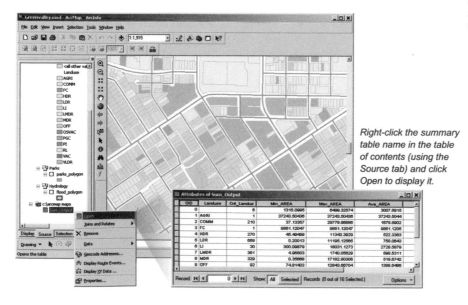

Right-click the summary table name in the table of contents (using the Source tab) and click Open to display it.

Right-clicking a field name in the table window in ArcMap also allows you to calculate summary statistics for the field—such as the minimum and maximum values, the mean value, and so on. The results are displayed in a window that also includes a histogram showing the distribution of values.

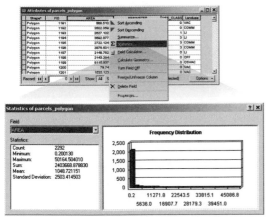

The Statistics window gives you information about the distribution of values.

When you open a table, by default ArcMap includes all the fields, with the values in their original data formats. To specify which fields to display in the table window, to assign an alternate name (alias), and to format data values (to show fewer decimal places, for example), use the Fields tab in the Layer Properties dialog box.

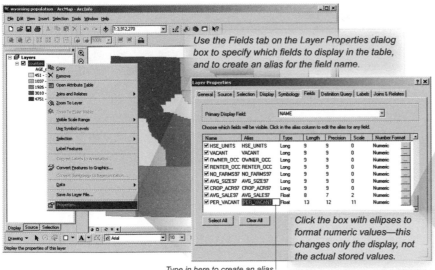

Use the Fields tab on the Layer Properties dialog box to specify which fields to display in the table, and to create an alias for the field name.

Click the box with ellipses to format numeric values—this changes only the display, not the actual stored values.

Type in here to create an alias.

349

You can also hide a field by right-clicking the column heading and clicking Turn Field Off.

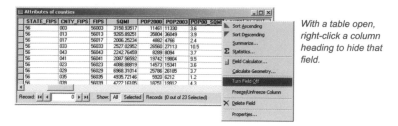

With a table open, right-click a column heading to hide that field.

Use the Options button on the table window to set the font type and size for the entire table—click Appearance on the menu, then change the settings in the Table Appearance dialog box.

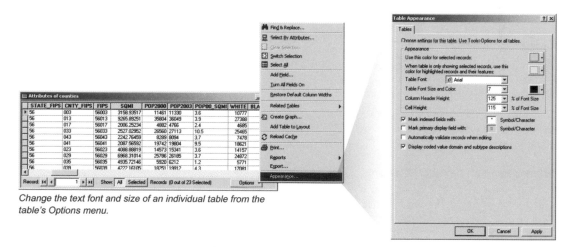

Change the text font and size of an individual table from the table's Options menu.

Use the Options settings on the Tools menu to specify the appearance of all tables in the map document.

Tabular data can be displayed graphically in ArcMap using graphs. Graphs present a visual summary of attribute values. ArcMap also lets you create a finished report from tabular data. Graphs and reports can be printed or added to a map layout. See 'Creating a graph' and 'Creating a report' in Chapter 4.

Exploring tabular data in ArcCatalog

You can also sort fields and get summary statistics in ArcCatalog, using the Preview tab. This is a quick way to get a sense of the distribution of values.

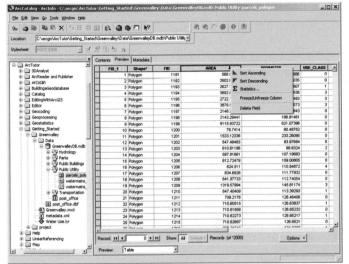

Right-click a field name in table preview mode to access sorting and statistics options.

ArcToolbox tools for working with tabular data

ArcToolbox includes tools for calculating summary statistics and a frequency table for a field. The results are written to tables you can add to a map or preview in ArcCatalog. Having the information in a table is useful if you need to save the information or use it in additional analysis. The tools are useful for including in models and scripts.

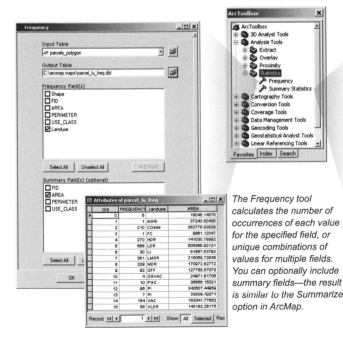

The Frequency tool calculates the number of occurrences of each value for the specified field, or unique combinations of values for multiple fields. You can optionally include summary fields—the result is similar to the Summarize option in ArcMap.

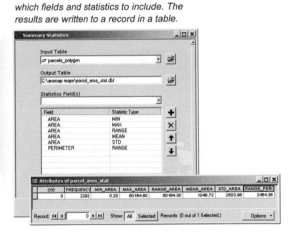

The Summary Statistics tool lets you specify which fields and statistics to include. The results are written to a record in a table.

Adding fields and calculating attribute values

Fields are usually added to attribute tables and populated with values when building a geodatabase. When performing analysis, though, you may find you need to add fields to a table and assign or calculate values. For example, you might reclassify detailed categories into general ones, or calculate percentages or densities from existing fields to map or use in your analysis. The usual process for this is to create a new field in the table and then calculate the new values for the field. In some cases—such as when reclassifying categories—you'll select subsets of features before calculating values.

Using ArcMap to add a field and calculate values

You'll likely be working in ArcMap to perform your analysis. To add a field, open the table, click Options, and click Add Field. Right-click the column heading for the newly added field to calculate values for the field.

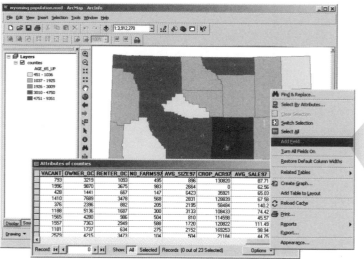
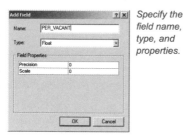

Specify the field name, type, and properties.

Use the Options menu on the table window to add a field.

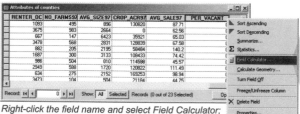

Right-click the field name and select Field Calculator; then use the calculator to build the expression.

When you calculate values, you'll get this warning, unless you're in an edit session.

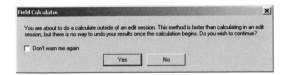

If you calculate values outside an edit session, you can't revert to the previous values for that field (you can always rerun the calculation and overwrite the values you just calculated). The advantage of calculating values in an edit session is that you can undo the calculation if necessary, using the Undo button on the Edit menu. You can't, however, add or delete fields while you're in an edit session—you'll need to add the field before starting the session. Editing a table also allows you to assign values to features individually (using the Edit Table button on the Editor toolbar). See 'Starting and managing and edit session' and 'Adding and editing attribute data' in Chapter 3.

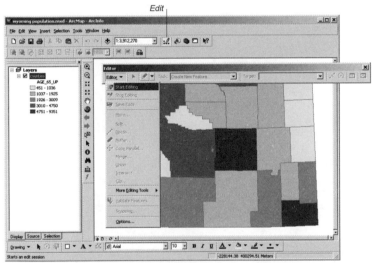

To edit a table in an edit session, click the Edit button to open the Editor toolbar, then select Start Editing from the drop-down menu.

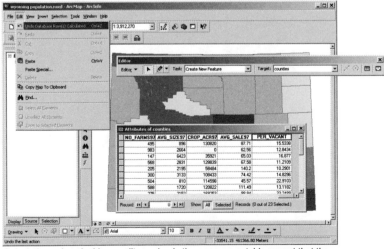

Calculating values inside an edit session is the same as outside except that the Undo button is available on the Edit menu.

Using ArcCatalog to modify a table

ArcCatalog also allows you to add fields to a table and calculate values, in the table preview window. You'd use ArcCatalog for this if you were reviewing and preparing your datasets prior to performing analysis in ArcMap and know there are certain fields you will need. If a layer is already open in ArcMap, you can't add or delete fields in ArcCatalog (a warning message is displayed). The reverse is also true.

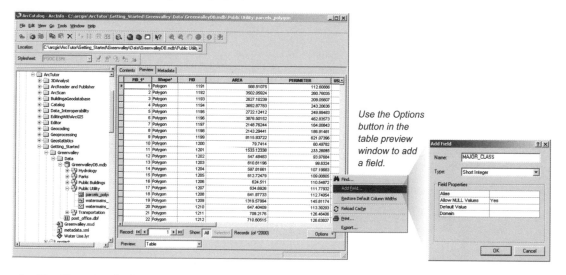

Use the Options button in the table preview window to add a field.

ArcToolbox tools for working with fields

ArcToolbox contains tools for adding and deleting fields in a table, calculating values, and setting a default value for a new field. The parameters are the same as for creating fields and calculating values using ArcMap or ArcCatalog. The ArcToolbox tools are particularly useful when you're working with tables in a script or model.

Tools for working with fields can be found in the Fields toolset, located in the Data Management toolbox.

Joining tables

Often in analysis you'll need to join the attributes contained in two separate tables. You'd do this when assigning the attributes in a standalone table to geographic features so you can map or analyze the features using the additional attributes. For example, you may want to join health statistics for a set of counties, stored in a standalone table, to the attribute table for a map layer of counties. You join the tables using a field they have in common, such as county name. You can then display the counties symbolized by the values for a particular statistic, such as the number of flu cases in each.

Another type of join—a spatial join—is used to join the tables of two map layers using the spatial relationship between features. Spatial join lets you, for example, assign demographic attributes to stores (point features) based on the census tract (polygon) they fall within.

Appending tables using a common field

Join appends the joined attributes to the original table for as long as the join is established (use Remove Join to delete the join). If you export the new layer to a dataset, the joined attributes will be saved in the dataset's attribute table. Join can be used with one-to-one or many-to-one relationships (see 'Building relationships between features and tables' in Chapter 2 for a discussion of types of tabular relationships).

Right-click a layer name, select Joins and Relates, and click Join.

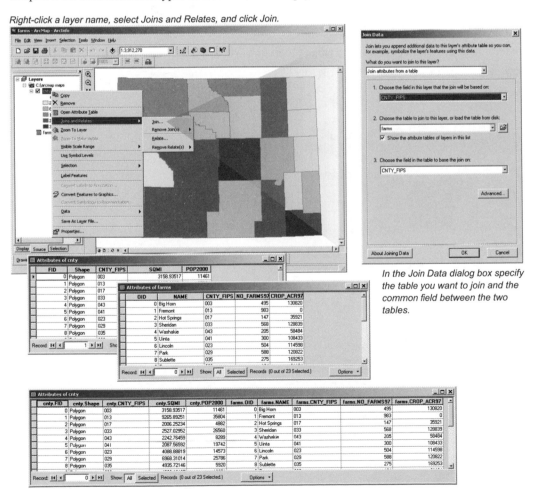

In the Join Data dialog box specify the table you want to join and the common field between the two tables.

The attributes of the join table are added to the input table.

Once the tables are joined, you can use the appended attributes anywhere you access attribute values—for example, to symbolize features (see 'Using attributes to symbolize features' in Chapter 4).

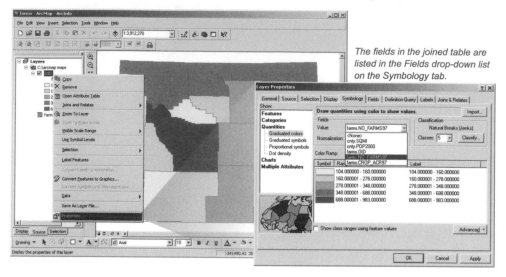

The fields in the joined table are listed in the Fields drop-down list on the Symbology tab.

To permanently save the appended attributes in a single table, export the layer to a new dataset.

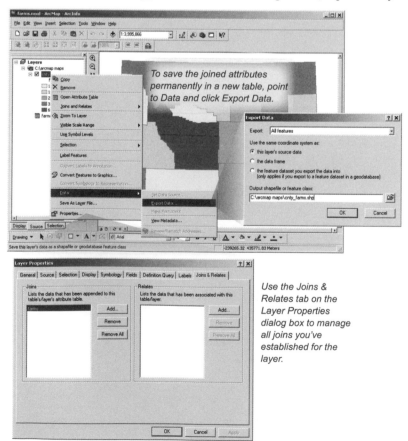

Use the Joins & Relates tab on the Layer Properties dialog box to manage all joins you've established for the layer.

To join tables within a script or model, use the ArcToolbox Add Join tool. In this case, the join is in effect only for the duration of the ArcMap or ArcCatalog session.

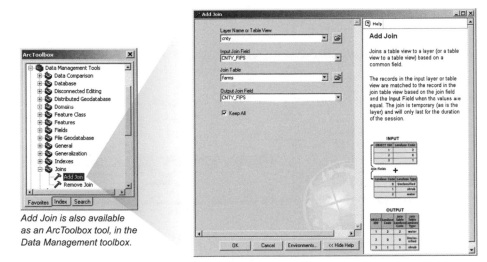

Add Join is also available as an ArcToolbox tool, in the Data Management toolbox.

Relating tables using a common field

Relate can be used with one-to-many or many-to-many relationships. Rather than appending the attributes, Relate only stores the relationship (or link) between the tables (it can't append the attributes to the original table since there may be many records in the related table pointing to a single record in the original table)—the related records are accessed on demand, when you select a feature or record in the original table.

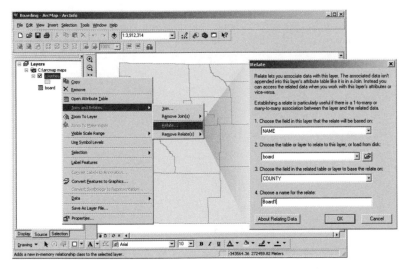

Relate is accessed by right-clicking a layer name. The relate is a link stored with the map—so in addition to specifying the related table and the common field between the two tables, you specify a name for the relate.

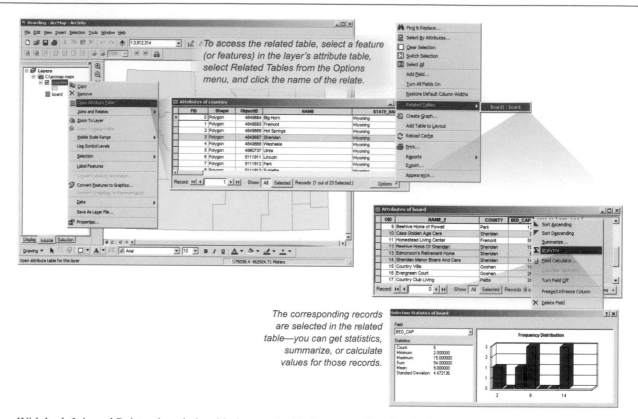

To access the related table, select a feature (or features) in the layer's attribute table, select Related Tables from the Options menu, and click the name of the relate.

The corresponding records are selected in the related table—you can get statistics, summarize, or calculate values for those records.

With both Join and Relate, the relationship is stored with the map, rather than in the database, so if you add the datasets to another map, the join or relate will not exist—you'll need to re-create it. If necessary, you can create relationships within your geodatabase that will persist from map to map (see 'Building relationships between features and tables' in Chapter 2).

Appending tables using spatial relationships

Spatial join allows you to assign the attributes from one set of features to another, based on the spatial relationship between the features—fully contained within, intersecting, or within a distance. The type of relationship available for the join depends on the types of data you're joining. The attributes of the joined dataset are appended to the table of the input dataset, and saved as a new dataset that is added to the map. One reason to do a spatial join is simply to add an attribute to a feature, such as adding the county name (in a polygon layer of county boundaries) to auto accidents (points). Another is to be able to summarize the data, such as summarizing the number of accidents in each county.

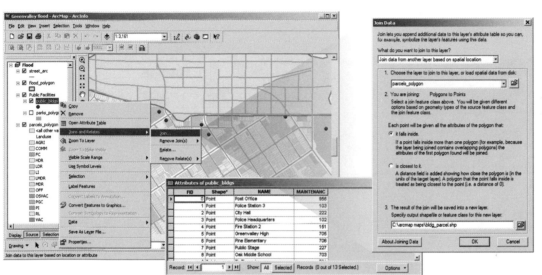

Spatial join is accessed from the Join option—use the drop-down menu to specify join based on spatial location.

Attributes of features that meet the spatial criteria are joined. In this example, information about the parcel each building sits on has been added to the building layer's attribute table.

Selecting a subset of features

Selection is used to extract a subset of existing features from a dataset. You'd select features to analyze the subset of features separately from the full dataset or to create a new dataset containing only the selected features. Selections are created by selecting features interactively on a map, by using features from other layers that overlap or are near the features you want to select, or by selecting features that match attribute values you specify. The selected set can be modified by adding to the selection, removing from it, switching it with the unselected set, and so on.

Selecting features interactively

Use the Select Features tool to select features interactively by pointing at them on a map in ArcMap. Click to select a single feature.

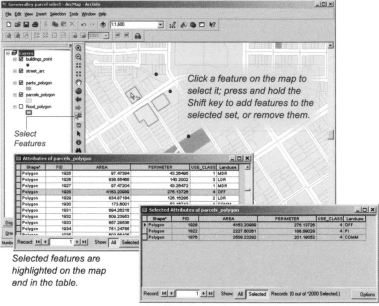

Click a feature on the map to select it; press and hold the Shift key to add features to the selected set, or remove them.

Select Features

Selected features are highlighted on the map and in the table.

Click Show Selected to view only the selected features.

Drag the tool to select features intersecting a rectangle.

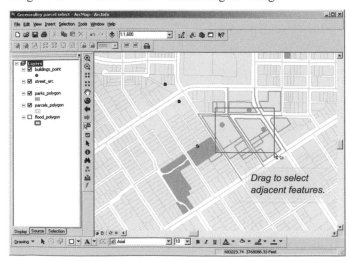

Drag to select adjacent features.

By default, layers are selectable when added to a map, so if you have multiple layers on your map, when you point at a feature or drag to create a selection rectangle, all features at that location—from any of the layers—will be selected. You can work with the selected features for each layer separately; however, you may want to select features only from a specific layer, rather than all layers. To specify which layer(s) to select features from, use the Set Selectable Layers option on the Selection menu, or use the Selection tab at the bottom of the table of contents. If a layer is selectable, features will not be selected unless it is also currently displayed (it is checked on in the table of contents).

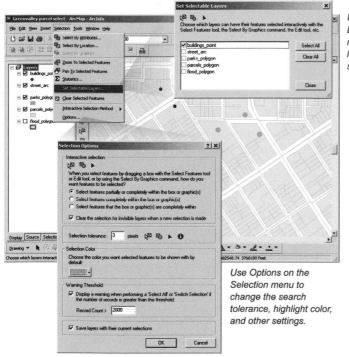

Use Set Selectable Layers on the Selection menu to specify which layers features can be selected from.

Use Options on the Selection menu to change the search tolerance, highlight color, and other settings.

The Selection tab at the bottom of the table of contents is another way of setting selectable layers.

A default color is used to highlight selected features. Change the selection highlight color for an individual layer using the Layer Properties dialog box for that layer.

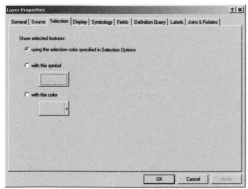

The Selection tab on the Layer Properties dialog box lets you specify a unique highlight symbol or color for an individual layer.

Selecting using feature geography

Use the Select By Location option on the Selection menu in ArcMap to select features in one layer based on their geographic relationship to features in another layer (to select parcels containing public buildings, for example)

Open the Select By Location dialog box from the Selection menu.

The dialog box lets you specify the layer(s) to select from, the spatial operator, and the layer to use to create the selection.

Spatial operators—available from the drop-down list—include overlay, adjacency and distance.

The Select Layer By Location tool in ArcToolbox (in the Data Management toolbox) performs the same function as Select By Location.

Selecting using feature attributes

Another way of extracting a subset of features is to select them based on an attribute value, or combination of values. This approach is often used to select features that meet some criteria you've defined. You create a query statement using the field name, Boolean operators ("equal to," "greater than," and so on), and the attribute value.

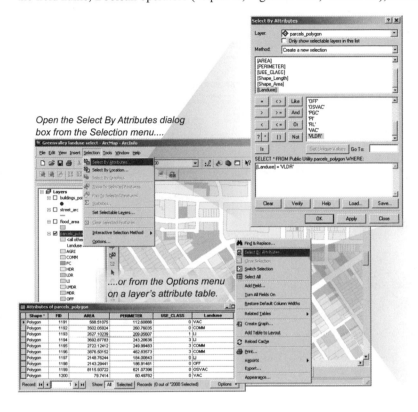

Open the Select By Attributes dialog box from the Selection menu....

....or from the Options menu on a layer's attribute table.

The dialog box lets you build a SQL query using logical operators—choose fields from the top panel and choose values from the list in the middle-right panel. Your query statement is constructed in the lower panel (you can also enter explicit values here).

Selecting using attributes is also available in ArcToolbox. The tool dialog boxes are similar to the ArcMap selection dialog boxes. The tools are useful for performing selections from within a script or model.

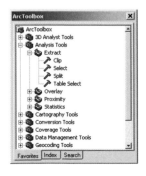

The Extract toolset in the Analysis toolbox contains two tools for selecting using attribute values. Use Select for feature attribute tables; Table Select can be used for feature attribute or standalone tables.

The Select Layer By Attribute tool is in the Layers and Table Views toolset in the Data Management toolbox.

Specifying the selection method

Once you've created a selected set, you can specify whether subsequent selections create a new selected set (the default), are added to the current set, removed from the set, or selected from the current set (to create a subset of the selection).

For interactive selection using the Select Features tool, the Interactive Selection Method is set on the Selection menu.

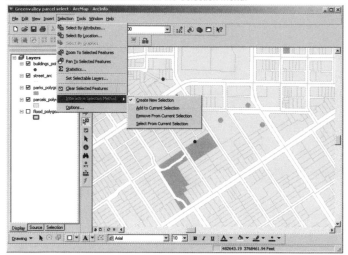

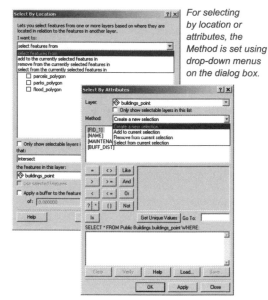

For selecting by location or attributes, the Method is set using drop-down menus on the dialog box.

Working with a selected set

Once you've created a selected set, options for working with and managing the set are available from the Selection menu in ArcMap and from the context menu for each layer for which there is an active selection.

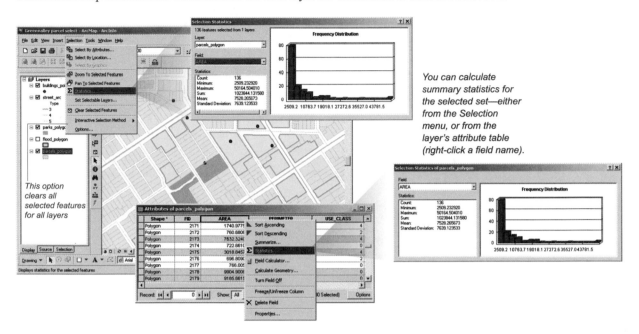

This option clears all selected features for all layers

You can calculate summary statistics for the selected set—either from the Selection menu, or from the layer's attribute table (right-click a field name).

Right-click a layer name and click Selection to access options for clearing the selection for that layer, for switching the selected and unselected features, or for selecting all features in the layer. The same options are also available from the layer table's Options menu.

Many of these options are also available from the Selection tab at the bottom of the ArcMap table of contents. Right-click a layer name to access the options. The Selection tab also shows you which features have active selections and how many features are selected, and lets you set selectable layers (using the check boxes).

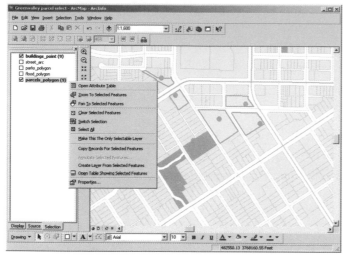

On the Selection tab, right-click a layer containing selected features to work with the selected set.

Saving the selection

When you save your map, any current selections are also saved and are active when you reopen the map. If you want to save the current selection to add to other maps, right-click the layer in the table of contents and click Save As Layer File (all the features in the layer will be saved, but the current selection will be active when you add the layer file to another map). To save only the selected features as a separate layer on your map, use Create Layer From Selected Features. You can then save this new layer as a layer file for use in other maps.

Use Create Layer From Selected Features to save only the selected features as a new layer on your map.

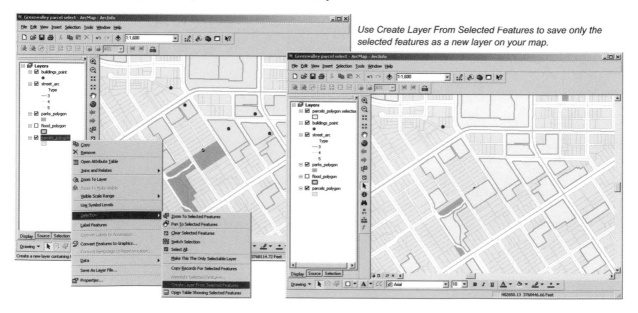

Exporting the selection

To save the selected features as a new dataset, export them. Do this if you want to use the subset of features in other analyses or distribute the dataset to other GIS users. Use Export on the layer's attribute table to export only the attribute data for the selected features.

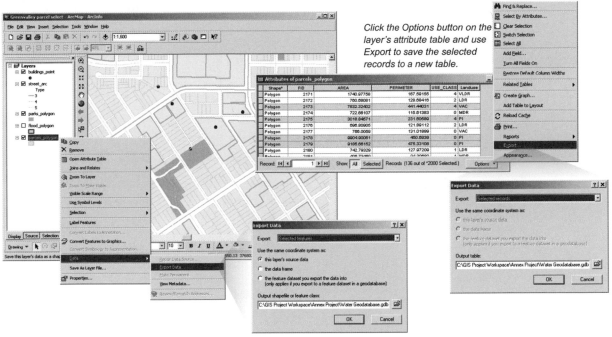

Click the Options button on the layer's attribute table and use Export to save the selected records to a new table.

Right-click a layer and use Export Data to save the selected features as a new dataset. Make sure the Export option is set to Selected features.

Other places the selected set is active

The current selection is active throughout your ArcMap session, including when summarizing or calculating attribute values in a table, and when printing a map.

When summarizing values you have the option of using only selected features.

Values can be calculated for selected features only.

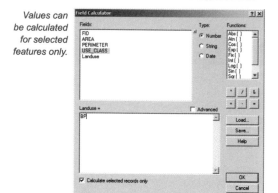

Selected features are active in Layout View and will be highlighted when you print a map.

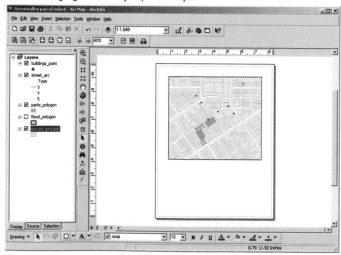

Extracting a portion of a dataset

Extraction uses an existing dataset, or geometry you define, to extract a portion of another dataset. Data extraction is used to clip data to a study area boundary, split a dataset into map sheets, or extract an area of interest for further analysis, such as when running a model for a portion of your study area. A new dataset is created containing the extracted data—the original dataset is not modified. Unlike data selection, which creates a temporary selected set, data extraction extracts data directly to a new dataset. Also unlike data selection, features are split or clipped where they are intersected by the geometry you're using for extraction. All of the data extraction tools are found within ArcToolbox.

Cropping feature datasets

The Clip tool allows you to crop a dataset using the boundary of a polygon dataset. Features are split where they intersect the cropping boundary, and the portion outside is discarded. Clip is mainly used to crop datasets to a study area boundary for mapping or analysis.

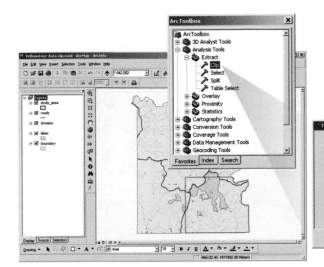

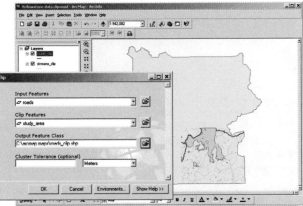

The Clip tool, in the Extract toolset (Analysis toolbox), crops datasets to a dataset boundary—in this example, roads, streams, and lakes have been clipped by the study_area dataset.

The inverse of Clip is the Erase tool. Erase discards the features (or portions of features) within the boundary and is used to remove portions of a dataset.

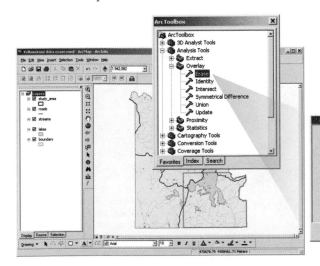

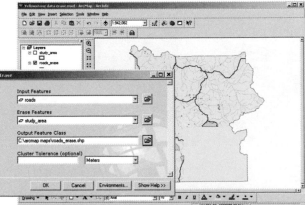

Erase, in the Overlay toolset (Analysis toolbox), removes features from the area inside the dataset boundary.

Splitting feature datasets

The Split tool divides a dataset into multiple datasets using polygon boundaries. It's often used to create map sheets from a single large dataset—a dataset of map sheet boundaries is used to split the dataset.

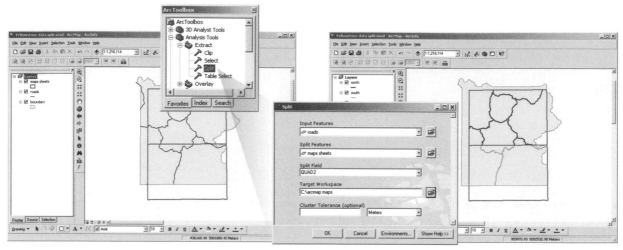

The Split tool, in the Extract toolset (Analysis toolbox), breaks a dataset into multiple output datasets. The values in the Split Field are used to define and name the output datasets (in this example the two map sheets were named "north" and "south").

Extracting raster data

Tools for extracting a portion of a raster dataset are provided as part of the Spatial Analyst extension. The tools allow you to use an existing feature or raster dataset, or a shape you define (a rectangle, circle, or polygon), to extract a portion of the raster dataset. These tools are mainly used to create a subset of the dataset for use in a model (perhaps for testing purposes) or other analysis, or to distribute to other GIS users.

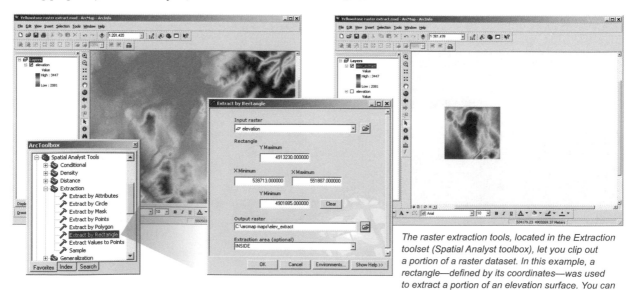

The raster extraction tools, located in the Extraction toolset (Spatial Analyst toolbox), let you clip out a portion of a raster dataset. In this example, a rectangle—defined by its coordinates—was used to extract a portion of an elevation surface. You can also define a circle or polygon, use the boundary of an existing feature or raster dataset (Extract by Mask), or use a set of point features to extract raster data.

The Extract by Attributes tool allows you to extract cells based on an attribute value, or combination of values. You create a query statement using the field name, Boolean operators ("equal to," "greater than," and so on), and the attribute value(s). This is useful if you need a subset of values for your analysis—for example, you may want to analyze the relationship between vegetation and elevation for a certain elevation range.

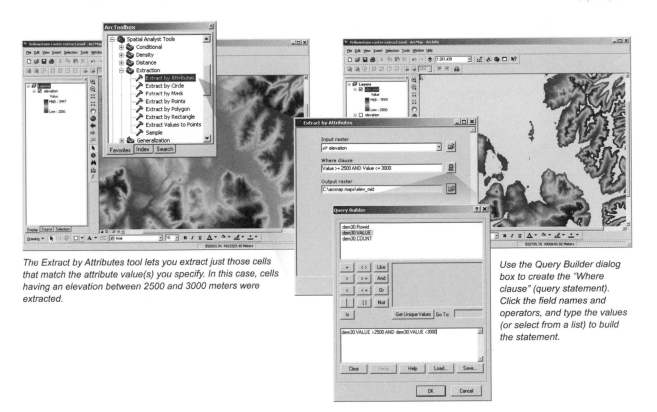

The Extract by Attributes tool lets you extract just those cells that match the attribute value(s) you specify. In this case, cells having an elevation between 2500 and 3000 meters were extracted.

Use the Query Builder dialog box to create the "Where clause" (query statement). Click the field names and operators, and type the values (or select from a list) to build the statement.

Sampling raster data

Spatial Analyst also includes tools for sampling a raster dataset. Sampling is useful for creating a subset of data for use in other, usually statistical, analyses, such as regression analysis. Rasters represent spatially continuous data—if you used the value of every cell, much of the data would be redundant (since adjacent cells often have the same or very similar values). This could skew the results of the analysis. Creating a sample from the raster allows you to capture the variation in data values without introducing redundant data.

A dataset of random point features is used to sample a raster dataset of vegetation. There are over 2 million cells in the raster, but only 11,300 sample points.

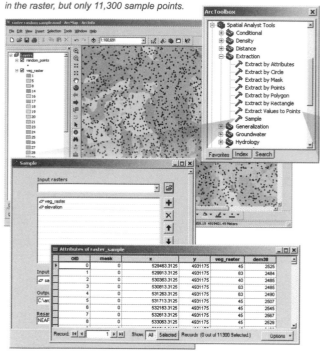

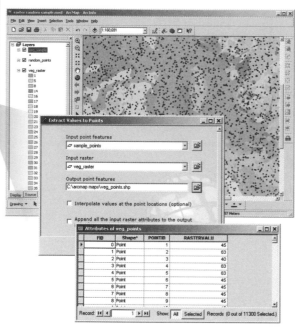

The Sample tool finds the values at each point for a list of rasters you specify. It writes the values—along with the x- and y-coordinates of each point—directly to a table you can use in other analyses.

The Extract Values to Points tool creates a new point feature dataset (containing all the input point features). It adds the value of the input raster at each point to the new dataset's attribute table.

Overlaying geographic datasets

Overlay analysis merges two or more coincident or overlapping datasets to create a new dataset having the attributes of all the input datasets. Overlay analysis is used to assign the attributes of features in one dataset to features in a coincident dataset, for example, to assign the adjacent land cover type to each segment of road. Overlay is also used to summarize the data in one dataset by the features in another—to calculate the total area of each landuse type within a flood zone you'd overlay the parcel layer with the flood zone layer and then sum the areas of the resulting polygons by landuse type. Another common use of overlay analysis is to combine the characteristics of several datasets into one. You can then find specific locations or areas that have a certain set of attribute values—that is, match the criteria you specify. For example, you'd overlay layers of vegetation type, slope, soil type, and so on, to find areas suitable for building a new subdivision. The type of data you're overlaying—features or rasters—determines the methods and tools you'll use and the results you'll get.

Overlaying feature datasets

The feature overlay functions split features in the input layer where they're overlapped by features in the overlay layer—new areas are created where polygons intersect; lines are split where polygons cross them. These new features are stored in the output layer—the original input layer is not modified. The attributes of features in the overlay layer are assigned to the appropriate new features in the output layer, along with the original attributes from the input layer. Feature overlay tools are located in ArcToolbox, in the Overlay toolset (in the Analysis toolbox).

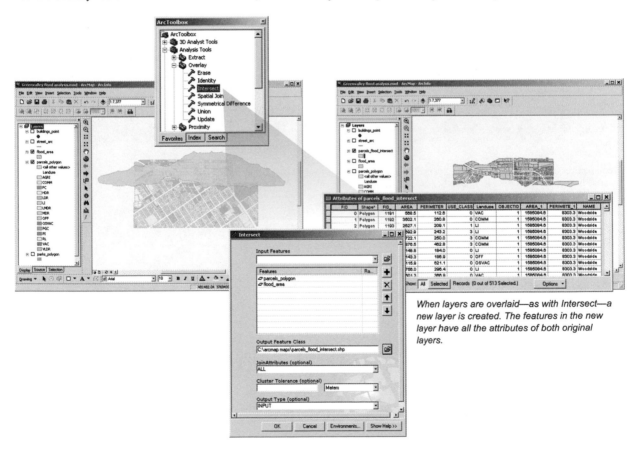

When layers are overlaid—as with Intersect—a new layer is created. The features in the new layer have all the attributes of both original layers.

373

Conceptually, the various tools are similar—they differ by the feature types they allow you to overlay, by whether you can overlay multiple layers at one time, and by which input and overlay features are maintained in the output layer.

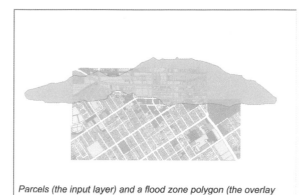

Parcels (the input layer) and a flood zone polygon (the overlay layer).

The output of Intersect is only features—or portions of features—common to both the input and overlay layers.

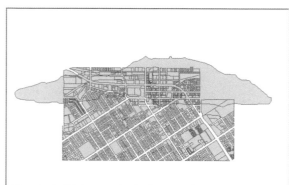

The output of Union contains the features of both the input and overlay layers—features are split where they overlap.

Identity maintains the input features—features are split where overlapped by the overlay features.

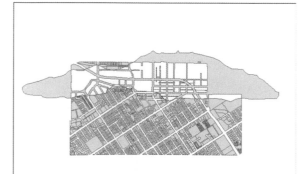

Symmetrical Difference is the inverse of intersect—it excludes features common to both input layers.

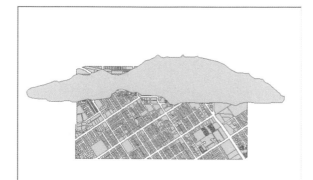

Update replaces the input features with the overlay features.

Intersect and Union can be used to overlay many layers at one time.

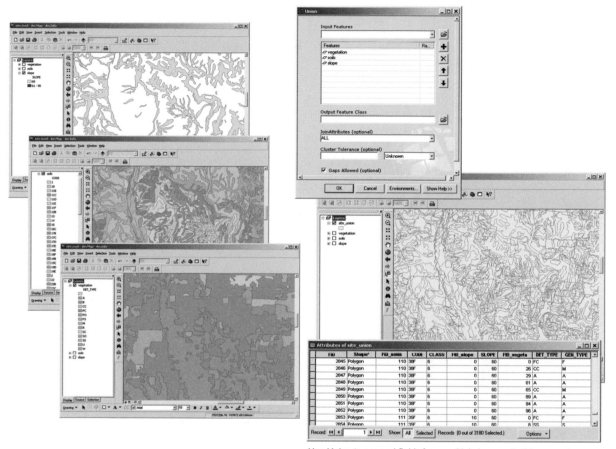

Use Union to append fields from multiple layers—in this example, slope, soil types, and vegetation types—to find features meeting specific criteria. New polygons are created where input polygons overlap.

375

Overlaying raster datasets

Raster overlay tools are located in several toolsets in the Spatial Analyst toolbox. The Combine tool (in the Local toolset) assigns a value to each cell in the output layer based on unique combinations of values from several input layers. The input values are also added to the output layer's attribute table.

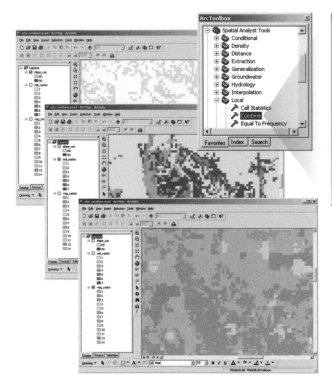

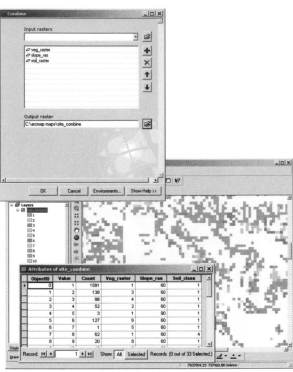

Combine assigns values based on unique combinations of values on the input rasters. You can then select or extract the cells that meet your criteria.

Another approach is to mathematically combine the layers and assign a new value to each cell in the output layer. This approach is often used to assign a suitability or risk value to each category in a layer and then add the layers, to produce an overall suitability or risk value for each cell. For example, to find areas suitable for development, you might assign values of 1 (low suitability) to 7 (high suitability) to the various slope values in a raster of slopes. You'd do the same for rasters of soil type and vegetation type. When you add the rasters (using the Map Algebra tool) the cells in the output raster have values ranging from 3 (not suitable) to 21 (highly suitable).

The various layers can also be assigned a relative importance (the values in each layer are multiplied by that layer's weight value before being summed with the other layers). The Weighted Overlay tool lets you do this.

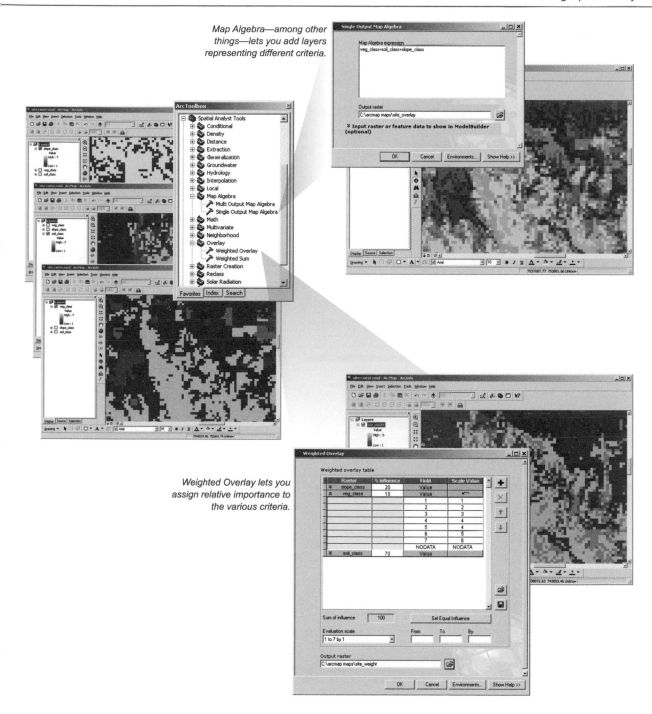

Map Algebra—among other things—lets you add layers representing different criteria.

Weighted Overlay lets you assign relative importance to the various criteria.

Spatial Analyst contains many other tools for processing, combining, and summarizing raster data. Some let you combine raster and feature data. For example, the tools in the Zonal toolset let you summarize the values in a raster by categories (or "zones"—all cells having the same category value, whether adjacent or not, constitute a zone) in another raster or feature layer. You'd use the Zonal Statistics tool to calculate the mean elevation for each vegetation type in a study area.

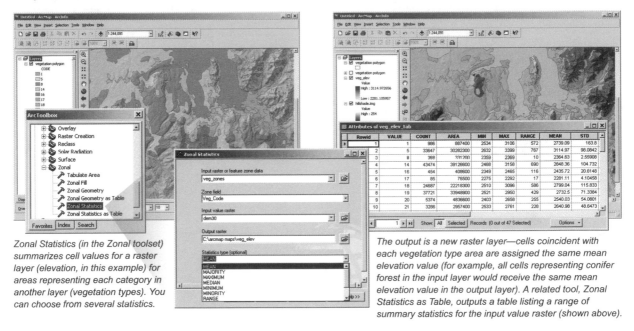

Zonal Statistics (in the Zonal toolset) summarizes cell values for a raster layer (elevation, in this example) for areas representing each category in another layer (vegetation types). You can choose from several statistics.

The output is a new raster layer—cells coincident with each vegetation type area are assigned the same mean elevation value (for example, all cells representing conifer forest in the input layer would receive the same mean elevation value in the output layer). A related tool, Zonal Statistics as Table, outputs a table listing a range of summary statistics for the input value raster (shown above).

The Tabulate Area tool, also in the Zonal toolset, calculates cross-tabulated areas between two datasets representing zones (or categories). These can be both raster, both feature, or one raster and one feature dataset. You'd use Tabulate Area to calculate the amount of each land cover type in each ownership category.

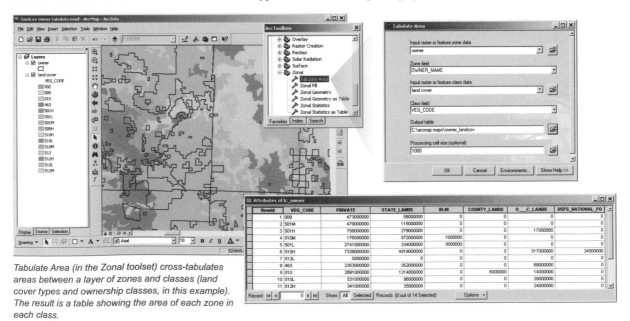

Tabulate Area (in the Zonal toolset) cross-tabulates areas between a layer of zones and classes (land cover types and ownership classes, in this example). The result is a table showing the area of each zone in each class.

Measuring distances between features

Finding distances is one of the most basic types of geographic analysis. ArcGIS Desktop provides a variety of tools for finding the distance between two locations, finding which feature or features are nearest another feature, and defining the area within a given distance of features.

Measuring distance on a map

The Measure tool in ArcMap lets you measure the distance between two locations or along a path. Click the start location and double-click at the end location. To measure a path, click as many locations as you want along the way, then double-click to end the path. The distance is displayed in the default display units of the map—you can change the units using the drop-down menu on the Measure dialog box. When measuring a path, the length of each segment is displayed along with a running total. Using the Measure tool is a quick way to interactively display distance. The Measure tool also lets you calculate the area of a polygon you draw, or display the coordinates of a point feature.

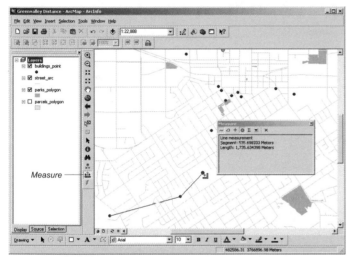

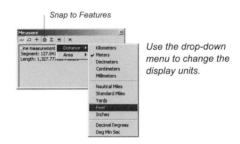

Use the Measure tool to quickly find the distance between features. The distance of each segment, and the total distance, are displayed in the Measure dialog box.

Calculating distance between features

ArcToolbox includes tools that calculate distances between features. The Near tool assigns to each input point the distance from that point to the nearest point or line in another feature class. You can then select, for example, all points within a certain distance of roads, or calculate the average distance of the points from a road. The Point Distance tool creates a table of distances between each point in one feature class and every point in another feature class.

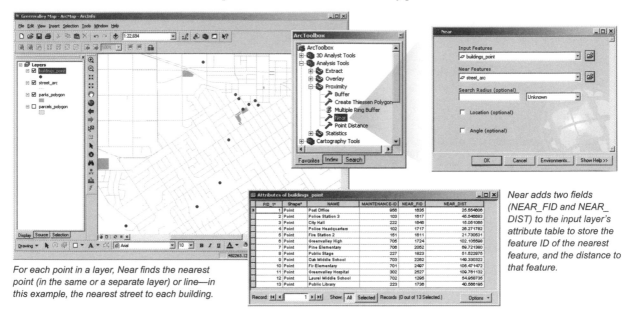

For each point in a layer, Near finds the nearest point (in the same or a separate layer) or line—in this example, the nearest street to each building.

Near adds two fields (NEAR_FID and NEAR_DIST) to the input layer's attribute table to store the feature ID of the nearest feature, and the distance to that feature.

Buffering features

A buffer identifies the area within a given distance of a feature or set of features. The Buffer tool in ArcToolbox creates a new geographic feature that defines the boundary of that area. You can add the buffer area to the map to create a graphic display of distance. You can also use the buffer area that's created to select other features—for example, all the parcels within 600 feet of a school.

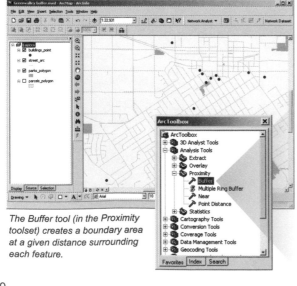

The Buffer tool (in the Proximity toolset) creates a boundary area at a given distance surrounding each feature.

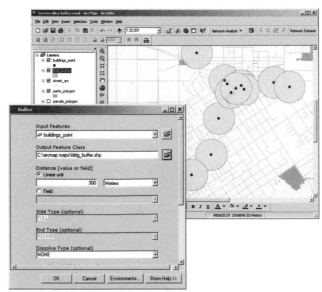

The Buffer tool provides several options—you can use an attribute value to define the buffer distance, and erase the intersecting buffer boundaries that may be created around multiple features.

Use the Field option on the Buffer dialog box to specify a field in the input dataset's attribute table containing the distance to buffer each feature. In this example, the BUFF_DIST field specifies the buffer distance, based on the type of building.

The Dissolve Type option on the Buffer dialog box lets you erase overlapping boundaries when buffering multiple features.

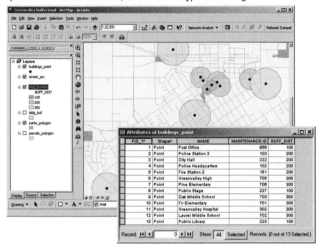

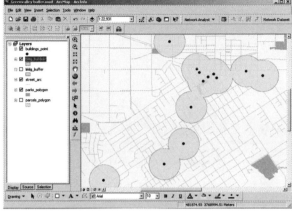

The Multiple Ring Buffer tool lets you create buffers of multiple distances at one time.

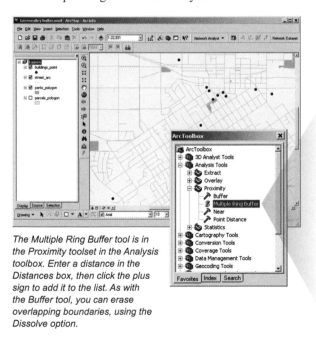

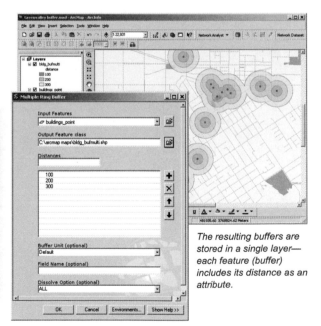

The Multiple Ring Buffer tool is in the Proximity toolset in the Analysis toolbox. Enter a distance in the Distances box, then click the plus sign to add it to the list. As with the Buffer tool, you can erase overlapping boundaries, using the Dissolve option.

The resulting buffers are stored in a single layer— each feature (buffer) includes its distance as an attribute.

Linear features and areas can also be buffered using the Buffer or Multiple Ring Buffer tools.

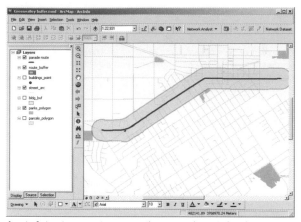

A set of street segments representing a parade route has been buffered to show the area within 200 meters of the route.

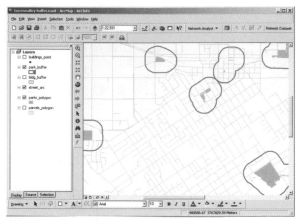

200-meter buffers around park polygons

The Select By Location option in ArcMap and the Select Layer By Location tool in ArcToolbox let you essentially create a temporary buffer for creating a selected set of features. No new buffer feature is created—the "buffer" is simply used to find features within the specified distance (see 'Selecting a subset of features' earlier in this chapter).

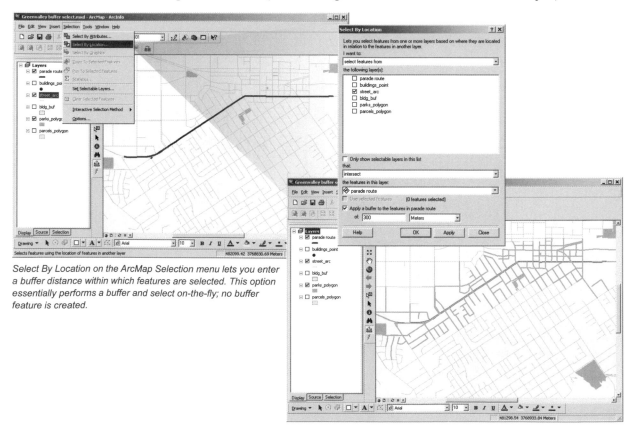

Select By Location on the ArcMap Selection menu lets you enter a buffer distance within which features are selected. This option essentially performs a buffer and select on-the-fly; no buffer feature is created.

Calculating distance over a surface

ArcGIS Desktop includes tools that let you calculate distance from features as a raster surface of continuous values. Each cell in the raster is assigned the distance to the nearest feature in another layer. For example, you can assign to each cell the distance to the nearest stream. Using a distance surface lets you perform your analysis with a finer gradation of distances than does a buffer (where you only know that a location is either within the buffer or outside it—you don't know the actual distance from the feature). It also gives you flexibility—you create the distance surface once, and specify the criteria in your analysis (as opposed to creating new buffers each time you want to change the distance criteria). The Euclidean Distance tool in the Spatial Analyst toolbox is used to create distance surfaces.

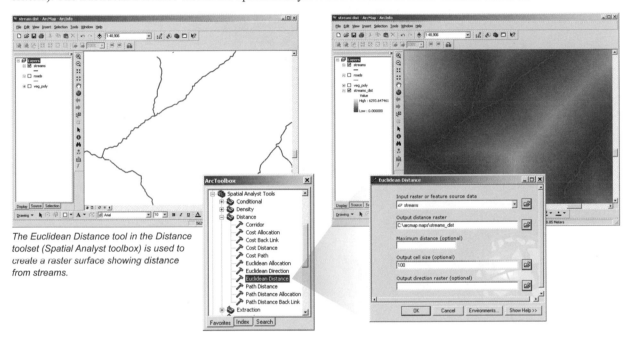

The Euclidean Distance tool in the Distance toolset (Spatial Analyst toolbox) is used to create a raster surface showing distance from streams.

In addition to Euclidean distance, you can create a surface based on other factors and combine that with distance to get a measure of the cost involved in traveling toward or from features. The cost could be time, money, or effort—for example, it's harder for deer to travel through thick brush than open grassland. Creating a cost distance surface is particularly useful for analyzing potential paths or corridors. The Spatial Analyst Cost Distance tool is used to create a cost surface, as illustrated on the next page.

A cost distance surface is created using the Cost Distance tool. The tool takes as input a cost surface (below) and the layer containing the features you're calculating distance to or from (streams, in this example).

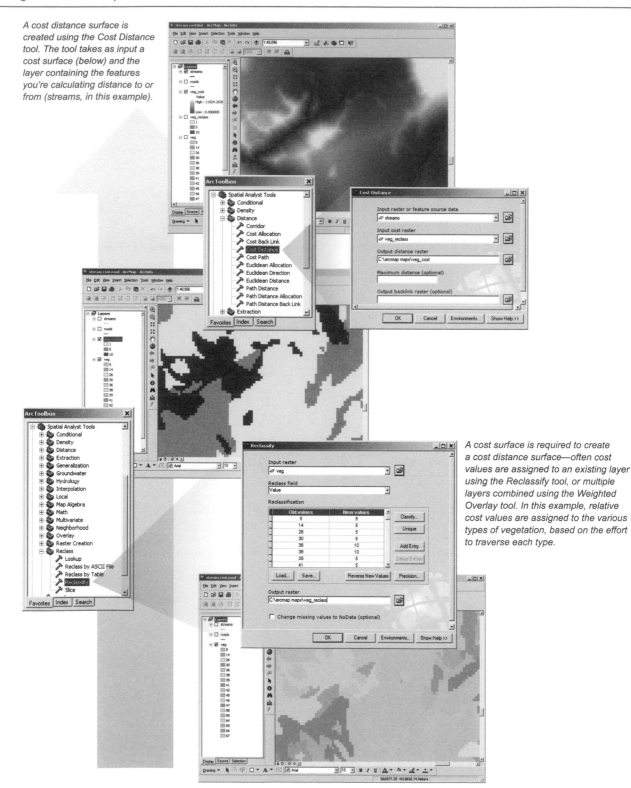

A cost surface is required to create a cost distance surface—often cost values are assigned to an existing layer using the Reclassify tool, or multiple layers combined using the Weighted Overlay tool. In this example, relative cost values are assigned to the various types of vegetation, based on the effort to traverse each type.

The Path Distance tool, also located in the Spatial Analyst Distance toolset, is similar to Cost Distance, but it allows you to specify additional parameters, including the cost of traveling up and downhill, and other vertical and horizontal factors.

The Euclidean Distance (Straight Line) and Cost Distance (Cost Weighted) functions are available on the Spatial Analyst toolbar in ArcMap, as well as in the Spatial Analyst toolbox.

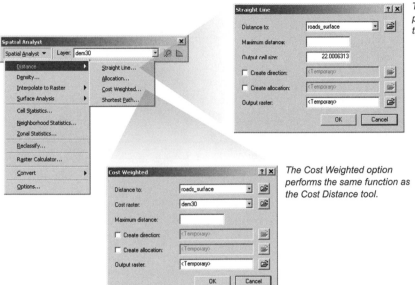

The Straight Line option performs the same function as the Euclidean Distance tool.

The Cost Weighted option performs the same function as the Cost Distance tool.

Another tool, Surface Length, which is provided with the ArcGIS 3D Analyst extension (in the Functional Surface toolset), measures the total length of a line over an elevation surface—taking into account elevation change—rather than over an assumed flat plane. This would be useful, for example, to predict actual miles traveled over mountainous terrain, and resulting fuel costs.

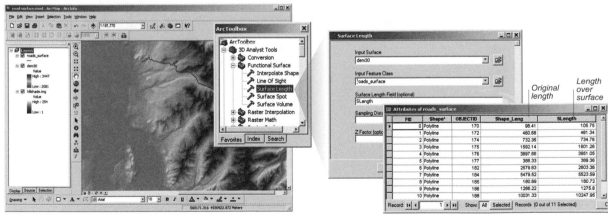

The Surface Length tool calculates the length of each line—or line segment—over an elevation surface. It adds a field (named SLength, by default) containing the new length values.

385

Creating paths and corridors

ArcGIS Desktop includes a number of functions that allow you to model the best path or corridor between two or more locations. These functions are based on distance and the resistance involved in traveling between the locations. In general, the goal is to find a solution that minimizes costs. Cost can be measured in terms of distance, money, time, effort, or even social values such as historical importance (a proposed highway that passes through a ruin may be too costly from a societal standpoint).

There are two types of paths you can model using GIS: paths over a surface, and network paths.

Modeling a path over a surface

Modeling a path over a surface is useful when creating new infrastructure, such as a highway, pipeline, or power line. It's also useful for modeling the movement of objects that don't travel over a fixed infrastructure. For example, you could create a managed wildlife corridor between two protected natural areas.

The main tool for creating a path over a surface is Cost Path. Cost Path requires, in addition to the location of the destination, two input layers: a cost distance layer and a backlink layer. (A backlink raster layer is an interim layer that several different distance functions use to calculate least cost. It essentially calculates the least cost direction from each cell toward the destination location.) These are in turn created using the Cost Distance tool, which requires the origin location and a cost surface layer (see the previous section, 'Calculating distance over a surface'). The cost distance and backlink layers can also be created using the Path Distance tool, which allows you to specify additional parameters such as wind resistance and the extra distance incurred in traveling uphill and downhill. These tools are located in the Distance toolset, in the Spatial Analyst toolbox (ArcGIS Spatial Analyst must be enabled to use them).

The output from Cost Path is a raster dataset. If necessary, you can convert the raster path to a line feature using the ArcToolbox Raster To Polyline tool, in the From Raster toolset (conversion toolbox). Creating a path using Cost Path is illustrated on the next page.

Similar functions are available from the Spatial Analyst toolbar in ArcMap. The Cost Weighted function takes the origin point and a cost surface as input, and creates a cost distance surface and a cost direction surface (comparable to a backlink layer). These then become input to the Shortest Path function, along with the destination point. The output from Shortest Path is a shapefile, rather than a raster.

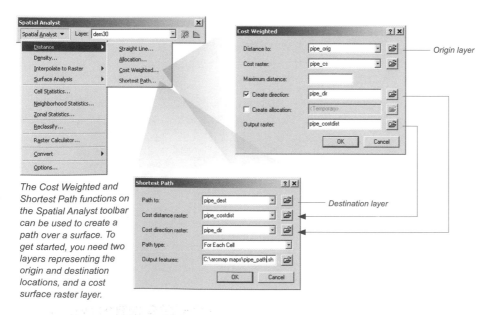

The Cost Weighted and Shortest Path functions on the Spatial Analyst toolbar can be used to create a path over a surface. To get started, you need two layers representing the origin and destination locations, and a cost surface raster layer.

386

A path over a surface is created using the Cost Path tool. The result is a raster surface containing the least cost path. Cost Path takes as input a layer that contains the destination (end point) of the path, a cost distance surface, and a backlink surface. Here, the path and destination are shown along with the cost distance and backlink layers in the background.

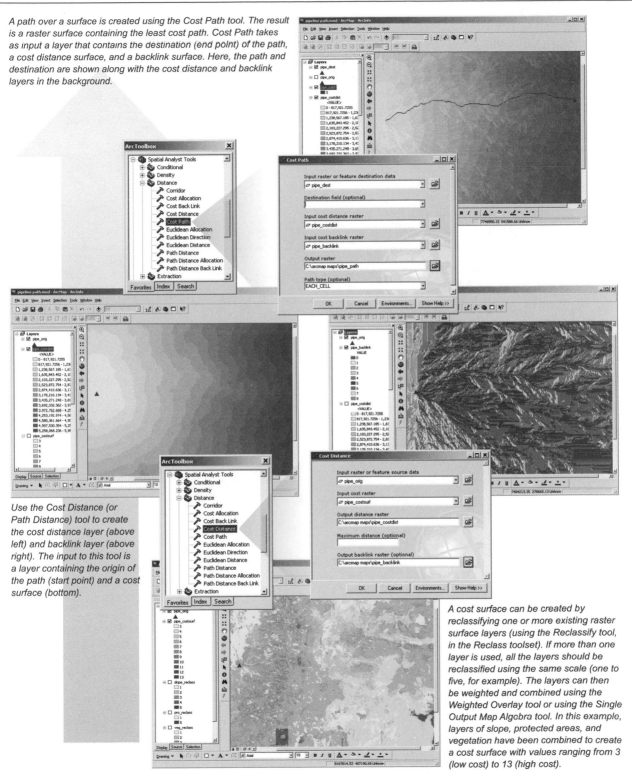

Use the Cost Distance (or Path Distance) tool to create the cost distance layer (above left) and backlink layer (above right). The input to this tool is a layer containing the origin of the path (start point) and a cost surface (bottom).

A cost surface can be created by reclassifying one or more existing raster surface layers (using the Reclassify tool, in the Reclass toolset). If more than one layer is used, all the layers should be reclassified using the same scale (one to five, for example). The layers can then be weighted and combined using the Weighted Overlay tool or using the Single Output Map Algebra tool. In this example, layers of slope, protected areas, and vegetation have been combined to create a cost surface with values ranging from 3 (low cost) to 13 (high cost).

The Cost Path tool creates the single least cost path over a surface between two locations. An alternative is the Corridor tool, which assigns each cell the cumulative cost involved in reaching that cell from two locations (or, a cost for reaching either of the locations from that cell). By classifying the cell cost values or selecting cells that have a value less than a certain cost, you can create potential corridors between the locations. This is useful for modeling the movement of wildlife or for creating several potential alternative paths for infrastructure (a highway or pipeline). The corridor tool takes two input cost distance rasters (created using Cost Distance or Path Distance) and creates a cumulative cost raster.

Use the Corridor tool in the Spatial Analyst toolbox to create a least-cost corridor between locations. In this example, the lightest areas represent the least cost corridors.

The input to Corridor is two cost distance surfaces—one created for each location you want to link. These are created using the Cost Distance or Path Distance tool (described earlier).

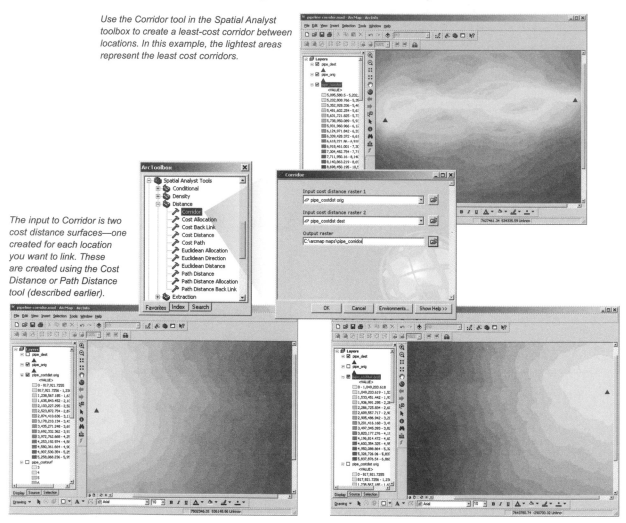

Modeling a path over a network

In ArcGIS Desktop, a network dataset is used to represent transportation infrastructure such as roads or railroads. Objects can move only along the lines that comprise the network. Examples of modeling paths over a transportation network include finding the best path for a truck from the fire station to a fire or the best route for a delivery truck. Network paths can simply connect two points, or can include stops along the way. See 'Adding specialized datasets to a geodatabase' in Chapter 2 for more on creating network datasets.

The Network Analyst extension allows you to create paths and routes. Open the Network Analyst toolbar in ArcMap click the View menu, point to Toolbars, and click Network Analyst (the extension must be enabled in order to use the toolbar).

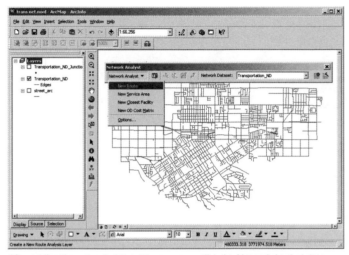

After adding the network dataset to your map, click the Network Analyst drop-down menu and click New Route. The new route—and all its elements—are added to the table of contents.

Click the Create Network Location tool, then add the origin and destination—and any stops along the way—by clicking network edges or junctions.

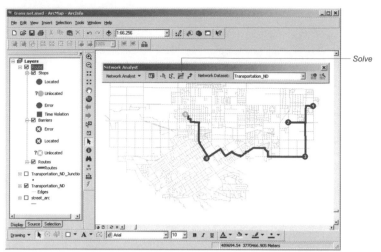

Solve

When you've added all the stops, click the Solve button to create the optimum path between all the stops.

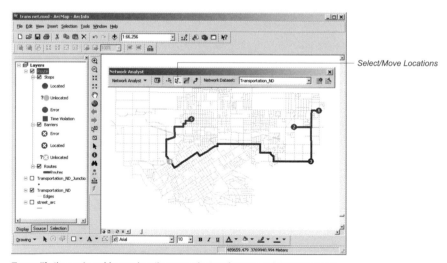

Select/Move Locations

To modify the route, add more locations or select and move or delete a location, and then click Solve again to calculate the new optimum path.

Any costs you built into your network when it was created—such as travel time—or any barriers you add (such as a closed street) will be taken into account when you create the path.

Allocating areas to centers

Allocation is used to delineate areas of influence, market areas, or service areas around a location or set of locations (referred to as "centers"). Often, the centers represent locations that people travel to (a library) or from (a fire station). Essentially, allocation assigns the area nearest each center to that center. As with other distance measures, "nearest" can be defined in terms of straight-line distance or cost (time, money, effort).

Creating areas around centers

The Create Thiessen Polygons tool in the Proximity toolset (Analysis toolbox) creates a polygon around each input location. The polygon represents the area closest to each location.

The Create Thiessen Polygons tool creates a layer of polygons around a set of input points—each polygon represents the area closest to the point at its center.

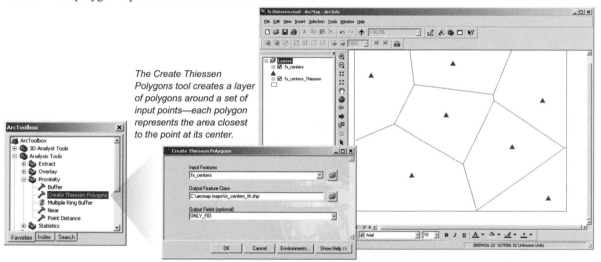

The Euclidean Allocation tool in the Distance toolset (Spatial Analyst toolbox) is similar to Thiessen—except it creates a raster (instead of polygons) and assigns each cell to its nearest center.

The Euclidean Allocation tool assigns each cell to its nearest center, using straight-line distance. The cell value is a unique identifier associated with each center (the fire station ID, in this example).

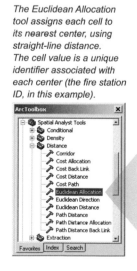

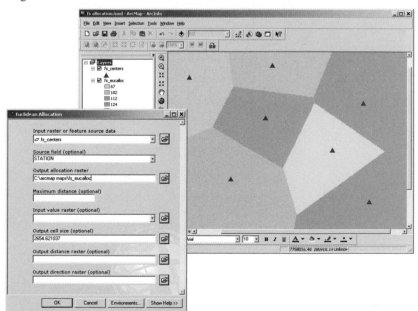

The same function is available on the Spatial Analyst toolbar in ArcMap (point to Distance on the drop-down menu, and click Allocation).

The Cost Allocation and Path Distance Allocation tools (in the Spatial Analyst Distance toolset in ArcToolbox) allow you to use costs rather than straight-line distance when assigning cells to their nearest center. The inputs for these tools are similar to the corresponding distance tools (Cost Distance and Path Distance).

The Path Distance Allocation tool allows you to use cost factors such as slope and elevation—in addition to straight-line distance—to assign cells to centers. The result is more representative of the effort required to travel from (or to) the center.

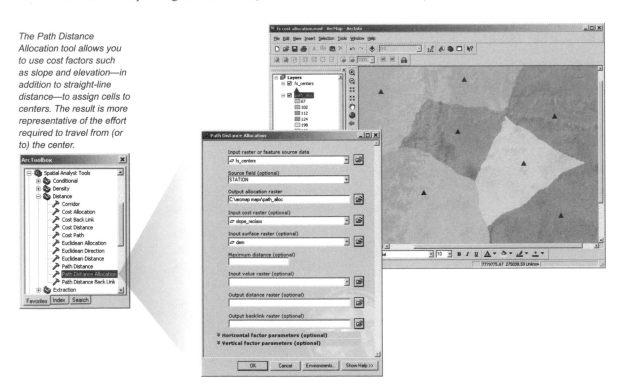

Creating service areas using a network

If you've built a network dataset, you can use the Network Analyst toolbar in ArcMap to create a service area delineated by traveling along streets (or other network features) to or from the center.

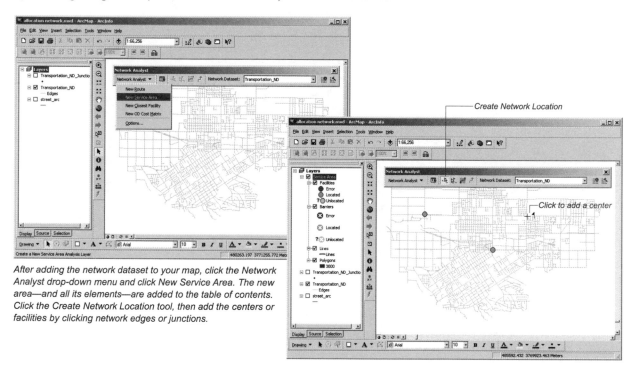

After adding the network dataset to your map, click the Network Analyst drop-down menu and click New Service Area. The new area—and all its elements—are added to the table of contents. Click the Create Network Location tool, then add the centers or facilities by clicking network edges or junctions.

When you've added all the centers, click the Solve button to create the service area around each center.

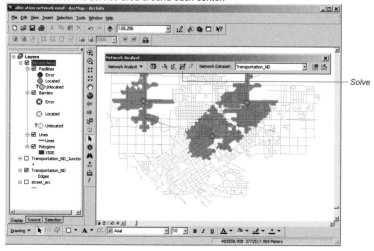

You can change the symbols used to delineate the service areas by clicking them in the table of contents. To change the parameters of the allocation, right-click the service area in the table of contents and click Properties. You can, for example, change the maximum distance for the service areas (on the Analysis Settings tab).

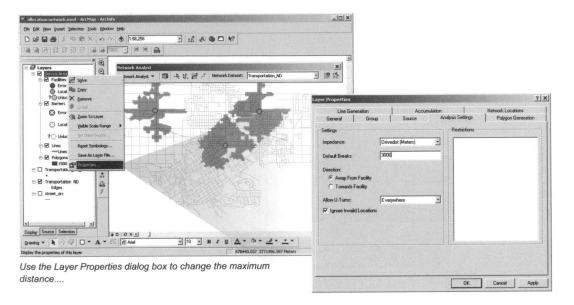

Use the Layer Properties dialog box to change the maximum distance....

....then click Solve to create the new service areas.

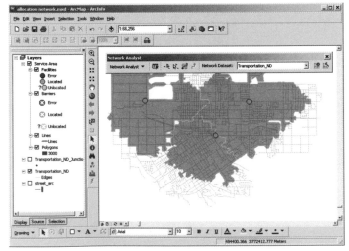

Modeling flow

Modeling flow lets you see how water or other materials move from a source point (or points) through a network or over a surface. You can see, for example, which portions of an electrical network will be affected if a transformer switches off, or where water falling on a hillside will accumulate.

Modeling flow over a network

Utility networks are represented in ArcGIS Desktop using geometric network datasets (see 'Adding specialized datasets to a geodatabasc' in Chapter 2). Once you've built a geometric network, you can trace the flow over the network from one or more source points. You can find connected features, find closed loops, trace upstream or downstream, and so on. To do this, you use the Utility Network Analyst toolbar in ArcMap. To open the toolbar, click the View menu, point to Toolbars, and click Utility Network Analyst.

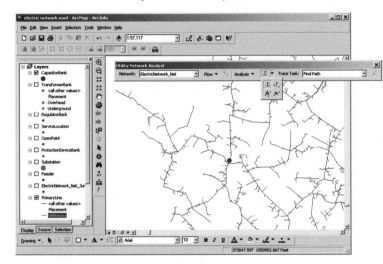

Click the Flags drop-down menu on the Utility Network Analyst toolbar to add a source at a junction or along an edge, or to place a barrier on the network. Select the flag, then click the location.

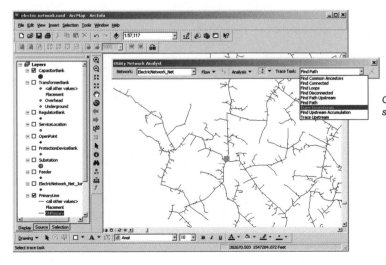

Once you've placed your sources, select the trace task.

395

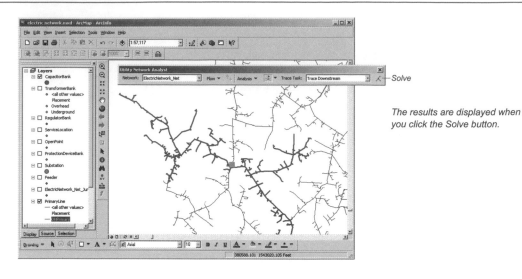

—Solve

The results are displayed when you click the Solve button.

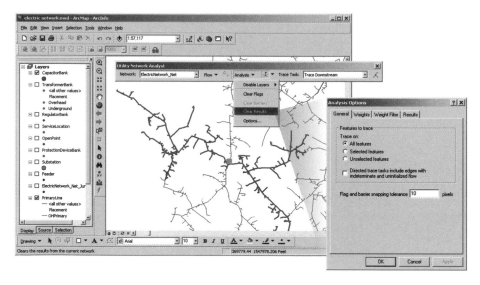

Click the Analysis drop-down menu to clear the results or flags, and to access the analysis options (for example, to limit the trace to selected features or to change the symbology for the results).

Modeling flow over a surface

The Hydrology toolset in the Spatial Analyst toolbox contains tools for modeling the flow of water over an elevation surface. You can, for example, define hydrologic basins, identify stream channels, or calculate the distance along a flow path. Another set of tools models the flow of water or other material (such as a contaminant) through the subsurface. These tools are included in the Groundwater toolset in the Spatial Analyst extension.

The Basin tool (left) calculates hydrologic basins, or watershed areas. The Flow Accumulation tool (right) can be used to identify and create stream networks. The results of the these tools are rasters—you can convert the basins to polygons and the streams to linear features.

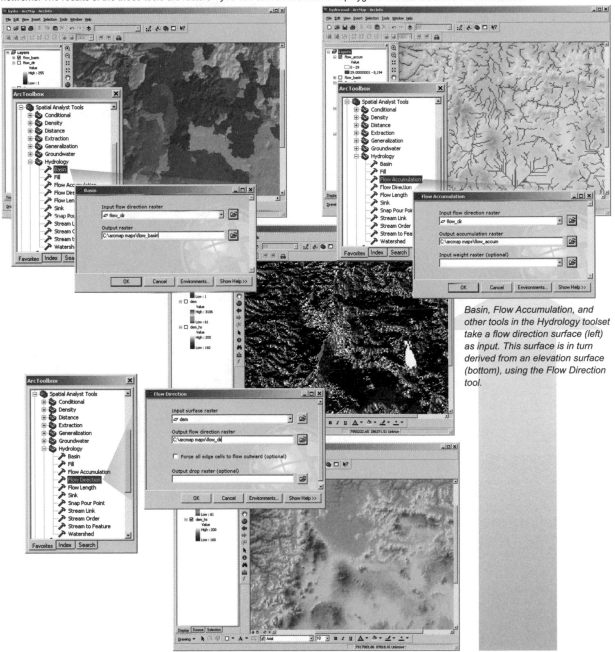

Basin, Flow Accumulation, and other tools in the Hydrology toolset take a flow direction surface (left) as input. This surface is in turn derived from an elevation surface (bottom), using the Flow Direction tool.

Creating raster surfaces

Raster surfaces represent phenomena that have values at every point across their extent. They are created from values sampled at a limited set of locations, such as surveyed height values (for an elevation surface), or temperatures collected at weather stations (for a temperature surface). ArcGIS Desktop includes tools for interpolating values between the sampled locations to create a continuous surface.

Another type of surface created from sample points shows concentration per unit area (density), such as crimes per square mile. Unlike an interpolated surface, a density surface doesn't predict a value at each location—there may, in fact, not have been any crimes within a particular square mile area during the time period being analyzed. Rather, the density surface provides an indication of the distribution of features or values.

Creating an interpolated surface

Interpolation tools create a continuous surface from samples with measured values, such as elevation or chemical concentration. There are several interpolation tools, and each has a variety of parameters that influence the resulting surface. The tools are included in both the Spatial Analyst toolbox (Interpolation toolset) and the 3D Analyst toolbox (Raster Interpolation toolset).

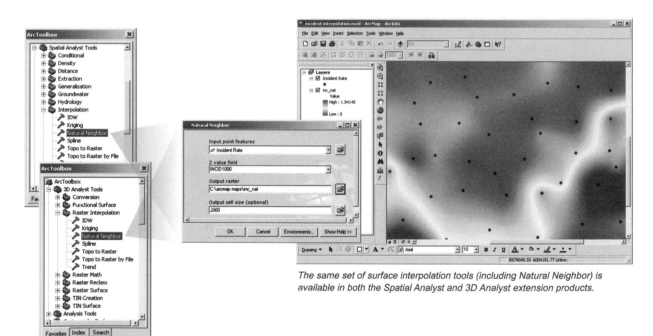

The same set of surface interpolation tools (including Natural Neighbor) is available in both the Spatial Analyst and 3D Analyst extension products.

The Topo to Raster tool is specifically designed to create elevation surfaces. It allows you to input elevation contours, spot heights, and streams to create an accurate digital elevation model (DEM).

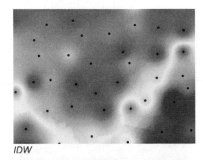

IDW

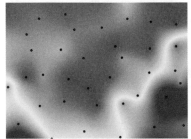

Natural Neighbor

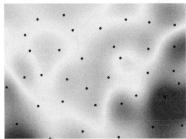

Spline

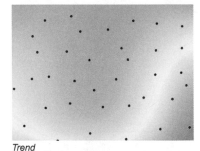

Trend

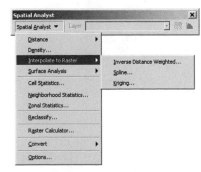

Kriging

Different interpolation techniques can produce different output surfaces from the same input data, although the broad pattern will be similar. The maps to the left show examples of each tool applied to a set of sample points representing readings at air pollution monitoring stations. The specific parameter choices will influence the results. A particular technique may be suited to particular data or applications.

Inverse Distance Weighted (IDW) and Natural Neighbor interpolation estimate surface values for each cell using the value and distance of nearby points.

The interpolated values for IDW surfaces are calculated as a weighted average of the values of a set of nearby points. The influence (weight) of nearby points is greater than that of distant points (the weight decreases as the distance increases).

Natural Neighbor interpolation is like IDW interpolation, except that the data points used to interpolate the surface values for each cell are identified and weighted using a Delaunay triangulation, as in a TIN. Natural Neighbors interpolation works reliably with much larger datasets than the other interpolation methods.

The Spline and Trend tools interpolate best-fit surfaces to the sample points using polynomial and least-squares methods, respectively.

Spline interpolation fits a mathematical surface through the points that minimizes sharp bending; it is useful for surfaces that vary smoothly, such as water table heights.

Trend surfaces are good for identifying coarse scale patterns in data; the interpolated surface rarely passes through the sample points.

Kriging is an advanced surface creation technique that is most useful when there is a spatially correlated distance or directional bias in the data. It is often used in soil science and geology.

Several of these tools are also available from the 3D Analyst and Spatial Analyst toolbars in ArcMap.

Geostatistical interpolation techniques allow the creation of predicted value surfaces and the interpretation of levels of certainty about the predictions based on confidence levels. The Geostatistical Analyst wizard (included in the Geostatistical Analyst extension) allows surface creation using a number of different methods, including Kriging, Cokriging, Radial Basis Function, Inverse Distance Weighted, Global Polynomial, and Local Polynomial interpolation methods. Geostatistical Analyst lets you analyze how well these various methods will predict values for your particular data.

Using Geostatistical Analyst for Inverse Distance weighting

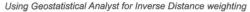

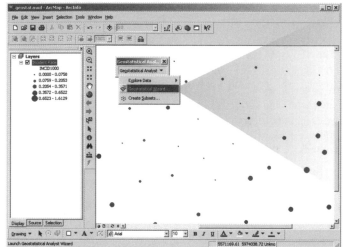

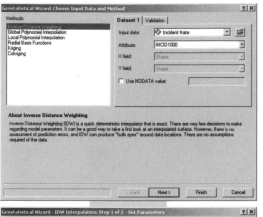

The wizard lets you specify the interpolation method to use and the model parameters, and shows you how well the model you've defined will predict the surface values. The specific parameters—and the corresponding wizard panels—depend on the method you specify.

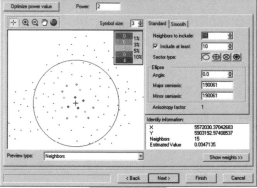

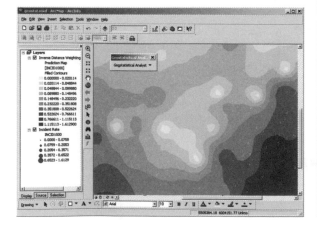

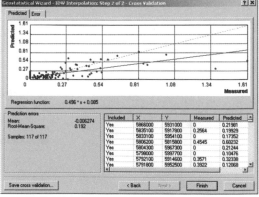

The Geostatistical Analyst toolbar also includes tools for detecting bias or patterns in your data, including histograms, normal QQ plots, and trend analysis.

Creating a density surface

Density tools produce a raster surface that represents how much or how many of something there are per unit area. You might use density surfaces to represent the distribution of a wildlife population from a set of observations, or the degree of urbanization of an area based on the number of roads.

The Density toolset in the Spatial Analyst toolbox includes tools for creating density surfaces for point and line features. Point Density and Line Density search around each cell (within a neighborhood you specify), calculate the density for that neighborhood, and assign the density value to the cell. This is known as a simple density surface. Kernel Density fits a smooth curved surface over each input feature, with the surface value diminishing from the feature and reaching zero at the maximum search radius distance. It adds the values of these kernel surfaces to calculate a value for each cell in the resulting density surface. The Kernel Density tool accepts either points or lines.

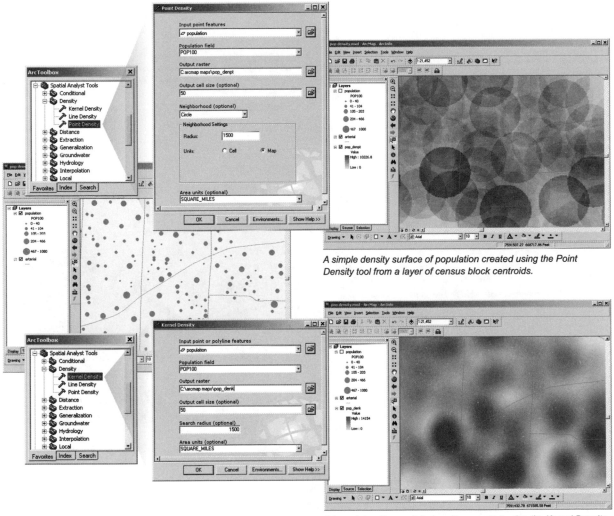

A simple density surface of population created using the Point Density tool from a layer of census block centroids.

A kernel density population surface created using the Kernel Density tool.

The Spatial Analyst toolbar in ArcMap also lets you create a density surface—the dialog box accepts either points or lines and will calculate a kernel density or a simple density surface.

Creating a TIN surface

A TIN, or triangulated irregular network, is a surface data structure composed of triangular facets defined by nodes and edges. They are usually used to represent terrain. The terrain heights are derived from spot elevations that are used as initial nodes in the triangulation. The shape of the TIN surface is controlled by the triangulation of these spot elevations. TINs capture the variation in a surface better than do rasters—the spot elevations can be irregularly distributed to accommodate areas of high variability in the surface and their values and exact positions are retained as nodes in the TIN. This makes TINs well-suited to engineering applications (such as calculating cut and fill). When creating the TIN, you can include other features, such as streams or ridge lines, to refine the TIN surface (these become breaklines that define the edges of triangular facets). Polygons, such as lakes, can be included to create flat planes in the surface.

TIN surfaces are created using the 3D Analyst extension. The Create/Modify TIN option on the 3D Analyst toolbar displays a dialog box that lets you specify the input datasets and parameters. The new TIN surface is automatically added to the display.

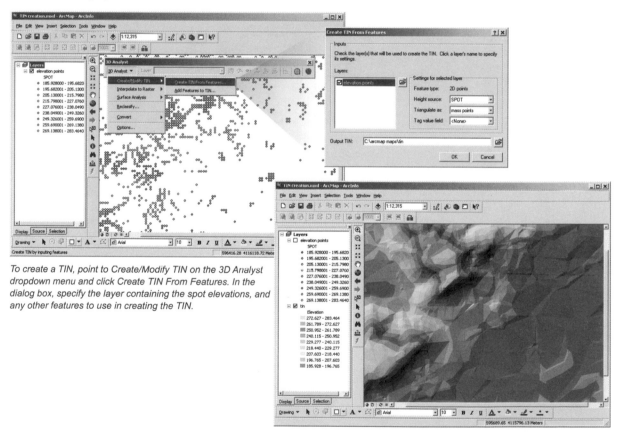

To create a TIN, point to Create/Modify TIN on the 3D Analyst dropdown menu and click Create TIN From Features. In the dialog box, specify the layer containing the spot elevations, and any other features to use in creating the TIN.

You can also create TINs using the Create TIN and Edit TIN tools in the 3D Analyst toolbox (TIN Creation toolset). Create TIN creates an empty TIN dataset—you specify the spatial reference for the dataset. You then use the Edit TIN tool to add points and breaklines to create the contents of the TIN (the faces, edges, and nodes). These tools are useful for creating TINs inside a script or model.

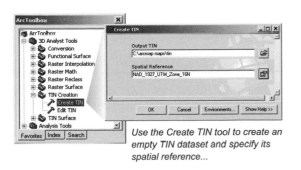

Use the Create TIN tool to create an empty TIN dataset and specify its spatial reference...

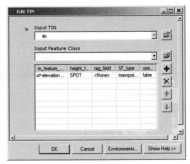

...then use Edit TIN to add points, breaklines, and other features to define the TIN surface.

TINs are often best visualized as a 3D surface in ArcScene. Once you've created the TIN (using ArcMap or ArcToolbox), add the TIN to the scene. Since the 3D Analyst toolbar is available in ArcScene, you can also create TINs within ArcScene.

When you add a TIN to a map or a scene, a default rendering is used. In ArcMap, the default is an elevation color ramp. In ArcScene, the faces of the TIN triangles are drawn using a single symbol (although the TIN is drawn in shaded relief). Use the Symbology tab on the Properties dialog box (in either ArcMap or ArcScene) to change the rendering. You can draw the faces using a color ramp for elevation, slope, or aspect; you can also draw the edges of the triangles, the nodes (derived from the original input points), and any breaklines you may have used to create the TIN.

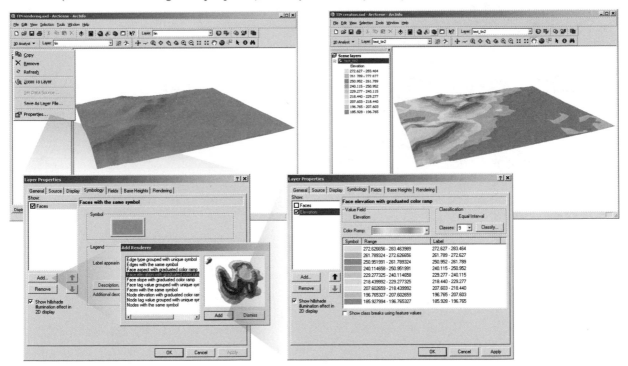

Click Add on the Symbology tab of the Layer Properties dialog box to display the Add Renderer dialog box. Select the renderers you want to add to the list, then click the Add button on the dialog box. Select a renderer from the list to display and modify the symbols.

You can create and store a TIN-based surface within a geodatabase by building a terrain dataset (see 'Adding specialized datasets to a geodatabase' in Chapter 2.

Deriving data from an elevation surface

Surfaces are constructed from x, y, and z (height) values. This allows you to perform geographic analysis that takes into account height above (or depth below) a flat plane. Once you've constructed an elevation raster surface or TIN, you can derive new datasets that represent characteristics of the surface, such as slope and aspect.

Tools that allow you to derive new surfaces from an elevation surface include Contour, Slope, Aspect, Hillshade, and Curvature. The derived datasets are useful for input to other analyses, such as overlay analysis, as well as for visualization and cartography. The tools are located in the Surface toolset in the Spatial Analyst toolbox and the Raster Surface toolset in the 3D Analyst toolbox.

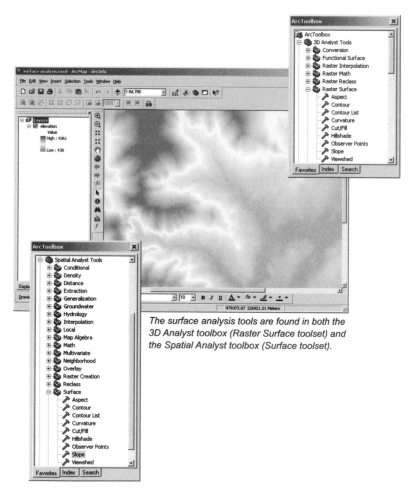

The surface analysis tools are found in both the 3D Analyst toolbox (Raster Surface toolset) and the Spatial Analyst toolbox (Surface toolset).

The Aspect tool calculates the direction of the slope face for each cell. The aspect of a surface typically affects the amount of sunlight it receives (among other factors).

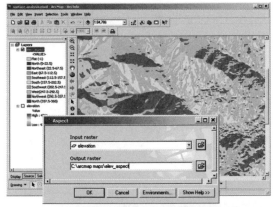

The Contour tool extracts lines of constant value (isolines) from a raster surface. The TIN Contour tool extracts a line feature class of contours from a TIN surface.

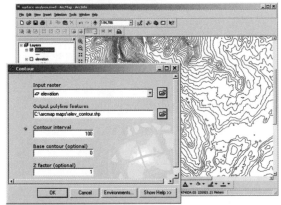

The tools use an elevation surface as input.

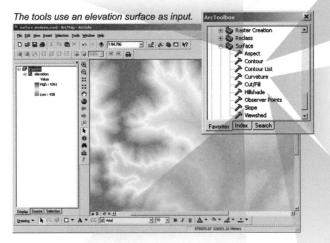

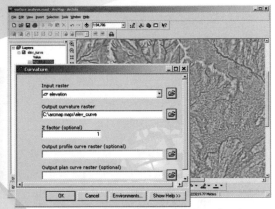

Curvature calculates whether a given part of a surface is convex or concave. Convex parts of surfaces, like ridges, are generally exposed and drain to other areas. Concave parts of surfaces, like channels, are generally more sheltered and accept drainage from other areas.

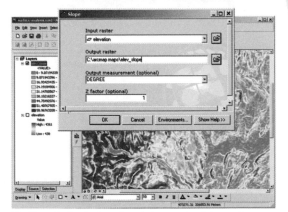

The Slope tool calculates the maximum rate of change from a cell to its neighbors, which is typically used to indicate the steepness of terrain.

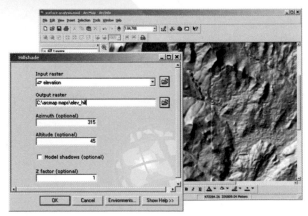

Hillshade shows the intensity of lighting on a surface given a light source at a particular location; it can model which parts of a surface would be shadowed by other parts.

The derived surfaces can be combined with the original elevation surface, or with each other.

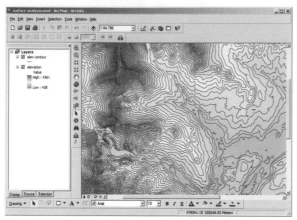

Displaying contours on top of the elevation surface adds detail to the map.

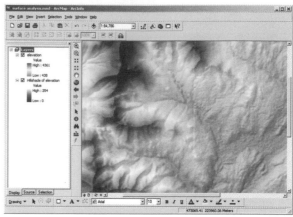

The hillshade surface is often displayed under the symbolized elevation surface to create a shaded relief map. Set the transparency of the elevation surface using the Display tab on the Layer Properties dialog box.

Viewing the surfaces in perspective, using ArcScene, can help you visualize the surface characteristics.

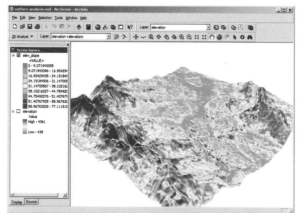

Displaying the Slope surface in perspective lets you easily see the areas of steepest and flattest slope (see "Creating relief maps and perspective views" in Chapter 4).

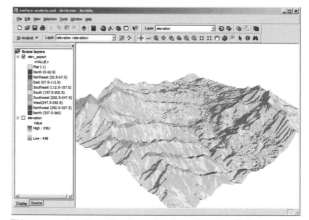

This perspective view of the Aspect surface shows north-facing slopes (blues) and south-facing slopes (yellows).

Contour, Slope, Aspect and Hillshade can also be accessed from the Spatial Analyst toolbar in ArcMap and the 3D Analyst toolbar in ArcMap or ArcScene.

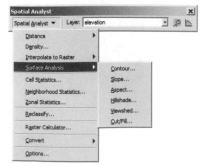

When accessing the tools via the toolbars, the default for the output is a "temporary raster," which is automatically added to the map or scene, but not saved. That allows you to preview the analysis parameters and preview the output. To make a temporary raster permanent, right-click the layer name in the table of contents, point to Data, and click Make Permanent. Alternatively, you can create a permanent raster initially by typing a name for the output raster in the dialog box—the raster will be saved in the working directory (set using Options on the Spatial Analyst drop-down menu). Or, type a full pathname to override the working directory setting.

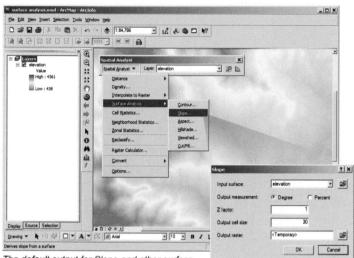

The default output for Slope and other surface analysis tools accessed from the toolbar is a temporary raster. Enter a raster name if you want to create a permanent output raster.

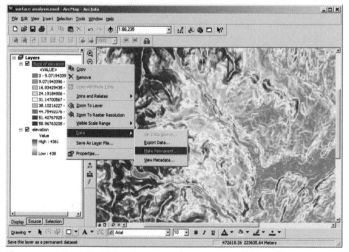

If you accept the default of a temporary output raster, and later want to save it, right-click the layer name, point to Data, and click Make Permanent. Alternatively, save the map to make all the temporary rasters permanent (they will be given a default name and stored in the working directory).

The tools on the 3D Analyst toolbar accept TINs as input, in addition to rasters. The output is still a raster surface for Slope, Aspect, and Hillshade, and line features for Contour.

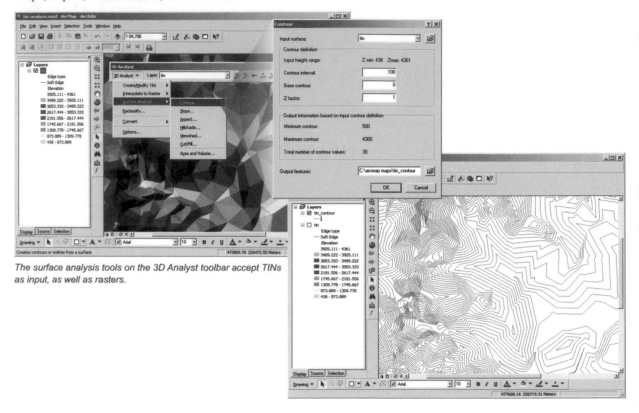

The surface analysis tools on the 3D Analyst toolbar accept TINs as input, as well as rasters.

The ArcToolbox versions of the TIN tools are located in the TIN Surface toolset, in the 3D Analyst toolbox.

Calculating surface volume

ArcGIS Desktop includes a set of tools used to calculate volume from surface information. The tools calculate the difference in volume between a raster or TIN surface and another surface. Depending on the tool, the other surface might be specified by a horizontal plane at a given elevation or by a second raster or TIN surface. Volume calculations are typically used in hydrology and civil engineering applications.

The Surface Volume tool is used to calculate volume of a surface above or below a horizontal plane at a specific elevation. You'd use this tool, for example, to calculate the volume of water in a section of river channel at a particular flood stage or to calculate the volume of additional water when a reservoir is near capacity versus its normal level. This tool is available on the 3D Analyst toolbar (as the Area and Volume function) and in the 3D Analyst toolbox (Functional Surface toolset), and can be used on raster or TIN surfaces. The output of the tool is the resulting surface area and volumes, which are displayed on the screen. You can optionally specify to write the results to a text file.

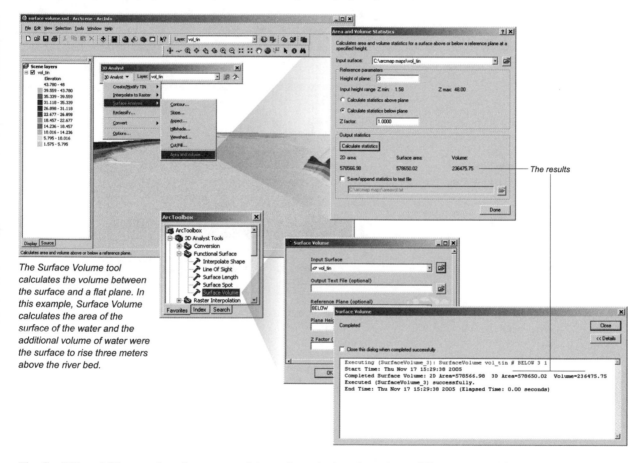

The Surface Volume tool calculates the volume between the surface and a flat plane. In this example, Surface Volume calculates the area of the surface of the water and the additional volume of water were the surface to rise three meters above the river bed.

The results

The Cut/Fill tool (illustrated on the next page) is used to calculate the volume difference—negative or positive—for before and after surfaces of the same area. This tool is used, for example, to calculate the volume of earth that must be dredged from a river channel to improve navigation. Cut/Fill is in the Spatial Analyst toolbox (Surface toolset) and the 3D Analyst toolbox (Raster Surface toolset). It's also available on the Spatial Analyst and 3D Analyst toolbars in ArcMap or ArcScene. The versions of the tools contained in Spatial Analyst accept rasters as input; the versions in 3D Analyst accept TINs (the toolbar version also accepts rasters). In all cases, the results of Cut/Fill are presented as a raster of the difference between the two layers. Cells are grouped into zones (contiguous cells representing cut areas, fill areas, or no difference areas), and the attribute table for the raster layer stores the volume for each zone.

This example shows elevation surfaces of a subdivision before and after grading for a new cul-de-sac.

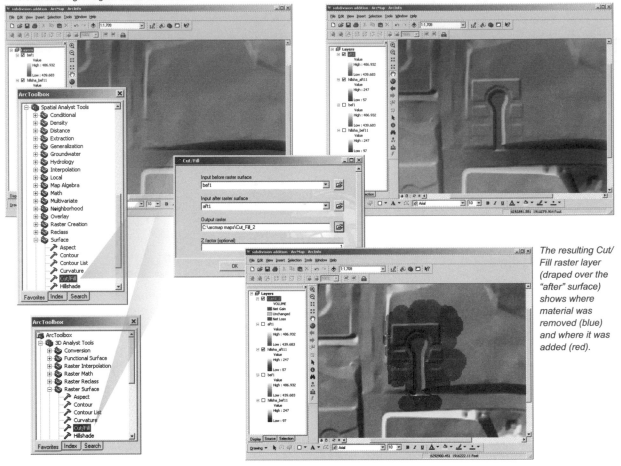

The resulting Cut/ Fill raster layer (draped over the "after" surface) shows where material was removed (blue) and where it was added (red).

The after surface is subtracted from the before surface, so if the surface has dropped (a cut), material has been removed and the calculated volume is positive. By summing the positive volume you get the total cut volume. Conversely, summing the negative volume gives you the total fill volume.

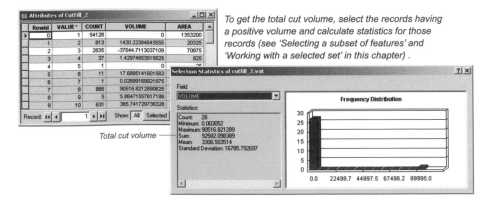

To get the total cut volume, select the records having a positive volume and calculate statistics for those records (see 'Selecting a subset of features' and 'Working with a selected set' in this chapter) .

Total cut volume

The TIN Difference tool compares two TINs and identifies each area where the second TIN is above, below, or at the same level as the first TIN. It creates polygon features corresponding to each of these horizontal areas, and codes each polygon as representing an area above, below, or the same. It also calculates volumes above or below these horizontal areas and the second TIN, and assigns them to each polygon.

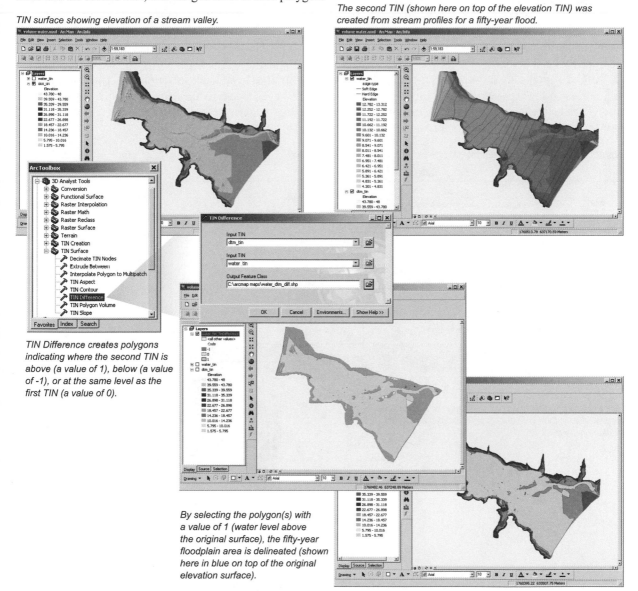

TIN surface showing elevation of a stream valley.

The second TIN (shown here on top of the elevation TIN) was created from stream profiles for a fifty-year flood.

TIN Difference creates polygons indicating where the second TIN is above (a value of 1), below (a value of -1), or at the same level as the first TIN (a value of 0).

By selecting the polygon(s) with a value of 1 (water level above the original surface), the fifty-year floodplain area is delineated (shown here in blue on top of the original elevation surface).

The TIN Polygon Volume tool calculates the volume difference and surface area for each polygon in a layer relative to a TIN surface. Each polygon represents a horizontal area at an elevation specified in a height field. The volume above or below this planar area to the TIN surface is added to the polygon layer's feature attribute table, along with the surface area of the polygon.

As with the other surface analysis tools, when the tool is accessed from the toolbar the default output is a temporary layer. Enter a file name to create a permanent layer initially, or—after creating the temporary layer (which is added to the map or scene automatically)—right-click it in the table of contents and click Make Permanent, if you want to save it.

Analyzing visibility

Several tools included with ArcGIS Desktop allow you to calculate which portions of a surface are visible from specific locations. These tools can be used, for example, to site fire lookout towers or find the route for a transmission line that is not visible from a scenic area. Some related tools measure the amount of solar radiation reaching the surface.

Measuring line of sight

The Line Of Sight tool identifies whether or not one location is visible from another, and whether or not the intervening locations along a line between the two locations are visible. Line Of Sight is available in 3D Analyst, and works with both raster and TIN surfaces. The tool supports offsets, which allows you to specify the height above the ground of the observer and target points. The Line of Sight button on the 3D Analyst toolbar lets you enter the observer and target points interactively. The result is a graphic line that is stored with the map.

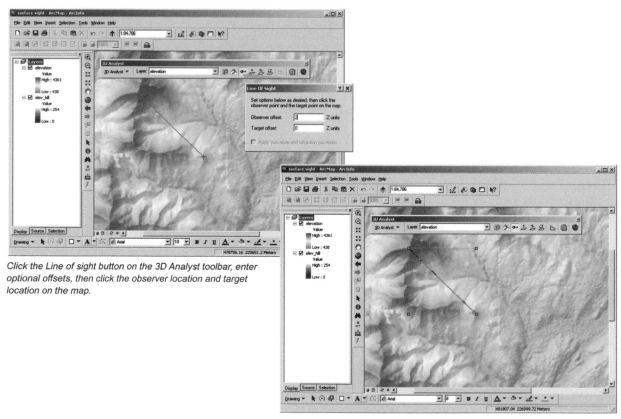

Click the Line of sight button on the 3D Analyst toolbar, enter optional offsets, then click the observer location and target location on the map.

The result is a graphic line showing which portions of the line of sight are visible from the observer location (green) and which are not (red). The target point is likewise color coded as visible or not.

The Line Of Sight tool is also included in the 3D Analyst toolbox (in the Functional Surface toolset). The input for the tool is a two-point line. The observer location and target location are defined by the direction the line was digitized—the start point is used as the observer location. The output is a line feature. The advantage of having an output line feature is that you can use the line in further analysis. For example, you could buffer the visible segments to create a view corridor, or overlay the line with land cover to find out which land cover types are visible from the observer point along the line of sight. You also can control the symbology for the line—to make it wider, for example, or change the color scheme.

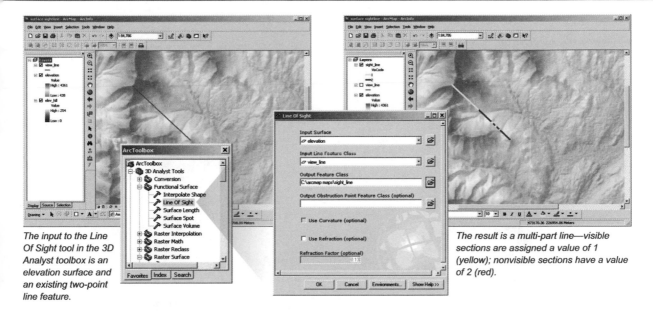

The input to the Line Of Sight tool in the 3D Analyst toolbox is an elevation surface and an existing two-point line feature.

The result is a multi-part line—visible sections are assigned a value of 1 (yellow); nonvisible sections have a value of 2 (red).

Creating a viewshed

The Viewshed tool shows which portions of a surface are visible from one or more observer points. The output is a new raster, with cells coded as either visible or not visible. Viewshed is available on the 3D Analyst and Spatial Analyst toolbars, as well as in both the 3D Analyst toolbox (Raster Surface toolset) and the Spatial Analyst toolbox (Surface toolset).

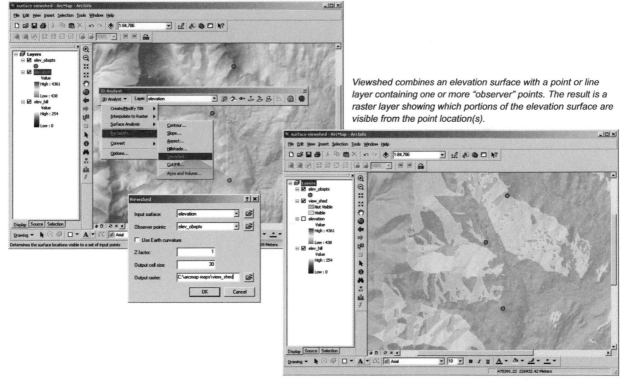

Viewshed combines an elevation surface with a point or line layer containing one or more "observer" points. The result is a raster layer showing which portions of the elevation surface are visible from the point location(s).

The Observer Points tool (available in both the 3D Analyst and Spatial Analyst toolboxes) is similar to Viewshed. However, it tracks which portions of the surface are visible from each point, or combination of points, and codes the output raster cells accordingly.

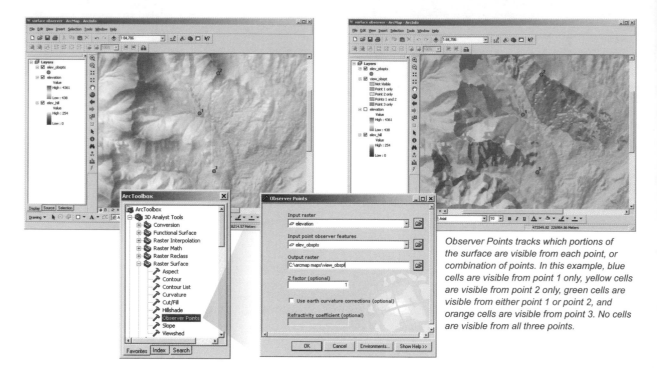

Observer Points tracks which portions of the surface are visible from each point, or combination of points. In this example, blue cells are visible from point 1 only, yellow cells are visible from point 2 only, green cells are visible from either point 1 or point 2, and orange cells are visible from point 3. No cells are visible from all three points.

Both the Viewshed and Observer Points tools also allow you to specify observer and target offsets, as well as parameters that let you limit the directions and distance each observer can view.

Measuring solar radiation

A related set of tools is used for measuring the amount of solar radiation (measured in watt hours per square meter) received at each location across a surface, or at specific locations. The tools, Area Solar Radiation and Points Solar Radiation, are located in the Solar Radiation toolset in the Spatial Analyst toolbox. In addition to the input elevation surface, you specify the time period for which to calculate the solar radiation, and the interval. For Area Solar Radiation, you can create a single, total solar radiation surface, or a separate surface for each interval.

Area Solar Radiation creates a raster surface showing the total amount of solar radiation received at each location (that is, for each cell).

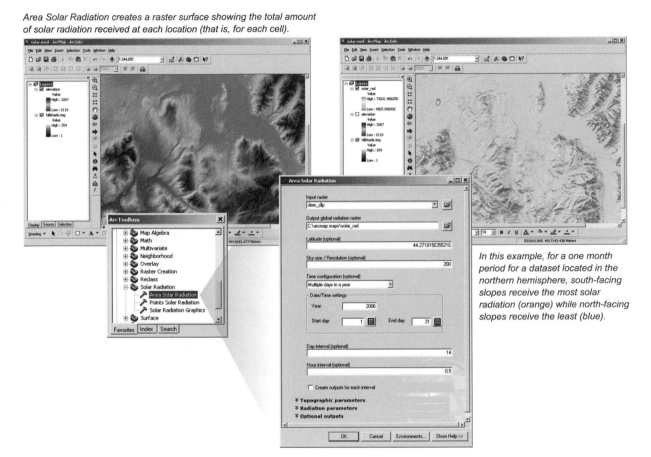

In this example, for a one month period for a dataset located in the northern hemisphere, south-facing slopes receive the most solar radiation (orange) while north-facing slopes receive the least (blue).

The output for the Points Solar Radiation tool is a dataset of point features, with the solar radiation readings stored as values in the dataset's attribute table.

Analyzing spatial distributions

ArcGIS Desktop includes statistical tools to analyze spatial distributions and trends. These tools allow you to go beyond visual analysis of maps—the calculations use the locations of features and the distance between them, as well as attribute values (in some cases). One set of tools calculates the center and dispersion of a set of features. Other tools calculate the directional trend of features.

Calculating the center and dispersion

The Mean Center tool calculates the average of the x-coordinates and y-coordinates of all the input features (usually points). The result is a new layer containing a single point (the center). The Standard Distance tool measures the dispersion or concentration of features around the mean center. These tools are located in the Spatial Statistics toolbox, in the toolset titled Measuring Geographic Distributions.

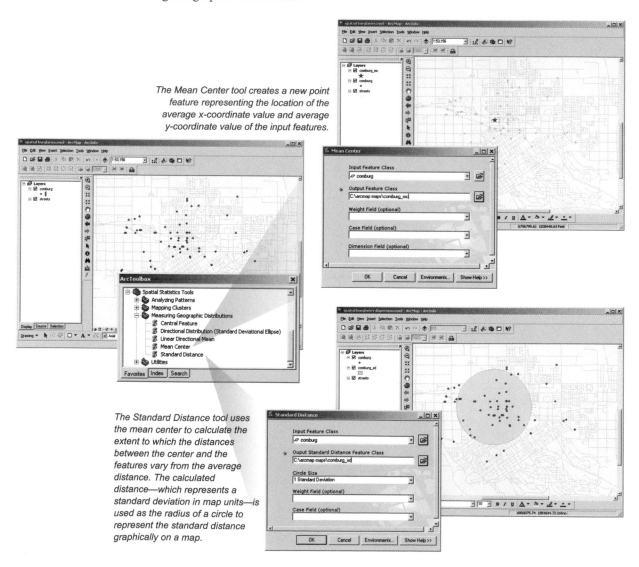

The Mean Center tool creates a new point feature representing the location of the average x-coordinate value and average y-coordinate value of the input features.

The Standard Distance tool uses the mean center to calculate the extent to which the distances between the center and the features vary from the average distance. The calculated distance—which represents a standard deviation in map units—is used as the radius of a circle to represent the standard distance graphically on a map.

You can specify an attribute value in the tool dialog box to calculate the weighted mean center (the center will be pulled toward the features with the highest values). For example, you might calculate the center of business locations weighted by the number of employees at each business to find a likely location for a transit stop. The weighted central feature and weighted standard distance can also be calculated by specifying an attribute value.

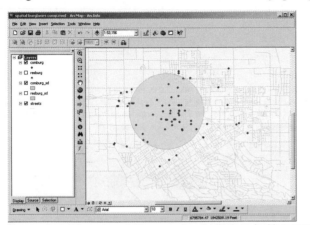 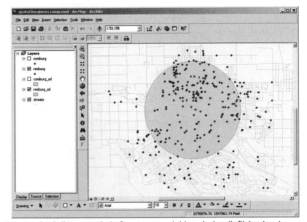

The standard distance is useful for comparing distributions. In this example, the standard distance circle for commercial burglaries (left) is clearly smaller than the one for residential burglaries (right), indicating that commercial burglaries are more concentrated around their mean center.

Analyzing directional trends

The Measuring Geographic Distributions toolset also includes tools for measuring spatial trends. The Standard Deviational Ellipse tool provides a measure of the directional trend of a set of features. The ellipse, which is created as a new feature, is calculated from the mean center. The attribute table for the ellipse includes the x- and y-coordinate of the center, along with the length of each axis, and the angle of rotation. You can specify that the ellipse be calculated using one, two, or three standard deviations. One standard deviation shows the area of concentration of features; three standard deviations shows the area covered by most of the features. The orientation of the ellipse is the same, regardless of the number of standard deviations—only the size is different. As with the standard distance, you can specify an attribute value to calculate the weighted standard deviational ellipse.

The standard deviational ellipse shows the orientation of discrete features (usually points). In this example,
the standard deviational ellipse for commercial burglaries (using two standard deviations) shows the area
where the majority of the burglaries occur. It could be used to decide where to deploy officers.

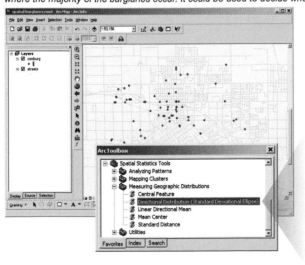 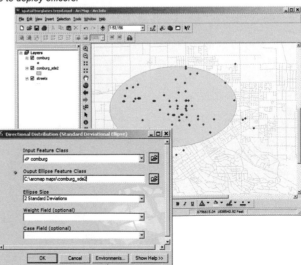

The Linear Directional Mean tool calculates the mean direction of a set of line features, based on the direction of each line. Optionally, the tool calculates the mean orientation—the direction the line points is not considered, only its trend (east–west, for example). Mean direction could be used to calculate the downstream trend of a stream network (in this case, the direction the stream segments point is important); mean orientation could be used to calculate the trend of elk migration paths (you don't care which direction the elk move, only the orientation of the paths). When you calculate the directional mean, the circular variance is also calculated. The circular variance is a measure of the extent to which the lines all point the same direction (or in different directions). The closer to 0, the more the lines point the same direction; the closer to 1, the more variability there is in the direction of the lines.

The linear directional mean shows the average direction (or orientation, optionally) of a set of line features. The output is a line feature, which you can draw as an arrow. The length of the line is the average length of the input features, and it's placed at the mean center. The attribute table for the directional mean line includes the angle of rotation, the coordinates of the center, and the length of the line. It also includes the circular variance.

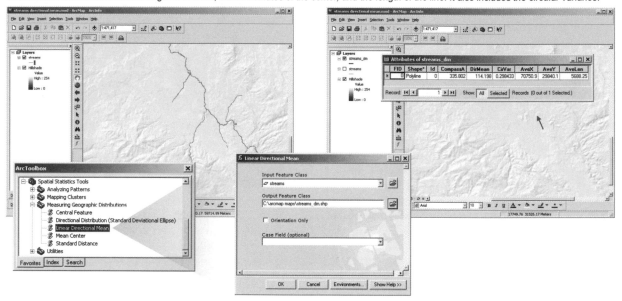

Identifying patterns and clusters

ArcGIS includes tools that allow you to identify spatial patterns in your data. Sometimes, apparent patterns you can see when you look at a map will vary depending on how features are symbolized or how values are classified into ranges. The Desktop tools use statistical methods to identify and analyze patterns in the underlying data. They also—in many cases—calculate the statistical significance of the results. This "score" tells you how confident you can be that any trend or pattern identified by the tool is not due to chance. All of these tools are located in the Spatial Statistics toolbox in ArcToolbox.

The tools in the Analyzing Patterns toolset identify whether a set of features (usually points) or values associated with features (usually polygons) form a clustered, dispersed, or random pattern.

The Average Nearest Neighbor tool is used to identify patterns in a set of discrete features such as points.

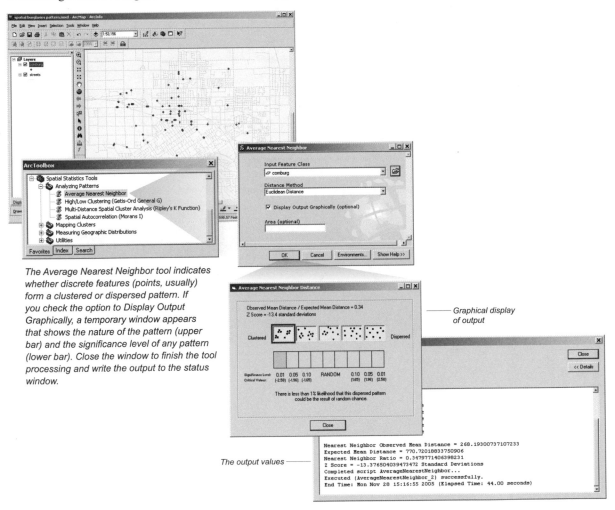

The Average Nearest Neighbor tool indicates whether discrete features (points, usually) form a clustered or dispersed pattern. If you check the option to Display Output Graphically, a temporary window appears that shows the nature of the pattern (upper bar) and the significance level of any pattern (lower bar). Close the window to finish the tool processing and write the output to the status window.

Graphical display of output

The output values

In the example above, the Nearest Neighbor tool has calculated that commercial burglaries in this area are clustered, and there is a less than 1 percent likelihood the pattern is due to pure chance. That is, you can be 99 percent sure the burglaries are, in fact, clustered.

Moran's I and Getis–Ord General G identify patterns formed by values associated with features—often contiguous features, such as census tracts or counties. They produce a single statistic that summarizes the pattern formed by the spatial distribution of values. Moran's I looks at whether features with similar values cluster or are interspersed. Getis–Ord General G identifies whether any clustered pattern is due to clustering of high values or low values.

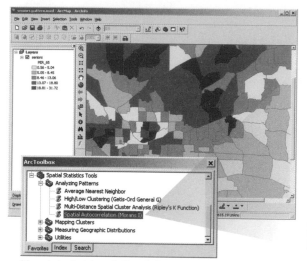

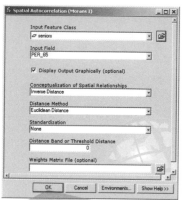

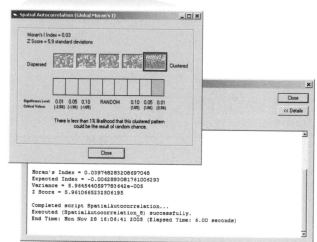

Moran's I calculates whether similar values cluster or are interspersed, more than you would expect due to random chance. In this example, census tracts having a high percentage of senior citizens occur in clusters, and there is a less than 1 percent likelihood that this is due to random chance. The results are written to the tool's status window and can optionally be displayed graphically.

The tools in the Mapping Clusters toolset show where clusters occur. The Anselin Local Moran's I tool calculates a statistic and significance value for each feature that indicates how similar that feature's value is to those of neighboring features. It shows areas (clusters) where neighboring features have similar values (either high values or low values) and areas where there is a mix of high and low values. The Getis–Ord Gi* tool also calculates a statistic and significance value for each feature. However, Gi* identifies clusters of high values and low values (hot spots and cold spots).

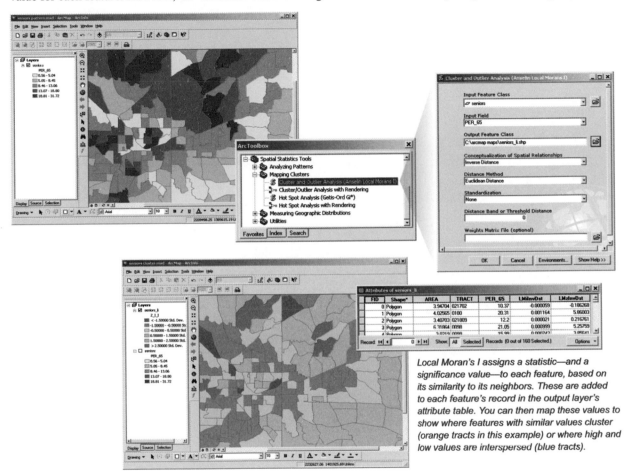

Local Moran's I assigns a statistic—and a significance value—to each feature, based on its similarity to its neighbors. These are added to each feature's record in the output layer's attribute table. You can then map these values to show where features with similar values cluster (orange tracts in this example) or where high and low values are interspersed (blue tracts).

Additional Resources for Learning and Using ArcGIS Desktop

Here are some additional sources of help and information available to you as you learn and use ArcGIS Desktop.

Data   ArcGIS comes with a number of geographic data sets you can use to start making maps quickly. These are found on the ESRI Data & Maps Media Kit. The data sets consist of global or national base map data, and include:

World

Continents
Countries
Cities
Lakes/Rivers
Ecoregions

Topography and bathymetry
Shaded relief
150 meter resolution satellite imagery
Latitude and longitude grids
Demographics

Europe

Countries
Provinces
Cities/Urbanized areas

Roads/Railroads
Waterbodies
Demographics

Canada

Provinces
Cities/Municipalities
Indian reserves

Highways/Railways
National/Provincial parks
Waterbodies

Mexico

States
Cities/Municipalities
Roads/Railroads

Elevation contours
Water bodies/Rivers and streams

United States

States
Counties
Cities/Populated places
ZIP Codes
Census tracts/Census block groups
County population data
Congressional districts

Cultural features
Highways/Roads
Detailed streets (StreetMap USA)
Water bodies/Rivers and streams
State Plane Zones
USGS Topographic Quad Series Indexes

See the data Media Kits for a complete list of datasets.

Tutorials   Quick-start tutorials are available for the various applications and functions within ArcGIS. They can be accessed from within the ArcGIS Desktop Help system—look under 'Getting more help' in the 'Getting Started' section of the Help contents (or search using the keyword "Tutorials"). The tutorials are in PDF format and require Adobe Acrobat to view them. The sample data to use in conjunction with the tutorials is installed optionally from the ArcGIS Desktop software installation media. The default location for the tutorial data is the arcgis\ArcTutor folder.

ArcGIS application overview tutorials

- Using ArcCatalog—organizing, previewing, and managing geographic datasets
- Using ArcMap—making maps, and querying and analyzing geographic data
- Using ArcReader—viewing and querying maps published with ArcGIS Publisher

Data management and processing tutorials

- Building geodatabases—designing and building a geodatabase for storing and managing geographic data
- Editing geodatabases—creating and editing specialized geodatabase feature classes
- Editing GIS features—creating and editing feature geometry and attributes, and performing spatial adjustment
- Geocoding in ArcGIS—assigning geographic coordinates to locations or events from a list of street addresses
- Geoprocessing in ArcGIS—working with tools for managing and analyzing geographic data
- Linear Referencing—defining, managing, and analyzing routes over GIS networks
- Representations—creating cartographic representations for rules-based symbology

Extension product tutorials

Tutorials are also available for most of the ArcGIS extension products.

Data compilation extensions

- ArcScan for ArcGIS—importing scanned data
- ArcGIS Data Interoperability—converting geographic data between various formats
- Using Survey Analyst—managing land survey data
- StreetMap—working with street and address data
- Schematics—creating schematic views of GIS networks and tabular data

Mapping and visualization extensions

- Maplex for ArcGIS—placing label text for cartographic production
- Using Publisher—creating and publishing map documents for use with ArcReader
- Using 3D Analyst—creating 3D perspectives and globe views
- Using Tracking Analyst—working with mobile features, and creating time-based displays and animations

Geographic analysis extensions

- Using Spatial Analyst—analyzing and modeling geographic data
- Geostatistical Analyst—modeling surfaces from sample points

Books ESRI Press publishes a variety of GIS-related books, including ESRI software workbooks, such as *Getting to Know ArcGIS Desktop*, and industry-specific case studies and applications. Several ESRI Press books cover the concepts and methods behind many of the geodatabase design, map design, and geographic analysis tasks presented in this book:

- *Modeling Our World: The ESRI Guide to Geodatabase Design* describes the various models for representing geographic data and the various components of a geodatabase.

- *Designing Geodatabases: Case Studies in GIS Data Modeling* describes the geodatabase design process in detail and provides examples from a variety of industries.

- *Designing Better Maps: A Guide for GIS Users* covers the basics of map design and production, including layout, fonts and text, symbols, and color selection.

- *The ESRI Guide to GIS Analysis, Volume 1: Spatial Patterns & Relationships* describes the use of maps for visual analysis, including types of maps, classification schemes, and use of perspective views. It also covers basic GIS analysis tasks, including feature selection, overlay analysis, and distance analysis.

- *The ESRI Guide to GIS Analysis, Volume 2: Spatial Measurements & Statistics* describes concepts, methods, and tools for statistical analysis of geographic distributions, patterns, clusters, and directional trends.

ESRI Press is online at *http://gis.esri.com/esripress*.

Courses from ESRI ESRI provides both instructor-led and online courses. These cover a wide range of topics and levels, from introductory courses on ArcGIS, to advanced database management and programming classes. Online offerings—at the Virtual Campus—also include courses on industry-specific applications. Go to Training at *www.esri.com*.

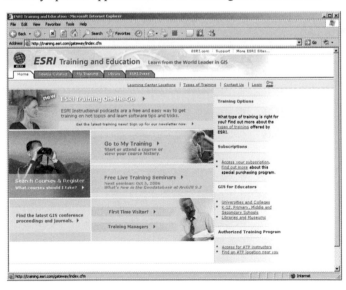

Conferences and user groups Finally, other ArcGIS users are a great source of information and help. ESRI user groups exist in many places around the world, and many of them hold local, regional, or national conferences and meetings. ESRI also sponsors an annual International User Conference, as well as other regional user conferences. These conferences provide a great opportunity to learn from other users' experiences. For more information see Events at *www.esri.com*.

Index